Positive Psychology

Remediating deficits and managing disabilities has been a central pre-occupation for clinical psychologists for much of the past 50 years. *Positive Psychology*, in contrast, is concerned with the enhancement of happiness and well-being, involving the scientific study of the role of personal strengths and positive social systems in the promotion of optimal well-being. The central themes of *Positive Psychology*, including happiness, hope, creativity and wisdom, are all investigated in this book in the context of their possible applications in clinical practice.

Positive Psychology is unique in offering an accessible introduction to this emerging field of clinical psychology. It will prove a valuable resource for undergraduate psychology students and lecturers who will benefit from the learning objectives and research stimuli included in each chapter. It will also be of interest to those involved in postgraduate training in related areas such as social work, counselling and psychotherapy.

Professor Alan Carr is the director of the doctoral training programme in clinical psychology at University College Dublin and Consultant Marital and Family Therapist at the Clanwilliam Institute for Marital and Family Therapy in Dublin. His previous publications include *The Handbook of Child and Adolescent Psychology: A Contextual Approach* (Routledge 1999), *What Works with Children and Adolescents? A Critical Review of Psychological Interventions with Children, Adolescents and their Families* (Routledge 2000) and *Prevention: What Works With Children and Adolescents? A Critical Review of Psychological Prevention Programmes for Children, Adolescents and their Families* (Brunner-Routledge 2002).

Positive Psychology

The science of happiness and human strengths

Alan Carr

Routledge
Taylor & Francis Group

LONDON AND NEW YORK

First published 2004 by Routledge
27 Church Road, Hove, East Sussex BN3 2FA

Simultaneously published in the USA and Canada
by Routledge
270 Madison Avenue, New York NY 10016

Reprinted 2004 and 2005

Routledge is an imprint of the Taylor & Francis Group

Typeset in 10/12pt Times by Graphicraft Limited, Hong Kong
Printed and bound in Great Britain by Biddles Ltd, King's Lynn, Norfolk
Paperback cover design by Lisa Dynan

This publication has been produced with paper manufactured to strict
environmental standards and with pulp derived from sustainable forests.

British Library Cataloguing in Publication Data
A catalogue record for this book is available from the British Library

Library of Congress Cataloguing in Publication Data
Carr, Alan, Dr.
    Positive psychology / Alan Carr.
        p. ; cm.
Includes bibliographical references and index.
    ISBN 1-58391-990-2 (hbk.) — ISBN 1-58391-991-0 (pbk.)
    1. Psychology. 2. Health. 3. Optimism.
    [DNLM: 1. Happiness. 2. Psychology, Applied—methods. 3.
Adaptation, Psychological. BF 575.H27 C311p 2004] 1. Title.

    BF121.C355 2004
    150–dc21
                                        2003009866

Contents

List of tables   ix
List of figures   xi
Acknowledgements   xiii
Foreword   xvii

1 Happiness   **1**

    Learning objectives   1
    Positive emotions   2
    Positive and negative affectivity   2
    Happiness   6
    Measuring happiness   6
    The effects of happiness   9
    Causes of happiness   16
    Culture and happiness   19
    Optimising well-being   19
    Relationships and happiness   20
    The environment and happiness   25
    Physical state and happiness   28
    Productivity and happiness   29
    Recreation and happiness   31
    Evolutionary perspectives on obstacles to happiness   31
    Happiness enhancement   36
    Related concepts   36
    Controversies   38
    Summary   39
    Questions   41
    Further reading   42
    Measures for use in research   43
    Glossary   45

2   Flow   **46**

Learning objectives   46
Intrinsic motivation   47
Signature strengths   50
Metamotivational states and reversal theory   55
Flow   58
Implications   66
Controversies   66
Summary   66
Questions   72
Further reading   73
Measures for use in research   73
Glossary   74

3   Hope and optimism   **76**

Learning objectives   76
Positive illusions   77
Self-deception   78
Optimism   82
Hope   88
Expectationism and risk homeostasis theory   93
Optimism, hope and health   97
The neurobiology of optimism and hope   98
Implications   100
Controversies   100
Summary   102
Questions   103
Further reading   104
Measures for use in research   104
Glossary   106

4   Emotional intelligence   **107**

Learning objectives   107
Emotional intelligence: ability or personality trait?   108
Enhancing emotional intelligence in adulthood   117
Development of emotional competence   120
Attachment and the development of emotional competence   124
Neurological basis for emotional intelligence   127
Related constructs   130
Implications   138
Controversies   138

Summary   141
Questions   142
Further reading   142
Measures for use in research   143
Glossary   143

5   Giftedness, creativity and wisdom   144

Learning objectives   144
Giftedness   145
Creativity   150
Wisdom   157
Implications   170
Controversies   175
Summary   176
Questions   177
Further reading   177
Measures for use in research   179
Glossary   179

6   Positive traits and motives   181

Learning objectives   181
Trait theories of personality and personal strengths   182
Motives as personal strengths   192
Implications   196
Controversies   196
Summary   197
Questions   198
Further reading   199
Measures for use in research   199
Glossary   200

7   Positive self   201

Learning objectives   201
Self as object and agent   203
Self-esteem   204
Self-efficacy   210
Coping strategies   213
Assessing coping   228
Defence mechanisms   230
Assessing defences   238
Implications   240

Controversies 240
Summary 242
Questions 243
Further reading 244
Measures for use in research 246
Glossary 249

8 Positive relationships **250**

Learning objectives 250
The family lifecycle 251
Lifecycle stages associated with separation and divorce 281
Assessing relationships 287
Implications 291
Controversies 291
Summary 293
Questions 294
Further reading 295
Measures for use in research 298
Glossary 299

9 Positive change **301**

Learning objectives 301
Bringing strengths to bear on opportunities and challenges 302
Stages of change 303
Change processes 311
Implications 323
Informal helping relationships 323
Psychotherapeutic relationships 326
The effectiveness of psychological therapies 327
Prevention of psychological problems 337
Controversies 341
Summary 341
Questions 344
Further reading 344
Measures for use in research 346
Glossary 346

Afterword 348
Bibliography 350
Index 382

List of tables

1.1	Positive Affectivity and Negative Affectivity Scale (PANAS)	5
1.2	Satisfaction with Life Scale	8
1.3	The Revised Oxford Happiness Scale	10
1.4	Components of subjective well-being	12
1.5	Cross-twin, cross-time and cross-twin and -time correlations based on scores from well-being scale of the multidimensional personality questionnaire taken at a 9-year interval	18
1.6	Strategies for enhancing happiness	37
2.1	Virtues and character strengths	52
2.2	Flow experience questionnaire	64
2.3	Experience sampling sheet for assessing flow in everyday life	67
2.4	Strategies for enhancing well-being using strengths, intrinsic motivation and flow	70
3.1	The Life Orientation Test – Revised	83
3.2	Time Horizon Questionnaire	95
3.3	Strategies for enhancing positive illusions, hope, optimism and positive expectations	101
4.1	Abilities assessed by Multifactor Emotional IQ Test and the Mayer, Salovey and Caruso Emotional Intelligence Test	111
4.2	Factors assessed by Reuven Bar-On's model of emotional intelligence	114
4.3	Factors assessed by the Emotional Competence Inventory	115
4.4	Factors assessed by the EQ Map	116
4.5	Development of emotional competence	121
4.6	Strategies for enhancing emotional intelligence	139
5.1	Erikson's psychosocial stage model	159
5.2	Implications of research on giftedness, creativity and wisdom	171
6.1	Strengths entailed by the Five-Factor Model of Personality	183
6.2	Temperament and personality traits	187
6.3	Strategies for promoting strengths and well-being based on research on traits and motives	197
7.1	Two aspects of self	203

7.2   Functional and dysfunctional, problem, emotion and
      avoidance focused coping strategies   216
7.3   Relaxation exercises   224
7.4   Subscales in selected coping style assessment instruments   229
7.5   Defence mechanisms at different levels of maturity   232
7.6   Strategies for promoting strengths and well-being based on
      research on self-esteem, self-efficacy, positive coping
      strategies and adaptive defences   241
8.1   Stages of the family lifecycle   252
8.2   Kansas Marital Satisfaction Scale   261
8.3   Five types of couples   262
8.4   Kansas Parental Satisfaction Scale   265
8.5   Factors associated with resilience in adolescence   271
8.6   False assumptions challenged in adulthood   273
8.7   Behavioural expressions of themes underlying grief processes
      following bereavement or facing terminal illness   278
8.8   Extra stages in the family lifecycle entailed by separation
      or divorce and remarriage   282
8.9   Strategies for promoting strengths and well-being based
      on research on the family lifecycle   292
9.1   The decisional balance questionnaire for assessing the pros
      and cons of change   309
9.2   Summary of strategies for making transitions from one
      stage of change to the next when using strengths to manage
      challenges and opportunities for change   324
9.3   Summary of research on psychological treatments that
      work for problems in adulthood   329
9.4   Summary of research on psychological treatments that
      work for problems in childhood and adolescence   334
9.5   Summary of research on psychological prevention
      programmes that work for problems in childhood
      and adolescence   338
9.6   Client Satisfaction Questionnaire   343

List of figures

1.1 Circumplex model of the emotions   4
1.2 Average happiness rating in 916 surveys involving over
     1 million people in 45 nations   7
1.3 The broaden-and-build theory of positive emotions   13
1.4 Marital status and happiness   21
1.5 Attendance at religious services and happiness in the USA   25
1.6 National wealth and life satisfaction   26
1.7 Increased wealth and happiness in the USA   27
2.1 Ryan and Deci's self-determination continuum   48
2.2 Telic and paratelic metamotivational states in reversal
     theory   56
2.3 Frequency of FLOW experiences in everyday activities   59
2.4 FLOW and other states related to levels of skill and
     challenge   60
3.1 Snyder's Hope Theory   89
4.1 Mayer, Salovey and Caruso's model of emotional intelligence   109
4.2 Reuven Bar-On's model of emotional intelligence   112
4.3 Characteristics of four attachment styles in children
     and adults   126
4.4 A framework for the analysis of emotional behaviour   135
5.1 Csikszentmihalyi's systems view of creativity   151
5.2 Baltes's predictors of wisdom-related performance in adults   166
5.3 Sternberg's balance theory of wisdom   169
6.1 Temperament and personality   186
7.1 Self-esteem and competence   208
7.2 Relationship between self-efficacy beliefs and outcome
     expectations   210
7.3 The coping process   214
7.4 Conflict, anxiety and defence mechanisms   236
8.1 Patterns of parenting   264
8.2 Circumplex model of interpersonal behaviour   289
9.1 Bringing strengths to bear on opportunities and challenges   304

9.2   Change processes, self-change techniques and therapeutic
       interventions associated with transition through stages
       of change   305
9.3   Relationship between levels of pros and cons of change
       and different stages of change   308
9.4   Factors which contribute to the improvement of clients
       during psychotherapy   326

Acknowledgements

Acknowledged with thanks permission to reproduce or adapt the following material:

Table 1.1 Positive Affectivity and Negative Affectivity Scale (PANAS) adapted from D. Watson, L. Clark and A. Tellegen (1988), Development and validation of brief measures of positive and negative affect: the PANAS scales, *Journal of Personality and Social Psychology* 44: 1063–70.
Table 1.2 Satisfaction with Life Scale adapted from E. Diener, R. Emmons, R. Larsen and S. Griffin (1985), The Satisfaction with Life Scale, *Journal of Personality Assessment* 49: 71–5.
Table 1.3 The Revised Oxford Happiness Scale adapted from M. Argyle (2001), *The Psychology of Happiness* (2nd edn), London: Routledge.
Table 1.4 Components of subjective well-being adapted from E. Diener, E. Suh, R. Lucas and H. Smith (1999), Subjective well-being: three decades of progress, *Psychological Bulletin* 125: 277.
Table 2.2 Flow experience questionnaire adapted from M. Csikszentmihalyi and I. Csikszentmihalyi (1988), *Optimal Experience: Psychological Studies of Flow in Consciousness*, Cambridge: Cambridge University Press, p. 195.
Table 2.3 Experience sampling sheet for assessing flow in everyday life adapted from M. Csikszentmihalyi and I. Csikszentmihalyi (1988), *Optimal Experience: Psychological Studies of Flow in Consciousness*, Cambridge: Cambridge University Press, pp. 257–8.
Table 3.1 The Life Orientation Test – Revised adapted from M. Scheier, C. Carver and M. Bridges (1994), Distinguishing optimism from neuroticism (and trait anxiety, self-mastery, and self-esteem): a re-evaluation of the Life Orientation Test, *Journal of Personality and Social Psychology* 67: 1063–78.
Table 3.2 Time Horizon Questionnaire, reproduced from Gerald J.S. Wilde (2001), Queen's University, Kingston, Ontario Canada. Home page: http://psyc.queensu.ca/faculty/wilde/wilde.html
Table 6.1 Strengths entailed by the five-factor model of personality adapted from P. Costa and R. McCrae (1992), *Revised NEO Personality Inventory*

(NEO-PI-R and NEO Five-Factor Inventory (NEO-FFI) Professional Manual, Odessa, FL: Psychological Assessment Resources, p. 49.

Table 8.2 Kansas Marital Satisfaction Scale adapted from W.R. Schumm, L.A. Paff-Bergen, R.C. Hatch, F.C. Obiorah, J.M. Copeland, L.D. Meens and M.A. Bugaighis (1986), Concurrent and discriminant validity of the Kansas Marital Satisfaction Scale, *Journal of Marriage and the Family* 48: 381–7.

Table 8.4 Kansas Parental Satisfaction Scale adapted from D.E. James, W.R. Schumm, C.E. Kennedy, C.C. Grigsby, K.L. Shectman and C.W. Nichols (1985), Characteristics of the Kansas Parental Satisfaction Scale among two samples of married parents, *Psychological Reports* 57: 163–9.

Table 9.1 The decisional balance questionnaire for assessing the pros and cons of change adapted from J. Prochaska, J. Norcross and C. DiClemente (1994), *Changing for Good*, New York: Avon, pp. 169–79.

Table 9.6 Client Satisfaction Questionnaire adapted from D. Larsen, C. Attkinson, W. Hargreaves and T. Nguyen (1979), Assessment of client/ patient satisfaction: development of a general scale, *Evaluation and Programme Planning* 2: 197–207.

Figure 1.2 Average happiness rating in 916 surveys involving over 1 million people in 45 nations adapted from D. Myers and E. Diener (1996), The pursuit of happiness, *Scientific American* 274 (May): 54–6.

Figure 1.3 The broaden-and-build theory of positive emotions adapted from B. Fredrickson (2002), Positive emotions, in C.R. Snyder and S. Lopez (eds), *Handbook of Positive Psychology* (p. 124), New York: Oxford University Press.

Figure 1.4 Marital status and happiness adapted from D. Myers (2000), The funds, friends and faith of happy people, *American Psychologist* 55: 63, based on data from 35,024 cases in General Social Survey, National Opinion Research Centre, USA, 1972–96.

Figure 1.5 Attendance at religious services and happiness in the USA adapted from D. Myers (2000), The funds, friends and faith of happy people, *American Psychologist* 55: 65, based on data from 35,024 cases in General Social Survey, National Opinion Research Centre, USA, 1972–96.

Figure 1.6 National wealth and life satisfaction adapted from E. Diener (2000), Subjective well-being: the science of happiness and a proposal for a national index, *American Psychologist* 55: 37.

Figure 1.7 Increased wealth and happiness in the USA adapted from D. Myers (2000), The funds, friends and faith of happy people, *American Psychologist* 55: 61. Income data from US Commerce Department, Bureau of the Census and Economic Indicators. Happiness data from 35,024 cases in General Social Survey, National Opinion Research Centre, University of Chicago USA.

Figure 2.1 Ryan and Deci's self-determination continuum adapted from R. Ryan and E. Deci (2000), Self-determination theory and the facilitation of intrinsic motivation, social development and well-being, *American Psychologist* 55: 72.

Figure 2.2 Telic and paratelic metamotivational states in reversal theory adapted from M. Apter (2001), *Motivational Styles in Everyday Life: A Guide to Reversal Theory*, Washington, DC: American Psychological Association, pp. 6–13 and 44.

Figure 2.3 Frequency of FLOW experiences in everyday activities adapted from M. Csikszentmihaly (1997), *Finding Flow: The Psychology of Engagement with Everyday Life*, New York: Basic Books, p. 37.

Figure 2.4 FLOW and other states related to levels of skill and challenge adapted from M. Csikszentmihalyi (1997), *Finding Flow: The Psychology of Engagement with Everyday Life* New York: Basic Books, p. 37.

Figure 3.1 Snyder's Hope Theory adapted from C.R. Snyder (2000), *Handbook of Hope*, Orlando FL: Academic Press, pp. 11–12.

Figure 4.1 Mayer, Salovey and Caruso's model of emotional intelligence adapted from J. Mayer, P. Salovey and D. Caruso (2000a), Emotional intelligence as zeitgist, as personality, and as a mental ability, in R. Bar-On and J. Parker (eds), *The Handbook of Emotional Intelligence* (pp. 92–117), San Francisco, CA: Jossey-Bass.

Figure 4.2 Reuven Bar-On's model of emotional intelligence adapted from R. Bar-On (1997), *BarOn Emotional Quotient Inventory (EQ-I): Technical Manual*, Toronto: Multi-Health Systems.

Figure 4.4 A framework for the analysis of emotional behaviour adapted from J. Averill (1997), The emotions: an integrative approach, in R. Hogan, J. Johnson and S. Briggs (eds), *Handbook of Personality Psychology* (pp. 522), New York: Academic Press, and J. Averill (2002), Emotional creativity: towards spiritualizing the passions, in C.R. Snyder and S. Lopez (eds), *Handbook of Positive Psychology* (p. 174), New York: Oxford University Press.

Figure 5.1 Csikszentmihalyi's systems view of creativity adapted from M. Csikszentmihalyi (1999), Implications of a systems perspective for the study of creativity, in R. Sternberg (ed.), *Handbook of Creativity* (p. 315), Cambridge: Cambridge University Press.

Figure 5.2 Baltes's predictors of wisdom-related performance in adults adapted from P. Baltes and U. Staudinger (2000), Wisdom: a metaheuristic (pragmatic) to orchestrate mind and virtue towards excellence, *American Psychologist* 55: 130.

Figure 5.3 Sternberg's balance theory of wisdom adapted from R. Sternberg (2000a), Intelligence and wisdom, in R. Sternberg (ed.), *Handbook of Intelligence* (p. 638), Cambridge: Cambridge University Press.

Figure 7.1 Self-esteem and competence adapted from C. Mruk (1999), *Self-esteem* (2nd edn), New York: Springer, pp. 164–5.

Figure 7.2 Relationship between self-efficacy beliefs and outcome expectations adapted from A. Bandura (1997), *Self-Efficacy*, New York: Freeman, p. 22.

Figure 7.3 The coping process adapted from C. Holahan, R. Moos, J. Schaefer (1996), Coping, stress, resistance, and growth: conceptualising adaptive functioning, in M. Zeidner and N. Endler (eds), *Handbook of Coping: Theory, Research, Applications* (p. 27), New York: Wiley.

Figure 8.2 Circumplex Model of Interpersonal behaviour adapted from J. Wiggins and P. Trapnell (1997), Personality structure: return of the big five, in R. Hogan, J. Johnson and S. Briggs (eds), *Handbook of Personality Psychology* (p. 749), New York: Academic Press.

Figure 9.3 Relationship between levels of pros and cons of change and different stages of change, adapted from J. Prochaska, J. Norcross and C. DiClemente (1994), *Changing for Good*, New York: Avon, p. 163.

Figure 9.4 Factors which contribute to the improvement of clients during psychotherapy based on M. Lambert and D. Barley (2002), Research summary on the therapeutic relationship and psychotherapy outcome, in J. Norcross (ed.), *Psychotherapy Relationships that Work* (pp. 17–32), New York: Oxford University Press.

Foreword

I stand for the reform of municipal morals. New worlds for old. Union of all. Three acres and a cow for all children of nature. Saloon motor hearses. Compulsory manual labour for all. All parks open to the public day and night. Electric dishscrubbers for all. Tuberculosis, lunacy, war and mendacity must now cease. General amnesty, weekly carnival, with masked licence, bonus for all. Esperanto the universal brotherhood . . . Free money, free love and a free lay church in a free lay state.

> (This is Leopold Bloom's vision of a better world from
> *Ulysses* by James Joyce, 1922).

Clinical Psychology has traditionally focused on psychological deficits and disability. It has rarely privileged our clients' resilience, resourcefulness and capacity for renewal. The critical psychology tradition in the UK has highlighted the shortcomings of this approach (Johnstone, 2000; Newnes, Holmes, and Dunn, 1999, 2001). In the USA Professor Martin Seligman and his colleagues have begun laying the foundations for a positive psychology to complement deficit-based approaches (Seligman, 2002; Seligman and Csikszentmihalyi, 2000b; Snyder and Lopez, 2002). This new branch of psychology is primarily concerned with the scientific study of human strengths and happiness. Like Leopold Bloom whose words open this foreword, it is concerned with identifying factors that promote well-being. However, unlike Leopold Bloom the mission of positive psychology is to base conclusions about what would make a better world on science rather than opinion or rhetoric. Unfortunately accessible textbooks on positive psychology for undergraduates are in short supply. It was this, along with my long-standing interest in human strengths, and a wish to offer an undergraduate course on positive psychology that prompted me to devote a sabbatical year to writing this text.

In the opening chapter findings from psychological research on happiness are outlined. The next four chapters deal with topics of central concern to positive psychology: flow, optimism, emotional intelligence, giftedness, creativity and wisdom. Chapter 6 is concerned with research on human strengths

associated with particular traits and motives. Chapter 7 focuses on four
aspects of the self-system that contribute to resilience. These are self-esteem,
self-efficacy, functional coping strategies and adaptive defences. Positive
relationships over the course of the lifecycle are addressed in Chapter 8.
Included here is a review of research on aspects of friendship, marriage and
parenting. Chapter 9 is concerned with how we can bring our strengths to
bear on opportunities for growth and challenges that require us to make
changes in our lifestyle. The stages-of-change model, which has underpinned
so much important research on prevention, is a central organising framework for this final chapter.

A number of features have been used to help students understand ideas
presented in this volume. Each chapter opens with a detailed chapter outline
and a set of learning objectives. Throughout all chapters, I have made lib-
eral use of headings and subheadings to help students make their way through
the material. With respect to the overall style of the prose, I may be guilty of
oversimplification from time to time in my attempts to make complex ideas
accessible. Towards the end of most chapters, a table is included which
summarises the implications of ideas discussed in the body of the chapter
for self-help and clinical practice. This is followed by a section highlighting
some of the controversial issues, debates and disagreements within the field.
Each chapter ends with a concise summary.

Questions at the end of each chapter are divided into those which focus
on self-development and research questions. The self-development questions
invite students to reflect on aspects of their own lives and to consider taking steps to enhance the quality of their lives using ideas discussed in the
chapter.

The research questions invite students to design and conduct research
studies. Of course in most instances students will probably only have the
time and resources to design studies. But there may be occasional opportunities for actually completing the suggested projects. In most chapters there
is a research question which is pitched at an introductory level and could be
suitably addressed in a second-year undergraduate psychology laboratory
course. I have also included more challenging questions that require students to conduct literature searches and to find articles describing studies
which they are invited to replicate. These questions are for students taking
an honours degree in psychology (or majoring in psychology) who wish to
do their undergraduate thesis on a topic in positive psychology. These complex research questions might also stimulate some undergraduates to undertake postgraduate research in the field of positive psychology. Lists of
measures or psychometric instruments for use in research are also given at
the end of each chapter. Again, this is done to stimulate undergraduates
into considering conducting their undergraduate thesis in positive psychology and also to signal that there are ample resources available to make
postgraduate work in this field viable.

Suggestions for further reading are also given at the end of each chapter and these are subdivided into academic readings and self-help material. Where available, I have listed academic texts that are authoritative and comprehensive. I hope that the suggestions for further reading in the self-help area will give students access to high quality material which is consistent with findings from rigorous scientific investigation rather than scientifically unfounded 'pop-psychology'. John Norcross's *Authoritative Guide to Self-Help Resources in Mental Health* was particularly useful in compiling these lists (Norcross, Santrock, Campbell, Smith, Sommer and Zukerman, 2000).

Finally a glossary of new terms is given at the end of each chapter.

Colleagues at the Psychology Department in University College Dublin and on the UCD Clinical Psychology Programme team kindly made it possible for me to write this book, relatively unfettered by day-to-day administrative and teaching duties. My thanks are due to all of them but particularly to Professor Ciarán Benson, Professor Aidan Moran, Dr Muireann McNulty, Dr Barbara Dooley, Dr Teresa Burke, Dr Gary O'Reilly and Muriel Keegan, MA. Finally, I wish to thank Gill, Davie and Hazel for their kindness and patience.

AC
October 2002

Chapter 1

Happiness

Learning objectives

- Learn about positive emotions, their conceptualisation and measurement.
- Be able to distinguish between pleasures and gratifications.
- Be able to distinguish between the hedonic and eudaimonic approaches to studying well-being.
- Be able to describe the effects of happiness on creativity, productivity and longevity.
- Understand the relative contribution of genetic and environmental factors to happiness.
- Be able to describe the role of relationships, the immediate environment, physical state, work situation and recreation on happiness.
- Appreciate the obstacles to happiness, notably habituation to pleasant stimuli, negative social comparisons, inequitable reactions to equal losses and gains and adaptive, but distressing emotions.
- Understand the implications of research on factors related to happiness for the enhancement of subjective well-being.
- Be able to identify research questions that need to be addressed to advance our understanding of the nature, causes and consequences of happiness.

Understanding and facilitating happiness and subjective well-being is the central objective of positive psychology (Seligman, 2002). Happiness and well-being, in this context, refer to both positive feelings, such as joy or serenity, and to positive states such as those involving flow or absorption. As a scientific enterprise, positive psychology focuses on understanding and explaining happiness and subjective well-being and accurately predicting factors that influence such states. As a clinical endeavour, positive psychology is concerned with enhancing subjective well-being and happiness, rather than remediating deficits. Thus, positive psychology complements rather than replaces traditional clinical psychology. In this chapter, after considering positive emotions and positive and negative affectivity, the nature and measurement of happiness will be discussed. This will be followed by an account of the main research findings on the effects of happiness and its causes.

POSITIVE EMOTIONS

Seligman (2002) in his book *Authentic Happiness* classifies positive emotions into three categories: those associated with the past, the present and the future. Positive emotions associated with the future include optimism, hope, confidence, faith and trust. Optimism and hope will be considered in detail in Chapter 3. Satisfaction, contentment, fulfilment, pride and serenity are the main positive emotions associated with the past. There are two distinct classes of positive emotions concerned with the present: momentary pleasures and more enduring gratifications. The pleasures include both bodily pleasures and higher pleasures. Bodily pleasures come through the senses. Feelings that come from sex, beautiful perfumes and delicious flavours fall into this category. In contrast higher pleasures come from more complex activities and include feelings such as bliss, glee, comfort, ecstasy and ebullience. Gratifications differ from pleasures in that they entail states of absorption or flow that come from engagement in activities which involve using our unique signature strengths. Sailing, teaching and helping others are examples of such activities. Signature strengths are personal traits associated with particular virtues defined in the Values in Action Classification of Strengths (Peterson and Seligman, 2001). Flow, signature strengths and gratifications are discussed in Chapter 2.

In the study of positive emotions and happiness a critical concern is finding a parsimonious way of distinguishing between reliable positive and negative affective states and it is to this that we now turn.

POSITIVE AND NEGATIVE AFFECTIVITY

There are between 550 and 600 words for different emotional experiences in the English language (Averill, 1997). There is good evidence that a dimensional approach accounts for much of the variability in emotional experiences (Larsen and Deiner, 1992; Watson and Tellegen, 1985). Studies of thousands of participants from a variety of cultures in which factor analyses of self-ratings for different emotional experiences were conducted have yielded a consensus. So too have the results of multivariate studies of ratings of emotional concepts and facial expressions of emotions. An extremely wide range of emotional experiences may be described in terms of the circumplex space defined by two broad dimensions. There has been controversy, however, over how best to conceptualise these two dimensions. Some researches, such as Larsen and Deiner (1992) and Averill (1997), have labelled these dimensions activation or arousal and pleasantness or evaluation. Activation or arousal ranges from highly activated or aroused to a low level of activation or arousal. Pleasantness or evaluation ranges from pleasant or positive to unpleasant or negative. These two dimensions constitute the vertical and horizontal axes in Figure 1.1. Other researchers, notably Watson and Tellegen (1985), have suggested a 45-degree rotation of these axes to yield dimensions of positive and negative affectivity. These two dimensions are represented by thin diagonal lines in Figure 1.1. Individual differences in positive and negative affectivity may be assessed reliably with the Positive and Negative Affectivity Scales presented in Table 1.1 (Watson et al., 1988).

A number of important findings have been made concerning positive and negative affectivity (Watson, 2000, 2002). Positive affectivity is correlated with the personality trait extraversion and negative affectivity is correlated with the trait neuroticism. Both of these traits are discussed further in Chapter 6. These correlations between affectivity and major personality traits are substantial and range from 0.4 to 0.9. Positive affectivity contains the subdimensions of joviality (e.g. cheerful, happy, lively); self-assurance (e.g. confident, strong, daring); and attentiveness (e.g. alert, concentrating, determined). Positive affectivity after the age of 30 is very temporally consistent. Negative affectivity peaks in late adolescence and then declines with age at least until middle adulthood. There are consistent individual differences in positive and negative affectivity and in the short-term variability of positive mood which follows a circadian rhythm (lower in the morning). Both positive and negative affectivity are partially heritable characteristics with heritability coefficients of about 0.5. However, environmental influences can improve positive affectivity. For example, over a 6-year period Headey and Wearing (1991) found that 31 per cent of participants in their study showed improvements in their positive affectivity scores by more than one standard deviation. Positive affectivity is associated with greater job satisfaction and marital satisfaction. The relationship between these variables is probably complex and bi-directional, with positive affectivity causing people to enjoy their jobs and relationships more and being happy in work and love increasing positive affectivity. Low positive affectivity is associated with a wide range of psychological disorders.

Both positive and negative affectivity represent the experiential components of neurobiological systems that have evolved to address different evolutionary tasks (Watson et al., 1995). Negative affectivity (like the personality trait, neuroticism) is one aspect of the avoidance-oriented behavioural inhibition system. The function of this system is to instigate avoidance-behaviour and inhibit approach-behaviour to keep the organism away from

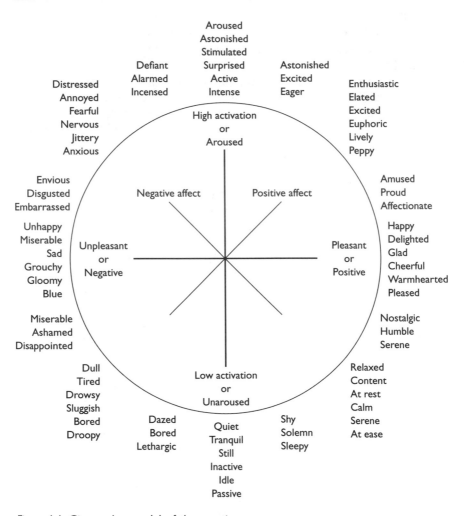

Figure 1.1 Circumplex model of the emotions

Sources: Adapted from Averill (1997); Larsen and Deiner (1992).

Note: The horizontal dimension represents evaluation (pleasant or positive versus unpleasant or negative). The vertical dimension represents activation (high activation or aroused versus low activation unaroused). The thin lines represent a 45 degree rotation of the axes as suggested by Watson and Tellegen (1985) Towards a consensual structure of mood. *Psychological Bulletin* 98: 219–35.

situations that may entail danger, pain or punishment. Positive affectivity in contrast is part of the behavioural facilitation system (like the personality trait – extraversion) which orients the organism toward potentially rewarding situations that may yield pleasure. The function of this system is to help the organism obtain resources necessary for survival such as food, shelter

Table 1.1 Positive Affectivity and Negative Affectivity Scale (PANAS)

This scale consists of a number of words that describe different feelings and emotions. Read each item and then circle the appropriate answer. Indicate to what extent you feel this way right now (that is, at the present moment).

1	Interested	Very slightly or not at all 1	A little 2	Moderately 3	Quite a bit 4	Extremely 5
2	Distressed	Very slightly or not at all 1	A little 2	Moderately 3	Quite a bit 4	Extremely 5
3	Excited	Very slightly or not at all 1	A little 2	Moderately 3	Quite a bit 4	Extremely 5
4	Upset	Very slightly or not at all 1	A little 2	Moderately 3	Quite a bit 4	Extremely 5
5	Strong	Very slightly or not at all 1	A little 2	Moderately 3	Quite a bit 4	Extremely 5
6	Guilty	Very slightly or not at all 1	A little 2	Moderately 3	Quite a bit 4	Extremely 5
7	Scared	Very slightly or not at all 1	A little 2	Moderately 3	Quite a bit 4	Extremely 5
8	Hostile	Very slightly or not at all 1	A little 2	Moderately 3	Quite a bit 4	Extremely 5
9	Enthusiastic	Very slightly or not at all 1	A little 2	Moderately 3	Quite a bit 4	Extremely 5
10	Proud	Very slightly or not at all 1	A little 2	Moderately 3	Quite a bit 4	Extremely 5
11	Irritable	Very slightly or not at all 1	A little 2	Moderately 3	Quite a bit 4	Extremely 5
12	Alert	Very slightly or not at all 1	A little 2	Moderately 3	Quite a bit 4	Extremely 5
13	Ashamed	Very slightly or not at all 1	A little 2	Moderately 3	Quite a bit 4	Extremely 5
14	Inspired	Very slightly or not at all 1	A little 2	Moderately 3	Quite a bit 4	Extremely 5
15	Nervous	Very slightly or not at all 1	A little 2	Moderately 3	Quite a bit 4	Extremely 5
16	Determined	Very slightly or not at all 1	A little 2	Moderately 3	Quite a bit 4	Extremely 5
17	Attentive	Very slightly or not at all 1	A little 2	Moderately 3	Quite a bit 4	Extremely 5
18	Jittery	Very slightly or not at all 1	A little 2	Moderately 3	Quite a bit 4	Extremely 5
19	Active	Very slightly or not at all 1	A little 2	Moderately 3	Quite a bit 4	Extremely 5
20	Afraid	Very slightly or not at all 1	A little 2	Moderately 3	Quite a bit 4	Extremely 5

Source: Adapted from Watson *et al.* (1988).

Note: For positive affectivity score sum responses to items 1, 3, 5, 9, 10, 12, 14, 16, 17, 19. For negative affectivity score sum responses to items 2, 4, 6, 7, 8, 11, 13, 15, 18, 20.

and a mate. The neurobiology of these two systems will be discussed in detail in Chapter 6 on personality traits.

Positive affectivity is associated with regular physical activity; adequate sleep; regular socialising with close friends; and striving for valued goals (rather than attaining them). So positive affectivity may probably be enhanced through engaging in regular physical exercise; maintaining a regular and adequate pattern of sleeping; making and maintaining strong friendships and socialising frequently with the supportive friends; and through working towards personally valued goals (Watson, 2002). Positive affectivity is one aspect of happiness which is our next area of concern.

HAPPINESS

How happy are most people? In an effort to answer this question, Professor Ed Diener from Minnesota University aggregated data from 916 surveys of happiness, life satisfaction and subjective well-being involving over a million people in 45 nations around the world (Myers and Diener, 1996). He transformed all the data onto a scale that went from 0 to 10 where 10 indicated extremely happy, 5 was neutral and 0 was very unhappy. From Figure 1.2 it may be seen that the average happiness rating was 6.75. So he concluded that the average person is moderately happy. Very few surveys found neutral mean ratings of 5 or an unhappy mean ratings of less than 5. These positive reports of happiness characterise all age groups, both genders and all races studied. Of course certain minority groups were unhappy: specifically hospitalised alcoholics; newly incarcerated prisoners; new therapy clients; South African blacks under apartheid; and students living under political oppression. Also, there are gender and age differences in the variability of happiness ratings (Diener *et al.*, 1999). More women and young people report extreme happiness and extreme misery compared with men and older people. Minor fluctuations in aspects of happiness have been found over the lifespan. Life satisfaction increased slightly with age, while positive affectivity decreases marginally. In US national opinion polls, 3 in 10 people describe themselves as 'very happy'; 1 in 10 say they are 'not too happy'; and the remaining 6 out of 10 describe themselves as 'pretty happy' (Myers, 2000).

MEASURING HAPPINESS

In studies of happiness a variety of techniques have been used to assess the construct. In many of the major national surveys single questions are used to measure happiness. These questions are framed in different ways such as 'How happy are you now?'; 'How satisfied are you with your life?'; 'How do you feel about your life as a whole?' Usually respondents are given a number

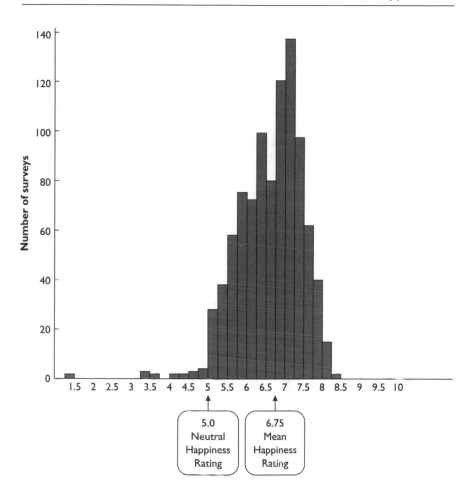

Figure 1.2 Average happiness rating in 916 surveys involving over 1 million people in 45 nations
Source: Adapted from Myers and Diener (1996).

of possible answers to choose from on 5-, 7- or 10-point scales. Fordyce (1988) developed a two-item happiness measure: (1) 'In general how happy or unhappy do you feel?' (with a 10-point response format from 10 = feeling ecstatic, joyous, fantastic to 0 = utterly depressed, completely down); (2) 'On average what percentage of the time do you feel happy (or unhappy or neutral)?' The average score for the first question is 6.9 and the average for the second is 54 per cent.

More sophisticated multi-item scales with good reliability and validity have also been used in recent research. These include the 29-item Revised Oxford Happiness Scale (Argyle, 2001) which has been widely used in the

Table 1.2 Satisfaction with Life Scale

Below are five statements you may agree or disagree with. Using the 7-point scale below indicate your agreement with each item by circling the answer that applies to you. Please be open and honest in your responding

	Strongly Disagree 1	Disagree 2	Slightly Disagree 3	Neither Agree nor Disagree 4	Slightly Agree 5	Agree 6	Strongly Agree 7
1 In most ways my life is close to my ideal	Strongly Disagree 1	Disagree 2	Slightly Disagree 3	Neither Agree nor Disagree 4	Slightly Agree 5	Agree 6	Strongly Agree 7
2 The conditions of my life are excellent	Strongly Disagree 1	Disagree 2	Slightly Disagree 3	Neither Agree nor Disagree 4	Slightly Agree 5	Agree 6	Strongly Agree 7
3 I am satisfied with my life	Strongly Disagree 1	Disagree 2	Slightly Disagree 3	Neither Agree nor Disagree 4	Slightly Agree 5	Agree 6	Strongly Agree 7
4 So far I have got the important things I want in life	Strongly Disagree 1	Disagree 2	Slightly Disagree 3	Neither Agree nor Disagree 4	Slightly Agree 5	Agree 6	Strongly Agree 7
5 If I could live my life over I would change almost nothing	Strongly Disagree 1	Disagree 2	Slightly Disagree 3	Neither Agree nor Disagree 4	Slightly Agree 5	Agree 6	Strongly Agree 7

Source: Adapted from Diener et al. (1985).

Note: Most people score in the 21–5 range on this scale.

UK, the 5-item Satisfaction with Life Scale (Diener *et al.*, 2002; Diener *et al.*, 1985; Pavot and Diener, 1993) which has been widely used in the US, and the 18-item well-being scale of the Multidimensional Personality Questionnaire which was used in the controversial Minnesota Study of Twins Reared Apart (Bouhard *et al.*, 1990; Lykken, 1999; Tellegen and Waller, In Press). Two of these scales are presented in Tables 1.2, and 1.3. The positive affect scale of the Positive and Negative Affect Scales in Table 1.1 (Watson *et al.*, 1988) and the positive feeling facet of the World Health Organisation Quality of Life scale (WHOQOL Group, 1998) are other widely used measures of subjective well-being. A multi-item bipolar depression-happiness scale has also been developed (Joseph and Lewis, 1998).

Factor analytic studies of measures of happiness and subjective well-being (SWB), as it is often called, show that happiness has at least two aspects. Such studies consistently yield affective and cognitive factors representing the emotional experience of joy, elation, contentment and other positive emotions on the one hand, and the cognitive evaluation of satisfaction with various life domains on the other (e.g. Andrews and McKennell, 1980). Cross-cultural data show that these two aspects of happiness are correlated at about $r = 0.5$ in individualist cultures such as the US and the UK, and as low as $r = 0.2$ in collectivist cultures where satisfaction depends on the state of others as well as oneself (Suh *et al.*, 1997). Thus, joy and satisfaction, the affective and cognitive components of happiness, are relatively independent of each other. To complicate the matter further, positive affect and negative affect are independent constructs or systems as shown in Figure 1.1. Furthermore, overall happiness is dependent upon cognitive evaluations of satisfaction within various life domains such as family or work setting and affective experiences within these. A framework is presented in Table 1.4 for conceptualising the various components of subjective well-being. To take account of the multiple domains which are associated with life satisfaction Alfonso *et al.*'s (1996) Extended Satisfaction with Life Scale uses five items in each of eight domains, i.e. self, family, sex, relationships, social, physical, work and college.

While single-item and multi-item scales measure global perceptions of personal happiness, experience sampling methods (ESM) provide moment-to-moment measures of happiness (Stone *et al.*, 1999). With ESM people are randomly signalled by a pager which they carry throughout an extended time period such as a week or a month. When the signal occurs they record their mood at that time point.

THE EFFECTS OF HAPPINESS

Martin Seligman (2002) has argued that positive and negative emotions may be distinguished from each other in terms of the degree to which they

Table 1.3 The Revised Oxford Happiness Scale

Below, there are groups of statements about personal happiness. Please read all four statements in each group and then pick out the one statement in each group that best describes the way you have been feeling in the past week, including today. Circle the letter (a, b, c, or d) beside the statement that you have picked.

1   a   I do not feel happy
    b   I feel fairly happy
    c   I am very happy
    d   I am incredibly happy

2   a   I am not particularly optimistic about the future
    b   I feel optimistic about the future
    c   I feel I have so much to look forward to
    d   I feel the future is overflowing with hope and promise

3   a   I am not really satisfied with anything in my life
    b   I am satisfied with some things in my life
    c   I am satisfied with many things in my life
    d   I am completely satisfied with everything in my life

4   a   I feel that I am not especially in control of my life
    b   I feel at least partially in control of my life
    c   I feel that I am in control most of the time
    d   I feel that I am in control of all aspects of my life

5   a   I don't feel that life is particularly rewarding
    b   I feel that life is rewarding
    c   I feel that life is very rewarding
    d   I feel that life is overflowing with rewards

6   a   I don't feel particularly pleased with the way I am
    b   I am pleased with the way I am
    c   I am very pleased with the way I am
    d   I am delighted with the way I am

7   a   I never have a good influence on events
    b   I occasionally have a good influence on events
    c   I often have a good influence on events
    d   I always have a good influence on events

8   a   I get by in life
    b   Life is good
    c   Life is very good
    d   I love life

9   a   I am not really interested in other people
    b   I am moderately interested in other people
    c   I am very interested in other people
    d   I am intensely interested in other people

10 a   I do not find it easy to make decisions
    b   I find it fairly easy to make decisions
    c   I find it easy to make most decisions
    d   I can make all decisions very easily

11 a   I find it difficult to get started to do things
    b   I find it moderately easy to start doing things
    c   I find it easy to do things
    d   I feel able to take anything on

12 a   I rarely wake up feeling rested
    b   I sometimes wake up feeling rested
    c   I usually wake up feeling rested
    d   I always wake up feeling rested

13 a   I don't feel at all energetic
    b   I feel fairly energetic
    c   I feel very energetic
    d   I feel I have boundless energy

14 a   I don't think things have a particular 'sparkle'
    b   I find beauty in some things
    c   I find beauty in most things
    d   The whole world looks beautiful to me

15		22	
a	I don't feel mentally alert	a	I do not have fun with other people
b	I feel quite mentally alert	b	sometimes have fun with other people
c	I feel very mentally alert	c	I often have fun with other people
d	I feel fully mentally alert	d	I always have fun with other people
16		**23**	
a	I don't feel particularly healthy	a	I do not have a cheerful effect on others
b	I feel moderately healthy	b	sometimes have a cheerful effect on others
c	I feel very healthy	c	I often have a cheerful effect on others
d	I feel on top of the world	d	I always have a cheerful effect on others
17		**24**	
a	I do not have particularly warm feelings towards others	a	I do not have any particular meaning or purpose in my life
b	I have some warm feelings towards others	b	I have a sense of meaning and purpose
c	I have very warm feelings towards others	c	I have a great sense of meaning and purpose
d	I love everybody	d	My life is totally meaningful and purposive
18		**25**	
a	I do not have particularly happy memories of the past	a	I do not have particular feelings of commitment and involvement
b	I have some happy memories of the past	b	sometimes become committed and involved
c	Most past events seem to have been happy	c	I often become committed and involved
d	All past events seem to have been extremely happy	d	I am always committed and involved
19		**26**	
a	I am never in a state of joy or elation	a	I do not think the world is a good place
b	I sometimes experience joy and elation	b	I do think the world is a fairly good place
c	I often experience joy and elation	c	I do think the world is a very good place
d	I am constantly in a state of joy and elation	d	I do think the world is an excellent place
20		**27**	
a	There is a gap between what I would like to do and what I have done	a	I rarely laugh
b	I have done some of the things I wanted	b	I laugh fairly often
c	I have done many of the things I wanted	c	I laugh a lot
d	I have done everything I ever wanted	d	I am always laughing
21		**28**	
a	I can't organise my time very well	a	I don't think I look attractive
b	I organise my time fairly well	b	I think I look fairly attractive
c	I organise my time very well	c	I think I look attractive
d	I can fit in everything I want to do	d	I think I look extremely attractive
		29	
		a	I do not find things amusing
		b	I find some things amusing
		c	I find most things amusing
		d	I am amused by everything

Source: Adapted from Argyle (2001).

Note: Sum scores where a = 0, b = 1, c = 2, d = 3. Most people score between 40 and 42.

Table 1.4 Components of subjective well-being

Cognitive component		Affective component	
Domain	Satisfaction	Positive affect	Negative affect
Self	Significant others' view of one's life	Happiness	Depression
Family	Satisfaction with current life	Elation	Sadness
Peer Group	Significant others' view of one's life	Ecstasy	Envy
Health	Satisfaction with past	Pride	Anger
Finances	Satisfaction with future	Affection	Stress
Work	Desire to change life	Joy	Guilt or shame
Leisure	Satisfaction with current life	Contentment	Anxiety

Source: Adapted from Diener *et al.* (1999).

prepare us for win–lose or win–win transactions, or zero-sum and non-zero-sum games. From an evolutionary perspective negative emotions such as fear or anger are our first line of defence against threats. For example, fear and anger tell us that danger is probable or that harm is imminent. Negative emotions narrow our attention to the source of the threat and mobilise us for fight or flight. Negative emotions prepare us for zero-sum games in which there is a winner and a loser and the amount lost and won is identical, so there is no net gain from the transaction. Hence the term, zero-sum game. In contrast positive emotions like pleasure or contentment tell us that something good is happening. Positive emotions broaden our attention so we become aware of the wider physical and social environment. This broadened attention prepares us to be open to new ideas and practices and to be more creative than usual (Isen, 2000). Thus positive emotions offer us opportunities to create better relationships and show greater productivity. Positive emotions prepare us for win–win or non-zero-sum games in which both parties conclude the transaction with more than they started. This link between non-zero-sum games and positive emotions is based on Wright's (2000) argument that the progress of civilisation is in the direction of increasing win–win interactions and institutions which support such non-zero-sum games.

From this analysis it is clear that negative emotions facilitate highly focused, defensive critical thinking and decision making, where the objective is to detect what is wrong and eliminate it. Positive emotions facilitate creative tolerant thinking and productivity. Studies of 'depressive realism' confirm that depressed people are more accurate judges of their own skills, and have a more accurate recall of positive and negative things that have happened to them and are more sensitive to risk-related information (Ackerman and Derubeis, 1991). In contrast, happy people overestimate their skills and remember more positive than negative events, but are better at making life planning decisions because they use important strategies such as seeking out health-risk-related information (Aspinwall *et al.*, 2001). The positive out-look that most people have and the realism associated with depression are both discussed in detail in Chapter 3.

Creativity and productivity: broaden-and-build theory

Professor Barbara Fredrickson (2002) at the University of Michigan has extended the idea that positive emotions lead to non-zero-sum games. She has developed the broaden-and-build theory of positive emotions to explain how positive affective experiences not only signal personal well-being but also contribute to personal growth and development. Many negative emotions such as anxiety or anger narrow people's momentary thought–action repertoires, so that they are ready to act in a particular self-protective way. Positive emotions, in contrast, broaden momentary thought–action repertoires. This broadening of momentary thought–action repertoires offers opportunities for building enduring personal resources, which in turn offers the potential for personal growth and transformation by creating positive or adaptive spirals of emotion, cognition and action. The process is diagrammed in Figure 1.3. For example, joy creates the urge to play and create in social and intellectual or artistic ways. Thus joy, through play, can strengthen social support networks and through creativity can lead to the production of art and science or to creative problem solving in day-to-day life. Increased social support, artistic and scientific productions, and successful

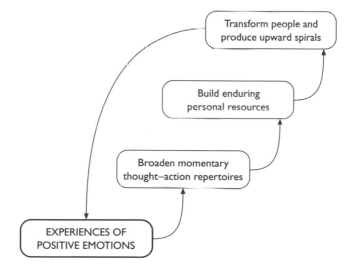

Figure 1.3 The broaden-and-build theory of positive emotions
Source: Adapted from Fredrickson (2002).

problem-solving experiences are all relatively enduring outcomes of joy and may contribute to personal transformation and development. This, in turn, may lead to more positive emotions. Contentment, another positive emotion, may create an urge to contemplate our life circumstances. This may lead to new and more positive ways of viewing ourselves and the world around us, and of carrying on our day-to-day lives. Further positive emotions may arise from these new and enduring insights and practices.

Empirical evidence from clinical and laboratory studies offer substantial support for the broaden-and-build theory of positive emotions (Fredrickson, 2002; Isen, 2000). There is good evidence that positive mood states broaden thought–action repertoires. Clinical studies of bipolar disorder show that manic and hypomanic states are associated with overinclusive thinking and that bipolar patients treated successfully with lithium show diminished creativity. In laboratory studies, a variety of methods have been found to reliably induce positive mood states for up to 15 minutes. These methods in order of effectiveness include asking participants to watch an arousing film and read an arousing story, receiving an unexpected gift (e.g. a bar of chocolate); reading positive self-statements; remembering a positive event; getting positive feedback; listening to music; and having positive social interaction with a cheerful person (Westermann et al., 1996). These mood induction methods have been used to show the positive effects of happiness on perception, cognition and social interaction in laboratory settings. Analogue studies show that a bias towards global visual processing and broadened attention is shown by people with positive mood states or people who receive success feedback on laboratory tasks. In contrast, people with negative mood states or people who receive failure feedback on laboratory tasks show a bias towards local visual processing. Laboratory studies of induced positive mood show that such induced mood states lead to more creative and flexible thought and behaviour. In Frederickson's own laboratory she has done a series of studies which lent support to the broaden-and-build theory. In one set of studies participants were shown film clips to induce positive emotions such as joy and contentment, and negative emotions such as fear and anger. After each clip participants listed as many things as they could think of that they would like to do if they had these emotions in real life. Positive emotions led to a far broader repertoire of thought–action tendencies.

Evidence from developmental and laboratory studies show that positive mood states help people build enduring personal resources. Developmental studies of securely and insecurely attached children, show that the former exhibit greater persistence, flexibility and resourcefulness in solving problems than the latter. They also show greater exploratory behaviour in novel situations and develop superior cognitive maps. Adults with secure attachment styles are more curious and open to new information than those with insecure attachment styles. Educational studies of children show that children in positive mood states learn faster. In her own laboratory Frederickson

(2002) has shown that over time positive emotions and broad minded coping mutually build upon each other. Broad minded coping entails considering a wide thought–action repertoire of responses. She has also shown that after the induction of a negative mood state involving increased heart rate, people who subsequently viewed short film clips to induce a positive emotional state had a faster cardiovascular recovery rate than those who viewed film clips to induce neutral or sad mood states. There are also individual differences in people's capacity to use positive emotions to effectively cope with stressful circumstances. People who obtain high scores on ego-resilience (Block and Kremen, 1996) show faster cardiovascular recovery following stress than those who obtain low scores and this recovery is mediated by experiencing positive emotions.

In view of this evidence which shows that positive emotions can facilitate creativity and problem solving, it is not surprising that happiness also increases work productivity. Staw *et al.* (1994) in a study of over 200 workers, found that over an 18-month period happier people obtained better evaluations and higher pay than their less happy counterparts.

Longevity

Evidence from longitudinal studies shows that happiness has important effects on longevity. In a follow-back study of 180 nuns in the USA, Danner *et al.* (2001) found that the happiness expressed in essays that the nuns wrote as they entered the order was associated with their longevity. This was a carefully controlled study. All of the participants had similar lifestyles. They were all unmarried nuns who worked as teachers, did not smoke or drink and ate a simple balanced diet throughout their adult life. When they wrote their essays as they entered the order, they gave a biographical sketch and stated their hopes for the future, but had no idea that these essays would be used in a study of happiness and longevity. More than half a century later, the amount of positive emotions in the essays was judged by trained raters who did not know the age of the participants. Of the happiest quarter 90 per cent lived past the age of 85 compared with only 34 per cent of the least happy quarter.

Maruuta *et al.* (2000) conducted a follow-back study of over 800 patients, 200 of whom had died. These patients had attended the Mayo Clinic forty years previously. As part of their intake assessment they had answered questions to show whether their outlook was optimistic or pessimistic. Forty years later, of the 200 patients who had died, the optimists showed 19 per cent greater longevity than pessimists. Thus, patients who reported that they were optimistic when they first attended the clinic, lived considerably longer than those who did not.

Ostir *et al.* (2000) in a longitudinal study of more than 2000 Mexican Americans over 65 years of age, found that after two years, positive emotions at the start of the study predicted who lived or died, and who showed greater functional independence or disability. After controlling for age, socio-economic status, drug use and diseases, the happy participants were twice as likely to survive and to remain functionally independent compared with their unhappy counterparts.

From the foregoing it is clear that happiness enhances creativity, product-ivity and longevity. Having considered the effects of happiness, let us now turn to research on the causes of happiness and subjective well-being.

CAUSES OF HAPPINESS

Identifying factors that contribute to happiness is not a simple matter (Diener, 2000; Diener et al., 1999). Pleasure and the pursuit of pleasure may sometimes, but not always, lead to happiness. For example, the repeated short-term pleasures of smoking cigarettes or using other drugs may lead to the long-term unhappiness associated with illness. Acts of murderous revenge, assault, rape, or theft may bring immediate satisfaction or short-term pleasure but in the long term they may reap social, psychological or physical conse-quences which lead to misery and despair. As a species we have evolved so that certain types of situations make us happy while others lead to the experience of distress. Individual differences in happiness may be partly accounted for by differences in personality which are partially genetically determined. There is also little doubt that certain kinds of environments are conducive to happiness or to providing people with opportunities to develop the skills required to achieve happiness. There are also important lessons to be learned from evolutionary psychology about obstacles to hap-piness and ways that these may be circumvented (Buss, 2000). These issues will be addressed in the remainder of this chapter.

Personality traits and happiness

Trait theories of personality (elaborated in Chapter 6) argue that a limited number of dimensions may be used to characterise important aspects of behaviour and experience and that particular personality trait profiles are associated with happiness. Traits are normally distributed within the population. So, for any given trait (for example extraversion), most people show a moderate level of the trait, but a few people show extremely low or extremely high levels of the trait. Because traits are normally distributed and because only a specific profile of traits is associated with happiness, not everyone will be able to achieve happiness.

Personality studies of happiness show that happy and unhappy people have distinctive personality profiles (Diener et al., 1999). In western cultures happy people are extraverted, optimistic and have high self-esteem and an internal locus of control. In contrast unhappy people tend to have high levels of neuroticism. Extraversion correlates about 0.7 with happiness or positive affectivity while neuroticism correlates above 0.9 with negative affectivity. Interestingly, intelligence is not related to happiness. The associations between personality traits and happiness are not universal across all cultures, an observation that will be discussed below.

There are a number of factors which offer partial explanations for the link between extraversion and happiness (Diener *et al.*, 1999). Extraverts may have a better fit with the social environment, which requires most people to be involved in frequent social interactions. So they find themselves frequently in situations which meet their needs for socialising and thus are happier. Also there is good evidence that extraverts respond with greater happiness to stimuli designed to induce positive moods. There is also evidence that extraversion and neuroticism predispose people to experience more positive and negative events respectively. So if you have a high level of extraversion you are more likely to experience positive events and therefore experience more happiness. If you have a high level of neuroticism, you are more likely to experience more negative events and so be more unhappy.

Cultural factors partially determine the types of personality factors associated with happiness. In western individualistic cultures such as the USA, self-esteem and acting in a consistent way that is congruent with one's personal beliefs are personality factors associated with high levels of subjective well-being. However, subjective well-being is not correlated with these factors in eastern collectivist societies. So cultural values partially determine personality traits that affect subjective well-being, probably because these traits are associated with achieving culturally valued goals (Triandis, 2000).

Genetic and environmental basis for personality traits

The weight of evidence shows that 50 per cent of the variance in major personality traits such as extraversion and neuroticism may be accounted for by genetic factors (Paris, 1996; Riemann *et al.*, 1997). The mechanisms by which genetic factors influence personality traits are complex. Probably multiple genes determine temperamental characteristics, and these interact with environmental influences in the development of personality traits. There is considerable evidence from longitudinal studies of the link between temperament and personality traits. Children with high activity levels and positive affect become extraverted, and so are more likely to be happy. Children who are highly irritable and fearful show high levels of neuroticism in later life and so are more likely to show negative affectivity (Rothbart and Ahadi, 1994).

Optimism, self-esteem and locus of control are also personality traits which correlate with happiness. The relative contributions of genetic and environmental factors to the development of optimism, self-esteem and locus of control is less clear. However, there are good reasons to believe that secure attachment is an important precursor of these types of personal strengths (Thompson, 1999). Also there is good evidence that parents who blend warmth with a moderate level of control in bringing up their children help them to develop self-esteem and an internal locus of control (Darling and Steinberg, 1993). Finally, optimistic children learn their optimism from their parents who adopt an optimistic explanatory style (Seligman, 1998).

Heritability of a happiness set-point

Professor David Lykken (1999), in the Minnesota Study of Twins Reared Apart, has shown that about half of the variance in current happiness or subjective well-being (assessed by the Well-Being scale of the Multidimensional Personality Questionnaire) is due to genetic factors. However, the set-point for happiness – that is the stable point around which people's mood varies over periods such as a decade – is about 98 per cent genetically determined. Data on which these conclusions are based are given in Table 1.5. These data show that there are moderately high correlations

Table 1.5 Cross-twin, cross-time and cross-twin and -time correlations based on scores from well-being scale of the multidimensional personality questionnaire taken at a 9-year interval

	No. of twin pairs	Correlations
Cross twin correlation for monozygotic twins reared apart	69	0.53
Cross twin correlation for monozygotic twins reared together	663	0.44
Cross twin correlation for dizygotic twins reared apart	50	0.13
Cross twin correlation for dizygotic twins reared together	715	0.08
Conclusion: Well-being is 44–53% heritable		
Cross-time correlation after 9 years for monozygotic twins	410	0.55
Cross-time and twin correlation after 9 years for monozygotic twins	131	0.54
Cross-time and twin correlation after 9 years for dizygotic twins	74	0.05
Conclusion: Set-point for well-being is 98% heritable (0.55/0.54)		

Source: Based on Lykken (1999).

(0.44–0.53) between the well-being scores of monozygotic twins and negligible correlations (0.08–0.13) between scores of dizygotic twins. These findings support the conclusion that well-being is 44–53 per cent heritable. The correlation between the scores of monozygotic twins at the start of the study and their own scores nine years later was $r = 0.55$ and that between each monozygotic twin at the start of the study and his or her twin-sibling nine years later was $r = 0.54$. This remarkable finding allows us to conclude that the set-point for happiness is 98 per cent (0.55/0.54) heritable.

CULTURE AND HAPPINESS

Specific cultural and socio-political factors have also been found to play an important role in determining happiness (Triandis, 2000). In cross-cultural studies associations have consistently been found between subjective well-being and living in a stable democracy devoid of political oppression and military conflict. Cultures in which there is social equality have higher mean levels of subjective well-being. Subjective well-being is greater in individualist cultures than in collectivist cultures. Happiness is also associated with important features of government institutions. Subjective well-being is higher in welfare states; in countries in which public institutions run efficiently; and in which there are satisfactory relationships between the citizens and members of the bureaucracy.

OPTIMISING WELL-BEING

Despite the fact that the set-point for happiness is predominantly genetically determined, and the fact that the cultural environment may facilitate or place constraints on our sense of well-being, there is scope for us to develop skills and organise our environments so that we spend the bulk of our time at, or just above, our happiness set-points. In this way we optimise our sense of well-being. However, our set-points determine the typical overall level of happiness we can experience over our lifecycles.

In finding satisfaction and happiness, it is useful to be aware of those situations which evolution has ensured will bring us deep satisfaction, that is those situations in which we are biologically designed to experience happiness (Buss, 1999, 2000; Pinker, 1997; Zahavi and Zahavi,1997; Lykken, 1999). Evolution has ensured that we experience deep happiness under conditions that are good for the propagation of our particular genetic line. Mating, maintaining close kinship ties with family members, developing deep friendships with a relatively small number of people, maintaining co-operative coalitions with slightly larger groups, living in a safe and fertile environment, engaging in physical exercise, developing and using skills for goal-oriented activities and eating high-quality food all produce a sense of happiness probably because they contributed to our survival.

There is good evidence from empirical studies in the USA and Europe that happiness is related to most of these factors pinpointed within evolutionary psychology (Argyle, 2001; Diener, 2000; Diener *et al.*, 1999; Kahneman *et al.*, 1999; Lykken, 1999; Myers, 1992, 2000). Associations have been found between happiness and significant personal relationships; the quality of the environment in which people live; their involvement in physical activities; work practices; and involvement in certain recreational activities. Let us now further explore evidence for the relationships between all of these factors and happiness.

RELATIONSHIPS AND HAPPINESS

Within the broad domain of relationships marriage, kinship, close friendships, co-operation with acquaintances and involvement in religion and spiritual practices are all associated with enduring happiness and well-being.

Marriage

From Figure 1.4 it may be seen that married people are happier than unmarried people, be they divorced, separated or never married (Myers, 2000). However, the least happy of all are people trapped in unhappy marriages. The happiness gap between married and unmarried women is the same as that for men. So both men and women reap the same benefits in terms of personal happiness from marriage. There are two explanations for the link between happiness and marriage. One explanation is that more happy people get married while more unhappy people do not because happy people are more attractive as marital partners than unhappy people. Another explanation is that marriage confers a range of benefits on people that make them happy. Marriage provides psychological and physical intimacy, a context within which to have children and build a home, a social role as a spouse and parent, and a context within which to affirm identity and create posterity.

There is some evidence to support the view that more happy people form a satisfying marriage. Harker and Keltner (2001) found that middle-aged women whose college yearbook photographs showed them displaying a Duchenne smile had lived happier lives and had more fulfilling and long-standing marriages than women who showed a false smile in their college yearbook photos. In a Duchenne smile (called after Guillaume Duchenne who discovered it) the corners of the mouth turn up and the corners of the eyes crinkle into a pattern of skin creases like crow's feet. With a false smile, these features are absent. This was a well-controlled

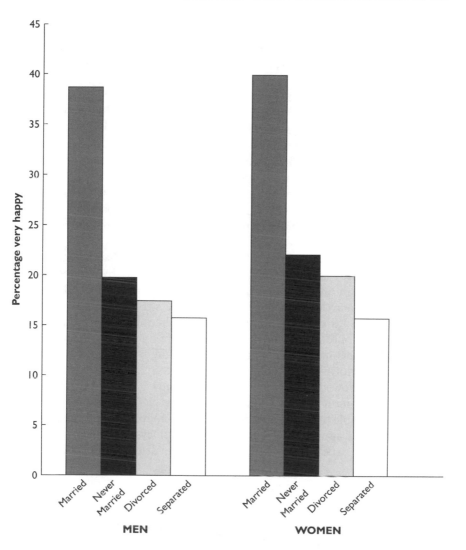

Figure 1.4 Marital status and happiness
Source: Adapted from Myers, E. (2000): 63, based on data from 35,024 cases in General Social Survey, National Opinion Research Centre, USA, 1972–1996.

study. The 141 participants had no idea that the quality of their smiles in their college yearbook photos would be judged by trained raters thirty years later. Also these raters were unaware of participants' satisfaction with life or marriage in middle life. Furthermore, when photos were rated for good looks, these were found to be unrelated to life or marital satisfaction.

A range of factors, besides happiness, have been identified as significant in the formation of stable and satisfying marriages. Partners similar in personality, ability, physical attractiveness, attitudes, interests, values and politics are more likely to experience marital satisfaction, remain married, avoid conflict and infidelity, and provide their children with a stable home environment (Newman and Newman, 1991; Buss, 2000). This may be because it is easier to empathise with people similar to ourselves and so partners similar to ourselves feel understood by us more easily. Also, where there is little difference between our 'mate value' and that of our partner, there is less likelihood of infidelity. So when choosing a mate, spouse or partner select someone who is similar to yourself on these attributes. Marriages in which people communicate respectfully and clearly and forgive each other's faults are typically associated with higher levels of satisfaction, so this type of communication is probably conducive to greater happiness (Harvey et al., 2002).

The association between marital status and happiness has been found in studies of 40 nations around the world regardless of the divorce rate or the effects of living in an individualist culture (Diener et al., 1999). However, the effects of unmarried cohabitation on happiness is affected by culture. In individualistic cultures, cohabiting couples are happier than even married couples, but in collectivist countries they are more unhappy than married or single people. This unhappiness may be due to the stresses associated with violating social norms about cohabiting in collectivist societies. In contrast, separated or widowed people in collectivist countries are happier than their counterparts in individualist cultures. This may be because greater social support is available to these single individuals in collectivist cultures and the additional social support leads to greater happiness. Marriage and mate selection, as one aspect of the family lifecycle, are discussed in greater detail in Chapter 8.

Kinship

Close supportive relationships between parents and children, between siblings, and between extended family members enhance the social support available to all family members. This social support enhances subjective well-being and from an evolutionary perspective we are 'hard-wired' to derive happiness from this contact with our kinship network (Argyle, 2001; Buss, 2000). There are certain things that we can do to enhance the benefits of kinship on our experience of happiness. Keep in regular contact with members of your family. Plan your lifestyle to allow you to maintain closer physical contact with your family. This planning refers to both stages of your yearly cycle and the longer time frame of your lifecycle. During periods when you are separated from your family use e-mail, the phone, and videotaped messages or videoconferencing or internet videolink to stay in touch. Maintaining contact with family members increases social support and this brings not only happiness but also improved immune system functioning, as will be outlined in the section on coping in Chapter 7. Maintaining contact with the extended family network reduces the chances of domestic violence and child abuse, because it pierces the veil of privacy that goes with being an isolated nuclear family so common in cases of domestic violence. A fuller discussion of the family lifecycle is given in Chapter 8.

Friendship

Maintaining a few close confiding relationships has been found to correlate with happiness and subjective well-being (Argyle, 2001, 2000). For example, in a study of the happiest 10 per cent of a group of 222 college students, Diener and Seligman (2002) found that their most distinctive attribute was their rich and fulfilling social life. These students spent a significant amount of their time socialising with friends and were rated by themselves and their friends at being outstanding in making and maintaining close friendships. Confiding relationships are probably associated with happiness for three reasons. First, happy people may be more often selected as friends and confidants, because they are more attractive companions than miserable people. They also help others more than depressed people who are self-focused and less altruistic. Second, confiding relationships meet needs for affiliation and so make us feel happy and satisfied. Third, close friendships provide social support. These research findings and insights on friendship from evolutionary psychology (Buss, 2000) have implications for how we can enhance our happiness through relationships with friends. Make a few good close friends and keep in touch with them. If you want to make good friends, choose work or leisure activities where you are likely to meet people who share similar interests to you and are similar in overall abilities, status and life experience to you, since friendships between people who are more similar have been shown to be deeper than those between dissimilar people. Where appropriate, find a match between your unique skills, characteristics and style and the needs or preferences of potential friends. Early on in friendships, this matching is important. If our profile of attributes and talents is unique and matches the needs of a new friend, we are less likely to be replaced. In evolutionary terms, we are fitter than other competitors for the role of being a friend to that person. To distinguish fair-weather friends from truly committed friends, once a friendship has developed, test the strength of the bond by disclosing some imperfection about yourself or putting yourself in a physically vulnerable situation in which your friend has to help you, for example in adventure sports such as climbing or sailing (Zahavi and Zahavi, 1997). Making and maintaining friendships is discussed in greater detail in Chapter 8 as one aspect of the family lifecycle. Social support as a benefit of friendship is discussed in the section on coping in Chapter 7.

Acquaintances

Co-operation with acquaintances, who are neither family nor close friends, is a potential source of happiness and a way of avoiding unhappiness due to loss of status and inequalities which inevitably arises from regular involvement in competition (Axelrod, 1984; Buss, 2000). It follows therefore that to enhance our own sense of well-being we should develop strategies for promoting co-operation with acquaintances, not competition. In all important relationships make sure that yourself and others are aware that the relationship will last indefinitely into the future and that long-term co-operation confers mutual benefits. When we keep in mind that we will have to co-exist with acquaintances for the long term and that working together will bring greater dividends than working alone, we are more likely to co-operate. In all important relationships, make a commitment to engage in equitable and reciprocal behaviour rather than exploitative behaviour. If another person does you a favour or helps you, return the favour or help with a gesture of similar (not lesser) value. This type of reciprocal behaviour builds trust whereas non-reciprocal behaviour dissolves trust. The co-operative or prosocial personality is discussed in detail in the section on altruism in Chapter 6.

Religion and spirituality

Moderate correlations have been found between happiness and involvement in religious activity in North American studies (Myers, 2000). This is illustrated by Figure 1.5. People involved in religion may be happier than others for many reasons. Three have been given serious consideration within psychology. First, religion provides a coherent belief system that allows people to find meaning in life and hope for the future (Seligman, 2002). Religious belief systems allow some of us to make sense of the adversities, stresses and inevitable losses which occur over the course of the lifecycle and to be optimistic about an afterlife in which these difficulties will be resolved. Second, involvement in routine attendance at religious services and being part of a religious community provides people with social support. Third, involvement in religion is often associated with a physically and psychologically healthier lifestyle characterised by marital fidelity; prosocial altruistic behaviour (rather than criminality); moderation in eating and drinking; and a commitment to hard work. Whether involvement in religion is associated with increased happiness in other cultures is not known. Meditation, which for some is a spiritual practice, has also been found to be associated with better personal well-being. Religion and meditation are discussed further in Chapter 7 in the section on coping.

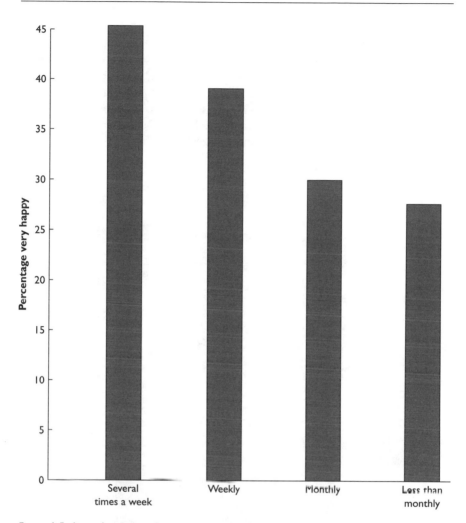

Figure 1.5 Attendance at religious services and happiness in the USA
Source: Adapted from Myers, E. (2000): 65, based on data from 35,024 cases in General Social Survey, National Opinion Research Centre, USA, 1972–1996.

THE ENVIRONMENT AND HAPPINESS

Broadly speaking more pleasant physical environments are moderately associated with happiness, although the way wealth, which determines the types of environments we can afford to live in, is associated with happiness is quite complex. Geographical location, housing, weather and the availability of music can all have short-term positive effects on well-being.

Wealth

Professor Ed Diener (2000) at the University of Illinois has found that
people in economically disadvantaged nations have lower set-points for happiness. In Figure 1.6 the relative levels of happiness in a number of different
countries may be seen along with their relative wealth. This is quantified in
the graph as purchasing power parity. Across nations, happiness and wealth
correlate about $r = 0.6$. Happiness rates are low in Russia and Turkey and
high in Ireland, Canada, Denmark and Switzerland. This is probably because

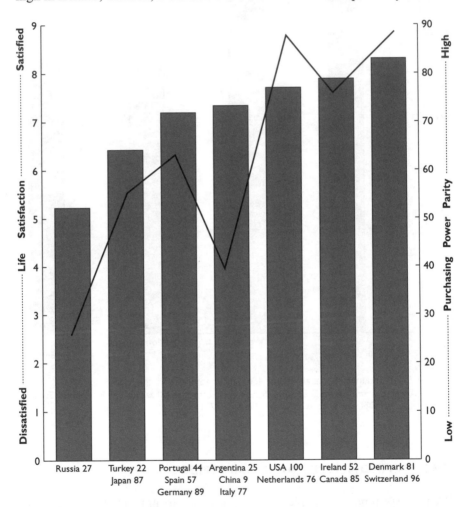

Figure 1.6 National wealth and life satisfaction
Source: Adapted from Diener, E. (2000): 37.
Note: Numbers after country names are purchasing power parity values. Bar graph is life
satisfaction and line graph is mean purchasing power parity for the group of countries in
that bar.

people in poorer countries are dissatisfied that they have not got the luxuries which they know from the media are available in the more affluent countries. However, from Figure 1.7 it may be seen that over time, in a wealthy nation such as the USA, increases in national income do not lead to an increase in the national level of subjective well-being. This is probably because increased wealth does not lead to increased power to become better off than one's neighbour. Within developed countries, very rich people have consistently been found to be slightly happier (although not a great deal

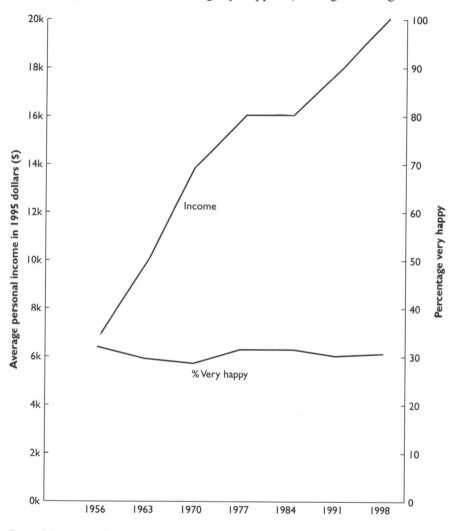

Figure 1.7 Increased wealth and happiness in the USA
Source: Adapted from Myers (2000): 61. Income data from US Commerce Department, Bureau of the Census and Economic Indicators. Happiness data from 35,024 cases in General Social Survey, National Opinion Research Centre, University of Chicago USA.

happier) than people on an average wage, probably because they view themselves as faring better than everyone else. These explanations are derived from social comparison theory which states that personal happiness is based on the perceived discrepancy between our own situation and that of others (Wood, 1996). Downward comparison, where the standard to which we compare our own situation is lower, results in greater satisfaction than upward comparison.

In economically advanced countries, people who value earning money more than other goals are less satisfied with their standard of living and their lives (Myers, 2000; Sirgy, 1998). This may be because the process and outcome of accumulating money may not be conducive to meeting social and psychological needs that enhance happiness once basic physical needs have been met. The degree to which this negative correlation between happiness and pursuit of money occurs in economically disadvantaged countries has not be studied.

Geographical location and other aspects of the environment

Strong positive feelings are associated with being in natural rather than artificial environments. People report positive feelings in geographical locations where there is vegetation, water and panoramic views (Ulrich *et al.*, 1991). Evolutionary factors probably contribute to preferences for these types of geographical locations (Buss, 2000). Such environments are both safe and fertile.

Good weather induces positive moods. When the sun is shining, when it's warm but not too warm, and when there is low humidity, people report more positive moods (Cunningham, 1979). However, people do adapt to unfavourable weather conditions and across nations there is no correlation between the climate and national happiness ratings.

Moderate correlations have been found between the quality of housing and life satisfaction. Indicators of the quality of housing include geographical location, rooms per person, room size and availability of heating (Andrews and Withey, 1976; Campbell *et al.*, 1976).

Music has been shown in surveys and mood induction experiments to induce short-term positive mood states and to reduce aggression (Hills and Argyle, 1998; Argyle, 2001). However, there is no evidence that music leads to enduring positive mood changes or life satisfaction.

PHYSICAL STATE AND HAPPINESS

Physical exercise leads to positive mood states but the link between physical health and happiness is quite complex.

Health

While subjective ratings of personal health correlate with happiness, object- ive health ratings made by physicians do not (except where people are se- verely disabled) (Diener *et al.*, 1999). Subjective ratings of personal health are influenced more by personality traits, such as neuroticism, and coping strategies, such as denial or reframing, than by objective physical health. People high on neuroticism may complain bitterly of ill-health and yet be rated as physically healthy by their physicians. In contrast, a person con- sidered quite ill by a physician may report feeling quite well because they are denying or reframing their physical ill-health. Also, positive emotions allow us to increase our tolerance for pain (Weisenberg *et al.*, 1998). With the exception of the severely disabled, most people adapt to their health prob- lems relatively quickly and develop self-perceptions of their health which are consistent with their level of happiness. However, there is a growing body of evidence which shows that happiness may influence our health via its effects on the immune system. The immune systems of happy people work more effectively than those of unhappy people (Kamen-Siegel *et al.*, 1991; Segerstrom *et al.*, 1998; Stone *et al.*, 1994). This in turn may account for the longevity of happy people discussed in an earlier section of this chapter.

Exercise

In the short term exercise induces positive mood states and in the long term regular exercise leads to greater happiness (Argyle, 2001; Sarafino, 2002). The short-term effects of exercise are due to the fact that exercise leads to the release of endorphins, morphine-like chemical substances produced in the brain. The longer-term increases in happiness associated with exercise are due to the fact that regular exercise reduces depression and anxiety, enhances the speed and accuracy of our work, improves our self-concepts, promotes fitness and leads to better cardiovascular functioning. Regular exercise also slows down or prevents weight gain with ageing. Regular exer- cise throughout adulthood reduces the risk of heart disease and cancer and is associated with longevity. In addition, people who exercise regularly often do so in the company of others, and so reap the benefits of this additional social support on their overall level of subjective well-being. Exercise is discussed more fully in Chapter 8 in the section on coping.

PRODUCTIVITY AND HAPPINESS

Employment status, job satisfaction, skill usage and goal-directed activity are all associated with subjective well-being and there is also an association between education and happiness in certain circumstances.

Work

Employment status is related to happiness, with employed people being happier than those who are unemployed, and people in professional and skilled jobs being happier than those in unskilled jobs (Argyle, 2001). Job satisfaction and happiness are moderately correlated at about $r = 0.4$ (Diener et al., 1999). This may be because work can potentially provide an optimal level of stimulation that people find pleasurable, an opportunity to fulfil their drive for curiosity and skills development, a social support network and a sense of identity and purpose. In jobs that are satisfying there is a good person–environment fit and such jobs have distinctive characteristics (Warr, 1999). People in such jobs are asked to fulfil functions and work in environments that are suited to their skills, talents and preferences. In such jobs they have considerable autonomy or decisional discretion about how they fulfil their work functions rather than being tightly constrained by frequent salient detailed directives from superiors. People tend to be more satisfied in jobs that entail completing intrinsically rewarding work tasks in which they use well-developed skills and work that brings social benefits. Such jobs also involve considerable task-variety. It follows from this that we should try to modify our work situation so that the functions we fulfil match our skills, strengths and preferences; so that we work on a variety of tasks that interest us; and so that we have a high level of autonomy at work. Other factors associated with job satisfaction include a clear role definition, supportive supervision, opportunities for interpersonal contact with colleagues, a socially valued position, physical safety and financial security (Warr, 1999). It has already been noted that happy people are more productive, so the link between happiness and productivity is bi-directional. Certain types of work situations facilitate happiness and happiness in turn facilitates greater productivity.

Education

Education level is positively correlated with happiness and this relationship is particularly strong for low-income groups in developed countries and populations in poorer countries (Diener et al., 1999). This may be because in underdeveloped countries education confers greater differential benefits. In underdeveloped countries, people with little education may not even be able to have their basic physical needs met whereas those with education may earn sufficient money to have their needs for food and shelter adequately met. In contrast, in developed countries in most instances even the poorly educated have their basic physical needs met.

Goal attainment

People report greater happiness on days when they achieve highly valued goals than on days when they achieve less valued goals (Diener *et al.*, 1999). These goals may be determined by many factors including personality traits. In keeping with this, extraverts experience more happiness on days when they do exciting things and introverts experience more happiness on days where they do things that bring contentment. When people's goals and aspirations are more coherently organised so as to be consistent with each other this leads to greater happiness than when their goals and aspirations are less clearly thought out. Having conflicting goals or ambivalence about certain goals reduces happiness. It follows from this that we should think carefully about our various goals and attempt to develop a set of life goals which are consistent with each other. We should then try to organise our time so that we can do at least some work towards these each day. The findings from research on goal attainment, work and job satisfaction are highly consistent with results of research on personal action constructs and subjective well-being discussed in Chapter 6 in the section on motives.

RECREATION AND HAPPINESS

Rest, relaxation, good food and leisure activities all have positive short-term effects on happiness (Argyle, 2001). During holiday periods people report greater positive moods and less irritability. Membership of leisure and sports groups, notably those that involve dancing, music, volunteer charity work or all-consuming sports have been found in surveys to be conducive to higher ratings of well-being. Membership of such leisure groups probably leads to increased well-being because it involves interaction with others, often within the context of a mini-culture that has its own ethos, values and a system for structuring time, activity and social relationships. Leisure groups that involve music, in addition to the foregoing, reap all the positive benefits of music for the induction of positive moods. Thus, group-based leisure activities may increase happiness by meeting certain needs such as: the needs for affiliation and altruism; the need for autonomous execution of skilled activity; the need for excitement; and the need for competition and achievement.

EVOLUTIONARY PERSPECTIVES ON OBSTACLES TO HAPPINESS

In western civilised countries our environment is in many respects luxurious compared to that of our cave-dwelling ancestors. We have reduced infant mortality, virtually eliminated many fatal infectious diseases, overcome food shortages and developed energy, housing and transport systems that have greatly reduced the destructive impact of extreme weather conditions. We have also developed ways of protecting ourselves from most predators, created machines to carry out many menial tasks, designed a lifestyle which includes education, sport, art and leisure activities, and doubled the average person's lifespan. However, we are still not happy some of the time and some people are unhappy much of the time. There are many obstacles to our happiness, and evolutionary psychology offers insights into some of these (Axelrod, 1984; Buss, 1999, 2000; Pinker, 1997; Zahavi and Zahavi, 1997).

Obstacles to happiness with evolutionary origins include our innate tendencies to habituate or adapt to pleasurable situations and to have inequitable reactions to equal losses and gains. Another obstacle to happiness is the tendency to make comparisons between the self and others, which in ancestral times was adaptive but can be maladaptive in modern society where highly salient and unrealistically positive images of others are presented in the media. A further obstacle to happiness is the fact that we have been naturally selected through the process of evolution to experience certain distressing emotions such as anxiety, depression and anger because they were adaptive for the survival of our species before the development of our modern society. Let us consider each of these obstacles to happiness in turn.

Habituation and adaptation to pleasurable situations

We have evolved in a way that we are designed to quickly habituate or adapt to situations that give us pleasure because it was adaptive for our hunting and gathering ancestors (Buss, 2000; Frederick and Lowenstein, 1999). People who quickly habituated to the pleasures of any gains they made in obtaining better food or shelter were naturally selected. Those who rested on their laurels for a long time on each occasion when they achieved a goal that entailed the experience of long-lasting pleasure did not survive. In modern times this evolutionary design feature of humans underlies the tyranny of consumerism. People believe that they will be happy when they get this new type of food, clothing, household appliance, car or house but once they have it for a while, they habituate or adapt and want one that is bigger or better.

Brickman and Campbell (1971) coined the term 'hedonic treadmill' to describe this process of rapid adaptation whereby people react strongly to both positive and negative recent events with sharp increases or decreases in happiness but in most instances return to their happiness set-point over relatively short periods of time (e.g. a few weeks or months). Subsequent research (e.g. Diener et al., 1999; Diener, 2000) has shown that while rapid habituation occurs for some positive and negative events (e.g. imprisonment or winning the lottery), people adapt more slowly to certain types of events (such as marriage or death of a spouse) and do not adapt at all to others (e.g. noise and sex). Why this occurs is not fully understood. It follows from our knowledge of habituation that an acceptance of its inevitability may reduce the disappointment and dysphoria that comes with expecting increases in happiness arising from material gains to be enduring.

A second important finding concerning adaptation is that habituation to discrete pleasures, such as eating a favourite food or hearing a favourite piece of music, occurs less rapidly if the pleasurable experiences are spaced apart. Such discrete pleasures have a greater positive effect if the craving for a further episode of pleasure is allowed to dissipate before the pleasure is indulged in again. This finding is based on animal studies of addictive processes (Shizgal, 1997). It follows from this that to increase our happiness we should indulge ourselves in pleasures at optimally spaced intervals, so that each time we listen to our favourite music or eat our favourite food, we do so after our craving to do so based on past indulgence of the pleasure has passed (Seligman, 2002).

Negative social comparisons

Our level of happiness is influenced by how we rate ourselves and our current circumstances, not only in comparison with our recent circumstances, but also in comparison with those of others (Wood, 1996). We compare ourselves with other people in terms of health, personal attractiveness and that of our partners and children, wealth, social status, academic and athletic achievement, and so forth. This process of social comparison in ancestral times was adaptive because it led us to strive to be the best and to have the best resources in our group and so propagate our genetic line. In ancestral society, it was possible for a handful of people within each human group (which typically numbered about 50 to 200) to have the best lifestyle, to be the most attractive male or female and to be the best at work, sport or relationships. Thus a handful of people in each human grouping were happy because they were the best in their group in some particular domain. Also, it was realistic for many people within the group to aspire to be the best in their group at something at some point in their lifecycle. Modern media, including TV, films, video, magazines, newspapers and the internet, present images of lifestyles, physical attractiveness and levels of excellence in work, sport and human relationships which most people will never be able to attain. When we measure our success against the standards presented in the media, rather than the best in our immediate reference group, this can lead to unhappiness because we cannot attain the standards set by media images (Buss, 2000). This is due in some instances to the fictitious nature of the standards. For example, the images of physical attractiveness and happiness portrayed by film stars or musicians are partially fictitious. In other instances, standards set by the media are unattainable because, for most of us, the constraints of our lifestyles do not allow us to devote all our energy to one thing such as singing, playing chess, or ballet dancing and all of us are not equally gifted. When we judge ourselves as failing to meet very high standards set by media images, we can experience low self-esteem and unhappiness. Also, the media's presentation of images of dominant males and attractive females can weaken people's commitments to their own partners who do not compare favourably with media images. This, in turn, in some instances can impact negatively on marital satisfaction, family stability and the health and well-being of offspring (Myers, 1992).

According to multiple discrepancy theory (Michalos, 1985) our level of satisfaction is determined by comparisons we make between our current circumstances and multiple standards. These include: people who are better and worse off than ourselves; our past circumstances; our future aspirations and ideals; and our needs and personal goals. This theory suggests that we have a choice about improving our happiness and low self-esteem associated with negative comparisons with media images. We can value the relationships, personal strengths, achievements and acquisitions that we have, compared to those worse off than ourselves. We can judge our circumstances against realistic personal goals and aspirations which are consistent with our personal abilities and resources. We can judge ourselves against our immediate local reference group, not the false images of the media. We can also check out the validity of the health, wealth, happiness, and so forth, of media images. There is evidence that we have the flexibility to choose to make these alternative comparisons and so improve our sense of well-being (Diener *et al.*, 1999).

Inequitable reactions to equal losses and gains

We are also designed in evolutionary terms so that losses lead to more intense emotional experiences than gains of the same magnitude, because this was adaptive for our ancestors (Buss, 2000). So, loss of an animal that had been hunted long and hard and got away led to a far more intense emotional experience than that associated with successfully killing the same animal after a long chase. Those who experienced intense emotions following loss were strongly motivated to work hard to avoid loss and so survived. Those that did not experience intense emotions in response to loss were not motivated to work hard to avoid loss and probably experienced multiple losses of food, shelter and other things necessary for survival and so died out. In modern times, this legacy remains with us. The despair experienced at losing €100 is not matched in magnitude by the satisfaction of earning or winning €100. One outcome of being designed in this way by the process of natural selection is that to achieve intense satisfaction a great deal must be acquired. However, to experience intense distress, only a little needs to be lost. Both of these factors compromise our capacity for happiness. Furthermore our disappointment at the small increments in happiness that arise from big gains and the large decrements in happiness entailed by small losses may further detract from our happiness. However, if we accept that this is the way we are designed, then we will not be disappointed when moderate achievements bring only small increases in happiness. We can also take steps to enhance the support available to us from friends and family when we anticipate or experience moderate losses.

Adaptive but distressing emotions

As a species we have evolved in such a way that we are designed to have certain distressing emotions such as anxiety, depression, jealousy or anger in certain circumstances because these reactions were adaptive for our ancestors (Buss, 2000). When faced with certain dangers or threats (e.g. snakes or separation from a parent) our ancestors experienced anxiety. This motivated them to avoid the threat and so survive. When faced with loss of status or power in a social hierarchy or close relationships they experienced depression. This motivated others within their group not to challenge or attack them and so they survived. When faced with the threat of spousal infidelity, they, like us, experienced jealousy. This motivated them to be vigilant and protective of their spouses so that their children could survive. When faced with obstacles to attaining a valued goal such as food or sex they experienced anger. This motivated them to remove obstacles and so survive. We have inherited this distressing emotional legacy from our ancestors, because it was adaptive for them. Thus, we all have some propensity to experience anxiety in the face of threat; depression following loss; jealousy in response to possible infidelity; and anger in response to obstruction. This distressing emotional legacy is an obstacle to happiness. Advances in psychotherapy, particularly cognitive-behavioural and systemic therapies suggest ways of managing distressing emotions by making changes in the way we think, act and manage relationships (Carr, 2000c; Nathan and Gorman, 2002).

For depression, avoid distressing situations. If this is not possible, focus on the non-distressing aspects of the situation. If this is not possible, assertively ask others who are distressing you to behave in less stressful ways. If you begin to feel depressed, challenge pessimistic and perfectionistic thinking and look for evidence to support more optimistic alternative ways of making sense of each situation. Increase your activity level by engaging in regular exercise and schedule events that you find stimulating and pleasurable. Meet regularly with close friends and family members whom you can count on to offer you social support.

For anxiety, challenge threat-oriented thinking and look for evidence to support less threatening ways of interpreting these distressing situations. Practise being courageous by actively going into situations that frighten you and remaining there until your anxiety subsides. When you take on these challenges, ask close friends and family members to support you and celebrate your success. Prepare well for challenges by practising coping skills such as relaxation exercises, listening to calming music, and so forth.

For anger, avoid anger-provoking situations. If this is not possible, focus on the non-distressing aspects of the situation. If this is not possible, assertively ask others who are provoking you to behave in less stressful ways. If you begin to feel anger, stand back from the situation and allow your physiological arousal level to decrease, so you can think more efficiently. We cannot think efficiently when we are highly physiologically aroused by anger, fear or excitement. Then try to hear, understand and empathise with the other person's point of view. This may allow you to see that there are no grounds for being aggrieved, or, if there are, you will be better able to see more constructive ways of settling the grievance.

HAPPINESS ENHANCEMENT

A summary of happiness-enhancement strategies suggested by the material reviewed in this chapter is presented in Table 1.6. Fordyce (1977, 1983), Fava *et al.* (1998) and Lichter *et al.* (1980) have all developed and evaluated community-based training programmes for enhancing happiness which include elements of the overall set of happiness-enhancement strategies presented in Table 1.6. In addition, Seligman has developed a highly effective programme to promote optimism in children and adults and this will be discussed more fully in Chapter 3 on optimism (Seligman, 1998). However, Seligman (2002) argues that an important distinction may be made between the pleasant life and the good life. The pleasant life may be achieved by pursuing positive emotions using strategies such as those outlined in Table 1.6. In contrast, the good life involves using signature strengths to obtain gratifications in important areas of life such as family relationships and work. Activities in which signature strengths are used are intrinsically motivated and result in experiences such as flow and absorption. These issues are discussed in Chapter 2.

RELATED CONCEPTS

Psychological well-being, social well-being and health-related quality of life are constructs related to, but distinct from, subjective well-being.

Psychological well-being

Psychological well-being refers to the achievement of one's full psychological potential. The construct is central to the humanistic tradition. Professor Carol Ryff is the leading researcher in this area and her psychological

Table 1.6 Strategies for enhancing happiness

Domain	Strategy
Relationships	• Mate with someone similar, communicate kindly and clearly and forgive faults • Maintain contact with your extended family • Maintain a few close friendships • Co-operate with acquaintances • Engage in religious or spiritual practices
Environment	• Secure physical and financial safety and comfort for yourself and your family, but don't get on the hedonic treadmill of consumerism • Periodically enjoy fine weather • Live in a geographically beautiful environment • Live in an environment where there is pleasing music and art
Physical state	• Maintain good health • Engage in regular physical exercise
Productivity	• Use skills that are intrinsically pleasing for tasks that are challenging • Achieve success and approval at work that is interesting and challenging • Work towards a coherent set of goals
Recreation	• Eat quality food in moderation • Rest, relax, and take holidays in moderation • Do co-operative recreational activities with groups of friends like music, dance, physical work projects, exhilarating activities (sailing/surfing)
Habituation	• For excessive striving for material gain to increase happiness, accept that you will inevitably habituate to material goods and situations that initially bring increases in happiness
Comparisons	• For low self-esteem due to negative comparisons with media images, judge yourself against your immediate local reference group and those worse off than yourself, not the false images of the media; check the validity of resources and happiness of media images; set realistic personal goals and standards consistent with your abilities and resources
Inequitable reactions to losses and gains	• For disappointment associated with inequity of reactions to gains and losses, expect to get small increases in happiness from large gains and successes; and large reductions in happiness from small losses and failures
Distressing emotions	• For depression, avoid distressing situations, focus on non-distressing aspects of difficult situations, assertively challenge distressing people, challenge pessimistic and perfectionistic thinking, be active and get support • For anxiety, challenge threat-oriented thinking and practise courage by entering threatening situations and using coping strategies to reduce anxiety • For anger, avoid provocative situations, focus on non-distressing aspects of difficult situations, assertively ask provocative people to be less provocative, stand back and practise empathy

Source: Based on Argyle (2001); Seligman (2002); Diener et al. (1999); Buss (2000); Myers (1992); Lykken (1999).

well-being scales evaluate six dimensions: autonomy; environmental mastery; personal growth; positive relations with others; purpose in life; and self-acceptance (Ryff, 1989; Ryff and Keyes, 1995). Keyes *et al.* (2000) in a factor analytic study involving over 3,000 Americans aged 25–74 found that psychological well-being and subjective well-being were related, but distinct, constructs which correlated differentially with socio-demographic variables and personality. Both psychological and subjective well-being increased with age, education, emotional stability, extraversion and conscientiousness. However, compared with adults with higher subjective than psychological well-being, adults with higher psychological than subjective well-being were younger, had more education and showed more openness to experience.

Social well-being

Social well-being refers to positive states associated with optimal functioning within one's social network and community. Keyes's (1998) social well-being scales evaluate five dimensions: social integration, social contribution social coherence, social actualisation and social acceptance. These scales correlate with measures of anomie, generativity, perceived social constraints, community involvement, neighbourhood quality and educational level. Social well-being as evaluated by these scales is distinct from measures of subjective well-being.

Quality of life

Quality of life is a far broader construct than subjective well-being. It is a complex construct which covers a variety of domains including health status, capacity to carry out activities of daily living, work-role status, availability of opportunities to pursue recreational interests, social functioning in friendships and relationships, access to health-care resources, standard of living and general well-being. Not all quality-of-life measures cover all of these domains. Various quality-of-life measures have been developed, including measures for general quality of life, health-related quality of life, and disease-specific quality of life, to evaluate a variety of populations, including: adults with physical illnesses (Gill and Feinstein, 1994); children with physical illnesses (Eiser and Morse, 2001); adults with psychiatric and psychological problems (Lehman, 1999); and people with intellectual disabilities (Hughes *et al.*, 1995).

CONTROVERSIES

One of the major debates within the field concerns the distinction between the hedonic and eudaimonic traditions in research on well-being (Ryan and

Deci, 2001). The hedonic approach defines happiness and the good life in terms of pleasure seeking and pain avoidance. This tradition has had many adherents throughout the history of philosophy and psychology and may be traced back to Aristippus, a Greek philosopher from BC fourth century. Currently this tradition is exemplified by the work of contributors to such volumes as *Well-being: The Foundations of Hedonic Psychology* edited by Professors Kahneman, Diener and Schwartz (1999). The eudaimonic tradition, in contrast, defines happiness and the good life in terms of achieving one's full potential. This tradition has found favour in many religious and spiritual movements. It is central to Aristotle's view that true happiness comes not from satisfying our appetites, but from doing what is morally worth doing: that is, from the expression of virtue. Thus, while the pursuit of pleasure through the satisfaction of needs and appetites may sometimes lead to well-being, this is not always the case, and in some instances the pursuit of pleasure may prevent well-being. Currently this tradition is exemplified by the work of Carol Ryff whose work on psychological well-being was mentioned in the previous section (Ryff, 1989; Ryff and Keyes, 1995). Factor analyses of multiple measures of well-being conceptualised from hedonic and eudaimonic perspectives show that subjective well-being and personal growth are distinct but related factors (Compton *et al.*, 1996; Keyes *et al.*, 2000). This supports Seligman's (2002) distinction between the (hedonic) pleasures and the (eudaimonic) gratifications.

SUMMARY

Understanding and facilitating happiness and subjective well-being is the central objective of positive psychology. Seligman classifies positive emotions into three categories: those associated with the past, the present and the future. There are two distinct classes of positive emotions concerned with the present: momentary pleasures; and more enduring gratifications. The pleasures include both bodily pleasures and higher pleasures which come from positive sensual experiences. Gratifications which entail states of absorption or flow come from engagement in activities that involve exercising signature strengths.

An extremely wide range of emotional experiences may be described in terms of the circumplex space defined by either arousal (high v low) and evaluation (positive v negative) or positive affectivity and negative affectivity. Positive affectivity is correlated with extraversion and negative affectivity is correlated with neuroticism. Positive and negative affectivity are probably subserved by the same neurobiological mechanisms that underpin extraversion and neuroticism and both types of affectivity are partially heritable. Positive affectivity is associated with greater job satisfaction and marital satisfaction and may be enhanced through regular physical activity, adequate sleep, regular socialising with close friends and striving for valued goals.

International surveys consistently show that most people are happy and the average happiness rating is 6.75 on a 10-point scale. Single questions with multiple-response categories, multi-item scales and experience-sampling methods have been used to assess happiness in empirical studies of the construct.

Negative emotions prepare us for win–lose, zero-sum transactions, while positive emotions prepare us for win–win, non-zero-sum games. The broaden-and-build theory of positive emotions explains how positive affective experiences not only signal personal well-being but also facilitate creative tolerant thinking and productivity. Evidence from longitudinal studies shows that happiness has a positive impact on longevity.

Personality studies of happiness show that happy people are extraverted and optimistic, and have high self-esteem and an internal locus of control. In contrast, unhappy people tend to have high levels of neuroticism. Fifty per cent of the variance in extraversion and neuroticism is due to genetic factors, and there is a strong link between temperament, which is largely genetically determined, and personality traits. Children with temperamentally high activity levels and positive affect become extraverted, and so are more likely to be happy. Children who are temperamentally highly irritable and fearful show high levels of neuroticism in later life and so are more likely to show negative affectivity. Secure attachment, an authoritative parenting style and good role modelling are probably important in the development of optimism, self-esteem, and an internal locus of control, all of which are associated with happiness. Twin studies show that about half of the variance in current happiness is due to genetic factors, but the set-point for happiness is about 98 per cent genetically determined. Despite the fact that the set-point for happiness is predominantly genetically determined, evidence from empirical studies supports insights from evolutionary psychology which point to ways for optimising happiness. Associations have been found between happiness and significant personal relationships; the quality of the environment in which people live; their involvement in physical activities; work practices; and involvement in certain recreational activities. We can optimise our sense of well-being by taking some of the following courses of action. With respect to relationships, mate with someone similar, communicate kindly and clearly and forgive faults; maintain contact with extended family; maintain a few close friendships; co-operate with acquaintances; and engage in religious or spiritual practices. With respect to the environment, secure physical and financial safety and comfort for yourself and your family, but don't get on the hedonic treadmill of consumerism; live in a geographically beautiful environment where there is fine weather and where there is pleasing music and art. With respect to physical well-being, maintain good health and engage in regular physical exercise. With respect to productivity, use skills that are intrinsically pleasing for tasks that are challenging; achieve success and approval at work that is interesting and challenging; and work towards a coherent set of goals. With respect to leisure, eat quality food in moderation; regularly rest, relax and take holidays in moderation; and engage in co-operative recreational activities with groups of friends. Some of the more significant obstacles to happiness with evolutionary origins include our innate tendencies to habituate to pleasurable situations; to make negative comparisons with others; to have inequitable reactions to equal losses and gains; and to experience depression, anxiety and anger. For excessive striving for material gain to increase happiness, accept that you will inevitably habituate to material goods and situations that initially bring increases in happiness. For low self-esteem due to negative comparisons with media images, judge yourself against your immediate local reference group and those worse off than yourself, not the false images of the media; check the validity of resources and happiness of media images; and set realistic personal goals and standards consistent with your abilities and resources. For disappointment associated with inequity of reactions to gains and losses, expect to get small increases in happiness from large gains and successes; and large reductions in happiness from small losses and failures. For depression, we should challenge pessimistic and perfectionistic thinking, be active and get support from family and close friends. For anxiety, we should challenge threat-oriented thinking and practise courage. For anger, we should stand back and practise empathy.

Psychological well-being, social well-being and health-related quality of life are constructs related to, but distinct from, subjective well-being.

One of the major debates within the field concerns the distinction between the hedonic and eudaimonic traditions. The hedonic approach defines happiness and the good life in terms of pleasure seeking and pain avoidance. The eudaimonic tradition in contrast defines happiness and the good life in terms of achieving one's full potential.

QUESTIONS

Personal development questions

1. What factors are present in your life that contribute to happiness?
2. What factors are absent?
3. What could you do to enhance your happiness?
4. What would be the costs and benefits of adopting these happiness-enhancing strategies?
5. Adopt some of these strategies and assess the impact it has on your well-being by assessing yourself before and afterwards on one of the well-being scales contained in the chapter.

Research questions

1. Replicate and extend this or a similar survey-type study: E. Diener and M. Seligman (2002). Very happy people. *Psychological Science*, 13, 81–4.
2. Replicate and extend a mood induction study such as those described in B. Fredrickson (2002). Positive emotions. In C.R. Snyder and S. Lopez (eds), *Handbook of Positive Psychology* (pp. 120–34). New York: Oxford University Press.

FURTHER READING

Academic

Argyle, M. (2001). *The Psychology of Happiness* (2nd edn). London: Routledge.
Aspinwall, L. and Staudinger, U. (2003). *A Psychology of Human Strengths. Fundamental Questions and Future Directions for a Positive Psychology*. Washington, DC: American Psychological Association.
Kahneman, D., Diener, E., and Schwartz, N. (1999). *Well-being: The Foundations of Hedonic Psychology*. New York: Russell Sage Foundation.
Keyes, C. and Haidt, J. (2001). *Flourishing: The Positive Person and the Good Life*. Washington, DC: APA.
Snyder, C. and Lopez, S. (2002). *Handbook of Positive Psychology*. New York: Oxford University Press.

Self-help: Happiness

Lykken, D. (1999). *Happiness. The Nature and Nurture of Joy and Contentment*. New York: St Martin's Press.
Myers, D. (1992). *The Pursuit of Happiness*. New York: Morrow.
Seligman, M. (2002). *Authentic Happiness*. New York: Free Press.

Self-help: Overcoming depression

Burns, D. (1980). *Feeling Good: The New Mood Therapy*. New York: Morrow. A practical cognitive behavioural guide to overcoming depression, backed by good research.
Burns, D. (1989). *The Feeling Good Handbook: Using the New Mood Therapy in Everyday Life*. New York: Harper Row and later published by Penguin as a Plume book. A very detailed practical cognitive-behavioural guide to overcoming depression, backed by good research.
Greenberger, D. and Padesky, C. (1995). *Mind Over Mood: A Cognitive Therapy Treatment Manual for Clients*. New York: Guilford. A practical cognitive-behavioural guide to overcoming depression, backed by good research.
Lewinsohn, P., Munoz, R., Youngren, M. and Zeiss, A. (1996). *Control Your Depression*. Englewood Cliffs, NJ: Prentice Hall. A practical cognitive-behavioural guide to overcoming depression, backed by good research.

Self-help: Anxiety management

Barlow, D. and Craske, M. (1994). *Master Your Anxiety and Panic II*. Albany, NY: Graywind. A research-based guide to managing anxiety and panic attacks.

Bourne, E. (1995). *The Anxiety and Phobia Workbook*. Oakland, CA: New Harbinger. A research-based guide to overcoming fears and phobias.

Foa, E. and Wilson, R. (1991). *STOP Obsessing. How to Overcome Your Obsessions and Compulsions*. New York: Bantam. A research-based guide to managing OCD.

Ingham, C. (1993). *Panic Attacks: What They Are, Why They Happen, and What You Can Do about Them*. London: Thorsens (Harper Collins). A research-based guide to managing anxiety and panic attacks.

Steketee, G. and White, K. (1990). *When Once Is Not Enough: Help for Obsessive Compulsives*. Oakland, CA: New Harbinger. A research-based guide to managing OCD.

Self-help: Anger management

Beck, A. (1999). *Prisoners of Hate*. New York: Harper Collins.

Bilodeau, L. (1992). *The Anger Workbook*. Minneapolis, MN: Compcare. A good anger workbook with practical exercises.

Potter-Efron, R. and Potter-Efron, R. (1995). *The Ten Most Common Anger Styles and What to Do about Them*. Oakland, CA: New Harbinger. A good anger workbook with practical exercises.

Tavris, C. (1989). *Anger: The Misunderstood Emotion* (revised and updated). New York: Touchstone. This book is rightfully critical of pop-psychologists who advocate 'letting it all out'.

MEASURES FOR USE IN RESEARCH

Strengths

Peterson, C. and Seligman, M. (2001b). Values in Action Inventory of Strengths (VIA-IS) Manual. Department of Psychology, University of Pennsylvania, 3815 Walnut Street, Philadelphia, PA 19104 215-898-7173, chrispet@umich.edu, http://www.positivepsychology.org/viastrengthsinventory.htm

Happiness

Alfonso,V., Allinson, D., Rader, D. and Gorman, B. (1996). The Extended Satisfaction with Life Scale: development and psychometric properties. *Social Indicators Research* 38: 275–301.

Argyle, M. (2001). *The Psychology of Happiness* (2nd edn). London: Routledge. (Contains the Revised Oxford Happiness Inventory.)

Diener, E., Emmons, R., Larsen, R. and Griffin, S. (1985). The Satisfaction with Life Scale. *Journal of Personality Assessment* 49: 71–5.

Fordyce, M. (1988). A review of research on the happiness measure. A sixty second index of happiness and mental health. *Social Indicators Research* 20: 355–81.

Joseph, S. and Lewis, C. (1998). The Depression-Happiness Scale: reliability and validity of a bipolar self-report scale. *Journal of Clinical Psychology* 54: 537–44.

Lykken, D. (1999). *Happiness*. New York: St Martin's Press. (On p. 35 of this book the well-being scale from the Minnesota Personality Questionnaire is given.)

Pavot, W. and Diener, E. (1993). Review of the Satisfaction with Life Scale. *Psychological Assessment* 5: 164–72.

Stone, A., Schiffman, S. and DeVries, M. (1999). Re-thinking self-report methodologies. An argument for collecting ecologically valid, momentary measurements and selected results of EMA studies. In D. Kahneman, E. Diener and N. Schwartz (eds), *Well-being: The Foundations of Hedonic Psychology* (pp. 26–39). New York: Russell Sage Foundation.

Psychological well-being

Ryff, C. and Keyes, C. (1995). The structure of psychological well-being revisited. *Journal of Personality and Social Psychology* 69: 719–27. For further details on the psychological well-being scales: cryff@facstaff.wisc.edu

Social well-being

Keyes, C.L. (1998). Social well-being. *Social Psychology Quarterly* 61: 121–40.

Quality of life

Frisch, M.B. (1994). *Manual and Treatment Guide for the Quality of Life Inventory*. Minneapolis, MN: National Computer Systems.

Gottschalk, L. and Lolas, F. (1992). The measurement of quality of life through the content analysis of verbal behavior. *Psychotherapy and Psychosomatics* 58(2): 69–78. Further information available from http://www.gb-software.com/develop.htm

WHOQOL Group (1998). The World Health Organization Quality of Life scale (WHOQOL): development and general psychometric properties. *Social Science and Medicine* 46: 1,569–85.

Emotions

Block, J. and Kremen, A. (1996). IQ and ego-resilience: conceptual and empirical connections and separateness. *Journal of Personality and Social Psychology* 70: 349–61. (Describes a measure of ego-resilience used to test Frederickson's broaden-and-build theory of positive emotions.)

Izard, C., Libero, D., Putnam, P. and Hayes, O. (1993). Stability of emotion experiences and their relations to states of personality. *Journal of Personality and Social Psychology* 64: 847–60. (Contains the Differential Emotions Scale.)

McNair, D., Lorr, M. and Doppleman, L. (1971). *Manual for the Profile of Mood States*. San Diego, CA: Educational and Industrial Testing Service.

Watson, D. and Clark, L. (1994). 'The PANAS-X: Manual for the Positive and Negative Affect Schedule – Expanded Form'. Unpublished Manuscript: University of Iowa, Iowa City.

Watson, D., Clark, L. and Tellegen, A. (1988). Development and validation of brief measures of positive and negative affect: the PANAS scales. *Journal of Personality and Social Psychology* 44: 1,063–70.

Zukerman, M. (1985). *Manual for the MAACL-R. The Multiple Affect Adjective Checklist – Revised.* San Diego, CA: Educational and Industrial Testing Service.

GLOSSARY

Broaden-and-build theory.   Fredrickson's view that positive emotions broaden momentary thought–action repertoires and provide opportunities for increased creativity and productivity which cumulatively lead to the enhancement of psychological resources and personal growth.

Eudaimonic.   The eudaimonic approach to studying well-being defines happiness and the good life in terms of achieving one's full potential.

Happiness.   A positive psychological state characterised by a high level of satisfaction with life, a high level of positive affect and a low level of negative affect.

Happiness set-point.   The genetically determined stable point around which a person's mood varies over extended time periods.

Hedonic.   The hedonic approach to studying well-being defines happiness and the good life in terms of pleasure seeking and pain avoidance.

Hedonic treadmill.   A process of rapid habituation or adaptation whereby people react strongly to both positive and negative recent events with sharp increases or decreases in happiness but in most instances return to their happiness set-point over relatively short periods of time.

Negative affectivity.   A dimension along which unpleasant emotional feelings of different intensities fall.

Positive affectivity.   A dimension along which pleasant emotional feelings of different intensities fall.

Psychological well-being.   Achievement of one's full psychological potential.

Quality of life.   A complex construct which covers health status, capacity to carry out activities of daily living, work-role status, availability of opportunities to pursue recreational interests, social functioning in friendships and relationships, access to health-care resources, standard of living and general well-being.

Social comparison.   The process of comparing oneself to others. Downward social comparisons (with those worse off than ourselves) increase happiness but upward social comparisons (with those better off than ourselves) decrease happiness.

Social well-being.   Optimal functioning within one's social network and community.

Subjective well-being.   Happiness as defined above.

Chapter 2

Flow

Learning objectives

- Be able to describe intrinsic motivation and the self-determination continuum.
- Be able to distinguish between virtues, character strengths and enabling themes.
- Be able to describe possible links between signature strengths and subjective-well-being.
- Understand reversal theory and its significance for intrinsically motivated actions.
- Be able to describe the characteristics of flow experiences and the conditions that lead to such experiences.
- Understand the implications of research on intrinsic motivation, reversal theory, signature strengths, and flow for enhancing subjective well-being.
- Be able to identify research questions that need to be addressed to advance our understanding of intrinsic motivation, signature strengths, flow and happiness.

Professor Mike Csikszentmihalyi at Claremont Graduate University has shown through extensive research that when people are engaged in challenging but controllable tasks that are intrinsically motivating they experience a unique psychological state, referred to as Flow (Csikszentmihalyi and Csikszentmihalyi, 1988; Csikszentmihalyi, 1990, 1997; Nakamura and Csikszentmihalyi, 2002). In this chapter, before discussing the concept of flow in detail, Ryan and Deci's (2000) intrinsic motivation theory will be addressed. Then Seligman's (2002) theory on the link between the use of character strengths and flow will be considered, since activities involving the use of such strengths are typically intrinsically motivated. Apter's (2001) reversal theory will also be outlined, since challenging tasks which lead to flow experiences are sometimes associated with reversals between states of anxiety and excitement, or goal-directed means-end thinking and activity-focused thinking.

INTRINSIC MOTIVATION

A distinction may be made between extrinsic and intrinsic motivation. With extrinsic motivation we do things because the outcomes of these activities will bring about situations that we like or which allow us to avoid unpleasant events. For example, some times we work to earn money to pay for food, accommodation and entertainment and to avoid being destitute. With intrinsic motivation we do things because we like the activities themselves. For example, art, sport or adventure.

Self-determination theory was developed by Professors Richard Ryan and Edward Deci at Rochester University to explain conditions that foster intrinsic motivation (Deci and Ryan, 1985; Ryan and Deci, 2000). Within this theory, intrinsic motivation is conceptualised as the inclination we have towards spontaneous interest, exploration and mastery of new information, skills and experiences. The theory predicts that when our needs for competence, relatedness and autonomy are satisfied, intrinsic motivation is likely to occur, but self-motivation is less likely when these needs are thwarted. The theory does not explain the genesis of these needs, but assumes that they are an evolved propensity.

Compared with people who are extrinsically motivated, those who are intrinsically motivated show more interest, excitement and confidence about the tasks they are intrinsically motivated to do. They also show enhanced performance, persistence and creativity concerning these tasks, and more generally report higher self-esteem and subjective well-being. These benefits of intrinsic motivation occur even when people with intrinsic and extrinsic motivation have the same levels of perceived competence and self-efficacy (Ryan and Deci, 2000).

People's intrinsic motivation is strengthened by offering them choices about how they complete tasks, opportunities for self-direction, and feedback which confirms that they have performed a task well. However, feedback which indicates that negative performance has occurred weakens intrinsic motivation. Positive feedback strengthens intrinsic motivation because it increases perceived competence concerning the task in question.

Intrinsic motivation, quite unsurprisingly, is weakened by punishment, threats of punishment, pressured evaluation and by imposing, goals, deadlines and directives. The surprising and controversial finding is that intrinsic motivation is also weakened by giving people rewards for completing interesting tasks, particularly if these rewards are perceived as controlling (Deci et al., 1999). Both punitive and positive incentives reduce intrinsic motivation because they reduce people's perception of autonomy and increase their perception that their performance was caused or controlled by external rather than internal factors. That is, they perceive their performance as being a response to the promise of external rewards or the threat of external punishment rather than arising from internal interest.

The self-determination continuum

After early childhood, opportunities for engaging in intrinsically motivated activities diminish, and much of what we do is dictated by parents, teachers, peers, partners, colleagues, customs and legislation. Between the extremes of intrinsic motivation and amotivation a variety of gradations of extrinsic motivation may be distinguished. In Figure 2.1, on Ryan and Deci's (2000) self-determination continuum, distinctions are made between four different extrinsic motivation regulatory styles. These differ in the degree to which actions are viewed as being more extrinsically or intrinsically motivated. Where activities are carried out because compliance is rewarded and non-compliance is punished, these activities are said to be externally regulated. This is the type of extrinsic motivation of interest to operant psychologists and historically compared with intrinsic motivation in the original laboratory experiments on intrinsic motivation. The regulation of activities is introjected when they are carried out under self-control in an ego-involved way to gain internal rewards such as increased self-esteem and avoid internal self-imposed punishments such as a low sense of self-worth. Here, the activities are carried out so that the person is living up to introjected standards

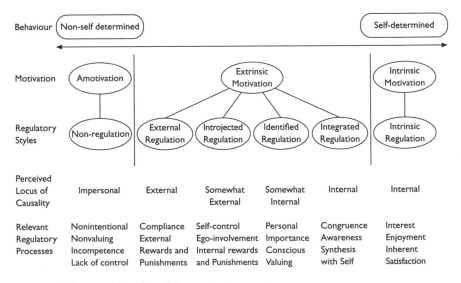

Figure 2.1 Ryan and Deci's self-determination continuum
Source: Adapted from Ryan and Deci (2000): 72.

learned from others. There may be some degree of ambivalence about completing the activities, but we complete them because we feel we should and if we don't our self-esteem decreases. Where people consciously value actions and view them as having personal importance, then regulation is based on identification or internalisation of views of others concerning the action. Where activities are congruent with a person's identity and synthesised with the self, then actions are regulated in an integrated way. We do these actions because we want to and because we view them as the sort of things that fit with our other personal values and needs. However, these actions are still viewed as extrinsically motivated because they are done to achieve particular outcomes rather than because they are experienced as inherently interesting and enjoyable.

The further along the continuum of self-determination we are, the greater the level of autonomy we experience in regulating our actions. Greater autonomy in extrinsic motivation is associated with better persistence at tasks, better task performance and greater subjective well-being. This holds for academic tasks, adherence to medical regimes in patients with chronic illnesses, obesity and addiction, physical exercise, environmental activism and intimate relationships.

Development of intrinsic motivation

Many activities which we find intrinsically motivating as adults, such as arts, sports and some types of work, were once abhorrent to us. We had to learn to be intrinsically motivated to do these things. This involved moving through the stages of extrinsic motivation entailed in the self-determination continuum in Figure 2.1, that is, progressing from external regulation through introjection and internalisation to integration. As children develop, they internalise and integrate more and more regulations and experience, increasing autonomy in carrying out various actions. Also, the range of regulations that they can internalise increases as their cognitive abilities develop.

Certain conditions promote the development of intrinsic motivation (Ryan and Deci, 2000). The development of intrinsic motivation is determined partly by the degree to which needs for relatedness, competence and autonomy are satisfied by children's parents, teachers, coaches and other significant members of their social networks. Evidence from developmental studies suggests that the needs for relatedness, competence and autonomy are to some degree constitutionally determined. Children show attachment behaviour from the earliest moments of life. From birth infants also strive to master skills and later to autonomously use them.

Children whose needs for relatedness are met in infancy and childhood show more intrinsic motivation. Studies of attachment in infants and children show that children with secure attachments to their parents engage in more intrinsically motivated exploratory behaviour. In childhood, a parenting style which is supportive rather than controlling engenders intrinsic motivation. Similarly in school, teachers who adopt a supportive rather than a critical style enhance pupils' intrinsic motivation.

Children whose needs for competence and autonomy are met by being given age-appropriate tasks and responsibilities develop integrated regulation for these tasks. In contrast, children who are given tasks that are too developmentally advanced for them remain externally motivated to do them or, at best, develop introjected regulation for these activities.

We develop intrinsic motivation to do activities that are: (1) moderately challenging; (2) that we feel we can do well; and (3) that give us satisfaction (Bandura, 1997). For very challenging complex tasks, intrinsic motivation may be developed by working initially towards moderately challenging subgoals. Once a series of subgoals have been mastered, the whole task or activity may be addressed. Intrinsic motivation is mediated partially by self-efficacy. That is, we are intrinsically motivated to do activities at which we believe we can succeed. Intrinsically motivating tasks bring personal satisfaction. Often this sense of satisfaction is associated with achieving personal standards of performance and experiencing the positive emotions that accompany such achievement.

The relationship between rewards and the development of intrinsic motivation is complex. While rewards that are perceived as controlling reduce intrinsic motivation for activities once such motivation has been established, such rewards may help people move along the continuum of self-determination towards intrinsic motivation. That is, rewards may help people persist at an activity initially until they achieve sufficient self-efficacy to reach a state where the activity is regulated in an integrated way. Rewards that are perceived as more informative than controlling may help us move along the continuum of self-determination towards intrinsic motivation, insofar as they let us know how well we are doing at a task.

One class of activities which are intrinsically motivated deserves particular mention because lifestyles which involve these activities may be profoundly rewarding. These are activities which entail the use of signature strengths (Seligman, 2002).

SIGNATURE STRENGTHS

Seligman (2002) distinguishes between two distinct classes of positive emotions concerned with the present: momentary pleasures and more enduring gratifications. While pleasures arise from sensual experiences, gratifications entail states of absorption or flow that come from engagement in activities which involve using signature strengths. Sailing, dancing, reading, creative writing and teaching are examples of such activities. Signature strengths are personal traits on which particularly high scores are obtained, associated with particular virtues, and defined in the Values in Action Classification of Strengths (Peterson and Seligman, 2001). The Values in Action Classification of Strengths is a system in which distinctions are made between virtues, strengths and enabling themes. Virtues are core characteristics valued by moral philosophers, such as wisdom or courage, and strengths are less abstract personality traits which may be used to achieve virtues. The 24 strengths associated with the 6 virtues of this classification system are presented in Table 2.1.

Virtues

The six virtues in the Values in Action Classification System are wisdom, courage, humanity, justice, temperance and transcendence (Peterson and Seligman, 2001). These were chosen because they recur in the writings of important moral philosophers such as Socrates, Plato, Aristotle, Augustan, Aquinas and others. Wisdom refers to strengths that entail the acquisition and use of knowledge. The will to accomplish goals in the face of opposition, external or internal, is the main feature of courage. Character strengths associated with the virtue humanity involve positive social interaction with friends and family members. The strengths of justice show up in positive interactions with the wider community. Temperance refers to strengths which protect us against excesses of all sorts in satisfying our needs. Strengths that connect us to the larger universe constitute the virtue of transcendence. These six broad categories of virtue which emerge consistently from historical surveys are definitely ubiquitous and probably universal. They may be grounded in biology through an evolutionary process and selected as a means of managing the important tasks necessary for survival of the species. Probably all six of these virtues must be present at above-threshold values for an individual to be deemed of good character.

Character strengths

Character strengths are routes for achieving virtues (Peterson and Seligman, 2001). To be included as a character strength in the Values in Action Classification, a positive characteristic had to satisfy most of the following criteria: be trait-like; lead to some form of fulfilment associated with the good life; be morally valued; not diminish other people; be supported by institutions; be displayed by highly valued societal role models; and be exemplified by prodigies. A further criterion was that the opposite of the character strength could not be phrased in a positive way: for example the opposite of flexible can be phrased as steadfast, so flexible would not qualify as a character strength. Talents and abilities (e.g. intelligence) and characteristics not valued across all cultures (e.g. cleanliness, forgiveness, frugality) were excluded from the classification system. Strengths in each virtue group are similar in that they all

Table 2.1 Virtues and character strengths

Virtue	Defining features	Character strengths	
1 Wisdom	Acquisition of and use of knowledge	1	Curiosity and interest in the world
		2	Love of learning
		3	Creativity, originality and ingenuity
		4	Judgement, critical thinking and open-mindedness
		5	Personal, social and emotional intelligence
		6	Perspective, seeing the big picture and wisdom
2 Courage	Will to accomplish goals in the face of internal or external opposition	7	Valour, bravery and courage
		8	Perseverance, industry and diligence
		9	Integrity, honesty, authenticity and genuineness
3 Humanity	Interpersonal strength	10	Kindness and generosity
		11	Capacity to love and be loved
4 Justice	Civic strengths	12	Citizenship, duty, teamwork and loyalty
		13	Fairness, equity and justice
		14	Leadership
5 Temperance	Strengths that protect us against excesses	15	Self-control and self-regulation
		16	Prudence, caution, carefulness, and discretion
		17	Modesty and humility
6 Transcendence	Strengths that connect us to the larger universe	18	Awe and appreciation of beauty and excellence
		19	Gratitude
		20	Hope, optimism and future-mindedness
		21	Spirituality, sense of purpose, faith and religiousness
		22	Forgiveness and mercy
		23	Playfulness and humour
		24	Zest, passion, enthusiasm and energy

Source: Adapted from Peterson and Seligman (2001a).

involve the core virtue, but they are also distinct from it. To be of good character, a person probably has to display one or two strengths within a virtue group.

The virtue of wisdom which involves the acquisition and use of knowledge can be achieved through the strengths of curiosity, love of learning, creativity, good judgement, emotional intelligence and the capacity to see the 'big picture' and take a wide perspective on life. The virtue of courage involves the will to accomplish goals in the face of internal or external opposition and can be achieved through the strengths of valour, perseverance and integrity. The virtue of humanity entails high interpersonal competence and can be achieved through the strengths of kindness and the capacity to love and be loved. The virtue of justice entails the capacity to relate well within the wider community and can be achieved through the strengths of teamwork, fairness and leadership. The virtue of temperance involves moderate expression of appetites and can be achieved through self-control, prudence and modesty. The virtue of transcendence connects us to the wider universe and can be achieved through the strengths of appreciation of beauty and excellence, gratitude, optimism, spirituality, forgiveness, playfulness and humour, and zest.

Enabling themes

Enabling themes are factors that lead people to manifest given character strengths in given situations and hence contribute to virtues (Peterson and Seligman, 2001). Enabling conditions may include educational and vocational opportunities, a supportive and consistent family, safe neighbourhoods and schools, political stability and democracy. The existence of mentors, role models and supportive peers inside or outside the immediate family are probably also enabling conditions. Some properties of settings may foster strengths and virtues, for example: features of the physical environment such as naturalness and beauty, features of the social environment such as empowerment as studied by community psychologists; and features of both such as predictability and controllability as studied by learning psychologists, or novelty and variety as studied by organisational psychologists.

Values in Action Inventory of Strengths

The 24 strengths associated with the 6 virtues of the Values in Action Classification System can be assessed with the Values in Action Inventory of Strengths (VIA-IS), a 240 item self-report questionnaire. The VIA-IS can be accessed at http://www.positivepsychology.org/viastrengthsinventory.htm (Peterson and Seligman, 2001). The character strength subscales of the VIA-IS all have good reliability and the inventory is currently undergoing validation. The subscales of the VIA-IS correlate in predicted ways with the scales which measure the Big Five personality traits, described in Chapter 6. For example, the trait openness to experience correlates with awe, curiosity and love of learning. The trait agreeableness correlates with teamwork. And the trait conscientiousness correlates with industry and self-regulation. Factor analyses of scale scores suggest five factors, which have tentatively been identified as cognitive strengths (curiosity, love of learning and creativity), emotional strengths (playfulness, zest and hope), conative strengths (judgement, perseverance, prudence and self-control), interpersonal strengths (leadership and teamwork), and transcendence strengths (awe, gratitude and spirituality).

The Values in Action Classification system offers researchers in the field of positive psychology a reliable framework for defining specific aspects of their subject matter, for framing and addressing research questions and for communicating coherently with each other. The VIA-IS offers a way for us to reliably identify signature strengths, a critical first step for increasing gratifications. A children's version of the inventory, the Children's Strengths Survey, is under development (Dahlsgaard, 2002).

Signature strengths and well-being

Seligman (2002) argues that each of us has a set of signature strengths and that if we use these every day in the main areas of our lives then we will experience gratification and authentic happiness. Signature strengths may be identified by completing the VIA-IS and then checking which of the top scoring half-dozen meet one or more of the following criteria:

- A belief that the strength is one of your core attributes;
- Excitement about using the strength;
- Rapid learning when the strength is first used;
- Continuous learning of new ways to use the strength;
- A yearning to find new ways to use the strength;
- A feeling that you will inevitably use the strength in many situations;
- Being invigorated rather than exhausted while using the strength;
- Creation of personal projects that revolve around the strength; and
- Feelings of joy, zest, enthusiasm or ecstasy when using the strength.

The main areas of life in which it is important to use signature strengths are: (1) our relationships with our romantic partners; (2) our relationships with our children; (3) our work setting; and (4) in our leisure activities. The hypothesis that there is an association between the use of signature strengths and the experience of flow, absorptions and well-being deserves urgent testing.

In addition to activities that entail the use of signature strengths, other activities, notably those which are exceptionally exciting or those which are done for their own sake rather than to achieve a goal, may lead to the experience of flow or absorptions. Reversal theory offers a useful framework for conceptualising motivation to engage in these sorts of activities.

METAMOTIVATIONAL STATES AND REVERSAL THEORY

It is one of the peculiarities of the human condition that we can both love and hate the same situations; be excited by them and be frightened of them. We can also find that we flip-flop in a short space of time between wanting to do a task to get to a goal and wanting to do the same task because it is enjoyable. That is, we may find that we oscillate between being intrinsically motivated and extrinsically motivated to do the same activity. Reversal theory offers a framework for understanding these apparent motivational paradoxes (Apter, 2001).

In reversal theory, it is assumed that at any given moment our motivation may be characterised by our status with respect to pairs of metamotivational states. In considering intrinsic motivation and flow experiences, our concern here is with what Apter refers to as the telic and paratelic metamotivational states associated with the means–ends domain. That is, when we are doing a task we may find ourselves extrinsically motivated, primarily focused on achieving a goal in a planned and serious way. This type of experience characterises being in a telic state. Alternatively we may find ourselves intrinsically motivated, primarily focused or doing the activity in a spontaneous way because the task itself is exciting, with minimal regard for the goal of the activity. These are the hallmarks of the paratelic state. In the telic state we focus on doing an activity to achieve a goal, but in the paratelic state we carry out activities primarily for their own sake. The telic state is associated with seriousness and achievement, while the paratelic state is associated with playfulness and fun. (Within reversal theory, other pairs of metamotivational states are associated with other domains such as dealing with rules, managing transitions and addressing relationships. Refer to Apter (2001) for a discussion of these, which are not immediately relevant to the theme of the present chapter.)

Emotions, both positive and negative, are explained within reversal theory as the outcome of metamotivational states. A diagram of the relationship between emotions associated with the telic and paratelic states is presented in Figure 2.2. In the telic state, where a low level of physiological arousal and a positive hedonic tone are experienced, then the dominant emotion is relaxation. As arousal increases and hedonic tone becomes more unpleasant, relaxation gives way to anxiety. In contrast, in the paratelic state, where there is a low level of arousal and an unpleasant hedonic tone, the dominant emotion is boredom and this gives way to excitement as arousal increases and the hedonic tone becomes more pleasant.

Reversals or shifts from one metamotivational state to another may occur at any level of arousal due to frustration, satiation or changes in the situation or social context. This will be associated with a sudden change in emotion, for example from relaxation to boredom or from anxiety to excitement.

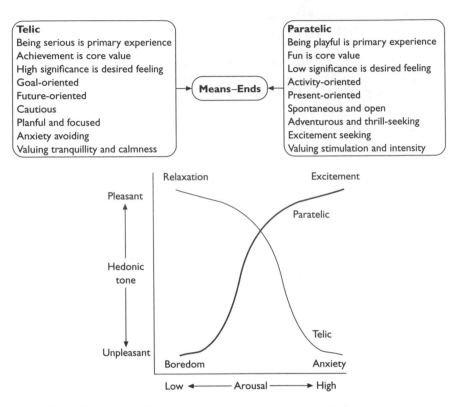

Figure 2.2 Telic and paratelic metamotivational states in reversal theory
Source: Adapted from Apter (2001): 6–13 and 44.

On a rollercoaster where a high level of arousal is experienced in the paratelic state, the predominant emotion is excitement, but if a person as a result of frustration associated with heightened perception of danger flips into the telic state, then the excitement is replaced by anxiety. Apter and his colleagues have documented paratelic–telic reversals in parachutists on either side of the moment of maximum danger; in dancers in the moments before and after curtain-up; in experimental participants faced with completing exceptionally frustrating puzzles; and in experimental participants given the option of shifting from a telic to a paratelic laboratory-based task when satiated.

Young (1998) in a study of professional tennis players found that absorbing flow experiences (described below) may be associated with either telic or paratelic metamotivational states. So paratelic states and flow experiences are not identical.

Reversal theory also proposes that people have dominant metamotivational states (Apter, 2001). Dominance is the tendency to spend more time in one metamotivational state than another. A telic dominant person spends more time in the telic than the paratelic state. Telic dominance has been found to be associated with less intrinsic motivation; more intense work motivation; stronger association between work and life satisfaction; more organised lifestyle; greater fear of failure and less hope of success; less teenage delinquency and drug abuse; less adventurous sexual behaviour; more stress in response to daily hassles or major life changes; and the use of problem-focused coping strategies.

Being in the telic state is associated with a distinctive psychophysiological profile. Compared with people in the paratelic state, those in the telic state show greater build-up in tonic muscle tension (EMG) during tasks requiring concentration; greater tonic physiological arousal in response to threat indexed by increased heart rate and respiration rate; and a more focal and localised pattern of cortical activation. In contrast, the paratelic state is associated with greater phasic fluctuations in muscle tension when completing a psychomotor task; greater phasic fluctuations in heart rate in response to comedy; and greater phasic changes in respiration amplitude in response to comedy.

Measures of metamotivational constructs

A variety of measures have been developed to measure metamotivational states and profiles of dominant metamotivational arrays (Apter, 2001, ch. 3). For research on telic and paratelic states which are of particular relevance here, the instruments listed below may be useful.

Telic State Measure (Kerr, 1997)

This measures current or recent status on the telic–paratelic dimension. It contains five six-point rating scales: serious – playful; planful – spontaneous; low-preferred arousal – high-preferred arousal; low arousal – high arousal; and low effort – high effort.

Telic–Paratelic State Instrument (Kerr, 1999)

This 12-item inventory measures current or recent status on the telic–paratelic dimension (7 items); and the arousal–avoidance – arousal-seeking dimension (5 items). The scales have good reliability.

Metamotivational State Interview and Coding Schedule (O'Connell et al., 1991)

This interview includes questions about pairs of metamotivational states and the coding system allows transcripts of the interview to be coded reliably when the interview is completed. It yields scores for eight metamotivational states, i.e. telic and paratelic states associated with the means–ends domain; negativistic, and conformist states associated with the rules domain; mastery and sympathy states associated with the transactions domain; and the autic and alloic states associated with the relationships domain.

Apter Motivational Style Profile (Apter International, 1999)

This reliable and valid 40-item inventory measures telic dominance along with dominance on three other pairs of metamotivational states, i.e. negativistic–conformist, mastery–sympathy and autic–alloic. It also yields subscale scores for all eight metamotivational states, i.e. telic, paratelic, negativistic, conformist, mastery, sympathy, autic and alloic.

Paratelic states, using signature strengths, and intrinsically motivating activity may all be associated with flow experiences, and it is to these that we now turn.

FLOW

Flow experiences occur when we become engaged in controllable but challenging tasks or activities that require considerable skill and which are intrinsically motivating (Csikszentmihalyi and Csikszentmihalyi, 1988; Csikszentmihalyi, 1990, 1997). For flow experiences to occur we must have a good chance of completing these tasks. There must be clear goals and immediate feedback. These tasks require total concentration so we become deeply and effortlessly involved in them, so much so that we no longer think of the worries and frustrations of everyday life. Our sense of self disappears when involved in these tasks and paradoxically the sense of self emerges as strengthened after the task is completed. Time perception is altered during flow experiences. Hours can pass in what seem to be minutes and minutes can seem like hours.

Flow experiences may occur during reading, sports, involvement in creative arts and music or involvement in certain types of work. Examples of activities that have been shown in scientific psychological studies to lead to flow experiences include reading, sailing, chess, rock climbing, dancing, writing and gang motorcycling. The frequency of flow experiences in everyday activities is diagrammed in Figure 2.3. The defining characteristic of activities that lead to flow experiences is that they become an end in themselves. While the tasks may initially be done for other reasons, ultimately they are done because they are intrinsically rewarding. Writers often say that they write not for financial or occupational advancement but because it is so enjoyable. Sailors may spend a lot of money and time getting their boats

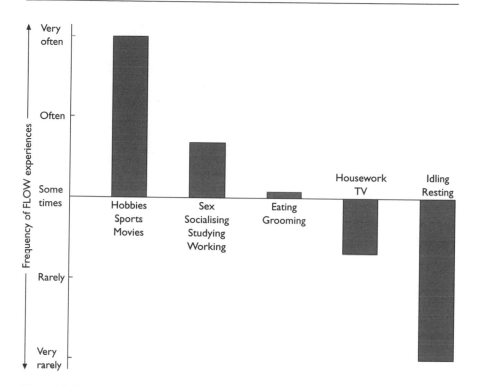

Figure 2.3 Frequency of FLOW experiences in everyday activities
Source: Adapted from Csikszentmihalyi (1997): 37.

into good condition, not because they want to win sailing competitions or maintain contact with other sailors, but because, for them, nothing compares with the flow experience of being out sailing.

Activities that lead to flow experiences are said to be 'autotelic'. Autotelic comes from the Greek words self (auto) and goal (telos). Autotelic experiences are those that arise from activities which are not done for some anticipated future benefit but because the activity in itself is intrinsically and immediately rewarding.

Challenging activities that require skill

The tasks which lead to flow experiences must demand that we use our skills almost to their limits. It is also important that the task be completable, for example, finishing reading or writing a piece of prose, completing a piece of music or finishing a game. In flow experiences the ratio of the challenge entailed by an activity and the skill required for the activity is close to 1:1, and we are operating at an above average level of challenge and skill. This

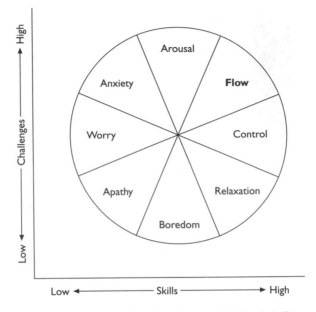

Figure 2.4 FLOW and other states related to levels of skill and challenge
Source: Adapted from Csikszentmihalyi (1997): 37.

is illustrated in Figure 2.4, where the high challenge/high skill quadrant is designated the flow domain. The low skill/low challenge domain is associated with apathy. In highly challenging situations where we have a low level of skills, anxiety may occur because the activities are experienced as uncontrollable. Boredom occurs in situations where there is a low level of challenge and we are at least moderately skilled.

Clear goals and immediate feedback

Tasks that lead to flow experiences have clear, not vague, goals and feedback about movement towards these goals is immediate, not delayed. Sports such as competitive sailing or tennis involve extremely clear goals such as rounding marks before other boats or scoring points and in all sports feedback is immediate. The competitor knows on a moment-to-moment basis if they are winning or losing.

Concentration and lack of self-awareness

Because tasks that lead to flow experiences involve working towards clear goals and receiving immediate feedback about movement towards these goals, a deep level of concentration on the task is essential. This results in a loss of awareness of the self. We stop being aware of ourselves as separate from the tasks in which we are involved. The dancer becomes the dance. The singer becomes the song. The sailor becomes one with the boat. Lapses in concentration or diversion into self-criticism can erase the flow experience and the quality of skilled task performance. So during flow experiences we do not ask ourselves should we be doing this, or is some other alternative better, because to do so would disrupt the flow experience. One outcome of this temporary loss of self-awareness is that after flow experiences our sense of self is strengthened.

Transformation of time

When we are involved in flow experiences our perception of time is distorted. For example, if we are fully engrossed in reading a good book hours may fly by in what seems like minutes. The experience of elapsed time in such instances is condensed. In other flow experiences the experience of elapsed time is extended. For example, executing rapid skilled manoeuvres in competitive sailing in windy conditions may take no more than seconds but during flow experiences these manoeuvres seem to occur almost in slow motion.

Conditions that lead to flow

Certain cultures and types of families are conducive to flow experiences (Csikszentmihalyi and Csikszentmihalyi, 1988). Some cultures afford more opportunities for flow experiences. Some families offer socialisation experiences that allow children to develop personality traits that make it easier for children to have flow experiences.

Culture

All cultures evolve goals to which citizens aspire and social norms, roles, rules and rituals which specify the ways in which these goals may legitimately be achieved. Cultures in which the goals, norms, roles, rules and rituals closely match the skills of the population afford citizens more opportunities for flow experiences. This position is supported by scientific surveys which show that greater life satisfaction is reported by citizens of nations in which there are more stable governments and in which people are more affluent and better educated. The frequency with which flow experiences occur in different cultures may vary depending upon prevailing practices in a variety of areas associated with flow experiences including work, religion and sport. Work-based flow experiences are more common in cultures that permit people to have work roles that are neither monotonously boring nor overly challenging and stressful, but where role demands meet workers' skills levels. Flow experiences are more common in cultures where religious rituals involving dance, singing or meditation, which promote flow experiences, are widely practised. Flow experiences are more common in cultures where skilled games against well-matched competitors are widely practised.

Within our own culture we can increase the frequency of our flow experiences by taking steps to develop work roles in which the demands of our jobs challenge us to use our skills to the limits of our abilities. We can increase our ritualistic-based flow experiences by developing skills for dance, music, rhythmic exercise or meditation and practising these skills regularly. We can increase our sports-based flow experiences by involving ourselves in one or more sports, becoming skilled in these and then practising them regularly so that our skills are moderately challenged. We can increase the frequency of flow experience associated with intellectual activities by having a commitment to lifelong learning and to maintaining an inquiring mind.

Creating flow in relationships with our children

Certain types of families have been found in a study by Dr Kevin Rathunde (1988) at the University of Chicago to promote the experience of flow. Adolescents in families characterised by optimal levels of clarity, centring, choice, commitment and challenge reported more frequent flow experiences. In families with optimal levels of clarity, goals and feedback were unambiguous and children knew clearly what was expected of them. In families with optimal levels of centring, children knew that their parents were interested in what they were doing and experiencing now in the present, and were not preoccupied with whether they would get a good job or a place in a good college after they finished school. In families with optimal levels of choice, children believed that they had a degree of choice over how they behaved and that different choices, including breaking parental rules, were associated with different consequences. In families with optimal levels of commitment children felt that the family was sufficiently safe for them to unself-consciously become involved in activities and sports that really interested them without fear of being judged negatively, criticised or humiliated. Thus, for children to be fully committed to activities in which they had flow experiences, they had to feel a high level of trust in their parents. In families where there was an optimal level of challenge, parents were dedicated to providing children with increasingly complex opportunities for exercising their unique and developing skills as they became older and more skilful.

The results of this study suggest that there are specific things we can do to help our children have more flow experiences. We can provide them with clear goals and feedback. We can respect what interests them now, rather than exclusively focusing on what might be good for them in the distant future. We can give them opportunities to make choices about what they do and to be mindful of the consequences of these choices. We can encourage them to unself-consciously try their best at activities they choose. We can offer them opportunities to face bigger challenges as they get older.

Creating flow in intimate relationships

Sexual relationships for most of us are initially very pleasurable and satisfying. However, with time, sex can deteriorate from being a positive experience into a boring routine or an addictive dependency. In the short term sexual relationships can continue to be a source of flow experiences if we make them increasingly erotically complex by experimenting with a variety of sexual practices. The ancient book the *Karma Sutra* and the modern text *The Joy of Sex* are manuals that outline ways for making our sexual relationships more erotically complex. However, for sexual relationships to retain their vitality over the long term, it is vital that the psychological as well as the erotic dimension of the relationship become more complex (Csikszentmihalyi, 1990). How is this done? By caring deeply for our partners as companions. By sharing valued interests, hopes and dreams with them. By embarking on adventures with them. By raising children with them. By facing all life's chaos, stress and losses with them.

How to create flow in physical activities

To develop the capacity to experience flow in carrying out physical activities like walking, running or swimming, there are some straightforward guidelines to follow. First, set an overall goal and break this down into a number of subgoals. Second, decide on a way of measuring progress towards the goals that you have chosen. Third, concentrate on doing the activity as well as you can when you are doing it and noting how well you are achieving your subgoals. Fourth, gradually increase the difficulty or complexity of the subgoals you are aiming for, so that the challenge you face matches your level of growing skill.

How to measure flow

Two main ways of measuring flow experiences have been developed (Csikszentmihalyi and Csikszentmihalyi, 1988). The first involves completion of a questionnaire on one occasion only. The second is called the experience-sampling method. In the questionnaire method, quotations from people who have had flow experiences are given, e.g. 'My mind isn't wandering. I am not thinking of something else. I am totally involved in what I am doing. My body feels good. I don't seem to hear anything.' Respondents are then asked to indicate if they have had such experiences, and if so how often and in what contexts. They then are invited to rate flow experiences they have had on a series of scales and these are listed in Table 2.2.

Table 2.2 Flow experience questionnaire

'My mind isn't wandering. I am not thinking of something else. I am totally involved in what I am doing. My body feels good. I don't seem to hear anything. The world seems to be cut off from me. I am less aware of myself and my problems.'

'My concentration is like breathing. I never think of it. I am really oblivious to my surroundings after I really get going. I think that the phone could ring and the door bell could ring or the house burn down or something like that. When I start I really do shut out the whole world. Once I stop I can let it back in again.'

'I am so involved in what I am doing. I don't see myself as separate from what I am doing.'

Have you had experiences like those described in these three quotations?

How often have you had such experiences?

What were you doing when you had these experiences?

What started the experiences?

What kept them going?

What stopped them?

For these experiences, indicate the degree to which you agree or disagree with the following statements:

I get involved	Strongly Disagree	1	2	3	4	5	6	7	8	Strongly agree
I get anxious	Strongly Disagree	1	2	3	4	5	6	7	8	Strongly agree

	Strongly Disagree	1	2	3	4	5	6	7	8	Strongly agree
I clearly know what I am supposed to do	Strongly Disagree	1	2	3	4	5	6	7	8	Strongly agree
I get direct clues as to how well I am doing	Strongly Disagree	1	2	3	4	5	6	7	8	Strongly agree
I feel I can handle the demands of the situation	Strongly Disagree	1	2	3	4	5	6	7	8	Strongly agree
I feel self-conscious	Strongly Disagree	1	2	3	4	5	6	7	8	Strongly agree
I get bored	Strongly Disagree	1	2	3	4	5	6	7	8	Strongly agree
I have to make an effort to keep my mind on what is happening	Strongly Disagree	1	2	3	4	5	6	7	8	Strongly agree
I would do it even if I didn't have to	Strongly Disagree	1	2	3	4	5	6	7	8	Strongly agree
I get distracted	Strongly Disagree	1	2	3	4	5	6	7	8	Strongly agree
Time passes more slowly or more quickly	Strongly Disagree	1	2	3	4	5	6	7	8	Strongly agree
I enjoy the experience and the use of my skills	Strongly Disagree	1	2	3	4	5	6	7	8	Strongly agree

Source: Adapted from Csikszentmihalyi and Csikszentmihalyi (1988): 195.

In the second way of assessing flow experience, participants are invited to carry electronic pagers which give signals periodically for participants to fill in a page in notebooks they carry. The pager gives about eight signals at random intervals per day and participants carry the pager for a week in most studies. Each of the pages of the notebook that participants fill in when the pager sends a signal is the same. A copy of one such page is given in Table 2.3. The information from these sheets is combined to give scores for various dimensions of the flow experience in the following way: affect (happy, cheerful, sociable); system negenthropy (clear, open, co-operative); activation (alert, active strong, excited); cognitive efficiency (concentration, ease of concentration, unself-consciousness, clear); motivation (wish to do the activity, control of actions, involved); and self-concept (feel good about self, meeting own expectations, satisfied with performance) (Csikszentmihalyi and Csikszentmihalyi, 1988).

IMPLICATIONS

A summary of self-help strategies for enhancing well-being using strengths, intrinsic motivation and flow is given in Table 2.4. These can be incorporated into clinical practice.

CONTROVERSIES

The main controversy in this area concerns the effects of rewards on intrinsic motivation. An extreme statement of the intrinsic motivation hypothesis entails the view that intrinsic and extrinsic motivation are distinct phenomena coupled to specific tasks and that all forms of rewards reduce intrinsic motivation. This position is no longer tenable (Ryan and Deci, 2000). Rather, motivation falls along a continuum from intrinsic motivation through various forms of extrinsic motivation to amotivation. Furthermore, at different times we may be intrinsically or extrinsically motivated to carry out the same activity. Finally, rewards that are perceived as giving feedback (rather than controlling behaviour) do not have a detrimental effect on intrinsic motivation.

SUMMARY

In self-determination theory Ryan and Deci distinguish between extrinsic motivation, where we do things because the outcomes of these activities will bring about situations that we like, and intrinsic motivation, where we do things because we like the activities themselves. Intrinsic motivation leads to enhanced performance, persistence and creativity and also to higher

Table 2.3 Experience sampling sheet for assessing flow in everyday life

A	Date		Time beeped			Time filled out						
B	Where were you?											
C	What were you doing?											
D	Why were you doing this?		I had to do it	I wanted to do it	I had nothing else to do							
E	What other things were you doing when you were beeped?											
1	How well were you concentrating?		0 Not at all	1	2	3 Somewhat	4	5	6 Quite	7	8	9 Very well
2	Was it hard to concentrate?		0 Not at all	1	2	3 Somewhat	4	5	6 Quite	7	8	9 Very well
3	How self-conscious were you?		0 Not at all	1	2	3 Somewhat	4	5	6 Quite	7	8	9 Very well
4	Did you feel good about yourself?		0 Not at all	1	2	3 Somewhat	4	5	6 Quite	7	8	9 Very well
5	Were you in control of the situation?		0 Not at all	1	2	3 Somewhat	4	5	6 Quite	7	8	9 Very well
6	Were you living up to your own expectations?		0 Not at all	1	2	3 Somewhat	4	5	6 Quite	7	8	9 Very well
7	Were you living up to expectations of others?		0 Not at all	1	2	3 Somewhat	4	5	6 Quite	7	8	9 Very well
	Describe your mood as you were beeped:											
8	Alert		Very 0	Quite 1	Some 2	Neither 3	Some 4	Quite 5	Very 6	Drowsy 7		
9	Happy		Very 0	Quite 1	Some 2	Neither 3	Some 4	Quite 5	Very 6	Sad 7		

Table 2.3 (Cont'd)

A Date		Time beeped		Time filled out				
10 Irritable	Very 0	Quite 1	Some 2	Neither 3	Some 4	Quite 5	Very 6	Cheerful
11 Strong	Very 0	Quite 1	Some 2	Neither 3	Some 4	Quite 5	Very 6	Weak
12 Active	Very 0	Quite 1	Some 2	Neither 3	Some 4	Quite 5	Very 6	Passive
13 Lonely	Very 0	Quite 1	Some 2	Neither 3	Some 4	Quite 5	Very 6	Sociable
14 Ashamed	Very 0	Quite 1	Some 2	Neither 3	Some 4	Quite 5	Very 6	Proud
15 Involved	Very 0	Quite 1	Some 2	Neither 3	Some 4	Quite 5	Very 6	Detached
16 Excited	Very 0	Quite 1	Some 2	Neither 3	Some 4	Quite 5	Very 6	Bored
17 Closed	Very 0	Quite 1	Some 2	Neither 3	Some 4	Quite 5	Very 6	Open
18 Clear	Very 0	Quite 1	Some 2	Neither 3	Some 4	Quite 5	Very 6	Confused
19 Tense	Very 0	Quite 1	Some 2	Neither 3	Some 4	Quite 5	Very 6	Relaxed
20 Competitive	Very 0	Quite 1	Some 2	Neither 3	Some 4	Quite 5	Very 6	Co-operative
21 Did you feel any physical discomfort as you were beeped?	None 0	1	2	Slight 3	4	5	Bothersome 6	7	8	9 Severe

Please specify

	Alone	Mother	Father	Sister/Brother	Male friends (How many?)	Female friends (How many?)	Strangers	Others	
22 Who were you with?										

Indicate how you felt about your activity:

	Alone	Mother	Father	Sister/Brother	Male friends (How many?)	Female friends (How many?)	Strangers	Others		
23 Challenges of the activity	Low 0	1	2	3	4	5	6	7 8	9	High
24 Your skills in the activity	Low 0	1	2	3	4	5	6	7 8	9	High
25 Was this activity important to you?	Not at all 0	1	2	3	4	5	6	7 8	9	Very much
26 Was this activity important to others?	Not at all 0	1	2	3	4	5	6	7 8	9	Very much
27 Were you succeeding at what you were doing?	Not at all 0	1	2	3	4	5	6	7 8	9	Very much
28 Do you wish you had been doing something else?	Not at all 0	1	2	3	4	5	6	7 8	9	Very much
29 Were you satisfied with how you were doing?	Not at all 0	1	2	3	4	5	6	7 8	9	Very much
30 How important was this activity in relation to your overall goals?	Not at all 0	1	2	3	4	5	6	7 8	9	Very much
31 If you had a choice who would you be with?										
32 If you had a choice what would you be doing?										
33 Since you were last beeped has anything happened or have you done anything which could have affected the way you feel?										

Source: Adapted from Csikszentmihalyi and Csikszentmihalyi (1988): 257–8.

Table 2.4 Strategies for enhancing well-being using strengths, intrinsic motivation and flow

Domain	Strategy
Using signature strengths	• Complete the VIA-IS and identify your signature strengths. • Decide to complete activities and tasks that allow you to use your signature strengths every day. • For each signature strength list a series of activities you could do that would allow you to use your strength. Some will be skilled activities and some will not. • For skilled activities follow the guidelines for task selection, moving along the continuum, reversals and flow outlined below.
Task selection for intrinsic motivation	• Select skilled activities that you would like to be intrinsically motivated to engage in. These activities should be moderately challenging but you should feel that you could do them well, and that they could give you satisfaction. • For very challenging complex tasks, work first towards moderately challenging subgoals. Once a series of subgoals have been mastered, the whole task or activity may be addressed.
Moving along the continuum	• Accept that for many skilled activities there is movement from extrinsic motivation towards intrinsic motivation. • To move along the continuum towards intrinsic motivation practise skills regularly in an extrinsically motivated way using the most informative rewards available, not rewards that you perceive to be controlling. • Once the skills become well-developed, decide to do the skilled activity for its own sake rather than for rewards or to avoid aversive situations (but acknowledge that sometimes you will be rewarded for your achievements even though your activities were intrinsically motivated).
Reversals	• When you are carrying out a highly skilled absorbing activity acknowledge that you may periodically flip from a paratelic state, in which you are doing the activity in a playful way for the sake of doing it, into a telic state where you are doing the activity to achieve a goal in a serious-minded way. • Reversal may occur when you are frustrated with the situation, when you are satiated and have had enough of the activity, or when there is a change in the social or physical context in which you are doing the activity.
Creating flow experiences	• To create flow experiences select controllable but challenging tasks or activities that require considerable skill, complete concentration and which are intrinsically motivating. • Select tasks that there is a good chance of completing within the time available to you. • Select tasks where there are clear goals and immediate feedback. • Focus on the task, not yourself, your feelings, or the potential external rewards of the task or activity. • Expect to be no longer conscious of yourself and to experience time-distortion. • Gradually increase the difficulty or complexity of the activities or tasks, so that the challenge you face matches your growing level of skill.
Helping children develop flow	• Provide them with clear goals and positive informative, non-critical feedback. • Respect what interests them now rather than exclusively focusing on what might be good for them in the distant future. • Give them opportunities to make choices about what they do and to be mindful of the consequences of these choices. • Encourage them to unself-consciously try their best at activities they choose. • Offer them opportunities to face bigger challenges as they get older.

Source: Based on Apter (2001); Csikszentmihalyi (1990); Ryan and Deci (2000): 68–78; Seligman (2002).

self-esteem and subjective well-being. Between the extremes of intrinsic motivation and amotivation on Ryan and Deci's self-determination continuum distinctions are made between four different extrinsic motivation regulatory styles: extrinsic, introjected, identified and integrated. Greater autonomy is associated with integrated regulation than with the other three styles. As children develop, they internalise and integrate more and more regulations and experience increasing autonomy in carrying out various actions. We develop intrinsic motivation to do activities that are moderately challenging, that we feel we can do well and that give us satisfaction. Intrinsic motivation occurs when needs for competence, relatedness and autonomy are met. Intrinsic motivation is strengthened by offering opportunities for self-direction and positive feedback.

Seligman classifies positive emotions into three categories: those associated with the past, the present and the future. There are two distinct classes of positive emotions concerned with the present: momentary pleasures and more enduring gratifications. The pleasures include both bodily pleasures and higher pleasures which come from positive sensual experiences. Gratifications which entail states of absorption or flow come from engagement in activities that involve exercising signature strengths. Signature strengths are personal traits associated with particular virtues defined in the Values in Action Classification of Strengths. The Values in Action Classification of Strengths is a system in which distinctions are made between virtues, strengths and enabling themes. Virtues are the core characteristics valued by moral philosophers and strengths are less abstract personality traits which may be used to achieve virtues. Enabling themes are the specific habits that lead people to manifest given character strengths in given situations and hence contribute to virtues. The 24 strengths associated with the 6 virtues of Values in Action classification system can be assessed with the Values in Action Inventory of Strengths.

In addition to activities that entail the use of signature strengths, other activities, notably those which are exceptionally exciting or those which are done for their own sake rather than to achieve a goal, may lead to the experience of flow or absorptions. Reversal theory offers a useful framework for conceptualising motivation to engage in these sorts or activities. Reversal theory focuses predominantly on transient metamotivational states such as the telic and paratelic states. The former motivates goal-oriented behaviour and the latter motivates task-focused activity. Reversals or shifts from one metamotivational state to another may occur at any level of arousal due to frustration, satiation or changes in the situation. Reversals are associated with a sudden change in emotion, for example from relaxation to boredom or from anxiety to excitement. Flow experiences may be associated with either telic or paratelic metamotivational states. Reversal theory also proposes that people have dominant metamotivational states. Telic and paratelic dominance are associated with distinct psychological and psychophysiological profiles.

Flow experiences occur when we become engaged in controllable but challenging tasks or activities that require considerable skill and which are intrinsically motivating. These activities typically entail clear goals and immediate feedback. They demand a high level of concentration and consequently during them we no longer think of our everyday lives or our selves. Time perception is also altered during flow experiences. Flow experiences may occur during reading, sports, involvement in creative arts and music, rituals or involvement in certain types of work. Activities that lead to flow experiences are said to be autotelic because they are intrinsically and immediately rewarding. Cultures in which the goals, norms, roles, rules and rituals closely match the skills of the population afford citizens more opportunities for flow experiences. Children from families characterised by optimal levels of clarity, centring, choice, commitment and challenge have more flow experiences. For sexual relationships to retain their vitality over the long term, it is vital that the psychological as well as the erotic dimension of the relationship become more complex by sharing valued interests, hopes and dreams; embarking on joint adventures; raising children; and by jointly facing all life's challenges.

QUESTIONS

Personal development questions

1. Complete the VIA-IS on the website and find out your personal strengths.
2. What activities are you intrinsically motivated to do that involve using your personal strengths and flow experiences?
3. Are you satisfied with the amount of time you spend doing these activities at present?
4. How could you change your daily or weekly schedule so that you engaged in more intrinsically motivated activities that involve using strengths and flow experiences?
5. What would be the costs and benefits of making these changes?
6. Make some of these changes and assess the impact this has on your well-being by assessing yourself before and afterwards on one of the well-being scales contained in Chapter 1.

Research questions

1. Design and conduct a study to test the hypotheses that when people engage in activities that involve using their signature strengths and meet the criteria for flow-inducing tasks, they are more likely to be intrinsically motivated and to experience flow than when they engage in equally demanding activities that do not involve the use of their signature strengths.

2. Conduct a PsychInfo search covering literature published in the past couple of years using the terms 'flow', 'intrinsic motivation', and 'signature strengths' individually and in combination. Identify a study that interests you and that is feasible to replicate and extend. Conduct the replication.

FURTHER READING

Academic

Apter, M. (2001). *Motivational Style in Everyday Life: A Guide to Reversal Theory.* Washington, DC: APA.

Csikszentmihalyi, M. and Csikszentmihalyi, I. (1988). *Optimal Experience: Psychological Studies of Flow in Consciousness.* Cambridge: Cambridge University Press.

Self-help

Csikszentmihalyi, M. (1990). *Flow: The Psychology of Optimal Experience.* New York: Harper Row.

Csikszentmihalyi, M. (1997). *Finding Flow: The Psychology of Engagement with Everyday Life.* New York: Basic Books.

MEASURES FOR USE IN RESEARCH

Motivational styles

Apter International (1999). Apter Motivational Style Profile, Manual and Workbook. Uppingham, UK: Author. http://www.apterinternational.com/main.htm email: <Marieshelton@apterinternational.com> Apter International Limited, Glaston Road, Uppingham, Rutland LE15 9EU England. Phone: (+44) 01572 821111 Fax: (+44) 01572 813113.

Kerr, J. (1997). *Motivation and Emotion in Sport: Reversal Theory.* Hove, England: Psychology Press (Telic State Measure is in appendix F.)

Kerr, J. (1999). *Experiencing Sport: Reversal Theory.* Chichester, England: Wiley (the Telic-Paratelic State Questionnaire is in appendix B.)

O'Connell, K., Potocky, M., Cook, M., and Gerkovich, M (1991). *Metamotivational State Interview and Coding Schedule Instruction Manual.* Kansas City, MO: Midwest Research Institute.

Strengths

Dalsgaard, K. (2002) *Values in Action Inventory of Strengths for Youth (VIA-Y).* Cincinnati, OH: Values in Action Institute. For information, contact dahlsgaa@CATTELL.psych.upenn.edu Department of Psychology, University of Pennsylvania, 3815 Walnut Street, Philadelphia, PA 19104 215-898-7173.

Peterson, C. and Seligman, M. (2001b). *Values in Action Inventory of Strengths (VIA-IS) Manual*. Department of Psychology, University of Pennsylvania, 3815 Walnut Street, Philadelphia, PA 19104 215-898-7173, chrispet@umich.edu, http://www.positivepsychology.org/viastrengthsinventory.htm

Flow

Csikszentmihalyi, M. and Csikszentmihalyi, I. (1988). *Optimal Experience: Psychological Studies of Flow in Consciousness*. Cambridge: Cambridge University Press. (Contains the flow experience questionnaire.)

GLOSSARY

Autotelic activities. Activities that lead to flow experiences and which are intrinsically motivating.

Character strengths. Personal traits which serve as routes for achieving virtues, for example curiosity is a strength associated with the virtue of wisdom.

Enabling themes. Factors that lead us to show particular character strengths in specific situations. For example, mentors may enable us to develop the strength of curiosity and so foster the virtue of wisdom.

Extrinsic motivation. Engaging in activities for external reward or to avoid punishment.

Flow experiences. Czikszentmihalyi's term for experiences which occur when we become engaged in controllable yet challenging activities that require considerable skill, complete concentration and which are intrinsically motivating. During flow experiences we become unself-conscious and time perception is altered.

Intrinsic motivation. Engaging in activities for their own sake rather than for external reward or to avoid punishment.

Reversal theory. Apter's view that at any given moment our motivation may be characterised by our status with respect to pairs of metamotivational states, the most important of which are the telic and paratelic states. Reversals from one metamotivational state to another may occur due to changes in external stimuli; frustration; or satiation and will lead to a sudden change in emotion, for example from relaxation to boredom or from anxiety to excitement.

Self-determination continuum. A dimension ranging from intrinsic motivation to amotivation, along which a variety of gradations of extrinsic motivation may be distinguished.

Signature strengths. A person's VIA-IS character strengths on which particularly high scores are obtained.

Telic and paratelic states. Apter's view that in the telic state we are externally motivated and focus on doing an activity to achieve a goal but in the paratelic state we are intrinsically motivated to carry out activities primarily for their own sake. The telic state is associated with seriousness and achievement, while the paratelic state is associated with playfulness and fun. In the telic state, where a low level of psychological arousal and a positive hedonic tone is experienced, then the dominant emotion is relaxation. As arousal increases and hedonic tone becomes more unpleasant, relaxation gives way to anxiety. In contrast, in the paratelic state, where there is a low level of arousal and an unpleasant hedonic tone, the dominant emotion is boredom and this gives way to excitement as arousal increases and the hedonic tone becomes more pleasant.

Values in Action Inventory of Strengths (VIA-IS). A self-report questionnaire which evaluates 24 strengths associated with the 6 virtues of the VIA classification system developed by Petersen and Seligman.

Virtues. Core characteristics valued by moral philosophers, such as wisdom, courage, humanity, justice, temperance and transcendence.

Chapter 3

Hope and optimism

Learning objectives

- Be able to describe positive illusions and the psychological processes of self-deception, denial, repression, selective attention, and benign forgetting.
- Distinguish between dispositional optimism and optimistic explanatory style.
- Understand hope theory.
- Be able to describe expectationism.
- Give an account of current knowledge concerning the neurobiological basis for optimism.
- Understand the implications of research on positive illusions, optimism, hope and expectationism for facilitating happiness.
- Be able to identify research questions that need to be addressed to advance our understanding of positive illusions, hope, optimism and happiness.

Up until the end of the 1970s optimism was considered to be a psychological deficit, a sign of immaturity or weakness of character while making a balanced even-handed appraisal of one's future prospects was considered to be a sign of mental health, maturity and strength (Petersen, 2000a). This negative view of optimism is to be found in the work of Voltaire (1759), whose Dr Pangloss naively insisted that we live in the best of all possible worlds, Porter's (1913) Pollyanna, who celebrated misfortune, and Sigmund Freud's (1928) analysis of religion as an optimistic illusion.

In *Future of an Illusion* Freud (1928) argued that the optimistic belief in a benevolent father-like God who would reward us in the afterlife if we controlled our aggressive and sexual instincts, was an illusion essential for civilisation. Without this illusion, people would be tempted to act out their aggressive and sexual instincts. However, this optimistic illusion came at a price. It entailed denial of the reality of sexual and aggressive instincts. Through the process of psychoanalysis, people could attain insight into the various defences, neurotic compromises and optimistic illusions they used to balance their need to fulfil sexual and aggressive impulses with their need to behave in a socially acceptable way. The goal of analysis was to attain a level of psychological maturity, where reality could be clearly perceived and where optimistic illusions could be discarded.

In the late 1970s, cognitive psychologists had accumulated a wealth of research data, integrated by Margaret Matlin and David Stang (1978) in *The Pollyanna Principle* which showed that people's thinking processes were optimistic. So, most people recalled positive things sooner than negative things. In spoken and written language they used more positive than negative words. They also evaluated themselves more positively than others. The only exception to this is people with anxiety or depression who view themselves in more realistic or pessimistic ways. Tiger (1979) in *Optimism: The Biology of Hope* argued that the capacity to think in an optimistic way was a naturally selected characteristic of our species which evolved when we developed the capacity to reflect on our future. Members of our species who were realistic or pessimistic about their future and the inevitability of danger, illness and death were not motivated to do the things necessary for survival. Their optimistic counterparts, in contrast, were motivated to struggle for survival because they believed things would work out well for them.

Within positive psychology, three research traditions have thrown considerable light on how and why people take a positive view of the world. These traditions focus on positive illusions and self-deception; optimism; and hope. Each of these research traditions will be addressed in this chapter.

POSITIVE ILLUSIONS

Professor Shelly Taylor (1989) at the University of UCLA, in her book *Positive Illusions*, summarised research which showed that most people, especially healthy people, are biased towards viewing themselves in an optimistic way. Human thought is distinguished by a robust positive bias. That is, our minds are designed to think in positive rather than realistic or negative ways. Most people view themselves, the world and the future in positive terms. In many carefully designed experiments in social psychology Taylor and others have shown that there are three main ways in which people see themselves in a more positive light than is warranted by the facts of the situation, or other peoples' views of the situation. First, they see their past behaviour, personal attributes and self as a person in an enhanced light. That is, they experience the illusion of self-enhancement. Second, they have an unrealistic sense of personal control and an exaggerated and unfounded belief that they can make things turn out better rather than worse; but are never responsible for bad things that happen to them. Third, they have an unfounded sense of optimism that the future will be rosier than the facts suggest it will. That is, they believe that it will hold more opportunities for good things to happen rather than adversity, stress and chaos. Most people are not aware of these positive illusions, mainly because the illusions work so well that we do not become aware of their positive nature. People avoid engaging in positive illusions that can be easily disconfirmed.

SELF-DECEPTION

To maintain a positive view of the self and the world, results from laboratory and field studies show that we use a variety of defences and self-deceptive strategies to manage negative information (Taylor, 1989; Taylor and Brown, 1988, 1994). This negative information which is contrary to a positive world view includes the facts that our talents and attributes are broadly speaking normal, not exceptional; we have limited control over an unpredictable and chaotic world and over our own impulses, emotions, thoughts and actions; and our future is bleak. Our future is bleak insofar as it entails many losses including: the loss of youth and vitality; loss of health; loss of intellectual abilities and talents; loss of valued friendships; loss of work role; and inevitably our future entails our own deaths and the deaths of everyone we hold dear. The self-deceptive strategies we use to manage this awful information, which is contrary to an optimistic world view, includes defence mechanisms and positive illusions.

Denial and repression

Denial and repression are two widely used defence mechanisms which help us to maintain a positive or optimistic world view. Denial involves not acknowledging the existence or meaning of threatening or stressful events in the external world. Repression involves not acknowledging unacceptable aggressive or sexual impulses in a person's inner world. To be accepted into society only a limited range of impulses are permitted expression. Repression is one way of keeping unacceptable impulses that society demands we should not feel out of consciousness. Shelly Taylor (1989) argues that defences like denial and repression are maladaptive because they distort reality. One part of the brain becomes dissociated from another part that 'knows' the denied or distorted facts. Self-deceptive positive illusions, in contrast, allow people to know negative information about the self and manage this in a way that preserves a positive view of the self. Illusions are adaptive because they permit people to interpret reality in the best light possible. Extensive research has shown that positive illusions involve the cognitive processes of selective attention, benign forgetting, maintaining pockets of incompetence and maintaining negative self-schemas (Taylor and Brown, 1988, 1994).

Selective attention and benign forgetting

Selective attention involves noticing positive things and screening out negative things about ourselves, that is, filtering information in a biased way so that only positive news is registered and encoded. Benign forgetting is a process where negative information about the self is not easily recalled. In contrast, positive information that supports a positive view of the self is recalled in considerable detail.

Pockets of incompetence

Negative information about the self can also be managed by having clearly defined pockets of incompetence and accepting that in these areas one has few skills, for example saying 'I'm not good with numbers' but believing that one is of high intelligence. We then ring-fence these areas off as peripheral to the essential core of the self which is viewed as having predominantly positive attributes. By ring-fencing pockets of incompetence and not using information about our performance in these domains in evaluating our self-worth, self-esteem is preserved.

Negative self-schema

A further strategy for managing negative information about the self is to develop a negative self-schema (in addition to a positive self-schema). Self-schemas may be developed around characteristics like being shy or overweight. A negative self-schema is an organised set of beliefs that allows us to anticipate situations in which negative information is likely to be received about the self and then to develop strategies for dealing with these, for example announcing that we are shy and so do not talk much. A negative self-schema allows a person to put a boundary around a negative personal attribute, to anticipate situations that may be relevant to it or not and to plan for these. Negative self-schemas may also protect self-esteem by allowing a person to attribute any negative evaluation of the self to the negative characteristic at the core of the negative self-schema, e.g. 'I didn't do well in the exam because my shyness prevented me from asking questions in class, and only those who ask questions get good exam results.'

Development of positive illusions

The development of positive illusions is fostered by a parenting style where children are given information by their parents and encouraged to make choices within the context of a warm relationship, with clear behavioural limits. Permissive or authoritarian parenting or parenting that is very cold does not facilitate the development of positive illusions.

Positive self-perception begins early in life. Pre-schoolers see themselves as competent and popular and this tendency to have a positive view of the self continues throughout life, although its strength diminishes gradually. This view of the self as good is partially determined by the way memory works. Memory is egocentric. Most of us remember the past as a drama in which we were the protagonists or heroes. Furthermore the information to which we selectively attend and remember is determined by our self-schemas, that is, beliefs about the type of people that we are and our unique attributes. For example, a person whose self-schema includes the belief 'I am musical and athletic' may remember 'I ran quickly and was not out of breath. Then I made an informed comment about the musical show.' In contrast, a person who sees themselves as intelligent and kind may recall that the same person tried hard not to be late and even though he was puffed tried to put people at their ease with light banter about the music. Self-schemas determine which aspects of a situation we attended to, and then our impressions of the situation are reinforced by that very information. So the athletic, musical person remembers that he was athletic and musical in that situation. Or the kind intelligent person remembers that he was kind and intelligent.

Most people see themselves as responsible for good things such as passing an exam or helping someone and not responsible for bad things such as failure or hurting others, because good things like success and kindness are what we intend to do and bad things like failure and cruelty are rarely intended. People also exaggerate the degree to which they are responsible for good outcomes in joint ventures. They take more than their share of the credit. When you ask husbands and wives who does the most housework, the sum usually exceeds 100 per cent. The same is true for creative teams in the fields of science, writing or music.

People who evaluate themselves positively hold others in high esteem also and so are more popular with others. This is true across the lifecycle from pre-school to old age (Mruk, 1999). People who view themselves as having positive attributes, who are optimistic about their future and who believe they can control important events in their lives work longer and harder because they expect a positive outcome from their work. When they confront an obstacle they keep trying various different solutions until they succeed, because they believe eventually they will. Thus their work style is characterised by strong motivation to succeed, a high level of persistence at challenging tasks, more effective performance and greater overall success.

The need for control and the perception of the self as capable of controlling the environment is present from birth. From their earliest months of life children show a need to control and master the environment. As they master one aspect they become bored and move on to the next. For example, a child may be intrigued by a new mobile, but then tire of it and be more interested in a new rattle, and then tire of that when they find a new squeaky toy. For children moderately novel situations are more stimulating and interesting than very familiar ones or situations that are completely unfamiliar. Thus children like environments that contain new challenges that are just beyond the limits of their competence, not one that contains very easy or very hard tasks and challenges.

Most adults believe that the world is controllable. We believe that with hard work, careful planning, and the right tools, technology and science, there is little that cannot be accomplished. We believe that natural disasters, diseases, social and economic problems, and war are all solvable problems. We believe that we succeed through effort and fail through laziness; so success is a sign of effort and failure is a sign of laziness. Most people do not believe that chaos or the unexpected play a major role in determining the course of their lives. In his book *Denial of Death*, Ernest Becker (1973) argues that our belief in the controllability and orderliness of the world protects us from constantly having to face the reality of our mortality, that we all live one step away from death.

We maintain a belief in personal control for a variety of reasons. We mistakenly categorise many events that have a desired outcome as being due to our actions. So, 'I watered the plants and they grew' is an example of correctly categorising a desired outcome as due to my actions. I have a friend who leaves the light on in his garage in the winter because he believes this guarantees that his car will start in the morning. This is an example of incorrectly categorising a desired outcome as due to one's own actions. We misclassify events as controllable, because sometimes they co-occur. So my friend's car didn't start one winter morning after a night when the garage light was off. He left the light on by mistake that night and the next day it started. So he attributed the car starting to leaving the light on and has continued to do so ever since on cold nights. Every time his car starts after he has left the light on, his belief that he can control whether or not the car will start by leaving the light on is strengthened. This common error of searching for examples to confirm prior beliefs underpins a lot of superstitious behaviour. People have the tendency not to seek out negative instances, like turning the light off for a few nights in the winter and seeing if the car starts the next day on each occasion.

The belief in control reduces stress responses. In laboratory experiments where two groups of people are exposed to the same number of electric shocks or bursts of loud noise, but one group has a panic button (which they do not use), the group that perceives they have control shows less stress on physiological measures of heart rate and skin conductance (Carr and Wilde 1988). Furthermore, in games of chance, if there are any cues that suggest that winning is due to skill, like introducing a well-dressed expert at the game who shows how it is done, people behave as if rolling a dice or drawing a card is a skilled activity (Langer, 1975).

Modifying positive illusions

Positive illusions are stronger in children than in adults. They are probably hard-wired into our nervous systems because they are so adaptive from an evolutionary perspective. Illusions are best modified if they are maladaptive. Modifying positive illusions involves giving negative information in a way that is corrective but not devastating. Trauma, victimisation and loss can shatter positive illusions and prevent people from seeing the self as good, the self as in control, and the future as rosy and safe. People who have been traumatised by catastrophic events, victimised and abused by others, or who become suddenly seriously ill, or suddenly bereaved all question their own worth, power to control things and the safety of the future world. Where these events happen early in life people are vulnerable to depression and illness in later life.

OPTIMISM

Two main approaches to the measurement of optimism have been taken and these are based on distinct conceptualisations of optimism (Peterson, 2000a). At one extreme optimism has been conceptualised as a broad personality trait characterised by general optimistic expectations (Scheier and Carver, 1985) while at the other it has been construed as an explanatory style (Seligman, 1998), that is, researchers have made a distinction between optimistic explanatory style and dispositional optimism.

Dispositional optimism

Dispositional optimism is a global expectation that more good things than bad will happen in the future. Scheier and colleagues argue that optimistic people, in the face of difficulties, continue to pursue their valued goals and regulate themselves and their personal states using effective coping strategies so that they are likely to achieve their goals (Scheier, Carver and Bridges, 2000). To evaluate dispositional optimism, Scheier and Carver (1985) have developed a brief self-report Life Orientation Test (LOT), and subsequently revised this instrument (Scheier et al., 1994). A copy of this scale is given in Table 3.1. The type of optimism evaluated by the LOT is a personality trait characterised by favourable personal future expectations. Dispositional optimism is associated with good health and a positive response to medical interventions for conditions such as heart disease and cancer. The impact of dispositional optimism on recovery from medical procedures is mediated by

Table 3.1 The Life Orientation Test – Revised

Please circle the answer that applies to you to show how much you agree or disagree
with each of the following statements

1 In uncertain times I usually expect the best	Strongly agree	Agree	Unsure	Disagree	Strongly disagree
2 If something can go wrong for me it will	Strongly agree	Agree	Unsure	Disagree	Strongly disagree
3 I'm always optimistic about my future	Strongly agree	Agree	Unsure	Disagree	Strongly disagree
4 I hardly ever expect things to go my way	Strongly agree	Agree	Unsure	Disagree	Strongly disagree
5 I rarely count on good things happening to me	Strongly agree	Agree	Unsure	Disagree	Strongly disagree
6 Overall I expect more good things to happen to me than bad	Strongly agree	Agree	Unsure	Disagree	Strongly disagree

Source: Adapted with permission from Scheier and Carver and Bridges (1994).

Note: All items are scored 5-4-3-2-1 for SA-A-U-D-SD, except items 2, 4 and 5 which are scored in
the reversed direction.

effective coping strategies such as redefinition or reframing. Pessimists, in
contrast, use avoidant coping strategies or disengage from coping with problems. Coping strategies will be discussed fully in Chapter 7.

Optimistic explanatory style

Professor Martin Seligman (1998) and his colleagues have conceptualised
optimism as an explanatory style, rather than a broad personality trait.
Optimistic people, according to this perspective, explain negative events or
experiences by attributing the cause of these to external, transient, specific
factors such as the prevailing circumstances. In contrast, pessimists explain
negative events or experiences by attributing their cause to internal, stable,
global factors such as being a personal failure. So optimists are more likely to
say they failed an exam because the wrong questions came up or the atmosphere in the exam hall was not conducive to concentration. Pessimists, in
contrast, are more likely to attribute failure to not being any good at academic
work generally or to being stupid. Optimism and pessimism conceptualised
in this way may be measured with the Attributional Style Questionnaire
(ASQ), (Dykema *et al.*, 1996; Peterson *et al.*, 1982; Peterson and Villanova,
1988) and the Content Analysis of Verbal Explanations (CAVE), (Peterson
et al., 1992). With the ASQ, respondents are given a series of hypothetical
events which have positive and negative outcomes. They are asked to indicate
what they think would be the one major cause of each of these positive and

negative events if the situations happened to them. They then are invited to rate these causes on three multipoint scales to indicate the degree to which the causes are perceived as: (1) internal or external; (2) stable or transient; and (3) global or specific. Ratings are combined to give indices of optimism and pessimism. With the CAVE, explanations for positive and negative events are abstracted from diaries, interview transcripts, newspaper quotations, or indeed any documents and rated by experts using: the internal or external; stable or transient; and global or specific rating scales of the ASQ. Ratings are combined to give indices of optimism and pessimism.

In addition to the ASQ and the CAVE, a children's version of the ASQ has also been developed (Seligman *et al.*, 1984; Seligman, 1998). A Relationship Attribution Measure (RAM) has been developed to evaluate optimism within marriage (Finchman and Bradbury, 1992; Fincham, 2000). The Leeds Attributional Coding System provides a way of coding optimistic explanations for events from transcripts of marital and family therapy (Stratton *et al.*, 1986).

Development of optimism

The development of optimism is determined by parental mental health, the type of role modelling offered by parents and the degree to which parents encourage and reward optimism (Abramson *et al.*, 2000; Gillham, 2000; Seligman, 1998). Optimists are more likely to come from families in which neither parent had depression. Parents of optimists are good role models for using an optimistic explanatory style, attributing success to internal, global, stable factors and failures to external, specific, transitory factors. Optimists come from families where their parents are understanding of their failures and attribute them to external rather than internal factors. Where youngsters come from families that have experienced major traumas (such as unemployment and poverty), they develop optimism if their families cope and recover from adversity. Parents of optimists encourage their children to deal with setbacks in an optimistic way and differentially reinforce optimism and persistence. Pessimists are more likely to come from families in which parents are depressed, are role models for a pessimistic explanatory style, and differentially reinforce the development of pessimistic explanatory style. Where parents criticise children and attribute their failures to internal, global stable factors the children are more likely to grow up to be pessimists. Child abuse and neglect also renders children vulnerable to developing a pessimistic explanatory style and depression. Optimism is also related to the ability to delay gratification and to forgo short-term gains in order to achieve long-term goals, probably because optimistic people can have faith that long-term goals are achievable.

Prospective and retrospective studies have shown that individuals with an optimistic explanatory style are less likely to develop physical ill-health, depression or suicidality when they face major stressful life events than individuals with a pessimistic explanatory style. In contrast, pessimists who face major stressful life events as children (such as chronic parental conflict, divorce or maternal bereavement) are more likely to develop depression. This can be counteracted if they have one good socially supportive relationship. Or it can be exacerbated and maintained if their depression leads them to fail at school where they are criticised, with critical internal, global, stable attributions being made for their failure.

In adulthood optimism is associated with better academic achievement, sport performance, occupational adjustment and family life (Seligman, 1998; Gillham, 2000). Optimism predicts better performance at college and predicts it more accurately than ability measures such as the Scholastic Aptitude Test (Peterson and Barrett, 1987). Optimism predicts better performance at individual and team sports (Seligman et al., 1988). Optimism predicts success in various occupations such as sales. When insurance salesmen who scored in the top and bottom 10 per cent on the ASQ were compared, those with very optimistic explanatory styles sold 88 per cent more than those with very pessimistic styles (Seligman, 1998; Seligman and Schulman, 1986). Optimism within marriage, as assessed by the RAM, has been found to be associated with higher rates of positive interactions and to predict long-term marital satisfaction (Fincham, 2000).

Optimism also has an important impact on the way people deal with bereavement and loss. Susan Nolen-Hoeksema (2000) found that bereaved optimists tended to use coping strategies such as: reappraisal of the loss in positive terms; problem solving by seeking social support; and distraction through involvement in hobbies and exercise. Pessimists, in contrast, tended to use coping strategies such as denial or distraction through excessive drinking. Optimists construed bereavement as a 'wake-up call' to reprioritise their lives. They became aware of the fragility of life and lived more in the present than the past or the future. They focused more on important relationships and less on work and casual relationships. They resolved family conflicts that had been unresolved for years. They made important life changes they had been putting off, such as changing jobs or pursuing retraining. They became more tolerant of others. They became aware of strengths that they did not know they had and became less afraid of their own death. Optimists who found some positive benefit from their loss within six months of bereavement showed better psychological adjustment and fewer symptoms of depression or anxiety over the subsequent 18 months.

A series of studies in which the CAVE system for conducting content analysis of historical documents such as speeches, diaries and newspaper reports of prominent political and military figures has shown that optimism determines success in public life (Satterfield, 2000). An optimistic explanatory style has been found to be associated with electoral success in the USA, aggressive campaigning in the USA, resilience to stress among international leaders, and military aggression and risk taking in the Gulf War and the Second World War.

Attributional retraining

Seligman (1998) has developed programmes to help adults and children change their explanatory style from pessimism to optimism. The programmes are based on the cognitive therapy models developed by Dr Aaron T. Beck (1976) and Dr Albert Ellis (Ellis and Harper, 1975). In these programmes participants learn to monitor and analyse mood-altering situations and then to modify their pessimistic beliefs so that their explanatory style becomes more optimistic.

In the first part of these programmes participants learn to monitor mood changes associated with encountering adversity. In each adverse situation they conduct an ABC analysis which involves specifying the adversity, the beliefs and thoughts that occurred when the adversity was encountered, and the consequent mood changes. Here is an example of an ABC analysis of a specific situation.

Adversity: My friend didn't call.
Beliefs: He's not interested in our friendship any more because I'm always so boring to be with.
Consequent mood change: I changed from feeling OK to feeling fairly depressed (from 3 to 8 on a 10-point depression scale, where 1 = very happy and 1 = very depressed).

In these programmes you analyse a dozen such situations and then notice what beliefs precede mood changes involving depression or other negative mood states and how these beliefs differ from those that precede positive mood changes. You find that beliefs which precede negative mood changes are based on a pessimistic explanatory style while those that precede positive mood changes are based on an optimistic explanatory style. Where beliefs are based on a pessimistic explanatory style, internal, global and stable attributions will be made for adversity. Where beliefs are based on an optimistic explanatory style, explanations for adversity will involved external, specific and transient attributions. Three sets of skills for changing pessimistic explanations for adversity are practised once ABC analysis has been mastered. These include distraction, distancing and disputation.

Distraction involves doing something to stop the internal pessimistic explanation for the adversity from taking all your attention and preoccupying you. Specific techniques include: saying 'stop' loudly and hitting the table with your hand; snapping yourself with an elastic band worn on the wrist; looking at a flash card you carry with STOP written on it in large letters; concentrating your attention on an external physical object; postponing rumination until later that day; or writing down the pessimistic explanation for the adversity as soon as it occurs.

Distancing involves reminding ourselves that pessimistic explanations of adversity are only one possible interpretation of the situation, not true facts. While distraction is a strategy for 'turning off' pessimistic thinking, distancing is a strategy for 'turning down' their impact on mood by recognising that beliefs are not facts, they are just one 'spin' on the situation. Distancing sets the stage for disputation.

Disputation is the process of carrying on an internal dialogue, the goal of which is to show that there is an equally valid or more valid optimistic explanation for the adversity. When disputing pessimistic explanations we ask four questions that centre on evidence, alternatives, implications and usefulness.

1. What is the evidence for that explanation or belief and is there evidence that it is not true?
2. Are there alternative optimistic explanations for the adversity where I can attribute this adversity to external, specific, transient factors?
3. If I cannot justify an optimistic explanation for adversity, are the implications of the pessimistic explanation catastrophic with huge long-term negative consequences or just a bit of a temporary nuisance?
4. If I cannot decide whether there is more evidence for an optimistic or pessimistic explanation for adversity, which explanation or belief is most useful for me in terms of having a positive mood and achieving my goals?

Armed with ABC analysis skills and distraction, distancing and disputation skills, the next step is to put them together in ABCDE practice. ABCDE stands for Adversity, Beliefs, and Consequent mood changes, Disputation and Energisation. In each adverse situation, in addition to noting the adversity, beliefs and mood-change consequences, you also note how you disputed your pessimistic beliefs and the impact of this on your mood state: how the alternative optimistic explanation and beliefs energised you.

For example:

Adversity: My friend didn't call.
Beliefs: He's not interested in our friendship any more because I'm always so boring to be with.
Consequent mood change: I changed from feeling OK to feeling fairly depressed (from 2 to 7 on a 10-point depression scale, where 1 = very happy and 1 = very depressed).
Disputation: Evidence? There is evidence that he is interested in our relationship. We have seen each other two or three times a week for the past year. Alternatives? He may have other things on his mind? He may

be dealing with a crisis? Implications? Even if he is losing interest, it is not a catastrophe. I will survive. I have other friends. Usefulness? It's more useful to think that he didn't call because of some temporary thing, like a crisis, not because of some negative personal characteristic of mine. Energisation? I feel more upbeat now. Much less depressed (3 on a 10-point depression scale).

To develop your disputation skills, work with a close friend. Take adverse situations and ask your friend to present the pessimistic explanations and beliefs to you. Your job is to dispute these and examine the evidence for the negative beliefs, generate optimistic alternatives, examine the real rather than catastrophic implications if the pessimistic viewpoint seems valid, and evaluate the usefulness of optimistic and pessimistic beliefs.

The Penn Optimism Programme, an example of an attribution retraining programme, was designed to help school-age children develop optimistic rather than pessimistic explanatory attributional styles and so prevent depression (Jaycox et al., 1994; Gillham et al., 1995). This 12-week programme contains modules on analysing mood-altering situations in terms of antecedents, behaviour and consequent mood changes; analysing beliefs about causes along the three dimensions of explanatory style, i.e. internal–external; global–specific, stable–transient; generating alternative explanations for mood-changing situations and evaluating the evidence; and challenging catastrophic thinking. The programme also includes behavioural skills training modules drawn largely from behaviour therapy. These modules cover managing family conflict; assertiveness and negotiation training; problem-solving skills training; decision-making skills training; relaxation and coping skills training; dealing with procrastination; and social skills training. The programme is highly effective in reducing depression scores on standardised measures of helplessness, hopelessness and depression and these gains are maintained at two-year follow-up. The cognitive part of the programme helps children develop hope that they can solve problems that once seemed insurmountable. The behavioural aspect of the programme provides youngsters with the skills required to deal effectively with life difficulties.

HOPE

Hope, a construct closely related to optimism, has been conceptualised by Professor Rick Snyder (2000) as involving two main components: the ability to plan pathways to desired goals despite obstacles, and agency or motivation to use these pathways. Hope is the sum of these two components. This is illustrated in the lower panel of Figure 3.1. According to this conceptualisation, hope is strongest when it entails valued goals that there is

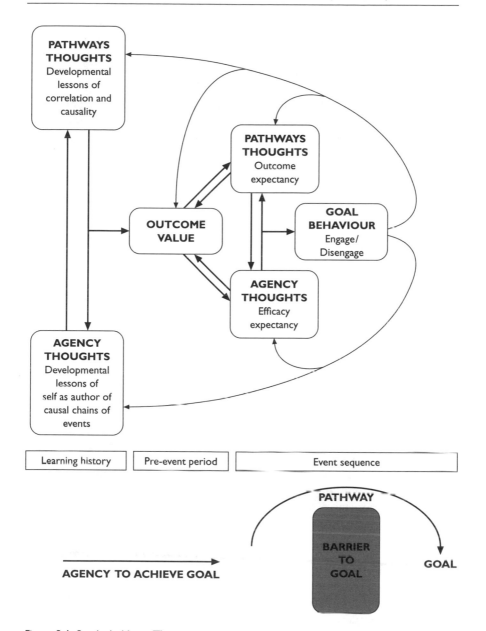

Figure 3.1 Snyder's Hope Theory
Source: Adapted from Snyder (2000): 11–12.

an intermediate probability of attaining due to challenging but not insurmountable obstacles. Where we are certain of achieving our goals, hope is unnecessary. Where we are certain that we will not, then we become hopeless. According to this conceptualisation, positive and negative emotions are by-products of goal-directed hopeful or hopeless thought.

Snyder's theory about the process of experiencing hope in a particular situation is diagrammed in the upper panel of Figure 3.1. In any situation where a valued goal is pursued, the hopeful goal-directed behaviour will be determined by the interaction of:

1. the degree to which the outcome or goal is valued;
2. thoughts about possible pathways to the goals and related expectations about how effective these will be in achieving the outcome or goal; and
3. the thoughts about personal agency and how effective one will be in following paths to goals.

All three of these factors will be dependent upon thoughts brought to the situation based on past experience and development in two areas:

1. thoughts about pathways to goals based on developmental lessons concerning correlations and causality; and
2. thoughts about agency based on developmental lessons about the self as author or causal chains of events.

In Figure 3.1 all of these relationships are expressed as thick arrows. The thin arrows in Figure 3.1 represent the feedback process in which goal-directed behaviour affects current and long-term thoughts about pathways to goals and the role of personal agency in achieving these; and the degree to which the current goal is valued.

Snyder's group have developed a series of scales to measure different aspects of hope (Lopez et al., 2000). The Adult Dispositional Hope Scale and State Hope Scale are brief trait-and-state self-report measures of hope for use with adults. The Children's Hope Scale has been developed for use with school-age children and the Young Children's Hope Scale is for use with pre-school children. Observational versions of the Adult Dispositional Hope Scale, the Children's Hope Scale and the Young Children's Hope Scale have been developed for completion by research raters, parents and teachers. All of these self-report and observational rating scales yield overall hope scores, in addition to scores for hope-related agency and hope-related pathways. In addition to these scales, an Adult Domain Specific Hope Scale has been developed which assesses hope in the following specific domains: social, academic, family, romantic relationships, occupation and leisure activities. Reliability and validity data are available for all scales.

Development of hope

Snyder (2000) suggests that hope develops in a clearly defined way over the course of infancy, childhood and adolescence. By the end of the first year of life, object constancy and cause-and-effect schemas allow infants to have anticipatory thoughts about pathways to goals. Pointing skills which are well developed by the end of the first year allow infants to indicate what their goals are.

In the second year, infants learn that they can instigate goal-directed activities to follow pathways to desired goals. The idea of self as an agent evolves during this period. During the second year, one of the most important hope-related skills learned is the idea that pathways around barriers may be planned and actively followed. This process of encountering barriers, planning ways around them, and then actively executing these plans is central to the genesis of hope. Professor Sir Michael Rutter (1994) at the Institute of Psychiatry in London has likened overcoming such barriers and adversities to a psychological immunisation process and referred to the outcome as resilience. The security of the child's attachment to caregivers and the interpersonal context within which youngsters cope with adversity is critical. Children who are securely attached to their parents or caregivers and are provided with sufficient social support to cope with adversity develop resilience and hope.

During the pre-school period from 3 to 6 years, the rapid development of language, pre-operational intuitive thinking, interest in story-telling, and predictable routines, allows for the further growth of hopeful pathway planning in the face of barriers and obstacles. Physical development allows for the growth of sophisticated skills for putting plans into action. As the ability to empathise with others begins to develop towards the end of the pre-school years, children become aware that planning and pursuing pathways towards valued goals may sometimes help and sometimes hinder others to pursue their valued goals. The development of perspective taking allows pre-schoolers to include the wishes of others in their plans.

In middle childhood and pre-adolescence there is a rapid growth in logical rather than intuitive thinking skills, memory skills, reading skills and advanced social perspective-taking skills. These allow for increasingly sophisticated hopeful planning and pursuing pathways towards valued goals, and doing so within a social context mindful of the wishes of their parents, siblings, peers and teachers.

In adolescence, youngsters develop abstract reasoning skills. These skills facilitate the management of complex issues including: increasing autonomy from parents; forming exclusive intimate relationships; and developing career plans. These challenges provide opportunities for hopeful planning and hopeful pursuit of plans despite setbacks and barriers.

Children who develop a hopeful disposition typically have parents who serve as hopeful role models and who coach them in developing and executing plans to circumvent barriers to valued goals. These children have secure attachment to their parents who provide them with a warm and structured family environment in which rules are consistently and predictably applied and conflict is managed in a predictable and fair way.

Some, but not all, children who are neglected, abused, bereaved or who are exposed to ongoing interparental conflict associated with separation or divorce may fail to develop a hopeful disposition. Children who grow up in a particularly stressful home environment are more likely to become resilient and hopeful under certain circumstances (Mahoney, 1991). First, these children become aware that their parents have difficulties and so categorise their parents' inadequate parenting as a parental shortcoming rather than a personal shortcoming. Second, these children find other adults who can routinely meet their needs for care, control and intellectual stimulation. Third, these children identify and refine a special talent or gift early in their lives which gives them access to new supportive social networks. Fourth, they have a high motivation to develop their talents marked by persistence and tenacity. Finally, they address adversity as a challenge or opportunity for development rather than an obstacle.

Hopeful adults have distinctive profiles (Snyder, 2000). Adults who have high levels of hope have experienced as many setbacks as others in their lives, but have developed beliefs that they can adapt to challenges and cope with adversity. They maintain an ongoing positive internal dialogue including statements such as 'I can do it, I will not give up', etc. They focus on success rather than failure. They experience fewer and less intense negative emotions when they encounter obstacles to valued goals. This may be because they creatively generate alternative routes to achieve their goals when they encounter barriers or flexibly select other more achievable goals. When people with low hope encounter insurmountable barriers their emotions follow a relatively predictable sequence from hope to rage; from rage to despair; and from despair to apathy. When faced with problems in adult life, people with high levels of hope tend to break large vague problems into small clearly defined and manageable problems.

Hope therapy

Hope therapy is derived from Snyder's hope theory and ideas drawn from cognitive-behaviour therapy, solution-focused therapy and narrative therapy (Snyder, 2000). Hope therapy aims to help clients formulate clear goals, produce numerous pathways to these, motivate themselves to pursue their goals and reframe obstacles as challenges to be overcome.

Hope therapy and attributional retraining help individuals or small groups develop optimism and hope-driven problem-solving strategies.

Expectationism, in contrast, provides a framework for helping whole populations develop safer future-oriented lifestyles. Let us examine expectationism in more detail.

EXPECTATIONISM AND RISK HOMEOSTASIS THEORY

Expectationism is the name of the preventive strategy for reducing lifestyle-dependent disease, accidents, violence and death rate per head of population by enhancing people's perceived value of the future. It is based on risk homeostasis theory (Wilde, 2001). Risk homeostasis theory argues that the degree of risk-taking behaviour and the magnitude of loss due to accidents and lifestyle-dependent disease in a population are maintained over time, unless there is a change in the target level of risk. Target risk is the level of risk a person chooses to accept in order to maximise the overall expected benefit from an activity. A nation's accident rate, per head of population, is the outcome of a closed-loop control process. In this process, fluctuations in the accident rate determine fluctuations in the degree of caution people subsequently apply in their behaviour. And fluctuations in the degree of caution are the cause of the ups and downs in the nation's *per capita* accident rate. Fluctuations in the accident rate are greatly reduced by people's ability to anticipate the potential consequences of health and safety interventions of the technological kind. Feedback about accident and illness rates and the riskiness of certain behaviour patterns (e.g. speeding or smoking) along with anticipation lead to adaptive behaviour which has a stabilising effect on accident risk. The homeostatic nature of the accident-production process means that only interventions which reduce our target level of risk will reduce the accident rate per head of population.

According to risk homeostasis theory, health and safety advances based on: engineering, such as designing better roads and vehicles; education, such as providing information on health and safety; legislation, such as punishing people occasionally for specific categories of unsafe behaviour; or medicine, such as developing better life-saving procedures for managing accidents and emergencies will have no significant effect on accident rates within a population. This prediction is based on the fact that none of these innovations influence the population's target level of risk. They fail to enhance the desire for health, safety and a longer life. This remarkable prediction of risk homeostasis theory is supported by a large body of empirical data. For example, the standardised mortality ratios due to violence from 1900 to 1975 (if periods of war are disregarded) changed remarkably little despite the enormous advances in roads and vehicle design, education safety legislation and medicine (Wilde, 1986, 2001).

However, accident rates can be changed, according to risk homeostasis theory, by reducing the target level of risk within a population. This can be achieved by four classes of interventions:

1. increase the perceived benefit of safe behaviour by for example highlighting the advantages of it;
2. decrease the perceived cost of safe behaviour;
3. increase the perceived cost of risky behaviour; and
4. decrease the perceived benefit of risky behaviour.

Of these four strategies, a large body of empirical evidence suggests that incentive programmes based on the first strategy are particularly effective in reducing industrial and road-user accidents (Wilde, 1986, 2001). An essential feature of an incentive – as distinguished from a reward – is that it is a pre-announced bonus that is promised on the condition that some behavioural requirements be fulfilled. Thus, instead of offering immediate gratification, incentives enhance the expectation of future enjoyment and therefore enhance the subjective value of future time. We will be more careful and take fewer risks today if we believe that the future holds a wealth of positive experiences for us. Thus, health and safety management, the prevention of lifestyle-dependent diseases and the prevention of violence depend on the extent to which countermeasures can enhance perceived value of the future.

Offering a person an incentive for remaining accident-free or safe implies offering that person a reason for looking forward to the future with increased expectations; hence the term expectationism for the preventive strategy for reducing lifestyle-dependent disease and death rate per head of population by enhancing people's perceived value of the future. The greater the perceived value of the future relative to the perceived value of the present, the more cautious a person would be expected to be. There is evidence that habits beneficial to health are more common among people who hold the future in high regard (Björgvinsson and Wilde, 1995; Strathman et al., 1994).

The Time Horizon Questionnaire (Table 3.2) may be used to assess the degree to which the future is valued over the present. An index to assess this variable may be computed by subtracting the mean item score on the present time value subscale from the mean item score on the future planning scale.

A distinction may be made between specific and general expectationist strategies. Specific expectationist strategies involve fulfilling particular requirements at some future point in time in order to qualify for a particular incentive. For example, people could be offered incentives for having a 12-month accident-free period at work or on the roads; or not suffering from alcohol-related cirrhosis of the liver at 50; or not suffering from smoking-related respiratory disease at 55. General strategies do not entail detailed criteria. All that is required to receive the incentive is to be alive at that future date at which the incentive has been promised, for example offering

Table 3.2 Time Horizon Questionnaire

By circling the appropriate answer, please indicate how much you agree or disagree with each of the following statements

	Strongly agree	Agree	Unsure	Disagree	Strongly disagree
1 It is more important to live for today than to worry about tomorrow	Strongly agree	Agree	Unsure	Disagree	Strongly disagree
2 I live for what is, rather than what will be	Strongly agree	Agree	Unsure	Disagree	Strongly disagree
3 I work below my capacity, and do less than I can	Strongly agree	Agree	Unsure	Disagree	Strongly disagree
4 I feel that I have insufficient time to accomplish everything that I must do	Strongly agree	Agree	Unsure	Disagree	Strongly disagree
5 It's more important to enjoy one's life now than to worry about how it may be in the future	Strongly agree	Agree	Unsure	Disagree	Strongly disagree
6 Each day seems to fly by	Strongly agree	Agree	Unsure	Disagree	Strongly disagree
7 The successes of tomorrow are the results of today's efforts	Strongly agree	Agree	Unsure	Disagree	Strongly disagree
8 I rarely schedule my time	Strongly agree	Agree	Unsure	Disagree	Strongly disagree
9 Let us live for today, nobody knows what the future holds	Strongly agree	Agree	Unsure	Disagree	Strongly disagree
10 I often feel pressure to speed up things	Strongly agree	Agree	Unsure	Disagree	Strongly disagree
11 I often find, after beginning a job, that it is more difficult than I had imagined	Strongly agree	Agree	Unsure	Disagree	Strongly disagree
12 I often have to do things faster than I am able to	Strongly agree	Agree	Unsure	Disagree	Strongly disagree
13 I am more concerned about how I feel now than how I may feel in the future	Strongly agree	Agree	Unsure	Disagree	Strongly disagree
14 I organise my daily activities so that there is little confusion	Strongly agree	Agree	Unsure	Disagree	Strongly disagree
15 I think a lot about what I am going to do in the future	Strongly agree	Agree	Unsure	Disagree	Strongly disagree
16 I often schedule too many things at once	Strongly agree	Agree	Unsure	Disagree	Strongly disagree
17 I am able to resist temptation when I know there is work to be done	Strongly agree	Agree	Unsure	Disagree	Strongly disagree
18 I am aware of a sense of continuity in my life	Strongly agree	Agree	Unsure	Disagree	Strongly disagree
19 I rarely think about the future	Strongly agree	Agree	Unsure	Disagree	Strongly disagree
20 It seems to me that my career path is pretty well laid out	Strongly agree	Agree	Unsure	Disagree	Strongly disagree
21 Today is much more important to me than a day in the future	Strongly agree	Agree	Unsure	Disagree	Strongly disagree
22 I work fast and efficiently according to schedule	Strongly agree	Agree	Unsure	Disagree	Strongly disagree

Table 3.2 (Cont'd)

	Strongly agree	Agree	Unsure	Disagree	Strongly disagree
23 I engage in behaviour now which I feel will have positive outcomes for me in the future	Strongly agree	Agree	Unsure	Disagree	Strongly disagree
24 I never seem to have enough time each day to get things done	Strongly agree	Agree	Unsure	Disagree	Strongly disagree
25 I know what I want to be and where I am going	Strongly agree	Agree	Unsure	Disagree	Strongly disagree
26 I waste lots of time before I finally settle down to business	Strongly agree	Agree	Unsure	Disagree	Strongly disagree
27 The future is more important to me than the 'here and now'	Strongly agree	Agree	Unsure	Disagree	Strongly disagree
28 The list of things I need to do seems to get bigger by the hour	Strongly agree	Agree	Unsure	Disagree	Strongly disagree
29 Thinking about the future is pleasant to me	Strongly agree	Agree	Unsure	Disagree	Strongly disagree
30 I rarely feel rushed	Strongly agree	Agree	Unsure	Disagree	Strongly disagree
31 I plan and schedule my time far in advance	Strongly agree	Agree	Unsure	Disagree	Strongly disagree
32 I can never find time to relax	Strongly agree	Agree	Unsure	Disagree	Strongly disagree
33 I think planning for the future is a waste of time	Strongly agree	Agree	Unsure	Disagree	Strongly disagree
34 I think I will feel less happy 10 years from now than I do now	Strongly agree	Agree	Unsure	Disagree	Strongly disagree
35 It is important to enjoy the moment and not worry about tomorrow	Strongly agree	Agree	Unsure	Disagree	Strongly disagree
36 I usually put off today what I can do tomorrow	Strongly agree	Agree	Unsure	Disagree	Strongly disagree
37 I live my life for today rather than worrying about the future	Strongly agree	Agree	Unsure	Disagree	Strongly disagree
38 It is important to get the most out of today and not worry about tomorrow	Strongly agree	Agree	Unsure	Disagree	Strongly disagree
39 When I want to achieve something, I set goals and consider specific means for reaching those goals	Strongly agree	Agree	Unsure	Disagree	Strongly disagree
40 I never plan further than one day in advance	Strongly agree	Agree	Unsure	Disagree	Strongly disagree

Source: Reproduced with permission from Gerald J.S. Wilde, Queen's University, Kingston, Ontario Canada. Home page: <http://psyc.queensu.ca/faculty/wilde/wilde.html>http://psyc.queensu.ca/faculty/wilde/wilde.html

Note: All items are scored 5-4-3-2-1 for SA-A-U-D-SD, except items 8, 19, 26, 27, 30, 33, 34, 36, and 40 which are scored in the reversed direction, 1-2-3-4-5 for SA-A-U-D-SD. The future time value scale contains items 7, 15, 18, 19, 20, 23, 25, 29, 33, 34. The present time value scale contains items 1, 2, 5, 9, 13, 21, 27, 35, 37, 38. The future planning scale contains items 3, 8, 14, 17, 22, 26, 31, 36, 39, 40. The time pressure scale contains items 4, 6, 10, 11, 12, 16, 24, 28, 30, 32.

a sum of money that equals ten times the average annual wage at 65 years of age.

The accident rate, the incidence of unhealthy habits and the level of violence depend on people's orientation towards their future. The more they expect from it, the more careful they will be. The level of risk taking in a society depends therefore, not on safety technology and education, but on prevailing societal values. According to expectationism, there are changes that could be made to our society that would give us good reason to look forward to our next birthday, our next decade and our later years. For youngsters we could increase their weekly pocket money at every birthday. For young adults we could reduce college fees after each year of study. For employees we could increase the minimum wage and the duration of annual leave as they grow older. The value of salaries and degree of job security could be made dependent on years of service. Tax advantages, retirement saving fund advantages and insurance discounts could be offered as we grow older so that we are motivated to contribute to the monetary value of our future. These financial incentives would go some way towards alleviating fears of becoming a burden upon others, or of being neglected, abused or lonely in our sunset years.

Expectationism entails the view that people can be motivated by incentives to save for later. One factor that contributes to the benefit of saving for later is a clean, green ecology and the conservation of natural resources. With incentives to live longer and save for the future, a society is more likely to protect the environment against pollution and destruction for short-term gains.

OPTIMISM, HOPE AND HEALTH

Optimism and hope as measured by the scales mentioned in preceding sections have been found to have important correlates (Peterson, 2000b; Snyder, 2000). Optimism and hope correlate negatively with measures of current psychopathology generally, and current depression in particular. Optimism and hope are predictive of physical and mental health as indexed and/or mediated by a variety of measures including self-reported health, positive response to medical intervention, subjective well-being, positive mood, immunological robustness, effective coping (reappraisal, problem solving, avoiding stressful life events, seeking social support) and health-promoting behaviour (Peterson, 2000; Snyder, 2000; Scheier et al., 2000; Taylor et al., 2000). Optimistic people are healthier and happier. Their immune systems work better. They cope better with stress using more effective coping strategies such as reappraisal and problem solving. They also actively avoid stressful life events and form better social support networks around themselves. They have healthier lifestyles which prevent them from developing illness, or if they develop illness they adhere to medical advice better and follow through with behaviour patterns that promote recovery. Optimism in early adulthood predicts health in later adulthood over periods of up to 35 years (Peterson *et al.*, 1988).

THE NEUROBIOLOGY OF OPTIMISM AND HOPE

Little research has been conducted on the neurobiology of optimism. However, findings from neurobiological research in three areas are of relevance: (1) pessimism, depression and anxiety; (2) optimistic goal-directed and incentive-driven behaviour; and (3) optimistic affiliative behaviour.

Neurobiology of pessimism

Pessimism is a key feature of depression and anxiety and so the neurobiology of these conditions provides a starting point for understanding the biological correlates of optimism and hope. Depression and anxiety are associated with abnormal functioning in the limbic system (particularly the amygdala), the paralimbic system and the lateral pre-frontal cortex. Depression is associated with the depletion of certain neurotransmitters (particularly serotonin and noradrenalin) or a decrease in the efficiency with which systems based on them function in the brain sites implicated in depression (Liddle, 2001). Antidepressants (tricylics, serotonin re-uptake inhibitors and monoamine oxidaise inhibitors) increase the efficiency with which systems involving these neurotransmitters operate. It is probable that optimism and hope is associated with efficient functioning of neurotransmitter systems involving serotonin and noradrenalin, although research in this area is in its infancy. Depression is also associated with abnormal functioning of the hypothalamic–pituitary–adrenocortical axis leading to the overproduction of cortisol, a depletion of endorphin secretion and immune suppression. There is growing evidence that optimism and hope are associated with more efficient functioning of the immune system (Peterson, 2000b).

Anxiety is associated with abnormal gamma aminobutyric acid (GABA) binding (Liddle, 2001). GABA is usually released automatically once arousal reaches a certain level. It then binds with GABA receptors on excited neurones which underpin the experience of anxiety. This binding process causes inhibition, a reduction in arousal and a decrease in experienced anxiety. Treatment of anxiety with benzodiazepines such as diazepam (Valium) reduces anxiety because these drugs bind to the GABA neuroreceptors with a consequent reduction in arousal. Research by Professor Robert Drugan (2000) demonstrates that animals who show resilience in the face of uncontrollable stress, have a unique pattern of GABA binding. Animals who show resilience in the face of uncontrollable stress, show increased gamma aminobutyric acid (GABA) binding (as if they had been given diazepam) and an impaired emotional memory for the stressful event. Animals who become helpless, in contrast, show reduced GABA activity and vivid memory for uncontrollable stressors.

Neurobiology of optimistic goal-directed behaviour

Snyder's conceptualisation of hope as involving the ability to plan pathways to desired goals despite obstacles and to be motivated to use these pathways suggests that research on the neurobiology of incentive-driven, goal-directed behaviour may throw light on the biological correlates of hope (Snyder, 2000). Professor Jeffrey Gray at the Institute of Psychiatry in London has proposed that much goal-directed behaviour is governed by two antagonistic control centres within the central nervous system (Pickering and Gray, 1999). These are the behavioural activation system (BAS) and the behavioural inhibition system (BIS). The BAS system is conceptualised as a system particularly responsive to rewards or reinforcement and the BIS as a system that is particularly responsive to punishment. The BAS is activated by signals of reward and controls approach behaviour. It is a 'go' system. The BIS is activated by signals of punishment and controls passive avoidance. It is a 'stop' system. The BAS, which probably is of central importance to optimistic behaviour, is subserved by mesolimbic and mesocortical dopamine pathways.

Professor Richard Depue (1996) at Cornell University New York has similarly shown that a behavioural facilitation system (BFS) activated by signals of reward, accounts for much of the animal and human data on incentive seeking. The BFS controls incentive-driven or goal-directed behaviour and activities associated with securing food, a sex partner and a nesting place, and seeking other important goals and rewards. It is sometimes loosely referred to as the neurobiological reward system. The BFS includes the mesolimbic dopamine pathways which arise in the ventral tegmental area of the midbrain and project to the amygdala, hippocampus and nucleus accumbens in the limbic system. The reward system also includes the mesocortical dopamine pathways that originate in the ventral tegmental area and projects onto all areas of the cortex. Individuals with an active BFS are strongly motivated by incentives and rewards to pursue goals. In personality trait models, the BFS corresponds approximately to extraversion (Eysenck and Eysenck, 1985) or positive affectivity (Watson and Tellegen, 1985). The efficiency with which the BFS operates is normally distributed within the population, and optimism is probably associated with more efficient functioning of the BFS.

Neurobiology of optimistic social interaction

A further line of research of relevance to the study of optimism in women within the context of socially supportive relationships focuses on oxytocin and endogenous opioids (Taylor, Dickerson and Cousino Klein, 2002). Oxytocin is a peptide released from the posterior pituitary following the birth of offspring. It facilitates milk ejection during nursing and uterine contractions during labour. It may facilitate the processes of attachment between mother and offspring and stress-management through social support seeking in women. Oxytocin is released in response to stress and social support. It down-regulates sympathetic hypothalamic–pituitary–adrenocortical activity and so reduces stress responses. It also stimulates (optimistic) contact with others who may potentially offer social support.

Low levels of endogenous opioid peptides can also act as an incentive to (optimistically) seek social contact. They, like oxytocin, are released during supportive and affiliate social contact. They down-regulate sympathetic hypothalamic–pituitary–adrenocortical activity in response to stress and separation, and so reduce stress responses. High levels of endogenous opioid peptides are intrinsically rewarding.

In summary, optimism and hope probably have many biological correlates. These may involve: (1) efficient functioning of neurotransmitter systems involving serotonin and noradrenalin; (2) efficient functioning of the immune system; (3) increased GABA binding and a capacity to forget or inhibit memories of stressful events; and (4) a particularly active or efficient behavioural activation or facilitation system involving mesolimbic and mesocortical dopamine pathways. In women, oxytocin and endogenous opioid-based systems may be associated with involvement in hopeful socially supportive relationships.

IMPLICATIONS

A summary of self-help strategies for enhancing positive illusions, hope, optimism and positive expectations is given in Table 3.3. These can be incorporated into clinical practice.

CONTROVERSIES

One of the interesting controversies in this field concerns risk homeostasis theory from which expectationism is derived. Professor Gerry Wilde (2001) has argued that the most effective way to reduce accidents and unhealthy lifestyles is to give people incentives so that they value the future more than the present. This strategy reduces the target level of risk that people are

Table 3.3 Strategies for enhancing positive illusions, hope, optimism and positive expectations

Domain	Strategy
Positive illusions	• When thinking about past experience, focus predominantly on details of positive events.
	• Psychologically, ring-fence areas where you have poor skills or personal characteristics that you have but do not like. Define these as exceptions to your predominantly competent and attractive self-image.
Optimism	• For any situation in which you attribute adversity to intrinsic, global stable attributes identify the Adversity, the pessimistic Beliefs, and Consequent negative mood change on a 10-point scale.
	• Distract yourself from adversity and rumination by saying STOP, by snapping yourself with an elastic band, or by focusing on another activity or object.
	• Distance yourself from the pessimistic explanation by noting that there are other explanations.
	• Dispute the pessimistic beliefs by checking the evidence for the pessimistic explanation and an optimistic alternative where you attribute adversity to extrinsic, specific and transient situational factors.
	• Notice how distraction, distancing and disputing lead your mood to change positively to Energise you.
Hope	• To generate hope in a particular situation, formulate clear goals, produce numerous pathways to these, pursue your goals and reframe obstacles as challenges to be overcome.
Positive expectations	• To reduce risk taking that may foreshorten your lifespan, develop incentives to help you to value the future more than the present.

Source: Based on Seligman (1998); Snyder (2000); Taylor (1989); Wilde (2001).

prepared to accept and so motivates them to live safer lives. However, opposition to this view comes from those who advocate engineering a safer environment by, for example, designing vehicles with better safety features or roads with better traffic signals. However, extensive research has shown that once people receive feedback that seatbelts, crash helmets or new road signals have led to a reduction in annual accident rates, they become more reckless in their driving behaviour and the annual accident rate returns to its previous level. Wilde argues that safety interventions based on engineering, environmental changes and education are ultimately ineffective because they do not modify the target level of risk within a population.

SUMMARY

Up until the end of the 1970s optimism was considered to be a psychological deficit. Freud argued that the optimistic belief in God was an illusion essential for civilisation.

In the late 1970s, cognitive psychologists had accumulated a wealth of research which showed that people's thinking processes were optimistic. Within positive psychology research on positive illusions and self-deception, optimism, and hope have been particularly important.

Research on positive illusions and self-deception has shown that human thought is distinguished by a robust positive bias. Most people view themselves, the world and the future in positive terms. The self-deceptive strategies we use to manage this negative information, which is contrary to an optimistic world view, includes defence mechanisms such as denial and repression and positive illusions. Positive illusions involve the cognitive processes of selective attention, benign forgetting, maintaining pockets of incompetence and maintaining negative self-schemas. The development of positive illusions is fostered by a parenting style where children are given information by their parents and encouraged to make choices within the context of a warm relationship, with clear behavioural limits. The tendency to have a positive view of the self continues throughout life, although its strength diminishes gradually. This view of the self as good is partially determined by the egocentric nature of memory and also by our self-schemas which determine which aspects of a situation we attended to. Modifying positive illusions involves giving negative information in a way that is corrective but not devastating.

Optimism has been conceptualised as a broad personality trait and as an explanatory style in which the causes of negative events are attributed to external, transient, specific factors rather than internal, stable, global factors. The development of optimism is determined by parental mental health, the type of role modelling offered by parents and the degree to which parents encourage and reward optimism. Individuals with an optimistic explanatory style are less likely to develop physical ill-health, depression or suicidality when they face major stressful life events than individuals with a pessimistic explanatory style. In adulthood optimism is associated with better academic achievement, sport performance, occupational adjustment and family life and response to bereavement and loss. Optimism contributes to success in public life. Effective programmes to help adults and children change their explanatory style from pessimism to optimism have been developed.

Hope involves the ability to plan pathways to desired goals, despite obstacles, and agency or motivation to use these pathways. Hope develops in a clearly defined way over the course of infancy, childhood and adolescence. Children who develop a hopeful disposition typically have parents who serve as hopeful role models and who coach them in developing and executing plans to circumvent barriers to valued goals. These children have secure attachment to their parents who provide them with a warm and structured family environment in which rules are consistently and predictably applied and conflict is managed in a predictable and fair way. Hope therapy aims to help clients formulate clear goals, produce numerous pathways to these, motivate themselves to pursue their goals and reframe obstacles as challenges to be overcome.

Expectationism is a preventive strategy for reducing lifestyle-dependent disease, accidents, violence and death rate by enhancing people's perceived value of the future. It is based on risk homeostasis theory which argues that the amount of risk-taking behaviour, accident-rate and lifestyle-dependent disease rate in a population are maintained over time, unless there is a change in the target level of risk and enhancing the degree to which the future is valued over the present is one way of altering target risk.

Optimism and hope correlate positively with, and are predictive of, physical and mental health as indexed and/or mediated by a variety of measures including self-reported health, positive response to medical intervention, subjective well-being, positive mood, immunological robustness, effective coping (reappraisal, problem solving, avoiding stressful life events, seeking social support) and health-promoting behaviour.

Optimism and hope probably have many biological correlates including efficient functioning of neurotransmitter systems involving serotonin and noradrenalin; efficient functioning of the immune system; increased GABA binding and a capacity to forget or inhibit memories of stressful events; and a particularly active or efficient behavioural activation or facilitation system involving mesolimbic and mesocortical dopamine pathways. In women, oxytocin and endogenous opioid-based systems may be associated with involvement in hopeful socially supportive relationships.

QUESTIONS

Personal development questions

1. In the domains of health, family, friends, romantic relationships, leisure activities, education and work what were your main success stories in the past year?
2. What is the evidence that these successes were due to your own personal strengths (rather than situational factors)?
3. In the domains of health, family, friends, romantic relationships, leisure activities, education and work what are your goals for the coming year?
4. What are some of the pathways that you can see to each of these goals?
5. What personal strengths have you got that will help you use some of these pathways to achieve your goals?
6. What incentives can you promise yourself to help you work towards these goals?

7. What would be the costs and benefits of pursuing some of the pathways that you can see to each of these goals?
8. Take some of these pathways and assess the impact it has on your well-being by assessing yourself before and afterwards on one of the well-being scales contained in Chapter 1.

Research questions

1. Design and conduct a study to test the hypotheses that there are significant correlations between self-deception, dispositional optimism, optimistic explanatory style, the trait hope, future-orientation and happiness. Which of these variables accounts for the greatest amount of variance in happiness?
2. Conduct a PsychInfo search covering literature published in the past couple of years using the terms 'self-deception', 'optimism', 'hope', and 'future orientation' individually and in combination. Identify a study that interests you and that is feasible to replicate and extend. Conduct the replication.

FURTHER READING

Academic

Gillham, J. (2000) *The Science of Optimism and Hope.* Philadelphia, PA: Templeton Foundation Press.
Snyder, C.R. (2000). *Handbook of Hope.* Orlando FL: Academic Press.
Wilde, G. (2001). *Target Risk 2: A New Psychology of Health and Safety: What Works, What Doesn't and Why* ... Toronto: PDE Publications. Available as e-book at <http://psyc.queensu.ca/faculty/wilde/wilde.html>

Self-help

Seligman, M. (1998). *Learned Optimism: How to Change Your Mind and Your Life.* New York: Pocket Books.
Taylor, S. (1989). *Positive Illusions: Creative Self-Deception and the Healthy Mind.* New York: Basic Books.

MEASURES FOR USE IN RESEARCH

Self-deception

Gur, R. and Sackeim, H. (1979). Self-deception: a concept in search of a phenomenon. *Journal of Personality and Social Psychology* 37: 147–69. Contains the Self-deception Questionnaire.

Dispositional optimism

Scheier, M. and Carver, C. (1985). Optimism, coping and health: assessment and implications of generalized outcome expectancies. *Health Psychology* 4: 219–47.

Scheier, M., Carver, C. and Bridges, M. (1994). Distinguishing optimism from neuroticism (and trait anxiety, self-mastery, and self-esteem): a re-evaluation of the Life Orientation Test. *Journal of Personality and Social Psychology* 67: 1063–78.

Optimistic explanatory style

Dykema, K., Bergbower, K., Doctora, J. and Peterson, C. (1996). An attributional style questionnaire for general use. *Journal of Psychoeducational Assessment* 14: 100–8.

Finchman, F.D. and Bradbury, T.N. (1992). Assessing attributions in marriage: the Relationship Attribution Measure. *Journal of Personality and Social Psychology* 62 (3): 457–68.

Peterson, C. and Villanova, P. (1988). An expanded attributional style questionnaire. *Journal of Abnormal Psychology* 97: 87–9.

Peterson, C., Schulman, P., Castellon, C. and Seligman, M. (1992). CAVE: Content Analysis of Verbal Explanations. In C. Smith (ed.), *Motivation and Personality: Handbook of Thematic Content Analysis* (pp. 383–92). New York: Cambridge University Press.

Peterson, C., Semmel, A., vonBaeyer, C., Abramson, L., Metalsky, G. and Seligman, M. (1982). The attributional style questionnaire. *Cognitive Therapy and Research* 6: 287–99.

Seligman, M., Peterson, C., Kaslow, N., Tanenbaum, R., Alloy, L. and Abramson, L. (1984). Attributional style and depressive symptoms among children. *Journal of Abnormal Psychology* 93: 235–8. Children's attributional style questionnaire is validated in this and is contained in full in Seligman, M. (1998). *Learned Optimism*. New York: Pocket Books.

Stratton, P., Heard, D., Hanks, H., Munton, A., Brewin, C. and Davidson, C. (1986). Coding causal beliefs in natural discourse. *British Journal of Social Psychology* 25: 299–311.

Hope

Lopez, S., Ciarlelli, R., Coffman, L., Stone, M. and Wyatt, L. (2000). Diagnosis for strength: on measuring hope building blocks. In C.R. Snyder (ed.), *Handbook of Hope* (pp. 57–88). Orlando FL: Academic Press. (Contains all Snyder's Hope Scales.)

Future orientation

Strathman. A., Gleicher, F., Boninger, D. and Edwards, C. (1994). The consideration of future consequences: weighing immediate and distant outcomes of behavior. *Journal of Personality and Social Psychology* 66: 742–52. Contains the 12-item

Consideration of Future Consequences scale which evaluates willingness to sacrifice immediate benefits like pleasure or convenience to achieve more desirable future states.

GLOSSARY

Attributional retraining.   Learning to detect and challenge pessimistic attributions for success and failure and replace them with optimistic ones.

Benign forgetting.   Not recalling negative information.

Denial. Not acknowledging the existence or meaning of threatening or stressful events in the external world.

Dispositional optimism.   A global expectation that more good things than bad will happen in the future.

Expectationism.   Wilde's preventive strategy for reducing lifestyle-dependent disease, accidents, violence and death rate per head of population by enhancing people's perceived value of the future.

Hope.   The ability to plan pathways to desired goals despite obstacles, and agency or motivation to use these pathways.

Negative self-schema.   An organised set of beliefs that allows us to anticipate situations in which negative information is likely to be received about the self and then to develop strategies for dealing with these, for example I don't talk much at parties because I'm shy.

Optimistic explanatory style.   Seligman's name for the tendency to explain negative events or experiences by attributing the cause of these to external, transient, specific factors such as the prevailing circumstances, for example attributing exam failure to the questions being unfair.

Pockets of incompetence.   Managing negative information about the self by defining circumscribed areas of incompetence but believing oneself to be otherwise competent.

Positive illusions.   Taylor's term for the tendency for us to view ourselves in a positive way.

Positive selective attention.   Noticing positive things and screening out negative things.

Repression.   Not acknowledging unacceptable aggressive or sexual impulses in a person's inner world.

Risk homeostasis theory.   Wilde's view that the degree of risk-taking behaviour and the magnitude of loss due to accidents and lifestyle-dependent disease in a population are maintained over time, unless there is a change in the target level of risk that members of the population choose to accept in order to maximise the overall expected benefit from their activities.

Chapter 4

Emotional intelligence

Learning objectives

- Be able to distinguish between emotional intelligence conceptualised as an ability and as a personality trait with reference to the models of Mayer, Salovey Caruso, Bar-On, Goleman and Cooper.
- Be able to describe the development of emotional intelligence through childhood and adolescence.
- Understand the importance of attachment in the development of emotional competence and resilience.
- Give an account of some aspects of the neurobiological basis for emotional intelligence.
- Be able to distinguish between emotional intelligence and related constructs such as practical intelligence, autistic spectrum disorder traits, openness to experience, alexithymia, psychological mindedness, levels of emotional awareness and emotional creativity.
- Understand the implications of research on emotional intelligence for enhancing subjective well-being.
- Be able to identify research questions that need to be addressed to advance our understanding of emotional intelligence and well-being.

In 1995 the American Dialect Society (1999) selected Emotional Intelligence as the most useful new term. The explosion of interest in the construct arose from Daniel Goleman's (1995) bestseller – *Emotional Intelligence: Why It Can Matter More than IQ*. This book popularised aspects of the academic work on emotional intelligence first published by Professor John Mayer, Peter Salovey and colleagues in 1990 (Mayer *et al.*, 1990; Salovey and Mayer, 1990) and the work of Professor Howard Gardner on intrapersonal and interpersonal intelligence first published in 1983. John Mayer and Peter Salovey presented research findings which suggested that processing information about emotions entailed abilities different from those required to process information about verbal, mathematical or visuo-spatial problems contained in traditional intelligence tests. Gardner argued that there were many other intelligences besides that measured by traditional IQ tests and these included the ability to understand and regulate one's own emotions (intrapersonal intelligence) and the ability to understand and manage relationships (interpersonal intelligence). The argument put forward in Goleman's book was that success at work and in achieving valued life goals was largely due, not to IQ, but to emotional intelligence – the capacity to recognise and manage one's own emotions and those of others in significant interpersonal relationships. Furthermore, while it is widely accepted that genetic factors set limits on IQ, implicit in Goleman's book was the idea that emotional intelligence is predominantly environmentally determined and could be improved by training. The American public was highly receptive to this idea, because it came at a time when Herrnstein and Murray's (1994) book *The Bell Curve* argued that high IQ was a key factor in determining occupational success and membership of higher social classes.

EMOTIONAL INTELLIGENCE: ABILITY OR PERSONALITY TRAIT?

In recent research emotional intelligence has been conceptualised in two distinct ways. First, it has been conceptualised as a set of abilities for processing emotional information. This position has been championed by Professors Jack Mayer, Peter Salovey and David Caruso at the University of New Hampshire (Mayer, Caruso and Salovey, 2000). Second, it has been conceptualised as a set of personality traits. This approach has been taken by Professor Reuven Bar-On (2000) in Denmark, author of the Emotional Quotient Inventory, by Daniel Goleman and colleagues (Goleman, 1995; Boyatzis *et al.*, 2000), and by Professor Richard Cooper (1996/1997) author of the EQ Map.

Mayer, Salovey and Caruso's ability model of emotional intelligence

According to Mayer, Caruso and Salovey's (2000) ability model, emotional intelligence refers to the abilities used to process information about one's own emotions and the emotions of others. Within the model, which is presented in Figure 4.1, there are four branches: emotional perception, emotional integration, emotional understanding and emotional management. The first of these – emotional perception – is the ability to register, attend to and decipher emotional messages as they are expressed in a variety of contexts including facial expressions, tone of voice and works of art. People who are skilled at perceiving emotions are better informed about their environment

Figure 4.1 Mayer, Salovey and Caruso's model of emotional intelligence
Source: Adapted from Mayer *et al.* (2000a): 92–117.

and so may adapt better to it. A person who can detect subtle facial expressions of irritability is in a better position to manage a potentially conflictual social situation than a person who does not have the ability to perceive such emotions.

The second branch of emotional intelligence in this model – emotional integration – refers to the ability to access and generate feelings which facilitate thought. Emotions can enter the cognitive system as explicit thoughts about specific feelings, such as 'I am happy', and as altered cognitions which are congruent with the emotional state, such as when a happy person thinks 'Today everything will go my way'. Thus emotions can facilitate thought by giving information about our mood state – letting us know if we are happy, sad, frightened or angry – and by making us think in a way that is congruent with our mood states. Thus, people skilled in emotional integration are more likely to view things from an optimistic perspective when happy, a pessimistic perspective when sad and a threat-oriented perspective when anxious or angry. This capacity to shift perspective depending upon mood state means that people with well-developed emotional integration skills can see things from multiple perspectives as their mood alters. This capacity to see things from multiple perspectives may facilitate very creative problem solving and may explain why people with mood swings show greater creativity than those with more stable moods. The degree to which mood swings are under voluntary control is dependent upon emotional management skills – the fourth branch of emotional intelligence in this model – which will be described below.

The third branch of emotional intelligence in this model – emotional understanding – is the ability to comprehend the implications of emotions. People with well-developed emotional understanding can understand how one emotion leads to another, how emotions change over time, and how the temporal patterning of emotions can affect relationships. For example, a person who understands that anger expressed as aggression which hurts others can lead to remorse if retaliation does not occur or to an escalation of anger if retaliation does occur may be better able to handle conflictual situations than someone who does not have the skill to understand these types of temporal emotional sequences.

The fourth branch of emotional intelligence in this model – emotional management – is the ability to regulate emotions, to choose to be open to experiencing emotions and to control the way in which these are expressed. A person with well-developed emotional management abilities has the option of choosing to experience emotions, or blocking the experience of them. For example, in normal day-to-day interactions it may enrich our lives and deepen our relationships to be open to emotions experienced by ourselves or expressed by others and to express our emotions freely. However, in emergency situations such as avoiding a car crash, being mugged, fire-fighting, or carrying out a risky medical operation it may be more adaptive to block the experience of emotions and restrict their expression. People with well-developed emotional management abilities are able to choose the degree to which they are open to experiencing emotions and expressing them.

Having well-developed abilities to perceive, integrate, understand and manage emotions does not necessarily mean that these abilities will routinely be used, any more than having a high IQ means that a person will usually read intellectually demanding books. For this reason, ability measures of emotional intelligence do not correlate highly with personality trait measures of emotional intelligence, which evaluate what people say about how they usually behave.

The abilities to perceive, integrate, understand and manage emotions may be measured by the *Multifactor Emotional Intelligence Scale* (MEIS), (Mayer

Table 4.1 Abilities assessed by Multifactor Emotional IQ Test and the Mayer, Salovey and Caruso Emotional Intelligence Test

Domain	Ability
Emotional perception	1. Identifying emotions in faces 2. Identifying emotions in designs 3. Identifying emotions in music 4. Identifying emotions in stories
Emotional integration	5. Translating feeling (synesthesia) 6. Using emotions to make judgements (feeling biases)
Emotional understanding	7. Defining emotions 8. Defining complex emotional blends 9. Defining emotional transitions 10. Defining emotional perspectives
Emotional management	11. Managing own emotions 12. Managing other's emotions

Source: Adapted from Mayer et al. (1997); Mayer et al. (1999).

et al., 1997) or the *Mayer, Salovey and Caruso Emotional Intelligence Test*, subtests of which are listed in Table 4.1 (MSCEIT), (Mayer et al., 1999). These tests include items which require complex judgements to be made about emotions and to which there are right and wrong answers. For emotional perception, respondents are asked to identify dominant emotions shown or evoked by a series of faces, landscapes and designs. For emotional integration, participants are asked to judge the similarity between an emotional feeling like love and other internal experiences such as temperatures and tastes. This is a synesthesia task. Emotional understanding is evaluated with a range of items such as 'Jamie felt happier and happier, joyful and excited. If this feeling intensified it would be closest to (a) challenge, (b) admiration, (c) pride, (d) peacefulness, (e) ecstasy'. Emotional management is evaluated by items such as 'If a sad person wanted to cheer up which would be the best course of action to take? (a) talking to friends, (b) seeing a violent movie, (c), eating a big meal, (d) taking a walk alone'. Responses on this item are scored according to a consensus criterion.

The MEIS and MSCEIT have good reliability and validity (Mayer, Caruso and Salovey, 2000). Factor analyses show that there is a single underlying factor and also that the four subfactors in the model are hierarchically beneath the single general factor. These tests correlate about 0.4 with vocabulary scores but not with non-verbal measures of intelligence. On these tests adults show greater emotional intelligence than children. Only moderate correlations of about 0.4 have been found between the MSCEIT (an ability measure of emotional intelligence) and the BarOn EQi (a personality trait measure of emotional intelligence). The MEIS correlates moderately (approximately

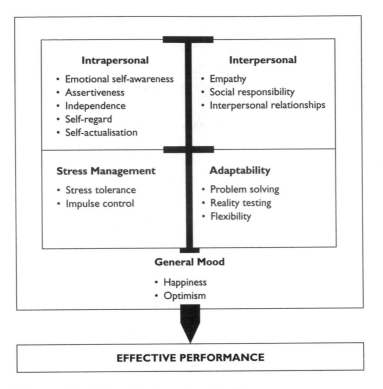

Figure 4.2 Reuven Bar-On's model of emotional intelligence
Source: Adapted from Bar-On, R. (1997).

0.3) with empathy, life satisfaction and self-esteem. The MEIS has weak but significant correlations (about 0.2) with self-reported parental warmth, extraversion and openness to feelings. The MEIS and MSCEIT have negligible correlations with measures of social desirability.

Bar-On's personality model of social and emotional intelligence

In Professor Reuven Bar-On's (2000) personality-trait model of emotional intelligence, presented in Figure 4.2, distinctions are made between five domains: the intrapersonal, the interpersonal, adaptability, stress management and mood. In each of these domains there are specific skills which collectively constitute what he refers to as emotional and social intelligence. The intrapersonal domain includes the following skills: emotional self-awareness, assertiveness, independence, self-regard and self-actualisation. The following skills fall into the interpersonal domain: empathy, social responsibility and management of interpersonal relationships. Problem solving, reality testing and flexibility are the skills which constitute the adaptability domain. Stress tolerance and impulse control are the main skills in the stress management domain. In the mood domain maintaining happiness and optimism are the principal skills.

In the intrapersonal domain, emotional self-awareness is the ability to recognise and understand one's own emotions. Assertiveness is the ability to express one's thoughts, beliefs and feelings in a non-aggressive way so as to defend one's rights. Independence is the ability to be self-directed and self-controlled in one's thinking and actions and to be free of emotional dependency. Self-regard refers to the ability to understand, accept and respect oneself. Self-actualisation is the ability to realise one's potential and to achieve goals that one wants to attain.

In the interpersonal domain empathy is the ability to be aware of, understand and appreciate the feelings of others. Social responsibility is the ability to co-operate and contribute constructively to one's social group. Maintaining interpersonal relationships refers to the capacity to make and maintain friendships characterised by emotional closeness and psychological intimacy.

In the adaptability domain, problem solving is the ability to identify social and interpersonal problems, define them in solvable terms and generate and implement effective solutions. Reality testing is the ability to evaluate the correspondence between subjective experiences and external objective situations. Flexibility is the ability to modify one's thoughts, feelings and behaviour to fit with changing situations.

In the stress management domain stress tolerance refers to the capacity to withstand the build-up of adversity, challenges, stresses and strong emotions without decompensating or emotionally 'falling apart'. Impulse control refers to the capacity to resist or delay acting on an impulse and to control one's emotions.

In the mood domain maintaining happiness is the ability to enjoy oneself and others, to have fun, to express positive feelings and to be satisfied with life. Optimism is the ability to look on the bright side of things even in the face of adversity.

Reuven Bar-On (1997) has developed a questionnaire – *The Emotional Quotient Inventory* – to evaluate emotional intelligence. The questionnaire contains 133 items. Each of these is a brief statement and the respondent indicates the degree to which each item describes them on 5-point scales where 1 = very seldom true and 5 = very often true. The *Emotional Quotient Inventory* yields an overall emotional quotient score and scores for the domains and specific abilities listed in Table 4.2. Different versions of the Emotional Quotient Inventory have been developed for adults, adolescents and children. Standardisation data have been collected from thousands of people in more than fifteen countries. So it is possible to say when somebody fills in the questionnaire where their scores stand with respect to those of other people. The Emotional Quotient Inventory has been shown in

Table 4.2 Factors assessed by Reuven Bar-On's model of emotional intelligence

Domain	Ability
Intrapersonal	1. Emotional self-awareness 2. Assertiveness 3. Independence 4. Self-regard 5. Self-actualisation
Interpersonal	6. Empathy 7. Social responsibility 8. Interpersonal relationships
Adaptability	9. Problem solving 10. Reality testing 11. Flexibility
Stress management	12. Stress tolerance 13. Impulse control
Mood	14. Happiness 15. Optimism

Source: Adapted from Bar-On (1997).

numerous studies to be reliable and to have some degree of validity. It reliably gives approximately the same score when filled in twice in the same six-week period. It validly yields similar ratings to those of expert judges and partially predicts the type of people who will excel in particular work situations. It is also distinct from cognitive intelligence assessed by routine intelligence tests. It is computer scored in such a way that compensations in scoring are made if the person's patterns of responses suggest that he or she is trying to describe themselves in an exceptionally positive or negative way.

Bar-On (2000) has shown that people of different ages and genders have differing EQs or EQ profiles. Emotional intelligence increases with age at least until middle life. People in their 40s and 50s have higher EQs than younger or older people. Males and females have similar overall EQs but males score higher in the intrapersonal, adaptability and stress management domains while females score higher in the interpersonal domain. Women are more aware of their emotions, demonstrate more empathy, relate better interpersonally and act more socially responsibly than men. Men, in contrast, have better self-regard, are more independent, cope better with stress (in the short term), are more flexible, solve problems better and are more optimistic than women. There is also considerable evidence that high EQ scores are associated with better mental health and low EQ scores with more mental health difficulties.

Goleman's model of emotional intelligence

Dr Daniel Goleman's model of emotional intelligence was initially articulated in his two bestselling books on the subject (Goleman, 1995, 1998) and later operationalised in the Emotional Competency Inventory (ECI), (Boyatzis *et al.*, 1999). The inventory, which has self-report and colleague-rated versions, was developed in collaboration with Professor Richard Boyatzis, an organisational psychologist at Case Western Reserve University. The aim of the inventory is to evaluate emotional intelligence competencies important for outstanding performance in commercial businesses.

Within the inventory distinctions are made between the competencies necessary for self-awareness, social awareness, self-management and social skills. The main scales and subscales of the inventory are listed in Table 4.3. Self-awareness competencies include emotional self-awareness, accurate self-assessment and self-confidence. Social awareness competencies include empathy, organisational awareness and having a service orientation. Competencies essential for self-management are self-control, trustworthiness, conscientiousness, adaptability, achievement orientation and initiative. Social skills competencies include developing others, leadership, influence, communication, change catalyst, conflict management, building bonds and teamwork.

Table 4.3 Factors assessed by the Emotional Competence Inventory

Domain	Ability
Self-awareness	1. Emotional self-awareness 2. Accurate self-assessment 3. Self-confidence
Social awareness	4. Empathy 5. Organisational awareness 6. Service orientation
Self-management	7. Self-control 8. Trustworthiness 9. Conscientiousness 10. Adaptability 11. Achievement orientation 12. Initiative
Social skills	13. Developing others 14. Leadership 15. Influence 16. Communication 17. Change catalyst 18. Conflict management 19. Building bonds 20. Teamwork

Source: Adapted from Boyatzis *et al.* (1999).

Research on experienced partners in a consulting firm showed that more partners with more scores above a tipping point or cut-off score on the dimensions of the ECI contributed more to the profits of the organisation (Boyatzis *et al.*, 2000).

Cooper's EQ Map

Dr Richard Cooper (1996/1997) developed an instrument called the *Emotional Quotient Map* or *EQ Map* which evaluates the respondent's current environment, emotional literacy, EQ competencies, EQ values and attitudes and EQ outcomes. The factors assessed by this instrument are given in Table 4.4. The current environment domain includes both life pressures and life satisfactions dimensions. The emotional literacy domain includes the dimensions of emotional self-awareness, emotional expression and emotional awareness of others. Intentionality, creativity, resilience, interpersonal connections and constructive discontent fall into the EQ competencies domain. In the EQ values and attitudes domain dimensions, which evaluate outlook, compassion, intuition, trust radius, personal power and integrated self are included. General health, quality of life, relationship quotient and optimal

Table 4.4 Factors assessed by the EQ Map

Domain	Ability
Current environment	1. Life pressures 2. Life satisfactions
Emotional literacy	3. Emotional self-awareness 4. Emotional expression 5. Emotional awareness of others
EQ competencies	6. Intentionality 7. Creativity 8. Resilience 9. Interpersonal connections 10. Constructive discontent
EQ values and attitudes	11. Outlook 12. Compassion 13. Intuition 14. Trust radius 15. Personal power 16. Integrated self
EQ outcomes	17. General health 18. Quality of life 19. Relationship quotient 20. Optimal performance

Source: Adapted from Cooper (1996/1997).

performance are the dimensions which constitute the EQ outcomes domain. The EQ map evaluates a very broad interpretation of the emotional intelligence construct, along with a variety of related dimensions such as current environment and EQ outcomes which are not strictly part of the EQ construct as interpreted by other researchers who take a personality trait approach to emotional intelligence, such as Reuven Bar-On or Daniel Goleman.

Because validation studies of ability and personality trait measures of emotional intelligence are in their infancy, the debate about which approach is the most useful, under which circumstances remains unresolved.

ENHANCING EMOTIONAL INTELLIGENCE IN ADULTHOOD

There has been a proliferation of programmes which claim to enhance emotional intelligence in schools and in the workplace (Salovey *et al.*, 2002). Empirical investigation of the effectiveness of these training programmes is currently at an early stage of development. Empirical findings from the field of cognitive-behaviour therapy, however, suggest that training in the skills for self-monitoring, self-regulation, communication and problem solving might usefully be included in programmes to enhance emotional intelligence (Carr, 2000c).

Self-monitoring to increase emotional awareness

Self-monitoring enhances awareness of emotions, the situations that elicit these and the thoughts and beliefs that accompany them. Self-monitoring involves keeping a diary of emotional mood change episodes containing the following columns (as was noted in Chapter 3 in the section on attributional retraining):

*   the Activity that led to the change in mood
*   the Beliefs that led to the change in mood
*   the Consequent mood change on a 10-point scale.

Reviewing this type of diary allows us to see that it is our beliefs or interpretation of events that contribute, in large part, to negative mood changes.

Self-regulation to manage distressing emotions

Well-developed routines for regulating depression, anxiety and anger have been developed within the cognitive-behavioural tradition. These have been mentioned in Chapter 1 in the section on managing adaptive but distressing emotions and in Chapter 3 in the section on attributional retraining, but will be recapped here. We can become aware of the situations in which episodes in which depression, anxiety and anger typically occur, and the beliefs we hold in such situations, by using the self-monitoring exercise outlined above.

For depression, we should avoid distressing situations. If this is not possible, we can focus on the non-distressing aspects of the situation. If this is not possible, we can assertively ask others whose behaviour we find distressing to behave in less stressful ways. The key to assertiveness is to say clearly what your preference is using an accurate and non-motive description of the situation that is problematic, a non-blaming 'I-statement' about how this makes you feel and a clear statement about what you would prefer. For example, 'When I'm trying to finish these reports on time and your part is late, I get worried that we will not meet the deadline. I'd prefer in future if you would give me your part by the time we agreed.' Alongside these strategies we should challenge pessimistic and perfectionistic beliefs that contribute to our low mood and look for evidence to support more optimistic alternative ways of making sense of each situation. Pessimistic beliefs can be identified by using the self-monitoring exercise outlined above. We can also reduce depression by increasing our activity levels. This involves engaging in regular exercise and scheduling events that we find stimulating and pleasurable. We should also meet regularly with close friends and family members who we can count on to offer social support.

For anxiety, the key to self-regulation is to challenge threat-oriented beliefs identified through self-monitoring and look for evidence to support less threatening ways of interpreting these distressing situations. We can also practise being courageous by actively going into situations that frighten us and remaining there until our anxiety subsides. It is vital not to leave these threatening situations while anxiety is still increasing. When we take on these challenges, we should ask friends and family members for support and celebrate success. We should prepare well for these challenges by practising coping skills such as the relaxation exercises described in Chapter 7, listening to calming music and so forth.

For anger, use the self-monitoring task to learn the types of situations that trigger anger for you, and avoid these. If this is not possible, focus on the non-distressing aspects of the situation. If this is not possible, assertively ask others who are provoking you to behave in less stressful ways using the assertiveness style outlined above. If you begin to feel anger, stand back from the situation, physically and psychologically, and allow your physiological arousal level to decrease, so you can think more efficiently. We cannot think efficiently when we are highly physiologically aroused by anger, fear or excitement. Then try to hear, understand and empathise with the other person's point of view. This will involve using the communication skills outlined below. When you do this, you may see that there are no grounds for being aggrieved, or if there are, that there are more constructive ways of settling the grievance. Usually this will involve using the problem-solving skills outlined below.

Communication

Communication skills are essential for empathising with others, for understanding their concerns and for setting the stage for interpersonal problem
solving. To enhance these skills, schedule specific times and places for conversations in which you wish to use these skills. These should be times when
there is no pressure to be elsewhere and in a place in which there are no
distractions. Issues and problems should be discussed one at a time. Take
turns fairly and make the speaking turns brief. Tell the other person that
you want to know their views on one particular issue or situation. Listen
carefully, to the other person's viewpoint. If their position is not fully clear,
ask them to say more about the details of their viewpoint. Then briefly
summarise what you have heard the other person say and check that your
summary is accurate. If your summary is not accurate, listen to their feedback and repeat the process of summarising and checking until you have
achieved an accurate understanding of the other person's position. Throughout this, try to listen without judging what is being said, and focus only on
accurately remembering what the other person is saying. Put your own
opinions and emotions on hold while you are listening. Avoid attributing
negative intentions to the other person (negative mind-reading), composing
your reply, defending yourself, interrupting or attacking the other person.
When you have reached an accurate understanding of what the other person
believes about the situation and what the situation looks like from their
perspective you have achieved empathy.

When you have empathised with the other person's position, then you
can invite them to listen to your reaction to it. When speaking, decide on
the exact points you want to make. Organise them logically. Say them clearly
and then check that you have been understood. It is helpful when speaking
to try to frame your points as congruent *I statements*, for example 'I feel
confused about what happened between you and me earlier today'. When
you are speaking, state your points without attacking or blaming the other
person and without sulking. When you are certain that the other person has
understood you accurately, allow space for a reply.

After an episode of clear communication we understand and empathise
with each other's points of view. We can distinguish between areas of agreement and areas where there are differences of opinion. This paves the way
for interpersonal problem solving.

Problem solving

Invariably when we collaborate with others to solve a problem, achieve a
goal or complete a task, we need to use communication skills to achieve
mutual understanding or empathy. However, we also need interpersonal
problem-solving skills for developing and implementing effective joint
action plans. Begin by scheduling a specific time and place where there are

no distractions. Break big vague problems into many smaller specific problems. Define these in solvable rather than unsolvable terms. Generate many possible solutions without judging the merits of these. Examine the pros and cons or costs and benefits of each of these before selecting the best course of action to follow. Agree to implement the action plan after the problem-solving session and schedule a time to meet and review progress. When you meet, evaluate the effectiveness of the plan against pre-set goals. If the problem remains unsolved, repeat the process in light of knowledge about why the attempted solution was ineffective. To avoid obstacles to clear joint problem solving show the people with whom you are trying to solve the problem that it is the problem (not the person) that makes you feel bad, if the problem is frustrating. Acknowledge your share of responsibility for causing the problem (if that is the case) and finding the solution. Do not explore the pros and cons of all of the possible solutions until you have finished brainstorming all the options. When you solve the problem, celebrate success.

While training in the skills for self-monitoring, self-regulation, communication and problem solving may enhance emotional intelligence in adolescents and adults, in the normal course of events, emotional intelligence follows a predictable developmental path as outlined in the next section.

DEVELOPMENT OF EMOTIONAL COMPETENCE

Research on the development of emotional competence offers insights into probable developmental precursors of emotional intelligence in adulthood. Emotional regulation skills, the skills for expressing emotions and the skills for managing relationships involving emotional give-and-take develop gradually from infancy to adolescence, as can be seen from Table 4.5 (Saarni, 1999, 2000).

Infancy

During the first year of life infants develop rudimentary self-soothing skills such as rocking and feeding for regulating their emotions. They also develop skills for regulating their attention to allow themselves and their caregivers to co-ordinate their actions to sooth them in distressing situations. They rely on their caregivers to provide emotional support or 'scaffolding' during such stress. During the first year of life there is a gradual increase in non-verbal emotional expression in response to all classes of stimuli including those under the infant's control and those under the control of others. At birth infants can express interest as indicated by sustained attention and disgust in response to foul tastes and odours. Smiling, reflecting a sense of pleasure, in response to the human voice appears at 4 weeks. Sadness and anger in response to removing a teething toy are first evident at 4 months.

Table 4.5 Development of emotional competence

Age	Regulation of emotions	Expression of emotions	Managing emotional relationships
Infancy 0 – 1y	• Self-soothing • Regulation of attention to allow-ordinated action • Reliance on 'scaffolding' from caregivers during stress	• Increased non-verbal emotional expression in response to stimuli under own control and control of others	• Increased discrimination of emotions expressed by others • Turn taking (peek-a-boo) • Social referencing
Toddlerhood 1 – 2y	• Increased awareness of own emotional responses • Irritability when parents place limits on expression of need for autonomy	• Increased verbal expression of emotional states • Increased expression of emotions involving self-consciousness and self-evaluation such as shame, pride or coyness	• Anticipation of feelings towards others • Rudimentary empathy • Altruistic behaviour
Pre-school 2 – 5y	• Language (self-talk and communication with others) used for regulating emotions	• Increased pretending to express emotions in play and teasing	• Increased insight into others' emotions • Awareness that false expression of emotions can mislead others about one's emotional state
Kindergarten 5 – 7y	• Regulating self-conscious emotions, e.g. embarrassment • Increased autonomy from caregivers in regulating emotions	• Presents 'cool' emotional front to peers	• Increased use of social skills to deal with emotions of self and others • Understanding of consensually agreed emotional scripts

Table 4.5 (Cont'd)

Age	Regulation of emotions	Expression of emotions	Managing emotional relationships
Middle childhood 7 – 10y	• Autonomous regulation of emotions is preferred to involving caregivers • Distancing strategies used to manage emotions if child has little control over situation	• Increased use of emotional expression to regulate relationships	• Awareness of feeling multiple emotions about the same person • Use of information about emotions of self and others in multiple contexts as aids to making and maintaining friendships
Pre-adolescence 10 – 13y	• Increased efficiency in identifying and using multiple strategies for autonomously regulating emotions and managing stress	• Distinction made between genuine emotional expression with close friends and managed display with others	• Increase understanding of social roles and emotional scripts in making and maintaining friendships
Adolescence 13 + y	• Increased awareness of emotional cycles (feeling guilty about feeling angry) • Increased use of complex strategies to autonomously regulate emotions • Self-regulation strategies are increasingly informed by moral principles	• Self-presentation strategies are used for impression management	• Awareness of importance of mutual and reciprocal emotional self-disclosure in making and maintaining friendships

Source: Adapted from Saarni, C. (2000): 75–6.

Facial expressions reflecting fear following separation become apparent at 9 months. Infants also show an increasingly sophisticated capacity to discriminate positive and negative emotions expressed by others over the course of their first year of life. The capacity for turn taking in games such as peek-a-boo develops once children have the appropriate cognitive skills for understanding object constancy. Social referencing also occurs towards the end of the first year where children learn the appropriate emotions to express in a particular situation by attending to the emotional expressions of their caregivers.

The second year

During the second year of life toddlers show increased awareness of their own emotional responses. They show irritability when parents place limits on the expression of their needs for autonomy and exploration. This irritability is often referred to as the 'terrible twos'. In their second year infants show increased verbal expression of emotional states, and increased expression of emotions involving self-consciousness and self-evaluation such as shame, pride or coyness. This occurs because their cognitive skills allow them to begin to think about themselves from the perspective of others. In relationships they can increasingly anticipate feelings they will have towards others in particular situations. They show rudimentary empathy and altruistic behaviour.

Pre-schoolers

Pre-schoolers between the ages of 2 and 5 years increasingly use language for regulating emotions. They use both internal speech and conversations with others to modulate their affective experience. During this period children increasingly pretend to express emotions in play when teasing or being teased by other children. There is increased insight into the emotions being experienced by others. During this period there is an increased awareness that we can mislead others about what we are feeling by falsely expressing emotions. More sophisticated empathy and altruistic behaviour also develops during the pre-school years.

Kindergarten

Children in kindergarten between the ages of 5 and 7 years increasingly regulate emotions involving self-consciousness such as embarrassment. There is also increased autonomy from caregivers in regulating emotions. Children at this age present a 'cool' emotional front to peers. There is also an increased use of social skills to deal with emotions of self and others. During this period children develop an understanding of consensually agreed emotional scripts and their roles in such scripts.

Middle childhood

Children in middle childhood between the ages of 7 and 10 years prefer to autonomously regulate their emotional states rather than involving caregivers in this process, as they would have done earlier in their lives. Distancing strategies are used to manage emotions if children have little control over emotionally demanding situations. There is increased use of emotional expression to regulate closeness and distance within relationships. Children become aware that they can feel multiple conflicting emotions about the same person, that they can be angry with someone they like. They use information and memories about the emotions of self and others in multiple contexts as aids to making and maintaining friendships.

Pre-adolescence

During pre-adolescence between the ages of 10 and 13 years children show increased efficiency in using multiple strategies for autonomously regulating emotions and managing stress. They make distinctions between genuine emotional expression with close friends and managed emotional displays with others. They develop an increasingly sophisticated understanding of the place of social roles and emotional scripts in making and maintaining friendships.

Adolescence

During adolescence from 13 to 20 years there is an increased awareness of complex emotional cycles, for example feeling guilty about feeling angry, feeling ashamed or feeling frightened. In adolescence, youngsters increasingly use complex strategies to autonomously regulate emotions. These self-regulation strategies are increasingly informed by moral principles, beliefs about what is right and good and what is wrong and evil. However, alongside this concern with morality, self-presentation strategies are increasingly used for impression management. Adolescents gradually become aware of the importance of mutual and reciprocal emotional self-disclosure in making and maintaining friendships.

ATTACHMENT AND THE DEVELOPMENT OF EMOTIONAL COMPETENCE

Children who develop secure attachments to their caregivers develop emotional competence. Children develop secure emotional attachments if their parents are attuned to their needs for safety, security and being physically cared for and if their parents are responsive to children's signals that they require their needs to be met. When this occurs, children learn that their parents are a secure base from which they can explore the world. John Bowlby (1988), who developed attachment theory, argued that attachment behaviour, which is genetically programmed and essential for survival of the species, is elicited in children between 6 months and 3 years when faced with danger. In such instances children seek proximity with their caregivers. When comforted they return to the activity of exploring the immediate environment around the caregiver. The cycle repeats each time the child perceives a threat and their attachment needs for satisfaction, safety and security are activated. Over multiple repetitions, the child builds an internal working model of attachment relationships based on the way these episodes are managed by the caregiver in response to the child's needs for proximity, comfort and security. Internal working models are cognitive relationship maps based on early attachment experiences which serve as a template for the development of later intimate relationships. Internal working models allow people to make predictions about how the self and significant others will behave within the relationship. Empirical research with mothers and children has shown that child–parent attachments may be classified into four distinct categories (Cassidy and Shaver, 1999). Later work on intimate relationships in adulthood confirms that these four relational styles show continuity over the lifecycle and significant adult relationships may be classified into four equivalent categories. There is also some evidence that these attachment styles characterise patterns of family organisation (Carr, 2000b). A summary of these four attachment styles is given in Figure 4.3.

Securely attached children and marital partners react to their parents or partners as if they were a secure base from which to explore the world. Parents and partners in such relationships are attuned and responsive to the children's or partner's needs. Families with secure attachment relationships are adaptable and flexibly connected. While a secure attachment style is associated with autonomy, the other three attachment styles are associated with a sense of insecurity. Anxiously attached children seek contact with their parents following separation but are unable to derive comfort from it. They cling and cry or have tantrums. Marital partners with this attachment style tend to be overly close but dissatisfied. Families characterised by anxious attachment relationships tend to be enmeshed and to have blurred boundaries. Avoidantly attached children avoid contact with their parents after separation. They sulk. Marital partners with this attachment style tend to be distant and dissatisfied. Families characterised by avoidant relationships tend to be disengaged and to have impermeable boundaries. Children with a disorganised attachment style following separation show aspects of both the anxious and avoidant patterns. Disorganised attachment is a common correlate of child abuse and neglect and early parental absence, loss or bereavement. Disorganised marital and family relationships are characterised by approach–avoidance conflicts, disorientation and alternate clinging and sulking.

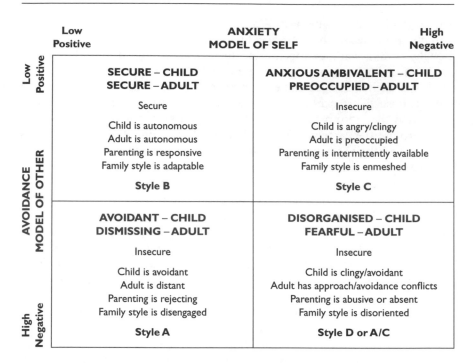

Figure 4.3 Characteristics of four attachment styles in children and adults
Source: Based on Cassidy and Shaver (1999) and Carr (2000b): 167.

Secure attachment is a central feature of resilience in the face of adversity, a topic which we will now address.

Emotional competence and resilience in the face of adversity

Some children show emotional resilience in the face of adversity and some do not (Ackerman *et al.*, 1999; Anderson and Cohler, 1987; Haggerty *et al.*, 1994; Luthar *et al.*, 1993; Masten and Coatsworth, 1998; Murphy and Moriarity, 1976). Those that do not are exposed to repeated challenges, stresses, difficulties and problematic situations that exceed their coping capacity in the absence of social support from their attachment figures and members of their caregiving network and oftentimes in the presence of a deviant peer group. In contrast, children who face difficult challenges, who are stretched to the limits of their coping capacity and who are offered sustained social support from their attachment figures and members of their caregiving network and their non-deviant peer group are strengthened by their experience of adversity and show marked resilience.

NEUROLOGICAL BASIS FOR EMOTIONAL INTELLIGENCE

Research on the mistakes of patients with brain damage who are required to make complex social judgements has thrown light on the neurological basis for emotional intelligence. Professor Antonio Damasio at the University of Iowa has studied decision-making errors of patients who suffer bilateral lesions of the ventromedial, pre-frontal cortex (Damasio, 1994; Bechara *et al.*, 2000). The impetus for doing so came from the clinical observation that previously well-adjusted patients who suffer bilateral lesions of the ventromedial, pre-frontal cortex show no significant deterioration in IQ, but major deterioration in planning work-related activities and relationships. Their actions lead to losses including financial losses, losses in social standing and loss of friendship. Damasio, in light of these clinical observations, has conducted a series of experiments, in which the performance on decision-making tasks of patients with these neurological lesions is compared with that of controls who have similar IQs but no brain damage. Thus, differences in performance may be attributed to functions subserved by the ventro-medial, pre-frontal cortex.

Decision making in these experiments is evaluated using a gambling task in which participants are asked to win as much play-money as they can by selecting cards from any of four decks (A,B, C and D). If they select win-cards from decks A and B they get $100 and if they select lose-cards from these decks they lose up to $350. In contrast, if they select win-cards from decks C and D they get $50 and if they select lose-cards they only lose up to $250 per card. They are not told these rules, nor are they told that they will have 100 chances to draw cards from any of the four decks. Normal control participants find out that drawing cards from decks C and D is the best strategy because, while the gains of $50 per win-card are relatively small, the losses incurred from drawing lose-cards are not great (only $250). Participants with lesions of the ventromedial, pre-frontal cortex, in contrast, typically draw most cards from decks A and B which yield relatively large gains of $100 per win-card, but these patients fail to learn that these short-term gains are offset by the very punitive long-term costs of losing up to $350 for lose-cards. Thus, patients with lesions of the ventromedial, pre-frontal cortex on the gambling task show a decision-making pattern similar to that shown in their day-to-day lives. They continually make decisions that lead to short-term gains without due regard for the more significant long-term losses these entail, especially in situations where exact information about long-term losses are not explicit and must be based on gut feelings or hunches.

In these gambling task experiments, the magnitude of skin conductance responses (SCR) prior to drawing cards – an index of anticipatory physiological arousal or 'gut feelings' – was measured. Normal participants produced more anticipatory SCRs as the experiment progressed. They also produced larger SCRs when drawing cards from the risky decks – A and B – than from the safer decks – C and D. Thus, as normal subjects became more experienced with the four decks in the experiment, their 'gut feelings' informed their decision making and they avoided the risky decks A and B. In contrast, patients with lesions of the ventromedial, pre-frontal cortex did not generate anticipatory SCRs and so their decision making was not informed by 'gut feelings'. These results show that effective decision making is guided by anticipatory emotional responses in complex situations where explicit information about risky outcomes is not available.

To determine whether these 'gut feelings' inform decision making only when people are fully aware of them, in one gambling task study, after every 10 card-draws, participants were asked to state their beliefs about the costs and benefits of drawing cards from each of the 4 decks. The results of this study showed that even before normal participants became consciously aware that decks A and B were riskier, they showed greater anticipatory SCRs when drawing from these decks and then greater preference for the safer decks C and D. In contrast, even when patients with lesions of the ventromedial pre-frontal cortex were fully aware that decks A and B were riskier, they showed no anticipatory SCRs and continued to show a preference for drawing from these decks. These results show that in complex situations effective decision making is guided by anticipatory emotional responses of which the person is not conscious.

Damasio (1994) has shown that the ventromedial, pre-frontal cortex is part of a neural network involving neural projections from the sensory sense organs; the amygdala; and the somatosensory and insular cortices. In a series of studies Damasio and his team compared the responses of three groups of patients each with different brain lesions to identify the effects of: (1) bilateral lesions of the ventromedial, pre-frontal cortex; (2) bilateral lesions of the amygdala; and (3) lesions of the right somatosensory/insular cortices. He found that damage to all three centres resulted in failure to generate anticipatory SCRs and failure to learn how to make safe decisions on the gambling task. Bilateral lesions of the amygdala and lesions of the right somatosensory/insular cortices led to errors in judging the intensity of emotions conveyed by facial expression. Only patients with bilateral lesions of the amygdala failed to develop a conditioned emotional response (SCRs) when a blue screen (UCS) was presented alone after repeated pairing with a startling sound (UCS). Only patients with lesions of the right somatosensory/insular cortices failed to re-experience emotions when thinking about memories of happy, sad, frightening or anger-provoking situations.

From these results it may tentatively be concluded that decision-making impairment arising from damage to the amygdala may be due to an impaired ability for developing conditioned emotional responses which inform us about the emotional significance of stimuli. Decision-making impairment arising from damage to the right somatosensory/insular cortices may arise from failure to remember emotions associated with particular events. Decision-making impairment arising from damage to ventromedial, pre-frontal cortex may be due to failure to inhibit responses that the person knows they should inhibit. Thus they have difficulty with higher-order conditioning where the contingency is remote and/or symbolic.

It seems that emotional intelligence requires the efficient functioning of the neural network involving the amygdala, the right somatosensory/insular cortices and the ventromedial, pre-frontal cortex.

Formative experiences and trauma may compromise the efficiency with which this neural network operates. Joseph LeDoux (1996) has produced evidence that the amygdala can operate independently of the pre-frontal cortex, and memories of the emotional significance of events stored in the amygdala can guide decision making without involvement of the pre-frontal cortex. Rats in whom the auditory cortex was ablated learned to fear a tone (CS) that was previously paired with an electric shock (UCS). LeDoux (1996) argues that while factual memory is subserved by the hippocampus, memory of the emotional significance of events is subserved by the amygdala. The hippocampus allows us to remember where the university exam hall is, but the amygdala permits us to remember how anxiety-provoking exams can be. In emergency situations or under stress, our perception and reactions are governed not by the hippocampus but by the amygdala.

From an evolutionary viewpoint, the lower sections of the human brain, in the brainstem, are structurally like that of phylogenetically earlier species such as reptiles; the next layer of the brain – the limbic system – is like that of early mammals; the next layer – the thin mammalian cortex – is like the brain of higher mammals; and the highest layer of the brain – the huge neocortex – is uniquely human. The amygdala is part of the limbic system and when we react to emergency situations or cues that remind us of previous emotionally intense events we are reacting like early mammals. The ventromedial pre-frontal cortex is part of the uniquely human part of the brain. It is this structure that allows us to deal in a measured way with emotional situations.

There are pros and cons to the fact that in emergencies or when reminded of past intense emotional experiences our rational brain is bypassed and we react like evolutionarily more primitive mammals. On the positive side, subtle signals in new situations remind the amygdala of past emergencies that involved similar signals and trigger intense emotional memories and rapid reactions without involving the pre-frontal cortex or consciousness in this, thus protecting us from harm. For example, the flicker of sunlight on the windscreen of a car on the very edge of the visual field can trigger a person to quickly step backwards onto the pavement to avoid being hit by a car without having to first weigh up the costs and benefits of doing so. On the negative side, some of the memories stored in the amygdala may trigger intense rapid emotional reactions that are completely inappropriate. For example, a young father told me that the first time he smelled his wife's breast milk he felt an inexplicably intense rage. He was unable to trace the memory of this but later found out from his older sibling that his breast feeding as a child had stopped abruptly due to his mother's illness and he subsequently had difficulty taking to a bottle or to being bottle-fed with expressed breast milk. The young husband's intense experience of rage made no sense in terms of his very positive relationship with his wife and his devotion to his child. However, his amygdala had encoded a memory of the smell of breast milk being associated with his mother's disappearance, replacement of her breast with a bottle that smelled like her breast milk, and with an intense experience of rage. This emotional memory, because of its great emotional significance, was triggered without the involvement of the pre-frontal cortex. People with high levels of emotional intelligence are probably aware of the possibility of these types of reactions and can predict them in themselves and others, avoid them, or modify them. In psychotherapy people learn to recognise and modify these types of reactions. However, direct research on the neurological correlates of people with high and low levels of emotional intelligence has not yet been done so that this hypothesis awaits testing.

RELATED CONSTRUCTS

Emotional intelligence is conceptually related to many other psychological constructs such as ego strength (Block and Block, 1980), constructive thinking (Epstein, 1998), hardiness (Kobasa, 1979) and sense of coherence (Antonovsky, 1993). However, there are a number of constructs related to emotional intelligence which deserve particular mention. These include: practical intelligence (Wagner, 2000); autistic spectrum disorders (Cohen and Volkmar, 1997); the factor of openness to experience from Costa and McCrae's Five Factor model of personality (McCrae, 2000); psychological mindedness from the literature on suitability for psychodynamic psychotherapy (McCallum and Piper, 1997, 2000); alexithymia from research on psychosomatic conditions (Taylor and Bagby, 2000); emotional awareness (Lane, 2000); and emotional creativity (Averill, 2000; Averill and Nunley, 1992).

Practical intelligence

Traditional IQ tests assess analytical and memory skills for solving verbal, numerical and visuo-spatial problems. In contrast to academic intelligence as assessed by traditional IQ tests, practical intelligence is the application of analytical and memory skills to solving everyday problems in family, work and leisure situations. People use practical intelligence to adapt to the current social environments, to change or shape current social environments or to select new social environments in which there is a better fit between their analytical abilities and the types of problems they must solve to adapt to those environments (Sternberg and Grigorenko, 2000; Wagner, 2000). Practical intelligence involves the skills for recognising problems, defining problems in solvable terms, forming mental representations of problems, formulating strategies for solving problems, allocating resources to implement these problem-solving strategies, monitoring the implementation of these strategies and evaluating the effectiveness of solutions. A well-validated measure of practical intelligence is the Sternberg Triachric Abilities Test (Sternberg, 1993). While academic intelligence is useful for solving clearly defined problems with a single right answer (like doing a maths problem), practical intelligence is useful for solving vaguely defined problems with multiple possible solutions, such as what to do about a friend who has a drug abuse problem or using a map to plan a route efficiently. Colloquially, practical intelligence is referred to as savvy, cop-on or being street-wise.

While academic intelligence as assessed by traditional IQ tests declines with age, practical intelligence (like emotional intelligence) does not, and people in middle age or older adulthood often show greater practical intelligence than adolescents or young adults with similar IQs. As academic intelligence declines, middle-aged and older people use practical intelligence to compensate for this. An important aspect of practical intelligence is tacit knowledge. Tacit knowledge is the procedural knowledge (knowing how to do something) needed to solve everyday problems important for achieving personal goals which is rarely explicitly taught or verbalised and accumulates with experience. There are good theoretical reasons for believing that there may be a moderate correlation between practical intelligence and emotional intelligence, since both may be required to solve complex interpersonal problems. According to Sternberg (1993) successful intelligence involves combining creativity with analytic and practical intelligence when solving problems to deal with life challenges.

Autistic spectrum disorder traits

The inability of people with autistic spectrum disorders (even those with very high IQs) to recognise and process information about the emotional states of others and to respond in emotionally appropriate ways suggests that there may be a conceptual similarity between the lower end of the emotional intelligence dimension and autistic spectrum disorder traits. Autistic spectrum disorders are a group of conditions which include Asperger's syndrome at the high functioning end of the spectrum and autism at the other. Autistic spectrum disorders are characterised by abnormalities in social development, language and behaviour (Cohen and Volkmar, 1997). Abnormalities in social development which first appear in infancy include:

the absence of eye-to-eye signalling; the absence of the use of social or emotional gestures; a lack of reciprocity in social relationships; attachment problems such as an inability to use parents as a secure base; little interest in peer relationships; lack of empathy; and little interest in sharing positive emotions such as pride or pleasure with others. Language development is usually delayed and may be characterised by a variety of abnormalities. People on the autistic spectrum rarely engage in extended conversations focusing on social or emotional topics and display little creativity in language use. The behaviour of people on the autistic spectrum is characterised by stereotyped repetitive patterns and confined in its range by the restricted interests. There is also a strong desire to maintain routines and sameness and a resistance to change, without regard for the impact of this on others. Imaginative or make-believe play is virtually absent. The traits which characterise people on the autistic spectrum are independent of analytic intelligence as assessed by IQ tests. About 75 per cent of people with autism have IQs below 70 but those with Asperger's syndrome have IQs that fall within or above the normal range. Genetic, prenatal, perinatal and constitutional factors, but not social factors have been implicated in the aetiology of autistic spectrum disorders. Research on the relationship between emotional intelligence and autistic spectrum disorders is urgently needed.

Openness to experience

Openness to experience is one of the factors within the Five Factor Model of Personality, described in Chapter 6, which has theoretical similarities to emotional intelligence (McCrae, 2000). Openness has the following six facets: openness to fantasy; openness to aesthetics; openness to novel feelings; openness to novel actions; openness to new ideas; and openness to different values. As predicted, moderate positive relationships have been found between openness to experience and emotional intelligence. An important research question is whether personality-trait models of emotional intelligence are really measuring facets of openness to experience.

Alexithymia

The term alexithymia was coined by the psychoanalyst Sifneos in 1973. The term alexithymia is from the Greek a = lack, lexis = word, and thymos = emotion. Sifneos, in his practice of psychodynamic psychotherapy, observed that many of his patients with psychosomatic complaints often had difficulty identifying and describing their emotions. In addition they reported little experience of fantasy and had an externally oriented cognitive style. Since the 1940s similar observations had been made by other clinicians working with psychosomatic patients having conditions such as hypertension or inflammatory bowel disease, patients with eating disorders, patients with post-traumatic stress disorder and drug abusers (Taylor and Bagby, 2000). Currently one of the most robust measures of the construct is the 20-item Toronto Alexithymia Scale (TAS) which evaluates three distinct dimensions: difficulty identifying feelings; difficulty describing feelings; and externally oriented thinking (Bagby *et al.*, 1994). There is good evidence that alexithymia is strongly associated with low emotional intelligence and the trait openness to experience from the Five Factor Model of Personality (Taylor and Bagby, 2000; Taylor *et al.*, 2000). As predicted, a large and significant negative correlation of about -0.7 has been obtained between the TAS total score and the total and subscale scores of the BarOn-EQi.

Psychological mindedness

Psychological mindedness is the disposition to be motivated to learn more about current and past cognitive, affective and behavioural factors that cause or arise from particular experiences. Psychologically minded people do not look exclusively to the current external environment or biological factors for explanations of their experiences, but are prepared to entertain complex psychological explanations (McCallum and Piper, 1997). In many respects psychological mindedness is the opposite of alexithymia. One of the most robust measures of psychological mindedness is the Psychological Mindedness Assessment Procedure (PMAP) in which the respondent views a videotape of two simulated therapist–patient interactions and then offers explanations for what is troubling the patient. The respondent's explanation is then rated for the degree to which it shows evidence for psychological mindedness (e.g. psychic determinism, intra-psychic conflict and use of defence mechanisms). The PMAP has good interrater reliability and predicts engagement in psychotherapy and outcome (McCallum and Piper, 2000). However, psychological mindedness has its downside. While it has been found to be associated with better behavioural adjustment, it has also been found to be associated with greater personal distress. Psychologically minded people are wiser but sadder than others, because their insight allows them to see the complexity of the world. They are aware, for example, that the joys of love entail the risk of abandonment and the strength of youth entails the fragility of ageing.

Levels of emotional awareness

Emotional awareness, according to Richard Lane (2000), is a cognitive skill that undergoes developmental changes in a manner similar to that described by Piaget for cognition in general. Individual differences in emotional awareness reflect differences in maturity level reached for this construct. A person's maturity in their capacity to recognise and describe emotions in themselves and others can by evaluated with the Levels of Emotional Awareness Scale

(LEAS), (Lane *et al.*, 1990). The scale contains 20 emotionally evocative scenes and, for each of these, respondents write a three- or four-sentence answer as to how people in the scene would feel. For example, in one scene respondents are told that they and their friends work hard in the same field for a prize and after a year's work the friend wins the prize. Respondents must say how they and their friend would feel. Answers are scored according to a 6-point rating system. A score of 0 is given for answers containing non-affective words such as 'I don't work hard to win prizes. My friend would feel that the judges knew their job.' A score of 1 is given for answers containing references to physiological states such as 'I would feel tired'. A score of 2 is given for answers containing words describing undifferentiated feeling states such as 'I would feel bad'. A score of 3 is given for answers containing one-word descriptions of differentiated feeling states such as 'My friend would feel happy'. A score of 4 is given for answers containing two words describing differentiated feeling states such as 'My friend would feel happy but concerned. I would feel sad for myself but pleased for my friend.' A score of 5 is given when statements about how the self and the other person would feel are clearly differentiated from each other and both include two words describing differentiated feeling states such as 'happy, sad, and angry'. The LEAS has good interrater reliability and validity. Lane and his colleagues have shown that scores on the LEAS correlate with activity in specific areas of the brain associated with emotional processing.

Emotional creativity

James Averill argues that emotionally creative people are able to have emotional experiences characterised by novelty, effectiveness and authenticity (Averill, 2000; Averill and Nunley, 1992). Emotional responses that are unconventional or atypical are novel. Emotional responses that express an experiential state and communicate this feeling clearly to others are effective. Emotional responses that are unique and stem from the self rather than from social expectations are authentic. Three levels of emotional creativity or transformation may be distinguished. First, a common emotion may be authentically and effectively expressed in a novel context. Second, a common emotion might be sculpted and refined to meet the needs of an individual or group. Finally a person may develop a new way of emotionally responding. The Emotional Creativity Inventory (ECI), (Averill, 1999) may be used to evaluate individual differences in emotional creativity. This 30-item inventory evaluates emotional preparation for responding to situations, emotional novelty, effectiveness and authenticity. The ECI has good reliability and validity. It is positively correlated with self-esteem, the trait of openness from the five-factor theory of personality; negatively correlated with alexithymia; and it is unrelated to extraversion and neuroticism.

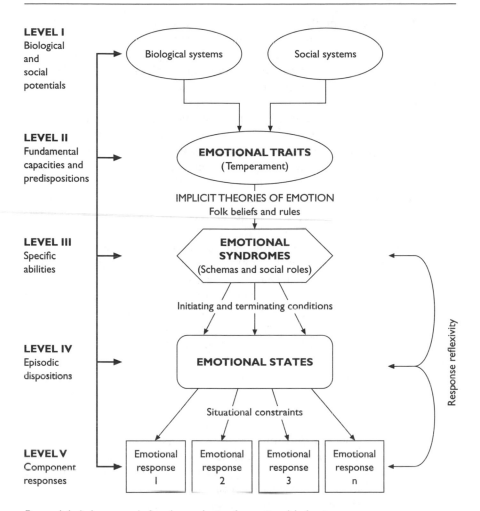

LEVEL I
Biological
and
social
potentials

Biological systems

Social systems

LEVEL II
Fundamental
capacities and
predispositions

EMOTIONAL TRAITS
(Temperament)

IMPLICIT THEORIES OF EMOTION
Folk beliefs and rules

LEVEL III
Specific
abilities

**EMOTIONAL
SYNDROMES**
(Schemas and social roles)

Initiating and terminating conditions

LEVEL IV
Episodic
dispositions

EMOTIONAL STATES

Situational constraints

LEVEL V
Component
responses

Emotional
response
1

Emotional
response
2

Emotional
response
3

Emotional
response
n

Response reflexivity

Figure 4.4 A framework for the analysis of emotional behaviour
Source: Adapted from Averill (1997); and Averill, J. (2002). Emotional creativity: towards
spiritualizing the passions. In C.R. Snyder and S. Lopez (eds), *Handbook of Positive Psychology*
(p. 174). New York: Oxford University Press.

This model of emotional creativity was developed from Averill's (1997)
framework for analysing emotional behaviour presented in Figure 4.4. Averill
argues that distinctions must be made between emotional responses (at
level V), such as laughing or fighting, and the emotional states (at level IV),
such as being happy or angry which give rise to these responses. The constraints entailed by particular situations will influence the emotional responses
that arise from a particular state. So a person in a happy state may laugh
out loud, long and hard when having a beer with a friend and listening to a

funny story, or laugh politely at work in response to the same joke. Emotional responses in addition to including behaviour, such as laughing or fighting, also include cognitive elements, such as appraisal (judging situations to be funny or threatening), affective elements (such as the momentary feelings that accompany laughing or fighting) and physiological responses. Different constraints lead to different responses, based on the same emotional state. Emotional states are in turn determined by emotional syndromes (at level III), provided certain initiating conditions occur (such as being told a joke or experiencing increasing physiological arousal), and emotional states are concluded when certain terminating conditions are met (after the joke and a brief spell of laughing is over and physiological arousal decreases). Emotional syndromes are states of affairs recognised in ordinary language by abstract nouns such as happiness or anger. They are social roles encoded as cognitive schemas. These specify the pattern of behaviour and experience that goes with a particular emotion such as happiness or anger. Emotional roles entail privileges, restrictions, obligations and entry requirements. For example, a man who feels paternal love for a pre-school child has the privilege of hugging and kissing the child; is restricted from having sex with them; has an obligation to meet the child's needs for care and control; and must have met the entry requirements of being the child's parent to do all this. The details of emotional syndromes, social roles and schemas are informed by implicit theories of emotion which people hold. Such implicit theories are grounded in folk beliefs and culturally determined rules. In this sense all emotions are social constructions. The degree to which particular emotional syndromes may be experienced is determined by emotional traits (level II) such as extraversion or agreeableness. Such traits place limits on the range of experiences that may occur within particular emotional syndromes. For example, people with high levels of the trait extraversion may be more capable of high levels of happiness. Emotional traits in turn are determined by biological systems (such as genetic endowment) and social systems (such as the process of socialisation within a particular social group and culture). These biological and social systems set limits on the range of emotional traits a person may display.

In some situations, levels in this model may be bypassed. For example, a trigger situation (such as slipping on ice) may lead to an instant fear response (screaming) and the emotional state of fear may be initially bypassed, but arise later when we perceive our behavioural and physiological fear responses. (This type of analysis was initially proposed by the American psychologist William James (1890) and the Danish physician Carl Lange in the James–Lange theory of emotions.) While the analysis outlined in the previous paragraph assumes that the direction of influence is typically from level I downward towards level V, in some situations the path of influence may run in the other direction, a process referred to in Figure 4.4 as response reflexivity. For example, our emotional responses (such as laughing uncontrollably) can heighten our emotional state (happiness) to the degree that we re-evaluate our concept of what the emotional syndrome of happiness means.

Distinctions may be made between three aspects of objects towards which emotions are directed: the instigation, target and objective (Averill, 1997). The instigation is the eliciting situation as appraised by the person. The target is the person or thing towards whom the emotion is directed. The objective is the goal of the emotion. For example, if Gráinne is feeling affectionate towards Diarmuid because he has given her a compliment, the instigation is the perceived compliment; the target is Diarmuid; the objective is to convey affection and deepen intimacy. With the exception of pathological conditions such as generalised anxiety, depression or mania almost all emotions have an object towards which they are directed, and different emotions are associated with different objects, e.g. making and maintaining attachment with love and affection; breaking off attachment bonds with grief and sadness; dangerous threats with anger or anxiety; and so forth.

Physiological responses associated with emotions prepare the organism for actions associated with those emotions, whether or not those actions are made (Averill, 1997). For example, increased cardiac output associated with anger prepares the organism for fighting. There are differences in the physiological response patterns associated with broad categories of emotions, since different categories of emotions require physiological preparation for different types of actions. For example, sexual arousal, fear and sadness each have quite distinct physiological response patterns to prepare the organism for reproduction, escape and mourning. However, within broad categories of emotions there is little evidence for differential physiological response patterning. For example, the physiological response patterns for anger and jealousy are indistinguishable.

However, physiological changes are not associated with all emotions and are not essential for emotion. For example, long-term emotions such as love and hope may not involve discernible physiological reactions but short-term emotions such as lust or excitement commonly involve clearly discernible physiological changes.

Distinctive, innate and universal facial expressions have been identified, but these are not invariably associated with the fundamental emotions of joy, surprise, sadness, anger, disgust and fear, a hypothesis first put forward by Charles Darwin (1872) and later by Eibl-Eibesfeldt (1975), both of whom recorded facial expressions of emotions in many cultures. Rather, the meaning of such expressions is culturally determined (Averill, 1997).

Whether distinctive neurobiological profiles will be found to be associated with distinct emotions remains to be seen (Gross, 1999). Preliminary evidence suggests that certain neural networks are associated with specific classes of emotions and many of these involve the amygdala.

Future research on emotional intelligence and related constructs

From the foregoing descriptions of constructs related to emotional intelligence, it is clear that research on the relationship between all of these constructs and emotional intelligence is required to further establish the convergent and discriminant validity of the construct of emotional intelligence.

IMPLICATIONS

A summary of self-help strategies for enhancing emotional intelligence is given in Table 4.6. These can be incorporated into clinical practice.

CONTROVERSIES

The validity of the construct of emotional intelligence is the most controversial issue in the field. Some studies have suggested that emotional intelligence may not be a valid construct. For example, Davies *et al.* (1998) administered a large battery of tests of abilities, aptitudes, personality traits and emotional intelligence to over 500 adults. The aim of the study was to evaluate the discriminant and convergent validity of the measures of emotional intelligence. They found that the construct of emotional intelligence may not be useful because it correlates so highly with measures of major personality traits in the Five-Factor Model of Personality and also with measures of verbal ability. Only certain ability tests of emotional intelligence (but not personality trait measures of emotional intelligence) were found to measure constructs other than those tapped by traditional measures of personality and cognitive ability.

Within the field of emotional intelligence there is an ongoing controversy about the precise definition of the construct. At one extreme there are those who define it as a set of abilities (Mayer, Caruso, and Salovey, 2000) while at the other there are those who view it as a set of personality traits (Bar-On, 2000; Goleman, 1995; Boyatzis *et al.*, 2000; Cooper, 1996/1997). This controversy remains unresolved (Mayer, Salovey and Caruso, 2000a). From a theoretical viewpoint, there are stronger grounds for adopting an ability model of emotional intelligence than a personality trait model. Programmes of research based on such models will eventually lead to the development of instruments that can identify people who are more skilled at understanding and managing emotions in themselves and others; handling stress; empathising with others; and making complex decisions in ambiguous social situations. This line of research will also identify factors that contribute to the development of such abilities and intervention programmes that enhance

Table 4.6 Strategies for enhancing emotional intelligence

Domain	Strategy
Self-monitoring	• Keep a diary of mood-change episodes and state the **A**ctivity that led to the change in mood, the **B**eliefs that led to the change in mood and the **C**onsequent mood change on a 10-point scale
Self-regulation	• For depression, avoid distressing situations, focus on non-distressing aspects of difficult situations, assertively challenge distressing people, challenge pessimistic and perfectionistic thinking, be active and get support • For anxiety, challenge threat-oriented thinking and practise courage by entering threatening situations and using coping strategies to reduce anxiety • For anger, avoid provocative situations, focus on non-distressing aspects of difficult situations, assertively ask provocative people to be less provocative, stand back and practise empathy
Communication	• **When listening**, listen without judging • Put your own opinions and emotions on hold • Summarise what you have heard the other person say • Check that your summary is accurate • **When speaking**, decide on the points you want to make • Organise them logically • Say them clearly • Check that you have been understood • State your points without attacking, blaming or sulking • Repeat as necessary
Problem solving	• Break big vague problems into many smaller specific problems • Define these in solvable terms • Focus on the problem, not the person • Generate many possible solutions • When all solutions are generated, examine the pros and cons of each • Select the best solution • Implement the solution • Review progress • Repeat as necessary • Celebrate success
Helping children develop emotional intelligence	• Be attuned to infants' needs for physical and emotional care; control and intellectual stimulation; and try to meet them reliably and predictably, since this will foster secure attachment • Help children understand their own emotions by acknowledging and discussing how particular situations lead them to think certain thoughts, and so to experience particular emotions • Help children learn self-regulation by modelling the use of avoiding triggers, distraction, humour, self-talk relaxation routines and other coping strategies and praising them for self-soothing and self-regulation in threatening or frustrating situations • Help children develop conversational turn taking, and empathy skills for understanding of others' emotions by acknowledging and discussing how particular situations lead to particular emotions in other people • Help children learn co-operative problem-solving skills by modelling and inviting them to participate in joint problem solving

such skills. It is unlikely that personality-trait models of emotional intelligence will yield assessment instruments with any greater predicative validity than currently available personality inventories. This is not surprising. Successful attempts to measure analytic intelligence have involved developing tests of skill rather than inventories which inquired about people's opinions of their own skill levels.

A third controversy concerns the role of environmental and genetic factors in determining individual differences in emotional intelligence. One of Goleman's (1995) arguments in his bestselling book *Emotional Intelligence* was that emotional intelligence is predominantly environmentally determined and may be improved by training. A subtext of this argument is that analytical intelligence assessed by traditional IQ tests is predominantly genetically determined and unaffected by training. In order to test this assertion we would need data from twin or adoptive studies and early intervention studies for both emotional intelligence and analytic intelligence. We have data from such studies for analytic but not emotional intelligence. The results show that about 50 per cent of the variance in analytic intelligence is accounted for by genetic factors and that the other 50 per cent is accounted for by environmental factors (Grigorenco, 2000). Also, early intervention studies of socially disadvantaged children show that IQ can be dramatically raised through intensive early intervention targeting both the child and the family (Lange and Carr, 2002).

Equivalent data for emotional intelligence are unavailable. There is evidence that social skills training for children and management, stress management or communications skills training for adults can have modest short-term effects on circumscribed areas of social functioning (Topping *et al.*, 2000; Cherniss, 2000). However, as yet there are no robust scientific studies to show that particular intervention programmes can significantly enhance emotional intelligence. Such studies would require the evaluation of emotional intelligence of people in intervention and control groups with a reliable and valid emotional intelligence test before and after the programme and at long-term follow-up.

Claims that emotional intelligence is twice as important for occupational success as IQ, such as those made by Goleman (1995) in *Emotional Intelligence: Why It Can Matter More than IQ*, have yet to be substantiated (Mayer, Salovey and Caruso, 2000a, b). IQ correlates at best about 0.45 with academic or occupational success and accounts for about 20 per cent of the variance. There is no sound scientific evidence to show that emotional intelligence can account for this amount of the variance in occupational success. A century of research using personality questionnaires to predict occupational success has rarely found any construct that is able to predict more than 5 per cent of the variance in occupational success, so it is unlikely that emotional intelligence will be able to do so (Mayer, Salovey and Caruso, 2000b).

Despite these controversies, the potential for using the findings of research on emotional intelligence to inform the development of prevention and therapy programmes is considerable, and this is one reason for the importance of the concept of emotional intelligence (Parker, 2000).

SUMMARY

Public interest in emotional intelligence arose in the 1990s from Daniel Goleman's bestseller, *Emotional Intelligence: Why It Can Matter More than IQ*. In academic research, emotional intelligence has been conceptualised as a set of abilities for processing emotional information by Mayer, Salovey and Caruso and as a set of personality traits by Bar-On, Goleman and Cooper. Research on the growth of emotional competence in childhood, which suggests how emotional intelligence may develop, has shown that emotional regulation skills, the skills for expressing emotions and the skills for managing relationships gradually develop from infancy to adulthood. The early development of secure attachments to caregivers is important for the later development of emotional competence. Stress in childhood does not always compromise the development of emotional competence. Children who receive social support during times of stress from their attachment figures show resilience in the face of adversity. The probable neural network which subserves emotional intelligence has been identified in research by Antonio Damasio on the mistakes of patients with brain damage when required to make complex social judgements. This neural network includes the amygdala, the ventromedial pre-frontal cortex, the right somatosensory and insular cortices, and neural projections from the sensory sense organs. Emotional intelligence is conceptually related to many other psychological constructs such as ego strength, constructive thinking, hardiness, practical intelligence, autistic spectrum disorders, openness to experience, psychological mindedness, alexithymia, emotional awareness and emotional creativity. Research on the relationship between all of these constructs and emotional intelligence is required to further establish the validity of the construct of emotional intelligence. This is important because it has been argued that the construct of emotional intelligence may not be valid because it correlates so highly with measures of well-established personality traits and measures of verbal ability. There are also ongoing controversies about: whether emotional intelligence is best conceptualised as an ability or a personality trait; the role of environmental and genetic factors in determining individual differences in emotional intelligence; the degree to which emotional intelligence can be increased by training; and the relative importance of IQ and emotional intelligence for occupational success.

QUESTIONS

Personal development questions

1. Describe a situation that occurred within the past month, in which you successfully identified and managed your own emotions and those of others.
2. What emotions did you identify in yourself and the other person or people?
3. What skills did you use to manage your emotions?
4. What skills did you use to manage the emotions of the other person or people?
5. Describe a situation that occurred within the past month, in which it was critical for you to identify and manage your own emotions and those of others, but you were not successful in doing so.
6. What emotions did you have difficulty identifying in yourself and the other person or people?
7. What skills would you like to have had so that you could have managed your emotions more effectively?
8. What steps can you take now to develop these skills?
9. What would be the costs and benefits of taking these steps?
10. Take some of these steps and assess the impact it has on your well-being by assessing yourself before and afterwards on one of the well-being scales contained in Chapter 1.

Research questions

1. Design and conduct a study to test the hypothesis that there is a significant correlation between emotional intelligence and happiness. Which aspect of emotional intelligence accounts for the greatest amount of variance in happiness?
2. Conduct a PsychInfo search covering literature published in the past couple of years using the term 'emotional intelligence'. Identify a study that interests you and that is feasible to replicate and extend. Conduct the replication. If you can't settle on a study to replicate and extend, try this one: M. Davies, L. Stankov and R. Roberts, (1998). Emotional intelligence: in search of an elusive construct. *Journal of Personality and Social Psychology* 75: 989–1,015.

FURTHER READING

Academic

Bar-On, R. and Parker, J. (2000). *The Handbook of Emotional Intelligence*. San Francisco, CA: Jossey-Bass.

Self-help

Goleman, D. (1995). *Emotional Intelligence: Why It Can Matter More than IQ*. New York: Bantam.

Goleman, D. (1998). *Working with Emotional Intelligence*. New York: Bantam.

Stein, S. and Book, H. (2000). *The EQ Edge. Emotional Intelligence and Your Success*. London, UK: Kogan Page.

MEASURES FOR USE IN RESEARCH

Bar-On, R. (1997). *BarOn Emotional Quotient Inventory (EQ-I): Technical Manual*. Toronto: Multi-Health Systems.

Boyatzis, R. Goleman, D. and Hay/McBer (1999). *Emotional Competence Inventory*. Boston, MA: HayGroup.

Cooper, R. (1996/1997). *EQ Map*. San Francisco, CA: AIT and Essi Systems.

Mayer, J. Salovey, P. and Caruso, D. (1997). *The Emotional IQ Test (CD-Rom)*. Needham, MA: Virtual Knowledge.

Mayer, J. Salovey, P. and Caruso, D. (1999). *MSCEIT Item Booklet (Research Version 1.1)*. Toronto: Multi-Health Systems.

Schutte, Malouff, J., Hall, L., Haggerty, D., Copper, J., Golden, C. and Dornheim, L. (1998). Development and validation of a measure of emotional intelligence. *Personality and Individual Differences* 25: 167–77.

GLOSSARY

Alexithymia.   Difficulty identifying and describing emotions.

Attachment theory.   Bowlby's view that when caregivers are attuned and responsive to children's needs children develop internal working models of themselves and their caregivers which entail the view that caregivers are secure bases from which they may safely explore the world. Such secure attachment does not occur when caregivers are poorly attuned or unresponsive to children's needs. Internal working models and attachment styles (secure or insecure) which develop in early childhood serve as templates for later intimate relationships in adulthood.

Autistic spectrum disorder traits.   The inability to recognise and process information about the emotional states of others and to respond in emotionally appropriate ways.

Emotional creativity.   The capacity to have emotional experiences characterised by novelty, effectiveness and authenticity.

Emotional intelligence.   The capacity to recognise and manage emotions of ourselves and others in relationships.

Practical intelligence.   The application of analytical and memory skills to solving everyday problems in family, work and leisure situations.

Psychological mindedness.   The disposition to be motivated to learn more about current and past cognitive, affective and behavioural factors that cause or arise from particular experiences.

Chapter 5

Giftedness, creativity and wisdom

Learning objectives

- Be able to define giftedness in terms of Renzulli's three-ring model of giftedness and Gardner's theory of multiple intelligence.
- Be able to describe the main research findings on gifted children concerning genetic and environmental factors in the genesis of giftedness, family backgrounds of gifted children and their psychological adjustment, and neurobiological aspects of giftedness.
- Understand Sternberg and Lubart's investment theory of creativity.
- Give an account of the main research findings on the stages of creativity, individual differences in creativity and the links between creativity and intelligence, personality, motivation and brain processes.
- Understand different conceptual models for explaining wisdom, including wisdom as the final stage of personality and cognitive development and balance theory of wisdom.
- Understand the clinical implications of research on giftedness, creativity and wisdom for facilitating happiness.
- Be able to identify research questions that need to be addressed to advance our understanding of giftedness, creativity and wisdom on the one hand and happiness on the other.

Giftedness in childhood, creativity in adulthood and wisdom in later life are the rubrics under which psychologists have studied a variety of types of outstanding achievements across the lifespan. Giftedness, creativity and wisdom all involve more than just a high level of analytic intelligence as assessed by traditional IQ tests. Gifted children are not just very bright. They have outstanding talent and may, for example, play musical instruments exceptionally well or perform complex mathematics from their pre-school years with minimal training (Callahan, 2000; Winner, 2000). Creative adults, too, are more than just intelligent (Sternberg, 1999). They break new ground and defy the conventions of their discipline through scientific discovery or producing outstanding works of art. Wise people, like Solomon in the Bible, make exceptionally sound judgements in a calm manner about highly complex social dilemmas using deep understanding, broad experience and profound compassion (Baltes and Staudinger, 2000). Giftedness, creativity and wisdom are all personal strengths which have the potential to lead to positive outcomes for ourselves and others. Research findings in these three domains and their implications will be considered in this chapter.

GIFTEDNESS

The earliest scientific studies of giftedness were Sir Francis Galton's (1869) retrospective investigation of the families of eminent people, *Hereditary Genius*, and Terman's 35-year longitudinal study of gifted children (Terman and Ogden, 1959). Galton found that eminence ran in families and concluded that giftedness was predominantly hereditary. Whether giftedness is innate or environmental continues to be a controversial issue. Some argue that the talents of gifted children are the product of intensive deliberate practice (Howe, 1999) while others argue that such talents are innate (Winner, 2000). Available evidence suggests that gifted children show outstanding innate talent before practice, but then are motivated to practise a great deal to master their talent and so environmental factors also contribute to the growth of their giftedness.

In the second major early study of giftedness, Terman used the Stanford–Binet intelligence test to screen more than 1000 children with IQs above 140 and followed them up over 35 years (Terman and Ogden, 1959). Terman found that this group of children with high IQs also showed exceptional physical health, behavioural adjustment and moral development. The idea that giftedness is associated with good overall adjustment has not been supported by recent studies in which a more stringent definition of giftedness has been used. For example, Morelock and Feldman (1997) found that children with IQs over 150 showed difficulties in developing good work habits at school and maintaining good peer relationships, and also showed emotional distress due to reaching an early understanding of major moral and existential problems before having the emotional maturity to cope with them.

Definitions of giftedness

Giftedness has been defined, following Terman's lead, as an IQ score above a particular level, but dissatisfaction with this, and a recognition that visual artists, musicians and others can show high levels of giftedness despite having

IQs in the average range, has led to broader definitions of giftedness. Such broader definitions of giftedness have been developed by Renzulli (1986) in his three-ring model of giftedness and Gardner (1983/1993) with reference to his multiple intelligence model.

Renzulli three-ring model of giftedness

Renzulli (1986) defined giftedness in his three-ring model as involving:

1. outstanding general ability as measured by IQ tests or specific aptitude tests for domains such as mathematical ability, musical talent or sculpture;
2. creativity in the domain of high ability; and
3. commitment and a high level of motivation to develop skills in the domain of high ability.

Renzulli's (1986) definition of giftedness is partially based on a hierarchical model of intelligence. This model has its roots in the work of Spearman (1927) and Thurstone (1938). Using factor analysis, Spearman examined the pattern of correlations among a large number of different types of ability tests given to a large sample of people. He found a single underlying factor of general intelligence which he called 'g'. Shortly after this, Thurstone (1938), using a wider range of tests and a slightly different method of factor analysis, failed to find 'g' and instead found a set of seven independent factors which he called primary mental abilities. These were: verbal comprehension; word fluency; number facility; spatial ability; perceptual speed; induction; and memory. Since the early work of Spearman and Thurstone, attempts to reconcile these two different models of the structure of intelligence have led to the development of various hierarchical models of intelligence with 'g' or aspects of 'g' at the top of the hierarchy and a greater number of factors representing specific abilities below this, the apex of the hierarchy (Cooper, 1999; Davidson and Downing, 2000).

Renzulli's (1986) definition of giftedness entails the view that gifted children may have high scores on 'g' or general intellectual ability or a high score on a factor lower in the hierarchy of abilities or both, along with creativity and task commitment.

Giftedness and multiple intelligence

Professor Howard Gardner (1983/1993, 1998) of Harvard University, following in the tradition of Thurstone (1938), has proposed that intelligence is not a unitary construct. Rather there are multiple intelligences and giftedness entails not high overall ability but outstanding ability in one of these multiple intelligences.

Gardner has identified eight types of intelligence: linguistic; logical-mathematical; spatial; musical; bodily kinesthetic; interpersonal, intra-personal; and naturalist. Linguistic intelligence refers to the production and comprehension of spoken and written language, the capacity to clarify, convince and explain, and a sensitivity to subtle nuances of meaning in language. Having a facility with numbers, a capacity to operate abstract symbol systems, and the ability to explore logical relationships between hypothetical statements are the central elements of logical-mathematical intelligence, which is important for mathematics, logic and science. Spatial intelligence refers to skills for perceiving and transforming visual–spatial relationships, and is important for architecture or visual art. Sensitivity to rhythm, pitch and timbre are the key components of musical intelligence. Bodily kinesthetic intelligence refers to sensitivity and control over body-movements, and is important for athletics and dance. A sensitivity to intentions and wishes of others and a capacity to influence others in desired ways are the main elements of interpersonal intelligence. Intrapersonal intelligence refers to understanding one's own psychological strengths and weaknesses and is important for making informed personal decisions. Naturalist intelligence involves understanding the patterns found in natural environments.

According to Gardner, each of the multiple intelligences follows a distinctive developmental course both ontogenetically and phylogenetically. Information relevant to each form of intelligence is encoded in a unique symbol system, e.g. letter, numbers, musical notation. Each form of intelligence is associated with unique core operations which can be analysed with experimental tasks and individual differences in these core operations can be evaluated with psychometric tests. Each form of intelligence can be isolated by brain damage, for example the case of Phineas Gage who had an iron bar pass through his pre-frontal lobes (Macmillan, 1986) showed that damage to the pre-frontal lobes of the cortex can lead to impaired interpersonal intelligence but leave other intelligences intact. Each form of intelligence can also be validated by the identification of exceptional cases, e.g. Freud was a prodigy in the field of intrapersonal intelligence, Gandhi in the field of interpersonal intelligence and Darwin in the field of natural intelligence. Giftedness, according to Gardner, represents the presence of outstanding ability in one domain of intelligence.

Research findings on gifted children

Reviews of the literature on giftedness allow a number of broad conclusions to be drawn about early gifted performance; genetic and environmental determinants of giftedness; families of gifted children; psychological adjustment of gifted children; brain processes related to giftedness; and adult creativity of gifted children (Howe, 1999; Miller *et al.*, 1999; Sternberg and Davidson, 1986; Subotnik and Arnold, 1994; Winner, 1996, 2000).

Early gifted performance

Gifted children, prodigies and savants (who excel in one area of talent but have IQs below the normal range) show extremely advanced skills in circumscribed areas very early in their lives. For example, before the age of 4 years gifted children may read fluently without instruction, or excel at playing a musical instrument, or solve complex mathematical problems for amusement. Gifted children defined in this way are different from children with fairly high IQs (of about 130–40) who show very good (but not outstanding) performance of a wide range of academic and non-academic pursuits.

Genetic and environmental factors of giftedness

An important question concerns the role of hereditary or constitutional factors on the one hand and environment or training factors on the other in the development of giftedness. The repeated observation that high ability runs in families supports the view that giftedness is partially hereditary. All gifted children exercise their talents a great deal and this has led to the view that giftedness may be partially environmentally determined. However, the high rates of practice shown by gifted children may be the result of having great talent rather than the cause of such precocity. That is, gifted children may be highly motivated to master their inherited talents and so practise a great deal.

Family backgrounds of gifted children

The family backgrounds of gifted children are typically benign. The idea that gifted children are driven to high levels of performance by their over-ambitious parents and become estranged, embittered and depressed as a result of this is not born out by empirical studies of gifted children. Gifted children, for the most part, report positive relationships with their parents. Gifted children typically grow up in child-centred families where parents model hard work and high achievement, provide an intellectually and artistically stimulating environment, offer their children a high level of autonomy, but expect a high level of excellence from them. Whether these parental behaviours are elicited by gifted children from otherwise normal parents or whether this type of parenting fosters giftedness we do not know. Gifted children from families in which there is a high level of nurturance and stimulation show better overall adjustment and more consistent use of their talents than other gifted children who have less supportive families.

Psychological adjustment of gifted children

There is some tentative support for the popular conception of a link between 'madness and genius'. Gifted children show double the rate of behavioural adjustment problems of non-gifted children. This may be due to the fact that their high performance can lead to them becoming bored with routine school work and socially isolated from their peers. Gifted children crave time alone to practise their talent but they also crave the company of like-minded peers (who are hard to find). They may also hide their talent to gain acceptance from non-gifted peers.

Brain processes and giftedness

Studies of neuropsychological and psychophysiological processes of gifted children show that some of these youngsters are biologically different from their normal counterparts. For example, a subgroup of gifted children with talents for art, music, maths and other non-language-based domains have atypical brain organisation which underpins their unusual talents. Specifically they have enhanced right hemisphere development. However, such constitutional advantage often entails a cost and such children typically have more language-related difficulties, such as dyslexia, auto-immune disorders and behavioural adjustment problems than non-gifted children.

Studies of the neuropsychological and psychophysiological correlates of overall intelligence also deserve mention here (Vernon et al., 2000). IQ is positively correlated with head circumference ($r = 0.2$) and brain volume ($r = 0.4$), suggesting that greater intelligence is subserved by greater brain mass.

IQ is negatively correlated with the latency of the P300 component of the event-related potential (ERP) waveform. The latency of the P300 waveform has been shown to be a reliable index of speed of information processing in the cortex associated with detection, recognition and classification of target stimuli. Thus, highly intelligent people have short P300 latencies and this is reflected in the fact that they make decisions quickly. (An event-related potential (ERP) is the averaged electroencephalographic activity (waveforms representing bioelectric brain activity) following the presentation of a stimulus. The latency of the P300 component of the waveform is the time taken for the component that appears at about 300 milliseconds after the stimulus to peak.)

IQ is also correlated with cerebral glucose metabolism, an index of the degree to which the brain is using glucose to compensate for expending energy involved in processing information. Glucose metabolism is assessed by positron emission topography (PET). IQ is positively correlated with cerebral glucose metabolism when participants are resting and free to engage in any mental activity they choose, but negatively correlated with cerebral glucose metabolism when participants are asked to solve a specific problem. Thus, when very intelligent people are free to engage in a mental activity of their choosing, they think a lot. However, when given a problem to solve they use their brains efficiently using a minimum of energy.

Childhood giftedness and adult creativity

The idea that child prodigies grow up to become highly creative adults has not been borne out by research. Most gifted children grow up to become well-adjusted successful experts in their fields. Only a minority of gifted children go on to become creative adults who make major innovative contributions to their field. This is not surprising, because showing creativity in adulthood would involve making the difficult transition from effortlessly achieving a high standard by conforming with the rules and practices of an established domain in childhood, to effortful disruption and transformation of the rules and practices of an established domain in adulthood. This type of transition would involve switching from predominantly using convergent thinking to predominantly using divergent thinking (Feist, 1999). Another possible reason why gifted children do not typically grow up to become creative adults is that the personality traits required to be a creative adult are quite different from those shown by gifted children. Gifted children are typically conforming and come from supportive stable families. Creative adults, in contrast, are typically rebellious and have a history of childhood stress and hardship which predisposes them to challenging the conventional rules and practices within their field (Simonton, 2000). There is also a disproportionately higher rate of bipolar affective disorder (manic depression) among creative adults.

CREATIVITY

Creativity is the capacity to produce work that is both novel and useful (Sternberg and Lubart, 1999). Early major contributions to the study of creativity were made in psychoanalysis, gestalt psychology and psychometrics. Freud (1908) underlined the importance of non-rational primary process thinking in creativity and saw creative output as a socially acceptable way of expressing unacceptable unconscious aggressive and sexual drives for power or love. Gestalt psychologists, notably Wertheimer (1945), focused on processes involved in insight learning such as transformation, figure–ground reversal and closure. In the psychometric tradition Guilford (1950, 1967) conceptualised creativity as a set of divergent thinking skills within his Structure of the Intellect Model which incorporated both convergent thinking skills evaluated by traditional IQ tests and divergent thinking skills. Modern studies of creativity have been conducted to throw light on cognitive processes, personal characteristics, psychophysiological processes, lifespan development and social contexts associated with creativity (Simonton, 2000). A number of fairly comprehensive theories of creativity have been developed, two of which deserve particular mention: Csikszentmihalyi's (1996, 1999) systems model of creativity and Sternberg and Lubart's (1999) investment theory of creativity.

Csikszentmihalyi's systems model of creativity

Csikszentmihalyi (1999, 1996) has argued that creativity is most usefully conceptualised as a systemic rather than an individualistic process which involves the dynamic interaction of three distinct systems:

1. the person with his or her talents, personality traits and motivations;
2. the domain which consists of the symbol-system, rules, techniques, practices and guiding paradigm; and
3. the field which consists of people working within the same domain (artists, scientists, critics, journal editors) whose activity is governed by the same domain-specific rules and practices.

Thus, the creativity process is an interaction between a creative individual who has become immersed in a field and come up with an original idea and an audience who may be ambivalent about accepting the idea. From Figure 5.1 it may be seen that for creativity to occur, a set of rules and practices must be transmitted from the domain to the individual. The individual must then produce a novel variation in the content of the domain. Motivation to produce this creative variation occurs when an appropriately talented individual responds to a tension between competing colleagues or critics within a field, or where there is a pronounced gap between the low demands of

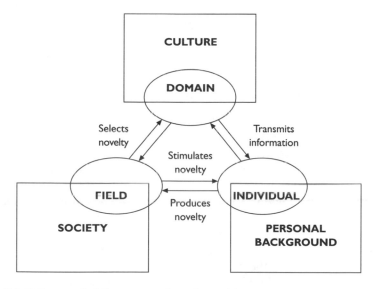

Figure 5.1 Csikszentmihalyi's systems view of creativity
Source: Adapted from Csikszentmihalyi (1999): 315.
Note: For creativity to occur, a set of rules must be transmitted from the domain to the individual. The individual must then produce a novel variation in the content of the domain which was stimulated by the field. The variation must then be selected by the field for inclusion in the domain.

routine work within a field and the high ability of the person entering the field. The variation must then be selected by the field for inclusion in the domain and must also be transmitted through time if it is to be accepted by the community who make up the field. This is analogous to evolution. To be creative, an idea has to be adapted to its social environment and transmitted through time.

The individual's creative work, the domain and the field are each parts of three wider systems. First, the creative individual's work arises within the context of that person's historical background and personal attributes. Second, the domain in which the work occurs (for example in a branch of science or art) is embedded within a wider culture. Third, the members of the field in which the creativity occurs are also members of a wider society. According to Csikszentmihalyi's theory, certain cultures, domains, fields, societies and personal attributes probably favour creativity.

Cultures which facilitate creativity

Cultures which promote creativity are probably those in which information is physically stored accurately rather than transmitted orally, and accessible to all members of the culture rather than kept secret from all but a few. The more differentiated the separate domains within the culture, such as religion, science and art, and the more loosely coupled these domains are, the more likely new ideas are to be accepted since the innovations will entail changes within only a circumscribed part of the culture. The more exposed the culture is to information from other cultures, the more likely the occurrence of creative innovation.

Domains which facilitate creativity

Domains in which clear and accurate symbol systems are used to record information probably promote greater innovation because of the ease with which they can incorporate new ideas into the existing knowledge base. Domains in which the information is very tightly organised and integrated probably are poor at accepting innovation and so are not conducive to creativity, nor are loosely organised domains where innovations may go unrecognised. Moderately well-organised domains probably foster creativity. Creativity within a domain, such as religion, politics or science, is probably made more difficult when the domain is central to the culture, closely linked to all aspects of the culture and accessibly to only an elite few, for cxample religion in the Middle Ages or physical science in the second half of the twentieth century. Where a domain is not central to a culture, only loosely linked to other aspects of the culture and open to many people, then innovation and creativity probably flourish, for example popular music in the second half of the twentieth century.

Societies which facilitate creativity

Societies in which there is surplus physical and mental energy are more likely to promote creativity than those in which all energy is devoted to survival. Societies that value change and innovation with mercantile economies are more likely to foster creativity than those committed to convention and maintaining the status quo. Societies in which there are external threats or internal strife foster creativity.

Fields which facilitate creativity

Fields are likely to promote creativity if their practitioners can obtain economic resources or status from society. Where a field is overly dependent for judgements about the value of new ideas on religious, political or economic considerations, it is less likely to promote creativity. Creativity also will not flourish where the field is very independent from other domains of society and has few links with them. Overly bureaucratic fields that are rigidly organised constrain originality. Domains that have lax criteria for admitting new ideas debase the domain and those that have too stringent criteria stifle creativity.

Family life which facilitates creativity

Individuals who have grown up in families which have surplus energy and resources to devote to curiosity and creativity are more likely to be creative than those that grow up in families where interest in anything but survival is discouraged. Creativity is fostered when there is respect within the family for learning. Creativity is more likely to occur where the family can introduce a child to a domain and field, through school placement, mentors or organised artistic or athletic pastimes. Creativity is more likely where individuals grow up in marginalised families and want to break out of this situation. Evidence from case studies shows that diversifying experiences, which serve to weaken the constraints entailed by conventional socialisation, and challenging experiences, which strengthen the person's capacity to persevere when obstacles or adversity are encountered, foster creativity (Simonton, 2000).

Personal characteristics which facilitate creativity

Personal attributes conducive to creativity include: special talents or aptitudes; intrinsic motivation to work hard in the field in which one is talented; well-developed divergent thinking skills; an openness to experience; flexibility; and an unconventional disposition. To make a creative contribution the individual must have internalised the rules of the domain and the opinions in the field, be dissatisfied with some aspect of these and then come up with a variety of new ideas. At this point, the kernel of creativity is recognising the good new ideas and being able to hold onto these and discard the less useful ideas.

Csikszentmihalyi's (1996) own case study research and the research findings presented below offer support for many of the hypotheses entailed in this elaborate systems view of creativity.

Sternberg and Lubart's investment theory

According to Sternberg and Lubart's (1999) investment theory of creativity, individuals make creative contributions to a field when they 'buy low and sell high' in a field of ideas. That is, they 'buy' or adopt poorly developed ideas which are unpopular or unfamiliar but which have growth potential, invest creatively in these and develop them into 'creative products' before moving on to 'new' unpopular ideas with growth potential.

A unique characteristic of the creative individual is persistence in developing a set of ideas despite resistance from the field to these new developments and a lack of acceptance.

Creativity, according to investment theory, requires a confluence of six factors. First, it involves the intellectual abilities required to see problems in novel unconventional ways and recognise which problems are worth pursuing, and the ability to sell one's ideas to others. Second, it requires sufficient knowledge about a field to move forward in it, but not so much that one is paralysed by conventional practices. Third, creativity requires the capacity to think in novel ways about effective problem solving and to think globally (about the big picture) as well as locally (about details). Fourth, creativity requires a personality characterised by sensible risk taking (particularly in the area of buying low and selling high), persistence in overcoming obstacles (in tolerating the field's resistance to one's new ideas), self-efficacy and a tolerance for uncertainty and ambiguity. Fifth, creativity requires intrinsic motivation to work in the field. Sixth, creativity requires a supportive environment which rewards creative contributions to the field.

Sternberg and Lubart's (1999) investment theory of creativity offers an elaboration of the way in which individuals select areas for innovation, and so fills in some of the detail absent from Csikszentmihalyi's (1999) broader framework. The six conditions necessary for creativity to occur are similar in both theories. A detail absent from both theories is the temporal sequence involved in creative production.

Research findings on creativity

Reviews of the literature on creativity allow a number of broad conclusions to be drawn about the stages of creativity; individual differences and creativity; intelligence, personality, motivation and brain processes involved in creativity (Simonton, 2000; Sternberg, 1999).

Stages of creativity

Since the gestalt psychologists' early formulations, numerous theorists have proposed that the process of creativity follows a series of stages (Simonton, 2000). Case studies of the lives of very creative people have thrown light on the stages involved in the creative process (Poicastro and Gardner, 1999). Such studies have focused on the lives of Darwin the naturalist and Piaget the polymath (Gruber and Wallace, 1999), Einstein the physicist, Freud the psychoanalyst, Gandhi the political activist, Picasso the painter, Stravinski the musical composer, T.S. Eliot the poet, Martha Graham the dancer (Gardner, 1993), John Stuart Mill, the philosopher, Norbert Weiner, the founder of cybernetics, George Bernard Shaw, the writer, and Michael Faraday, the scientist (Howe, 1999). Creative adults have a history of many years of training to gain expert knowledge in their field. After this apprenticeship or period of immersion, which usually lasts about ten years, they make their creative contributions which are often not a single product, but a network of interrelated enterprises. Creative output is curvilinear and follows an inverted-backwards J-shaped function. The best work is usually produced at the point of greatest productivity (Simonton, 2000).

Case studies have borne out Csikszentmihalyi's (1999) hypothesis that to make a creative contribution the individual must have internalised the rules of the domain and the opinions in the field, be dissatisfied with some aspect of these and then come up with a variety of new ideas.

Acts of creativity, which may appear as sudden insights into how particular problems may be solved, typically follow long and hard work on details related to the problem and its solution, and a period of incubation during which problem solving occurs in the cognitive unconscious.

Most creative people have a sense of their finished product before they start. Much of their work is publicly articulating and differentiating the detail entailed by this preliminary intuitive sense of the finished product.

Individual differences in creativity

Guilford (1967), who viewed creative abilities as a subset of skills within his Structure of the Intellect Model, developed divergent thinking skills tests to evaluate these. Torrance (1974) and others have continued this research tradition, by developing creative thinking tests modelled, in style, on intelligence tests which show that there are individual differences in creativity which are normally distributed within the population. Torrance's (1974) Test of Creative Thinking is still the most widely used psychometric research instrument in the field. This and other similar tests have been shown to have good reliability but only moderate predictive criterion validity. That is, the correlation between test scores in childhood or adolescence and the production of creative work in adulthood is small. Creativity as measured by creativity and divergent thinking tests is fairly stable over time, but in children there is a slump in late elementary school: the fourth-grade slump.

Creativity self-rating scales or parent and teacher rating scales; psychometric rating scales for judging the originality of creative products; and rating scales for quantifying aspects of environments, such as supervisor encouragement or freedom to choose assignments that promote creativity, have been developed and many show good reliability and validity (Plucker and Renzulli, 1999).

Intelligence and creativity

Creativity as measured by divergent thinking tests correlates moderately with measures of IQ measured by conventional intelligence tests. A certain basic level of analytical intelligence is essential for creativity, but beyond that critical base level, creativity and IQ are relatively independent sets of abilities.

Guilford's (1967) Structure of the Intellect Model and newer models, such as Sternberg's (1997) Triarchic Model, subsume creativity into a much broader definition of intelligence. Guilford (1967) included both convergent (analytical) thinking skills and divergent (creative thinking skills) within his overall model of the intellect. In Sternberg's (1997) triarchic theory of intelligence (described below in the section on wisdom) he argues that effective adaptation to the environment, and hence successful use of intelligence, involves combining analytic intelligence with practical intelligence and creative intelligence.

Personality and creativity

Feist (1999), in a thorough literature review of empirical studies, concluded that, compared with normal controls, creative artists and scientists have different personalities. They tend to be more open to new experiences; more self-confident, dominant, driven, ambitious and impulsive; more hostile; and less conscientious and conventional. While creative artists and scientists differ from normal controls in these respects, their personality profiles differ from each other insofar as scientists are more conscientious while artists are more emotionally unstable and unconventional. The creative personality profile is relatively enduring over time and the profiles that characterise creative adults is similar to that shown by creative children and adolescents. However, as has already been noted, giftedness in childhood (expert performance in conformity with rules of the domain) rarely leads to adult creativity (innovation which violates the rules of the domain).

Motivation and creativity

Intrinsic motivation, discussed in Chapter 2, is essential for creativity (Collins and Amabile, 1999). Intrinsic motivation refers to a willingness to engage in an activity for its own sake because it is challenging, interesting and enjoyable rather than to achieve some other end. In contrast, extrinsic motivation arises from a wish to achieve some external goal by engaging in an activity, such as receiving social or financial rewards, avoiding sanctions or obtaining feedback. Extrinsic motivators, such as providing feedback, rewards or sanctions that distract attention from the task or reduce perceived autonomy, hinder creativity. However, other types of extrinsic motivators, such as providing task-related feedback which enhance perceived competence and task-involvement, facilitate creativity. Task-related feedback may be a useful extrinsic motivator when 'getting up to speed' before making a major creative breakthrough or working out the fine details of a creative product after a major creative breakthrough. Extrinsic motivators such as receiving recognition for creativity may also be an important motivator for going through the steps necessary for bringing creative work to the attention of people within one's field. Thus, there may be a motivation–work cycle match where intrinsic motivation is critical during the period just prior to and during creative insight, but facilitative extrinsic motivators such as task-relevant feedback or the prospect of recognition may be important before and after this particular time period.

Brain processes and creativity

Psychophysiological studies of creativity indicate that creative people show low levels of cortical activation during the inspiration stage of creativity and higher levels of cortical activation when resting than non-creative people (Martindale, 1999). In these studies low levels of cortical activation are indexed by the percentage of time in EEG alpha state, with high percentages of alpha associated with low cortical arousal.

Psychophysiological studies show that attention is defocused, thought is associative and a large number of mental representations are activated during periods of low cortical activation associated with creative inspiration (Runco and Sakamoto 1999).

Within western cultures, giftedness is typically associated with childhood, creativity with adulthood, and wisdom, the focus of the next section, with middle and later life.

WISDOM

Distinctions are made between implicit and explicit theories of wisdom (Sternberg, 2000a). Implicit theoretical approaches to wisdom aim to articulate folk conceptions of the nature of wisdom. That is, psychologists conduct studies to find out what the man in the street thinks wisdom is. In contrast, theories or wisdom developed by psychologists may be classified as explicit theoretical approaches to wisdom. In studies of implicit theories of wisdom, participants are asked to rate the sorts of words that characterise wise people and these words are then collapsed into dimensions using multidimensional scaling techniques (e.g. Clayton and Birren, 1980). The results of these studies show that people have a clear understanding that wisdom is related to excellence and differentiated from other concepts such as social intelligence, maturity and creativity. Wisdom involves an exceptional level of personal and interpersonal competence including the abilities to listen, evaluate and give advice and is used for the well-being of self and others (Baltes and Staudinger, 2000). Explicit theories of wisdom include those that define wisdom as a stage of personality development (Erikson *et al.*, 1986); a stage of cognitive development (Basseches, 1984; Riegel, 1973); or a high level of skill development that entails both personality and cognitive processes (Baltes and Staudinger, 2000; Sternberg, 2000a).

Wisdom as the final stage of personality development

Erik Erikson, a Jewish psychoanalyst who fled Nazi Germany prior to the Second World War, has addressed the issue of wisdom within the context of his lifecycle model of personality development (Erikson *et al.*, 1986; McAdams and de St Aubin, 1998). Within this model, the lifecycle is divided into a series of stages each of which involves facing a challenge or crisis that requires resolution. If resolution occurs, a particular personal strength or virtue evolves and if not, a personal difficulty or vulnerability is engendered. The ease with which successive dilemmas are managed is determined partly by the success with which preceding dilemmas were resolved. Erikson's model is presented in Table 5.1. What follows is a summary of the main hypotheses entailed in this theory.

Trust v mistrust

The main psychosocial dilemma to be resolved during the first 18 months of life is trust versus mistrust. If parents respond to infants' needs in a predictable and sensitive way, the infant develops a sense of trust. In the long term, this underpins a capacity to have hope in the face of adversity and to trust, as adults, that difficult challenges can be resolved. If the child does not experience the parent as a secure base from which to explore the world, the child learns to mistrust others and this underpins a view of the world as threatening. This may lead the child to adopt a detached position during

Table 5.1 Erikson's psychosocial stage model

Stage	Dilemma and main process	Virtue and positive self-description	Pathology and negative self-description
Infancy 0–18m	**Trust v mistrust** Mutuality with caregiver	**Hope** I can attain my wishes	**Detachment** I will not trust others
Toddler years 18m–3y	**Autonomy v shame and doubt** Imitation	**Will** I can control events	**Compulsion** I will repeat this act to undo the mess that I have made and I doubt that I can control events and I am ashamed of this
Pre-school years 3y–6y	**Initiative v guilt** Identification	**Purpose** I can plan and achieve goals	**Inhibition** I can't plan or achieve goals so I don't act
Middle childhood 7y–11y	**Industry v inferiority** Education	**Competence** I can use skills to achieve goals	**Inertia** I have no skills so I won't try
Adolescence 12–20y	**Identity v role confusion** Role experimentation	**Fidelity** I can be true to my values	**Confusion** I don't know what my role is or what my values are
Young adulthood 21y–34y	**Intimacy v isolation** Mutuality with peers	**Love** I can be intimate with another	**Exclusivity** I have no time for others so I will shut them out
Middle age 34y–60y	**Productivity v stagnation** Person–environment fit and creativity	**Care** I am committed to making the world a better place	**Rejectivity** I do not care about the future of others, only my own future
Old age 60y +	**Integrity v despair** Introspection	**Wisdom** I am committed to life, I accept myself, my parents, my life but I know I will die soon	**Despair** I am disgusted at my frailty and my failures

Source: Adapted from Erikson, E. (1959). *Identity and the Life Cycle*. New York: International University Press.

later years and difficulties with making and maintaining peer relationships may occur.

Autonomy v shame and doubt

The main psychosocial dilemma in the pre-school years (18 months to 3 years) is autonomy versus shame and doubt. During this period children become aware of their separateness and strive to establish a sense of personal agency and impose their will on the world. Of course, sometimes this is possible, but at other times their parents will prohibit them from doing certain things. There is a gradual moving from the battles of the terrible twos to the ritual orderliness that many children show as they approach school-going age. If parents patiently provide the framework for children to master tasks and routines, autonomy develops. As adults such children are patient with themselves and have confidence in their abilities to master the challenges of life. If parents are unable to be patient with the child's evolving wilfulness and need for mastery and criticise or humiliate failed attempts at mastery, the child will develop a sense of self-doubt and shame. The lack of patience and parental criticism will become internalised and children will evolve into adults who criticise themselves excessively and who lack confidence in their abilities. In some instances this may lead to the compulsive need to repeat their efforts at problem solving so that they can undo the mess they have made and so cope with the shame of not succeeding.

Initiative v guilt

In the pre-school years (3–6 years) the main psychosocial dilemma is initiative versus guilt. When children have developed a sense of autonomy in the pre-school years, they turn their attention outwards to the physical and social world and use their initiative to investigate and explore its regularities with a view to establishing a cognitive map of it. The child finds out what is allowed and what is not allowed at home and at school. Many questions about how the world works are asked. Children conduct various experiments and investigations, for example by lighting matches, taking toys apart, or playing doctors and nurses. The initiative versus guilt dilemma is resolved when the child learns how to channel the need for investigation into socially appropriate courses of action. This occurs when parents empathise with the child's curiosity but establish the limits of experimentation clearly and with warmth. Children who resolve the dilemma of initiative versus guilt act with a sense of purpose and vision as adults. Where parents have difficulty empathising with the child's need for curiosity and curtail experimentation unduly, children may develop a reluctance to explore untried options as adults because such curiosity arouses a sense of guilt.

Industry v inferiority

In middle-childhood (6–12 years) the main psychosocial dilemma is industry versus inferiority. Having established a sense of trust, autonomy and initiative, the child's need to develop skills and engage in meaningful work emerges. The motivation for industry may stem from the fact that learning new skills is intrinsically rewarding and many tasks and jobs open to the child may be rewarded. Children who have the aptitude to master skills that are rewarded by parents, teachers and peers emerge from this stage of development with new skills and a sense of competence and self-efficacy about these. Youngsters who fail and are ridiculed or humiliated develop a sense of inferiority and in adulthood lack the motivation to achieve.

Identity v role confusion

The establishment of a clear sense of identity – that is, a sense of who I am – is the major concern in adolescence. Where a sense of identity is achieved following a moratorium in which many roles have been explored, the adolescent avoids the problems of being aimless as in the case of identity diffusion. Rather they develop a strong commitment to vocational, social, political and religious values – a virtue Erikson refers to as fidelity – and usually have good psychosocial adjustment in adulthood.

Intimacy v isolation

The major psychosocial dilemma for people who have left adolescence is whether to develop an intimate relationship with another or move to an isolated position. People who do not achieve intimacy experience isolation. Difficulties with establishing intimate relationships typically emerge from experiences of mistrust, shame, doubt, guilt, inferiority, and role-confusion associated with failure to resolve earlier developmental dilemmas in a positive manner.

Productivity v stagnation

The midlife dilemma is that of productivity versus stagnation. People who select and shape a home and work environment that fits with their needs and talents are more likely to resolve this dilemma by becoming productive. Productivity may involve procreation, work-based productivity or artistic creativity. Those who become productive focus their energy into making the world a better place for further generations. Those who fail to select and shape their environment to meet their needs and talents may become overwhelmed with stress and become burned out, depressed or cynical on the one hand or greedy and narcissistic on the other.

Integrity v despair

In later adulthood the dilemma faced is integrity versus despair. A sense of personal integrity is achieved by those who accept the events that make up their lives – the good and the bad – and integrate these into a meaningful personal narrative in a way that allows them to face death without fear. Those who avoid this introspective process or who engage in it and find that they cannot accept the events of their lives or integrate them into a meaningful personal narrative that allows them to face death without fear develop a sense of despair. This despair entails a sense of self-rejection for one's past failures and current frailties.

The process of integrating failures, disappointments, conflicts, growing incompetencies and frailty into a coherent life story is very challenging. The positive resolution of this dilemma in favour of integrity rather than despair leads to wisdom. So, people are more likely to develop wisdom if they already have developed virtues of hope, will, purpose, competence, fidelity, love and care in resolving psychosocial dilemmas faced at earlier stages of the lifecycle. For Erikson, wisdom is the acceptance of imperfection in one's self, one's parents and one's life. Wisdom is an acceptance of oneself with all one's achievements and failures, without major regrets; acceptance of one's parents as people who did their best, and so deserve love, but were not perfect; acceptance of one's own life as the best one could have lived; and acceptance of the inevitability of death.

Research on lifespan development shows that people do face the psychosocial dilemmas entailed by Erikson's theory and develop the virtues or vulnerabilities associated with the successful or unsuccessful resolution of them. However, the passage through the stages is more variable than the theory suggests and people can return to past stages in later life (Valliant, 1977).

From Erikson's theoretical perspective, wisdom is the final stage of personality development, and has little to do with intelligence, although presumably a minimum level of intelligence is required to resolve all of the lifecycle dilemmas. An alternative view is that wisdom is the final stage of cognitive and intellectual development characterised by sophisticated problem solving, an issue discussed in the next section.

Wisdom as the final stage of cognitive development

Riegel (1973) has suggested that in late adolescence, after people have passed through Piaget's (1976) four stages of cognitive development, they enter the stage of dialectical operations. The significance of dialectical thinking for problem solving in adulthood has been explored by Basseches (1984) and it is clear from this work that the extensive use of dialectical thinking to solve complex human problems in adulthood is one way of conceptualising wisdom.

Dialectical thinking will be described below after briefly summarising Piaget's stages of development.

Sensorimotor stage

According to Piaget, children progress through four main stages on the way to developing adult thinking skills. In the first of these – the sensorimotor period – which extends from birth until about 2 years of age, the child's approach to problem solving and knowledge acquisition is based upon manipulating objects and trial-and-error learning. The main achievements of this stage are the development of cause-and-effect sensorimotor schemas and the concept of object permanence, that is, the realisation that objects have a permanent existence independent of our perception of them.

Pre-operational stage

The second stage of development in Piagetian theory is the pre-operational period. During this stage the child moves from the use of sensorimotor schemas as the main problem-solving tool to the formation of internal representations of the external world. The ability to use internal representations of the world to solve problems underpins a number of important achievements readily observable in pre-schoolers. These include increasingly sophisticated language usage, engagement in make-believe or symbolic play, the ability to distinguish between appearance and reality and the ability to infer what other people are thinking. Reasoning in the pre-operational period is largely intuitive, with the child linking one particular instance to another rather than reasoning from general to particular. For example, a pre-operational child will say, *I'm tired so it must be night-time* rather than *It's getting dark so it must be night time*. The pre-operational child's attempts to solve problems are influenced to a marked degree by what is perceived rather than by what is remembered. The main limitations of the pre-operational period are an inability to take the visual perspective of another person, difficulty in retelling a story coherently (egocentric speech), a belief that inanimate objects can think and feel like people (animism), and an inability to focus on more than one dimension of a problem at a time. For example, if liquid is poured from a short wide glass into a tall narrow glass, the pre-operational child may say there is now more liquid because the level is higher, without making reference to the decreased width of the second glass. Piaget referred to the capacity to take account of two dimensions simultaneously as conservation of quantity.

Concrete operational stage

Conservation of quantity is one of the primary achievements of the concrete operational period which extends from between 5 and 7 years up until about

12 years. The concrete operational period is the third of Piaget's developmental stages. During this period the child develops the ability to classify objects, place objects in series, engage in rule-governed games, adopt the geographic perspective of another person and manipulate numbers using addition, subtraction, multiplication and division. These abilities involve the use of logic (rather than intuition) to solve concrete problems.

Formal operational stage

At about the age of 12 the child begins to use logic to solve abstract problems. That is, the child can develop hypotheses about what might be true and then make plans to test these hypotheses out. This is the primary characteristic of the formal operational period. This is Piaget's fourth and final developmental stage. There are many achievements which occur during this period. The adolescent can manipulate two or more logical categories such as speed and distance when planning a trip. Time-related changes can be projected so the adolescent can predict that her relationship with her parents will be different in ten years. The logical consequences of actions can be predicted, so career options related to certain courses of study can be anticipated. The adolescent can detect logical inconsistencies such as those that occur when parents do not practise what they preach. A final achievement of the formal operational period is the capacity for relativistic thought. Teenagers can see that their own behaviour and that of their parents is influenced by situational factors.

Piaget's developmental theory has been partially supported by empirical research, but it is clear that significant variability occurs in temporal development of children's thinking skills and that some children develop sophisticated thinking skills earlier than Piaget suggested (Chen and Siegler, 2000). There is also considerable evidence for a further stage of cognitive development which occurs in adulthood: the stage of dialectical operations.

Dialectical operational stage

Alongside the extraordinary achievements which typify the stage of formal operations, there are limitations which characterise thinking during this period. Just as egocentric pre-schoolers cannot take another person's perspective because they do not realise that others occupy a different geographical location from themselves, young adolescents do not realise that others occupy different (and less logical) philosophical positions from themselves. This cognitive egocentricism compromises the adolescent's capacity to solve interpersonal problems that entail logical conflicts and contradictions. Riegel (1973) has suggested that this limitation of the formal operational period is overcome in a final stage of cognitive development which he refers to as the period of dialectical operations, in which dialectical thinking develops.

Dialectical thinking may involve reasoning about time and space. In dialectical reasoning about problems involving different perspectives in space, there is a recognition that different people may hold different beliefs about what is right or true depending upon their perspective, their geographic and social context. When dialectical thinking occurs and involves taking account of different points in time, there is a recognition that people's ideas evolve over time in an unending process of thesis–antithesis–synthesis. So an idea that may seem absolutely true and right to a person at one point in time may later seem false in light of new evidence and ideas, and later still, the old and new ideas may be synthesised into a completely new idea that seems right and true. Wisdom, from this theoretical perspective, involves the application of dialectical thinking to solving complex problems.

Wisdom as expert knowledge

Baltes and Staudinger (2000) view wisdom as involving both personality and cognitive processes. Baltes and Staudinger (2000) define wisdom as an expert knowledge system concerning the pragmatics of life that links mind and virtue. This system includes knowledge and judgements about the meaning of life and the way to conduct one's life in the pursuit of excellence, with due regard to both personal well-being and the common good. Wisdom is an expert knowledge system concerned with the fundamental pragmatics of life, that is with understanding planning and managing a good life. Wisdom covers knowledge about human development in all its complexity and variations; about the multiple biological, psychological, social, cultural, physical and spiritual contexts associated with the human condition; and about the limits of one's own knowledge and expertise in making judgements about complex life events.

Baltes and Staudinger (2000) have developed five criteria by which the quality of a wise judgement or behaviour may be evaluated. First, wisdom entails a rich store of declarative knowledge, that is knowing facts about development, and the contextual nature of the human condition. Second, wisdom involves a rich repertoire of procedural knowledge, that is knowledge about how to perform certain skills and routines such as complex decision making about interpersonal problems or conflict resolution. Third, wisdom involves lifespan contextualism, that is an appreciation of the many themes and contexts of life such as the self, family, peer group, school, workplace, community, society and culture and the variations and interrelations among these across the lifespan. Fourth, wisdom entails a relativism of values and life priorities with a tolerance for differences in values and priorities held by individuals and society in the service of the common good. The wise person is respectful of the unique sets of values that other people hold, since the common good can be achieved by many routes. Fifth, wisdom entails a recognition and management of uncertainty and a tolerance for ambiguity (Kirton, 1981). It involves an appreciation that, when solving any problem, each of us has access to incomplete information about the past and present; uncertainty about the future; and limited information-processing capacity. Thus our problem-solving strategies must take account of these uncertainties.

In their research on wisdom, participants in Baltes's studies are given difficult dilemmas to resolve and asked to speak aloud about their decision-making process. For example, what should a person take into consideration and do if they receive a call from a suicidal friend? Or, what should people take into consideration and do if they realise that they have not achieved what they wished in their lives? Recordings of think-aloud answers are rated on 7-point scales (using a rating manual) for each of the five criteria for wisdom mentioned above. Scores above 5 in all areas are interpreted as indicative of wisdom. In addition, participants are asked to complete a battery of ability and personality tests and historical lifespan inventories. A summary of some of the results of Baltes's work is given in Figure 5.2. The

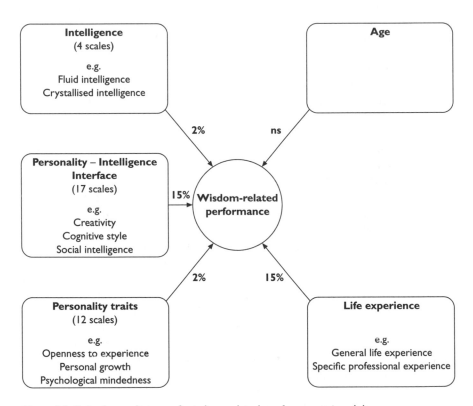

Figure 5.2 Baltes's predictors of wisdom-related performance in adults
Source: Adapted from Baltes & Staudinger (2000): 130.

results show that variables that combine aspects of analytical intelligence with aspects of personality such as social intelligence and cognitive style account for 15 per cent of the variance, as does life experience. Analytic intelligence as measured by formal IQ tests and personality traits from traditional personality inventories only accounted for 2 per cent of the variance each. In other studies where performance alone on the wisdom task mentioned above was compared with performance in situations where participants could consult with others about each problem, higher levels of wisdom were shown in the consultation condition. This underlines the idea that wisdom is facilitated by collaborative consultation.

Wisdom as balance

Sternberg's (2000a) balance theory of wisdom is derived from his triarchic theory of intelligence, which will be briefly described here.

Triarchic theory of intelligence

In Sternberg's (1997) triarchic theory of intelligence he argues that effective adaptation to the environment, and hence successful use of intelligence, involves combining analytic intelligence with practical intelligence and creative intelligence. Analytic intelligence consists of the information-processing skills that guide intelligent behaviour. Practical intelligence involves the skills required to create an optimal match between one's skills and the external environment. Creative intelligence involves the ability to capitalise upon experience to process novel or unfamiliar information.

Analytic intelligence

Three sets of information-processing components constitute analytic intelligence. These are: knowledge-acquisition components; performance components; and metacomponents. Knowledge-acquisition components include selective encoding (choosing what is important from a new set of information), selective combination (arranging new bits of information into a meaningful whole) and selective comparison (relating new ideas to what is known). Performance components include encoding the elements of a problem, comparing one's own solution with other possible solutions, justifying one's solution and implementing the solution. Metacomponents, which involve using knowledge-acquisition and performance components, include recognising problems, defining problems in solvable terms, forming mental representations of problems, formulating strategies for solving problems, allocating resources to implement these problem-solving strategies, monitoring the implementation of these strategies and evaluating the effectiveness of solutions.

Practical intelligence

While analytic intelligence is useful for solving clearly defined problems with a single right answer (like doing a maths problem), practical intelligence is useful for solving vaguely defined problems with multiple possible solutions, such as deciding what to do about a friend who has a drug abuse problem or using a map to plan a route efficiently. Practical intelligence is the application of analytical intelligence to solving everyday problems. People use practical intelligence to adapt to their current social environments; to change or shape current social environments so that they can adapt to them; or to select new social environments in which there is a better fit between their analytical abilities and the types of problems they must solve to adapt to those environments. An important aspect of practical intelligence is tacit knowledge. Tacit knowledge is the procedural knowledge (knowing how to do something) needed to solve everyday problems important for achieving valued goals, which is rarely explicitly taught or verbalised and accumulates with experience in specific environments.

Creative intelligence

Creative intelligence refers to the skills required to use experience to find procedures to solve novel or unfamiliar problems and automatise these procedures rapidly, so as to free up cognitive capacity to process more new information.

Sternberg's balance theory of wisdom

Sternberg's (2000a) balance theory of wisdom is derived from his triarchic theory of intelligence. According to balance theory, wisdom is the application of practical intelligence, and the tacit knowledge that such intelligence entails, to solve problems in a way that achieves a common good. This goal of achieving the common good is informed by ethical values. Such values entail information about what is right and good. The model is presented in Figure 5.3.

Balancing interests and responses

Wisdom involves applying tacit knowledge to problem solving in a way that achieves a balance among multiple interests:

1. intrapersonal interests (i.e. personal wishes);
2. interpersonal interests (i.e. things that would be good for relationships with others involved in the problem situation);
3. and extrapersonal interests (i.e. things that would be good for everyone affected by the problem situation within society).

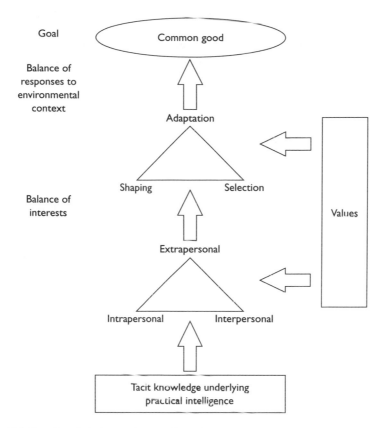

Figure 5.3 Sternberg's balance theory of wisdom
Source: Adapted from Sternberg (2000a): 638

Wisdom also involves applying tacit knowledge to problem solving in a way that achieves a balance among multiple types of responses to environmental contexts. These responses include:

1. adapting to the current social environment;
2. shaping the current social environment so that adaptation can occur; or
3. selecting a new social environment in which there is a better fit between analytical abilities and the types of problems that must be solved for successful adaptation to occur.

So wisdom, according to Sternberg's balance theory, is the use of practical intelligence in a way that balances one's own interests and those of others involved with the problem and the wider community to achieve a common good for all. Usually the outcome of wisdom is a judgement or advice on how to solve a complex problem involving multiple competing interests and this usually involves a statement about some people conforming or adapting to the environment; some people taking steps to shape the environment so they can fit into it with greater ease; and some people selecting a new environment which suits their skills and interests better.

Wisdom and tacit knowledge

Because wisdom involves the use of tacit knowledge, it cannot be taught. Tacit knowledge is acquired through personal experience and possibly through modelling, but not formal instruction. So, according to Sternberg's theory, although wisdom cannot be taught in a didactic way, people may be helped to become wise by becoming apprenticed to a person skilled in solving complex problems. Indeed, this is the way clinical psychologists, physicians and other professionals acquire wisdom. They undergo placements of supervised clinical practice in which they observe their supervisor solving complex problems and then try to do likewise and receive feedback on doing so. Because tacit knowledge and practical intelligence are specific to particular contexts, people develop wisdom in circumscribed domains. A person wise in our culture might not be wise in another culture. Because wisdom involves solving complex problems with no single right answer, it probably requires people to have progressed through the various stages of intellectual development outlined by Piaget and reached the neo-Piagetian stage of dialectical thinking mentioned above (Riegel, 1973).

Why are some people wiser than others?

According to balance theory, individual differences in wisdom may be due to many factors. People may differ in their commitment to the goal of solving problems to achieve a common good. People may differ in their values concerning what is good or right. There may be individual differences in people's capacity to balance multiple interests (intrapersonal, interpersonal and extrapersonal) and multiple responses (adapting, shaping and selecting environments). People may differ in their level of tacit knowledge and the breadth of domains in which they have tacit knowledge. All of these differences in factors that contribute to the balancing process involved in making wise judgements may be due to a range of antecedent factors such as age, experience, motivation, personality, and practical creative and analytic intelligence.

IMPLICATIONS

The material covered in this chapter has a series of implications for clinical practice which are summarised in Table 5.2.

Table 5.2 Implications of research on giftedness, creativity and wisdom

Helping gifted children	• Give gifted children mainstream schooling with an adapted curriculum and a teaching assistant to meet their unique profile of abilities. • Arrange access for gifted children to a peer group of similarly talented youngsters. • At home support the development of their special talents.
Focus on strengths	• For all clients, design homework tasks that require clients using their strengths and talents, since they will be more likely to do these.
Fostering personal creativity	• Provide yourself with environments in which there are many opportunities to select a domain or part of a domain in which to be creative. • Every day set yourself a problem to solve that is of interest to you. • Every day create a distraction-free environment in which to explore numerous framings of the problem. • Work on the problem for an uninterrupted period and then write down what you achieved. • Create a vision of what problem you want to solve or what art you wish to create. • In creating this intuitive vision, use metaphor, emotional language and vague or poetic language if you cannot be precise. • Develop basic skills to enter the domain (linguistic, mathematical, musical, artistic or athletic). • Master all the relevant domain-specific knowledge so you reproduce the domain in your mind. • Widen the span of your attention both to the inner and outer world and give up taking usual assumptions, rules and practices for granted. • Irreverently question orthodoxies and be playfully curious about why things are so. • Focus attention on doing the task and completing it to your own satisfaction, not for outside rewards. • Work to do your personal best rather than to beat the competition. • Take risks when you come up with possible ideas or tentative solutions, no matter how bizarre these might be. • Be optimistic that you can improve your creative output. • When you reach an *impasse* create subgoals by working backwards from the main goal; then work forwards step-wise from where you are to the goals. • When you reach an *impasse* list all the attributes of a problem or potential solution and then recombine them in different ways; consider extreme cases (small and large); use elimination, substitution, combination, modification, rearrangement, of one or all elements to rethink the solution. • When you reach an *impasse* consider an analogous problem; work with a number of metaphorical representations of the problem; consider the problem in terms of visual, auditory and verbal representations.

Table 5.2 (Cont'd)

	• When you reach an *impasse* set the problem aside and work on something else to allow incubation to occur and then return to the problem refreshed. • Produce a lot of creative efforts and your most creative work will come when you are most productive.
Making wise judgements	• When faced with a complex problem, remember that each of us has access to incomplete information about the past and present; uncertainty about the future; and limited information processing capacity so our judgements are always imperfect, constrained and should always be open to revision. • When trying to solve complex problems recognise that different people may hold different beliefs about what is right or true depending upon their perspective, their geographic and social context, and also remember that people's ideas evolve over time. • For complex problems consider the many themes and contexts of life such as the self, family, peer group, school, workplace, community, society and culture and the variations and interrelations among these across the lifespan. • When making judgements about a complex problem, balance your own interests and those of others involved with the problem and the wider community to achieve a common good for all and expect that the outcome of such decision making will usually involve a statement about some people conforming or adapting to the environment; some people taking steps to shape the environment so they can fit into it with greater ease; and some people selecting a new environment which suits their skills and interests better. • In later life when you look back consider integrating failures, disappointments, conflicts, growing incompetencies and frailty into a coherent life story, rather than opting for a legend based exclusively on mastery.

Giftedness

Within child and adolescent clinical psychology, the findings on giftedness may be used for psychoeducation, when parents are asking how to deal with gifted children. To help gifted children avoid adjustment problems they require mainstream schooling with an adapted curriculum and additional allocated staffing to meet their unique profile of abilities. In addition they require access to a peer group of similarly talented youngsters. At home they require space, time and support to make the most of their special talents. A second implication of the research on giftedness concerns the practice of clinical psychology generally. When we ask our clients to do homework assignments between sessions, we should always try to frame assignments that involve clients using their strengths and talents, since this makes it more likely that they will complete the assignment.

Creativity

For children, adolescents, adults and clinical psychologists who wish to be creative in their day-to-day lives, there are many implications from the research on creativity. Gardner (1993) distinguished between little 'c' creativity – relatively common small departures from daily routines – and big 'C' creativity – relatively rare major innovations which affect our culture. Small 'c' creativity can be enhanced (Nickerson, 1999).

The development of creativity involves a set of processes which can be practised (Nickerson, 1999). First, provide yourself with environments in which there are many opportunities to choose from, that is many opportunities to select a domain or part of a domain in which to be creative. If you want to find a creative solution to a particular problem, then create a distraction-free environment in which to explore numerous framings of the problem. You can do this every day by setting one goal you wish to achieve, working on that for an uninterrupted period and then writing down what you achieved.

Manage your time carefully. Make spaces in which you can be creative. Do more of what you like and less of what you hate.

Second, create a vision of where you want to go, what problem you want to solve, or what art you wish to create. Use metaphor, emotional language and vague or poetic language if you cannot be precise. Listen to your inner intuitions when getting a sense of this vision.

Third, develop basic skills to enter the domain. These may be linguistic, mathematical, musical, artistic or athletic.

The fourth process is to become immersed in the domain, master all the relevant domain-specific knowledge and reproduce the domain within the mind. In a sense you must come to master the domain. Begin with a simple representation of the domain but aim in the long term for increasing complexity.

The fifth process is to create a context that encourages curiosity and exploration. This involves practising being very observant, widening the span of attention both to the outer world and inner thoughts about the outer world and allowing oneself to wonder at the wide range of things one observes. This wonder involves: giving up taking usual assumptions, rules and practices for granted; irreverently questioning orthodoxies; like a child, being playfully curious about why things are so and how they might be otherwise. Each day try to notice three things that surprise you and write these down. Also try to surprise other people a couple of times each day and write these down.

The sixth process is to motivate yourself to be passionate about the area. This involves being genuinely interested in the task, and focusing attention on doing the task and completing it to your own satisfaction rather than being distracted by the pay-off for doing the task. Accept praise and rewards for remaining task-focused, but if your attention continually strays on to the rewards for doing the task, then passion for the task will suffer and less creativity will occur. Working for goals set by others is not conducive to creativity. However, accommodating the goals of others within your own vision of where a project is going is conducive to creativity.

The seventh process involves working to do your personal best rather than to beat the competition. You are more likely to come up with original ideas if your goal is to do better than you did the last time, rather than better someone else.

The eighth process is to develop a habit of taking risks. When you come up with possible ideas or tentative solutions, no matter how bizarre these might be, do not judge them and reject them too early. New ideas are to be highly valued, especially when they entail taking risks. If you do not take risks you will conform to conventions and so will not be original and creative.

The ninth process is to nurture the optimistic belief that you can improve your creative output. The idea that your creative potential is wholly genetically determined will stifle your creativity. There is good evidence that motivation, commitment and persistence are as important as genetic factors.

The tenth process involves developing strategies for breaking through *impasses*. Create subgoals; work backwards from the main goal; work forwards step-wise from where you are to the goals; do a means–end analysis; list all the attributes of a problem or potential solution and then recombine them in different ways; consider an analogous problem; work with a number of metaphorical representations of the problem; consider the problem in terms of visual, auditory and verbal representations; consider extreme cases (small and large); use elimination, substitution, combination, modification, rearrangement of one or all elements to rethink the solution. If you are still at an *impasse*, set the problem aside and work on something else, sleep on it, take a walk or do something distracting to allow incubation to occur. Then return to the problem refreshed.

The final process is to be patient. Creativity and originality take time. Produce a lot of creative efforts and products and your most creative work will come when you are most productive.

Wisdom

For adult clients and for ourselves as clinicians the research on wisdom has a number of implications. There is value throughout life in attempting to integrate failures, disappointments, conflicts, growing incompetencies and frailty into a coherent life story, rather than opting for a legend based exclusively on mastery. There is value in being open to achievements and failures; accepting of one's parents as people who did their best, and so deserve love, but were not perfect; accepting of one's own life as the best we can live; and accepting of the inevitability of death, particularly as we move into middle life.

For adult clients and for ourselves as clinicians there is value when reasoning about problems involving different perspectives in recognising that different people may hold different beliefs about what is right or true depending upon their perspective, their geographic and social context. There is also value in recognising that people's ideas evolve over time in an unending process of thesis–antithesis–synthesis. So an idea that may seem absolutely true and right to a person at one point in time may later seem false in light of new evidence and ideas, and later still, the old and new ideas may be synthesised into a completely new idea that seems right and true.

There is value in an appreciation of the many themes and contexts of life such as the self, family, peer group, school, workplace, community, society and culture and the variations and interrelations among these across the lifespan. There is value in recognising that the values and life priorities of different people may be different. There is value in appreciating that when solving any problem, each of us has access to incomplete information about the past and present; uncertainty about the future; and limited information-processing capacity. So our judgements are always imperfect, constrained and should always be open to revision.

When making judgements in complex situations, there is value in deliberately attempting to balance one's own interests and those of others involved with the problem and the wider community to achieve a common good for all. There is also value in accepting that the outcome of such decision making will usually involve a statement about some people conforming or adapting to the environment; some people taking steps to shape the environment so they can fit into it with greater ease; and some people selecting a new environment which suits their skills and interests better.

CONTROVERSIES

In the field of giftedness there is controversy over the relative importance of innate endowment and intensive practice. Some researchers argue that the talents of gifted children are the product of intensive deliberate practice (e.g. Howe, 1999) while others argue that the talents of gifted children are innate (Winner, 2000). There is evidence that most gifted children show outstanding talent before practice, but then are motivated to practise a great deal to master their talent. In the field of creativity, there is debate about whether intelligence and creativity are separate sets of abilities, overlapping or correlated sets of abilities, or whether creativity is a subset of the skills that along with other abilities make up intelligence (Sternberg, 1999). In the field of wisdom research, the construct has been conceptualised as a final stage of personality development, a final stage of cognitive development and as a high level of skill development that entails both personality and cognitive processes. Empirical studies offer greater support for these latter theories (Baltes and Staudinger, 2000).

SUMMARY

Giftedness in childhood, creativity in adulthood and wisdom in later life are three of the outstanding achievements across the lifespan that have been studied by psychologists. Gifted children's talents are largely inherited but these children typically engage in extensive practice which further enhances their performance. Gifted children usually grow up in child-centred families where parents model hard work and high achievement, provide an intellectually and artistically stimulating environment, offer their children a high level of autonomy, but expect a high level of excellence from them. Gifted children show double the rate of behavioural adjustment problems of non-gifted children. At a biological level they often have enhanced right hemisphere development, or if they have extremely high overall intelligence this is subserved by greater brain mass. When very intelligent people are free to engage in a mental activity of their choosing, they show high levels of cortical activity. However, when given a problem to solve they show lower levels of cortical activity than normal controls. Only a minority of gifted children go on to become creative adults who make major innovative contributions to their field.

Csikszentmihalyi has argued that creativity is a systemic process in which a creative individual who has become immersed in a domain develops an original idea and presents it to practitioners within the field. Certain domains and the culture within which they occur; fields and the societies within which they occur; and personal attributes probably favour creativity. According to Sternberg and Lubart's investment theory of creativity, individuals make creative contributions to a field when they 'buy' or adopt poorly developed ideas which are unpopular or unfamiliar but which have growth potential, invest creatively in these and develop them into 'creative products' before moving on to 'new' unpopular ideas with growth potential. Acts of creativity, which may appear as sudden insights into how particular problems may be solved, typically follow long and hard work on details related to the problem and its solution, and a period of incubation during which problem solving occurs in the cognitive unconscious. Torrance's (1974) Test of Creative Thinking is still the most widely used psychometric research instrument in the field and correlates moderately with IQ measured by conventional intelligence tests. Personality traits associated with creativity include openness to experiences, rebelliousness and ambition. Intrinsic motivation is essential for creativity. From a biological perspective creative people show low levels of cortical activation during the inspiration stage of creativity and higher levels of cortical activation when resting than non-creative people. From a theoretical perspective wisdom has been conceptualised as a final stage of personality development, a final stage of cognitive development and a high level of skill development that entails both personality and cognitive processes. Empirical studies offer greater support for these latter theories.

QUESTIONS

Personal development questions

1. Describe a situation that occurred within the past month, in which you successfully found a creative solution to a difficult problem or made a wise judgement.
2. What skills did you use to do this?
3. Describe a situation that occurred within the past month, in which it was critical for you to find a creative solution to a difficult problem or to make a wise judgement, but you were not successful in doing so.
4. What skills would you like to have had so that you could have found a creative solution or made a wise judgement?
5. What steps can you now take to develop these skills?
6. What would be the costs and benefits of taking these steps?
7. Take some of these steps and assess the impact it has on your well-being by assessing yourself before and afterwards on one of the well-being scales contained in Chapter 1.

Research questions

1. Design and conduct a study to test the hypotheses that there is a significant correlation between creativity and intelligence, but no significant correlation between happiness and either creativity or intelligence.
2. Conduct PsychInfo searches covering literature published in the past couple of years using the terms 'giftedness', 'creativity' and 'wisdom'. Identify a study that interests you and that is feasible to replicate and extend. Conduct the replication.

FURTHER READING

Academic

Sternberg, R. (1999). *Handbook of Creativity*. Cambridge, UK: Cambridge University Press. Ch. 8 on giftedness and ch. 28 on wisdom.
Sternberg, R. (2000b). *Handbook of Intelligence*. Cambridge, UK: Cambridge University Press.

Self-help: gifted children

Winner, E. (1996). *Gifted Children: Myths and Realities.* New York: Basic Books. For parents of gifted children.

Teaching creativity in schools

Adams, M. (1986). *Odyssey: A Curriculum for Thinking.* Watertown, MA: Mastery Education Corporation. (A programme containing about 100 lessons on thinking, including some on creative thinking.)

Covinton, M., Crutchfield, R., Davies, L., and Olton, R. (1974). *The Productive Thinking Program: A Course in Learning to Think.* Columbus, OH: Merrill. (A 15-booklet course for fifth and sixth graders which covers general thinking skills and creativity skills.)

De Bono, E. (1973). *CoRT Thinking.* Blanfort, UK: Direct Educational Services. (A six-unit programme for teaching school children thinking skills. Unit 4 deals with creative thinking.)

Self-help: lateral thinking

De Bono, E. (1971). *Lateral Thinking for Management.* New York: McGraw-Hill.

De Bono, E. (1985). *Six Thinking Hats.* Boston: Little Brown.

De Bono, E. (1992). *Serious Creativity: Using the Poser of Lateral Thinking to Create New Ideas.* New York: Harper Collins.

Self-help: brainstorming and creative problem solving

Cropley, A. (1992). *More Ways than One: Fostering Creativity.* Norwood, NY: Ablex.

Gordon, W. (1981). *The New Art of the Possible: The Basic Course in Synectics.* Cambridge, MA: Porpoise Books. (Describes an approach to creative problem solving based largely on using metaphor and analogy.)

Hayes, J. (1989). *The Complete Problem Solver* (2nd edn). Hillsdale, NJ: Erlbaum.

Isaksen, S. and Treffinger, D. (1985). *Creative Problem Solving: The Basic Course.* Buffalo, NY: Bearly. (A good book on creative problem solving.)

Osborn, A. (1963). *Applied Imagination: Principles and Procedures of Creative Thinking.* New York: Scribner's. (The original book on brainstorming.)

Parnes, (1981). *Magic of Your Mind.* Buffalo, NY: Bearly. (A book on creative problem solving.)

Sanders, D. and Sanders, J. (1984). *Teaching Creativity through Metaphor.* New York: Longman. (Describes an approach to creative problem solving based largely on using metaphor and analogy.)

Treffinger, D., McEwen, P. and Witting, C. (1989). *Using Creative Problem Solving in Inventing.* Noneoye, NY: Centre for Creative Learning.

Self-help: concentration and studying

Baddley, A. (1983). *Your Memory: A User's Guide.* Harmondsworth, UK: Penguin. Contains much practical advice on how to remember things along with scientific background to memory.
Moran, A. (2000). *Managing Your Own Learning at University: A Practical Guide.* Dublin: UCD Press.

MEASURES FOR USE IN RESEARCH

Hawley, G. (1999). *Measures of Psychosocial Development.* Odessa, FL: Psychological Assessment Resources. (Measures resolution of dilemmas entailed by Erikson's stages of development including the final stage which involves wisdom.)
Kirton, M. (1981). A reanalysis of two scales of tolerance to ambiguity. *Journal of Personality Assessment* 45: 407–14.
Torrance, E. (1974). *Torrance Tests of Creative Thinking: Norms-Technical Manual.* Lexington, MA: Ginn.

GLOSSARY

Analytic intelligence. The information-processing skills that guide intelligent behaviour.
Balance theory of wisdom. Sternberg's view that wisdom is the application of practical intelligence, and the tacit knowledge that such intelligence entails, to solve problems in a way that achieves a common good.
Creative intelligence. The ability to capitalise upon experience to process novel or unfamiliar information.
Creativity. The capacity to produce work that is both novel and useful.
Dialectical operations. Riegel's view that there is a form of reasoning which develops after the stage of formal operations in which there is a recognition that people's ideas evolve over time, space and different social contexts in an unending process of thesis–antithesis–synthesis.
Giftedness. Outstanding ability and performance in one or more domains.
Investment theory of creativity. Sternberg and Lubart's view that individuals make creative contributions to a field when they 'buy' or adopt poorly developed ideas which are unpopular or unfamiliar but which have growth potential, invest creatively in these and develop them into 'creative products' before moving on to 'new' unpopular ideas with growth potential.
Multiple intelligences. Gardener's view that there are eight distinct intelligences: linguistic; logical-mathematical; spatial; musical; bodily kinesthetic; interpersonal; intrapersonal; and naturalist.
Practical intelligence. Capacity to create an optimal match between one's skills and the external environment.
Systems model of creativity. Csikszentmihalyi's view that creativity arises from a process which involves the dynamic interaction of three distinct systems: (1) the

person with his or her talents, personality traits and motivations; (2) the domain which consists of the symbol-system, rules, techniques, practices and guiding paradigm; and (3) the field which consists of people working within the same domain (artists, scientists, critics, journal editors) whose activity is governed by the same domain-specific rules and practices.

Triarchic theory of intelligence.   Sternberg's view that effective adaptation to the environment involves combining analytic intelligence with practical intelligence and creative intelligence.

Wisdom.   Exceptional personal and interpersonal competence including the abilities to listen, evaluate and give advice, used for the well-being of self and others.

Chapter 6

Positive traits and motives

Learning objectives

- Be able to describe trait theories of personality, notably the five-factor theory.
- Be able to give an account of the assessment of trait-related strengths and the genetic and environmental basis for them.
- Understand the lifespan development of trait-related strengths, resilient personality profiles and the neurobiological basis for trait-related strengths.
- Be able to distinguish between trait-like and state-like motives.
- Appreciate how trait-like motives can be regarded as personal strengths and that particular constellations of state-like motives facilitate subjective well-being.
- Understand the clinical implications of research on traits and motive-related strengths for facilitating happiness.
- Be able to identify research questions that need to be addressed to advance our understanding of traits and motive-related strengths on the one hand and happiness on the other.

An important body of empirical research on positive traits and motives has developed which is of relevance to positive psychology. This research points to links between certain traits, and motives on the one hand and personal strengths or subjective well-being on the other. Traits and emotions are complex constructs so let us begin by defining these terms.

Traits

Traits are relatively enduring personal characteristics, which, along with situational variables, influence behaviour, cognition and affect. For example, if we have a high level of the trait of conscientiousness we will tend to complete academic assignments or occupational tasks in a reliable and punctual way. Personality traits differ from states. Traits, such as conscientiousness, are enduring. States, in contrast, are transitory and situation specific. For example, 'being busy' is a state. In this chapter our focus will be on the five-factor trait theory of personality, since this currently is one of the most influential and parsimonious trait theories (McCrae and Costa,1999).

Motives

Motives are dispositions that energise us to pursue particular sets of goals. For example, if we have a strong intimacy motive we strive to form close interpersonal relationships. Motives that are enduring and trait-like, such as the intimacy motive, or more transient and state-like, have been identified. Striving to ask a prospective romantic partner for a date is an example of a more transient state-like motive. In this chapter, frameworks for conceptualising enduring and transient positive motives will be addressed. Intrinsic and extrinsic motivation and metamotivational states associated with reversal theory which are particularly relevant to the study of flow experiences have already been discussed in Chapter 2.

TRAIT THEORIES OF PERSONALITY AND PERSONAL STRENGTHS

Trait theories argue that a limited number of dimensions may be used to characterise important aspects of behaviour and experience. Implicit in such theories is the idea that a person's status on some, or all, of these traits may be associated with certain personal strengths. Traits are normally distributed within the population. So for any given trait (for example extraversion) most people show a moderate level of the trait, but a few people show extremely low or extremely high levels of the trait. In recent years trait theory has come to be dominated by the Five-Factor Model of Personality (McCrae and Costa, 1999). This model includes the following dimensions: neuroticism; extraversion; openness to experience; agreeableness; and conscientiousness.

The five factors have been derived from the semantic clustering of an exhaustive list of adjectives describing personality traits abstracted from dictionaries in a number of languages and extensive factor-analytic studies of self-report and observer-rated items based on these lists (John and Srivastava, 1999; McCrae and Costa, 1999). Within the broad tradition of trait theory there has been considerable controversy over the precise number of traits that may appropriately be used to describe personality functioning. For example, Eysenck (1990) argued that three traits (neuroticism, extraversion and psychoticism) could account for most aspects of personality functioning. In contrast, Cattell (1990) argued that 16 traits were required.

Differences in the number of traits in these models are due to differences in the factor-analytic methods used and the range of items analysed.

The Five-Factor Model of Personality builds on the insights of Eysenck, Cattell and others (McCrae, 2000). The first two dimensions are the same as those proposed by Eysenck. Furthermore, the traits of agreeableness and conscientiousness are two aspects of Eysenck's psychoticism factor. Disagreeable people are interpersonally cold and people low on conscientiousness disregard social conventions. Openness to experience refers to a dimension that extends from imaginative creativeness to constriction. Furthermore, secondary factor analyses of Cattell's 16 factors yield broadband factors similar to some of those within the Five-Factor Model.

From Table 6.1 it may be seen that each of the factors within the Five-Factor Model comprises six facets (Costa and McCrae, 1992). High scores

Table 6.1 Strengths entailed by the Five-Factor Model of Personality

Factor	Components	Correlated positive trait adjective
Stability / Neuroticism	N1. Courage / Anxiety	Not tense
	N2. Calmness / Angry hostility	Not irritable
	N3. Happiness / Depression	Contented
	N4. Positive self-regard / Self-consciousness	Not shy
	N5. Impulse control / Impulsiveness	Not moody
	N6. Resilience / Vulnerability	Self-confident
Extraversion	E1. Warmth	Outgoing
	E2. Gregrariousness	Sociable
	E3. Assertiveness	Forceful
	E4. Activity	Energetic
	E5. Excitement seeking	Adventurous
	E6. Positive emotions	Enthusiastic
Openness to experience	O1. Fantasy	Imaginative
	O2. Aesthetics	Artistic
	O3. Feelings	Excitable
	O4. Actions	Wide interests
	O5. Ideas	Curious
	O6. Values	Unconventional
Agreeableness	A1. Trust	Forgiving
	A2. Straightforwardness	Not demanding
	A3. Altruism	Warm
	A4. Compliance	Not stubborn
	A5. Modesty	Not showing off
	A6. Tender-mindedness	Sympathetic
Conscientiousness	C1. Competence	Efficient
	C2. Order	Organised
	C3. Dutifulness	Not careless
	C4. Achievement striving	Thorough
	C5. Self-discipline	Not lazy
	C6. Deliberation	Not impulsive

Source: Adapted from Costa and McCrae (1992).

on these facets may be viewed as personal strengths. Strengths associated with the facets of the stability–neuroticism dimension are: courage; calmness; happiness; self-esteem; impulse control; and resilience. Strengths associated with the six facets of extraversion are: warmth; gregariousness; assertiveness; activity; excitement seeking; and positive emotions. Openness entails the following strengths: openness to fantasy; openness to aesthetics; openness to novel feelings; openness to novel actions; openness to new ideas; and openness to different values. The six facets of agreeableness involve the following strengths: trust; straightforwardness; altruism; compliance; modesty; and tender-mindedness. Strengths associated with the six facets of conscientiousness are: competence; orderliness; dutifulness; achievement striving; self-discipline; and deliberation.

Assessment of trait-related strengths

Personality questionnaires and adjective checklists have been developed to evaluate the five factors of the Five-Factor Model. The five factors and the six facets associated with each of these may be assessed with the 240-item Revised NEO Personality Inventory (NEO-PI-R), (Costa and McCrae, 1992). The five factors, but not their facets, can be assessed with the briefer 60-item NEO Five-Factor Inventory (NEO-FFI), (Costa and McCrae, 1992). Goldberg (1992) has developed 100-unipolar item and 50-bipolar item trait-descriptive adjective checklists to assess the five factors. Oliver John has developed a brief 44-item Big Five Inventory which includes very brief items each containing a single adjective (John and Srivastava, 1999). The Inter-personal Adjective Scale provides a system for assessing the Big Five factors in a way that is consistent with the circumplex model of interpersonal behaviour (Wiggins, 1995) All of these instruments have good reliability and validity (John and Srivastava, 1999).

Genetic and environmental basis for trait-related strengths

An important question concerns the determinants of the strengths entailed by personality traits. Are these strengths innate and/or learned through a process of socialisation? The weight of evidence from twin studies shows that 50 per cent of the variance in extraversion and neuroticism and 40 per cent of the variance in agreeableness, conscientiousness and openness to experience may be accounted for by genetic factors (Plomin and Caspi, 1999). Thus, the variance in the trait-related strengths listed in Table 6.1 is due to approximately equal proportions of genetic and environmental factors.

With respect to the environmental determinants of trait-related strengths, there are good reasons to believe that secure attachment is an important precursor of positive adjustment on each of the personality traits in the Five-Factor Model (Cassidy and Shaver, 1999) and that parents who blend warmth with a moderate level of control in bringing up their children promote positive adjustment on these factors also (Darling and Steinberg, 1993). Early life precursors of later positive development are discussed further in Chapter 8 on positive relationships across the lifecycle.

The mechanisms by which genetic factors influence personality traits are complex. Probably multiple genes determine temperamental characteristics, and these interact with environmental influences in the development of personality traits. Heritability of personality traits is estimated from studies in which the similarity of pairs of people sharing differing amounts of genetic material in common are compared. In twin studies, which is one of the most common methods for studying heritability, a specific trait is assessed using a personality inventory or rating scale in a group of monozygotic or identical twins and a group of dyzygotic or fraternal twins. The monozygotic twins have identical genetic codes, whereas the dyzygotic twins share only 50 per cent of genetic material. Heritability is estimated using the following formula: $h^2 = 2(r_{mz} - r_{dz})$. In this formula h^2 is heritability, r_{mz} is the trait correlation for monozygotic twin pairs, and r_{dz} is the correlation for dyzygotic twin pairs (Rowe, 1997). Thus heritability is double the difference between the two correlations. For the Big 5 personality traits, this is usually about 0.4–0.5. Other formulae for calculating heritability are described in Rowe (1997).

Lifespan development of trait-related strengths

The way personal strengths associated with personality traits develop over the lifespan is a central concern. Research on temperament and its links to personality traits throws some light on this issue. Personality traits are underpinned by temperamental characteristics, and continuities have been identified between early temperamental profiles and later personality trait profiles (Rothbart and Ahadi, 1994). Temperament refers to the characteristic affective response style which is present from infancy and due to predominantly constitutional or hereditary factors.

The idea that temperament is subserved by biological factors and is the bedrock on which adult personality is based was first proposed by Hippocrates in BC fourth century and later expanded in the second century AD by Galen. Both proposed a link between the four humours and four distinctive temperaments which formed the core of four personality types (Murray, 1983). According to this position, people with a sanguine temperament developed a cheerful, active personality due to an excess of the humour – blood – associated with the heart. The development of a calm personality was associated with a phlegmatic temperament which was subserved by an excess of the humour – phlegm – associated with the brain. People

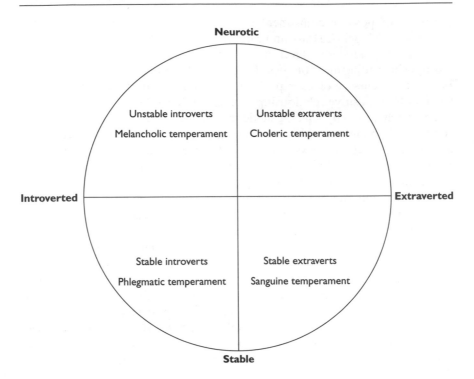

Figure 6.1 Temperament and personality
Source: Adapted from Eysenck and Eysenck (1975).

with a melancholic temperament developed a gloomy personality due to an excess of the humour – black bile – associated with the spleen. Finally, an excess of the humour – yellow bile – from the liver was thought to subserve a choleric temperament which led to the development of an aggressive personality. The late Professor Hans Eysenck at the University of London pointed out that these four temperaments correspond to the four quadrants defined by the orthogonal traits, neuroticism and extraversion (Eysenck and Eysenck, 1975). From Figure 6.1 it may be seen that using this two-factor model, stable introverts have phlegmatic temperaments while stable extraverts have sanguine temperaments. These are resilient temperamental styles. Melancholic temperaments characterise neurotic introverts, and unstable extraverts have choleric temperaments.

Table 6.2 offers a somewhat oversimplified representation of the correspondence between the factors in three of the more prominent models of temperament and the three- and five-factor theories of personality. The correspondences are based on both descriptions of the traits and temperament dimensions, and on research findings of continuity between temperament and personality traits. From Table 6.2 it may be seen that temperament has

Table 6.2 Temperament and personality traits

McCrae and Costa's (1999) Five-Factor Model of Personality	Eysenck and Eysenck's (1975) Three-Factor Model of Personality	Clark and Watson's (1999) Three-Factor Model of Adult Temperament	Buss and Plomin's (1975) Four-Factor Model of Childhood Temperament	Thomas and Chess's (1977) Nine-Factor Model of Infant Temperament
Stability–Neuroticism	Neuroticism	Negative temperament	Emotionality	Intensity of mood Sensory threshold Approach withdrawal Adaptability Rhythmicity
Extraversion–Introversion	Extraversion	Positive temperament	Sociability Activity	Predominant mood Activity level
Conscientiousness Agreeableness	Psychoticism	Disinhibition	Impulsivity	Attentional persistence Distractibility
Openness to experience				

Source: Based on Buss and Plomin (1975): 399–423; Clark and Watson (1999); Eysenck and Eysenck (1975); McCrae and Costa (1999): 139–53; Thomas and Chess (1977).

been classified in a variety of ways. Thomas and Chess's (1977) model of infant temperament contains nine factors which are rated by observers. Buss and Plomin's model (1975) of childhood temperament contains four factors which can be measured by the EASI Temperament Survey. The acronym EASI stands for the four factors in the model: emotionality; activity; sociability; and impulsivity. Clark and Watson (1999) have developed a three-factor model of adult temperament which is very similar to Eysenck's three-factor model of personality.

Evidence from modern longitudinal studies supports the link between temperament and personality traits (Rothbart and Ahadi, 1994). For example, children with high activity levels and positive affect become extraverted adults and reap the benefits of the strengths associated with extraversion. Children who show attentional persistence later develop high levels of conscientiousness and related personal strengths. Children who are highly irritable and fearful show high levels of neuroticism in later life. Children with extreme temperamental characteristics may be more vulnerable to environmental stressors or they may elicit reactions from parents and others that exacerbate their extreme temperamental characteristics.

In addition to the continuity between temperamental style and personality profile, there is also strong evidence that the Big Five personality traits follow a predictable lifespan trajectory and that this occurs within many cultures. Overall, personality traits are fairly constant across the lifespan. Individual differences are consistent across the lifespan for any individual, but all individuals are affected by general maturational trends. Between late adolescence and age 30, neuroticism, extraversion and openness to experience decline a little, while agreeableness and conscientiousness increase (McCrae et al., 1999). After age 30, change continues in the same direction but at a slower rate. Thus, young adults as a group have extraversion and openness as strengths, while older adults have stability, agreeableness and conscientiousness as strengths. However, major changes in personality traits do not occur over the lifespan and traits in early or midlife predict traits in later life.

Strengths of the resilient personality profile

Trait theory has led to the identification of a highly resilient personality profile, that is a profile which entails many personal strengths. Typological studies repeatedly identify three profiles associated with the Five-Factor Model. These are the resilient, overcontrolled and undercontrolled profiles (John and Srivastava, 1999). Resilient individuals show positive adjustment on all five factors. Overcontrolled people have high levels of agreeableness and conscientiousness coupled with low extraversion. Undercontrolled people have high scores on neuroticism, and low scores on agreeableness and conscientiousness. This profile is associated with delinquency.

The resilient profile is associated with all of the personal strengths listed in Table 6.1. Research on the correlates for the five factors shows that additional benefits are associated with high scores on each of the five dimensions (John and Srivastava, 1999). Extraversion is associated with good social adjustment and success in leadership, management and sales positions. Emotional stability (the opposite pole to neuroticism) is associated with good mental and physical health. Openness to experience is associated with creativity and a disposition towards absorption and peak experiences. Agreeableness is associated with altruism, good interpersonal relationships within work and social contexts. Conscientiousness is highly predictive of occupational performance (regardless of the occupation in question). Conscientiousness and openness together are predictive of good school performance.

Personality traits and well-being

Studies of the links between subjective well-being defined in both hedonic or eudaimonic terms show clear links between these constructs and personality dimension of the Big Five Model. In a meta-analysis of 197 samples containing over 40,000 adults, DeNeve and Cooper (1998) found that hedonically defined subjective well-being was consistently related to extraversion, emotional stability (the high functioning pole of the neuroticism dimension) and agreeableness. In a study of middle-aged adults, the relationship between the Big Five personality traits and the six dimensions of Carol Ryff's eudaimonic model of psychological well-being, Schmutte and Ryff (1997) found distinctive personality correlates for all dimensions of the model. Self-acceptance, environmental mastery and purpose in life were linked with emotional stability, extraversion and conscientiousness. Personal growth was linked with openness to experience and extraversion. Positive relations with others was linked with agreeableness and extraversion. Autonomy was linked with emotional stability.

Diener and Lucas (1999) point to five possible explanations for the association between personality traits and subjective well-being. Temperament models argue that the happiness set-point and personality traits are both predominantly genetically determined, hence the correlation between traits and well-being. In cognitive models it is assumed that genetically determined temperament influences the way we perceive and process information and this in turn influences subjective well-being. In socialisation models it is assumed that learning processes account for both the expression of personality traits and subjective well-being. In congruence models, the assumption is that subjective well-being occurs when there is a good fit between the person's personality trait profile and the environment, and certain personality profiles are associated with a greater facility for arranging a good person–environment fit. With goal models, it is assumed that the selection, pursuit and attainment of goals influence subjective well-being and certain personality profiles are associated with selecting, pursuing and attaining goals particularly conducive to happiness.

There is some evidence for each of these positions. In support of the temperament model, in Chapter 1 it was noted that about one half of the variance in current well-being and major personality traits is due to genetic factors and that over extended time periods the set-point for happiness is about 98 per cent genetically determined. In support of the cognitive model, in Chapter 3 it was noted that positive illusions, optimism and hope all influence levels of subjective well-being and it may be that these cognitive processes are partially grounded in genetically determined temperamental attributes. The literature on childhood attachment experiences and later adjustment mentioned in Chapter 4 lend some support to the socialisation model. With respect to the person–environment fit model, in Chapter 1 it was noted that there is evidence from studies of job satisfaction that good person–environment fit is associated with greater well-being, but evidence is lacking on whether certain personality profiles facilitate arranging this type of fit. Later in this chapter evidence for the relationship between certain patterns of explicit motives and subjective well-being is mentioned which offers some support for the goals model. Future research will refine our understanding of the psychological process which explains the link between personality and well-being.

Neurobiological basis for trait-related strengths

Research on the neurobiological basis of personal strengths associated with personality traits is still in its early stages. Professor Richard Depue (1996) at Cornell University, New York, in a synthesis of biological approaches to personality trait theory and a large body of empirical evidence from human and animal studies, argues that distinctions may be made between three neurobiological systems which roughly correspond to personality traits within the three- and five-factor models. The personality traits are extraversion, psychoticism, and neuroticism in Eysenck's system. In the Five-Factor Model they are extraversion, a combination of conscientiousness and agreeableness and neuroticism. Depue's synthesis builds on the earlier work of Professors Hans Eysenck (1967, 1990) and Jeffrey Gray (1987) in London and entails hypotheses about the possible neurobiological basis for trait-related strengths.

The first neurobiological system, the behavioural facilitation system (BFS), is activated by signals of reward. The BFS controls incentive-driven or goal-directed behaviour and activities associated with securing food, a sex partner, a nesting place and seeking other important goals and rewards. It is sometimes loosely referred to as the neurobiological reward system. The BFS includes the mesolimbic dopamine pathways which arise in the ventral tegmental area of the midbrain and project to the amygdala, hippocampus and nucleus accumbens in the limbic system. The reward system also includes the mesocortical dopamine pathways that originate in the ventral tegmental area and project onto all areas of the cortex. Individuals with an active BFS are strongly motivated by incentives and rewards to pursue goals. In personality trait models, the BFS corresponds approximately to extraversion. A high level of activity in the BFS is associated with extraversion while a low level of activity in the BFS is associated with introversion.

The second system in Depue's model corresponds to a combination of conscientiousness and agreeableness in the Five-Factor Model of personality theory and is at the low scoring end of Eysenck's psychoticism scale. This constraint system inhibits the flow of information to the brain. This system involves ascending serotonin pathways which provide a widespread diffuse pattern of innervation within the brain. The constraint system interacts with the BFS and its function is to modulate reward seeking. Where the constraint system is very active (and there are high levels of serotonin), it dampens the activity of the BFS, so stronger incentives are required to elicit goal-directed behaviour. In such instances goal-directed behaviour is inhibited and cautious. Where the constraint system is less active (and there are low levels of serotonin), it dampens the activity of the BFS (which involves dopamine), so intense goal-directed behaviour occurs even in response to minimal incentives. In such instances goal-directed behaviour is unstable, erratic, irritable and violent or self-destructive. The capacity to pursue long-term goals and a stable life plan becomes seriously disrupted. Low serotonin is common in people with antisocial or borderline personality disorders which lead to aggression and impulsive suicide.

The third system in Depue's model corresponds to the trait of neuroticism. Its function is to distinguish threatening from non-threatening stimuli and to inhibit or stop behaviour in potentially threatening or dangerous situations that may lead to punishment experiences. It is subserved by noradrenaline projections which arise in the locus ceruleus and which have a pattern of diverse innervation throughout many brain regions. Reductions in noradrenalin are associated with a breakdown in selective attention and the ability to distinguish threatening from non-threatening stimuli. This is associated with chronic overactivity of the locus ceruleus noradrenaline system accompanied by chronic uncertainty, worry, fear and hyperarousal.

From the foregoing, certain hypotheses about the neurobiological basis of personal strengths associated with four of the five factors in the Five-Factor Model may be offered. People with high levels of extraversion, emotional stability, conscientiousness and agreeableness may show a high level of activity in the BFS; a moderate to high level of activity within the constraint system; and moderate to high level of activity in the third noradrenalin-based system. These hypotheses deserve rigorous investigation.

MOTIVES AS PERSONAL STRENGTHS

Motives to pursue particular sets of goals may be viewed as personal strengths if these motives lead to positive outcomes. It was noted earlier that distinctions may be made between transient state-like motives (such as wanting to go sailing after work) and enduring motives (such as the need for achievement).

Trait-like motives

Of the many trait-like motives that have been identified, those for affiliation or intimacy, power and achievement have consistently emerged as three of the most important and are associated with significant personal strengths (Emmons, 1997; McClelland, 1985). Altruism, a uniquely positive motive, also deserves consideration in this context (Batson *et al.*, 2002; Schulman, 2002).

Affiliation motive

The affiliation intimacy motive is a recurrent preference for warm, close interpersonal communication as an end in itself rather than as a means to an end. If we have strong intimacy motives we are primarily concerned with making and maintaining close interpersonal relationships. The outcomes of acting upon this motive include developing a strong social support network, which in turn is a buffer against stress and conducive to good mental and physical health (Emmons, 1997). In this sense the intimacy is an extraordinarily positive form of trait-like motivation and an important personal strength.

Achievement motive

The achievement motive is a recurrent preference for working to very high standards. If we have strong achievement motivation, we work hard to achieve excellence. This motive in part is responsible for outstanding contributions in the arts, sciences, technology and industry (Emmons, 1997). So the achievement motive is a positive form of motivation also.

Power motive

The power motive is a recurrent preference to have an impact on others through attaining high status. People with strong power motives devote much energy to attaining prestige. They select people with low power motives as friends and are extremely sexually promiscuous. The power motive is important in some instances for successful leadership. Where such leadership produces positive outcomes for the group being led, the power motive may be viewed as a positive channelling of aggression into activities that may serve the greater good (Emmons, 1997). However, the power motive is associated with exploitation of those with low power motives and it is also associated with sexual exploitation, so it is not always a virtuous form of motivation.

Power and affiliation motive profiles have been shown to influence health (Jemmott, 1987). People with higher affiliation than power motives who do not inhibit the expression of their needs have particularly good health as indexed by normal blood pressure, well-functioning immune systems and fewer illnesses. This is a resilient motive profile. In contrast, people with low affiliation motives and high power motives who inhibit the expression of their strong need for power have high blood pressure, poorly functioning immune systems and poor health.

Altruism

Behaviour is motivated by altruism if our ultimate goal is to increase the welfare of another person. Altruistic motivation is defined by the intention of improving another person's situation, for that reason alone, and not for ulterior self-serving motives. The altruistic motive is distinct from egoistic motives which may also energise helpful behaviour. Altruistic motivation is evoked in many instances by empathic emotion, that is by the emotional reaction we have to seeing another person in distress and needing help. This emotional reaction is synonymous with sympathy, compassion and tenderness. Professor C. Daniel Batson and his colleagues have shown in a series of carefully designed experiments that altruistic helping behaviour is a response evoked by empathic emotion rather than the result of one of three types of egoistic motives. These are:

1. helping others so as to reduce aversive arousal associated with seeing others in distress;
2. helping others in need so as to avoid guilt, shame or social punishment for not doing so; and
3. helping others so as to obtain praise, honour, a sense of pride or personal joy.

(Batson, 1991; Batson *et al.*, 2002)

Certain factors predispose us to experience emotional empathy when we see others in distress or need of help. These include having a prosocial personality profile (Oliner and Oliner, 1988); having internalised prosocial values through the process of socialisation (Staub, 1974); and having reached the advanced stage of moral development (Kohlberg, 1976). A central feature of the prosocial personality, in terms of the Five-Factor Model described above, is agreeableness. People with a prosocial personality score high on this trait which is partially heritable and partially the result of socialisation and early life experiences. Specific socialisation experiences conducive to developing a prosocial personality profile have been identified (Graziano and Eisenberg, 1997; Schulman, 2002). People who grow up in families in which they have secure attachments to their parents, whose parents offer a warm and supportive home environment and who are good role models for altruistic behaviour are more likely to develop a prosocial personality. Other factors associated with the development of a prosocial personality include growing up in a family in which there are high moral standards, an expectation that children should help others, very clear rules, and where sensitivity, firmness and explanation for sanctions rather than corporal punishment are used to discipline children.

Schulman (2002) argues that we can help our children develop altruism by fostering empathy, moral affiliations and moral principles. Empathy is fostered by inviting children to reflect on the impact of their behaviour on others. Encouraging altruism through moral affiliations involves offering clear rules and sanctions within the context of a warm, supportive and sensitive relationship. Encouraging altruism through fostering moral principles involves engaging children in discussion about what sorts of principles would make a better world and how these principles could be put into practice.

State-like motives and subjective well-being

Motivation to follow particular courses of action may be conceptualised as being determined not only by implicit, broadband, trait-like motives, but also by explicit narrowband, state-like motives. Research on the role of state-like motives in promoting subjective well-being and happiness is of particular relevance to positive psychology, since particular characteristics of state-like motives, discussed later in this section, are associated with subjective well-being. State-like motives, or personal action constructs as they are typically called, include current concerns, personal projects, life tasks, and personal strivings. These four different ways of conceptualising personal action constructs have been developed by different groups of researchers, but have much in common (Emmons, 1997; Little, 1999).

Current concerns are motivational states that we experience between making a commitment to a goal and reaching it or abandoning it, for example finishing breakfast or getting promotion (Klinger, 1987, 1989). Personal projects are interrelated sequences of actions intended to achieve personal goals. In everyday life, people spend a considerable amount of time thinking about, planning and carrying out (or procrastinating about) personal projects such as doing the washing and the shopping, getting some exercise, doing lists of things at work, and so forth (Little, 1999). Life tasks are sets of problems that people see themselves as working on during specific periods in their lives, particularly during important lifecycle transitions such as leaving home or having a first child (Cantor, 1990). Managing life alone, succeeding academically, minding the baby are examples of life tasks. Personal strivings are motivational organising principles that represent what a person is typically trying to do (Emmons, 1997). A personal striving is a common theme that underpins a variety of apparently different actions, for example trying to appear attractive to potential partners or trying to be a good listener to friends.

Research on personal action constructs has led to the following important conclusions about motivation and subjective well-being (Emmons, 1997; Little, 1999). Subjective well-being is associated with pursuing projects that are personally meaningful; which are initiated by oneself rather than others and over which one has much control; which are supported by important people in our network; which are progressing well; and which are moderately challenging but not overly stressful or demanding. Subjective well-being is also associated with having non-conflicting sets of personal action constructs that are inconsistent with each other and coherently interrelated. Certain personality traits are associated with the development of personal action projects and their impact on subjective well-being. People with a high level of the trait of openness to experience tend to undertake more personal projects. People with a high level of the trait of neuroticism report more stress associated with their projects.

Assessment of motives

Trait-like motives may be assessed in a variety of ways, although content analysis of transcripts has been the most popular way of evaluating these motives (Smith, 1992; Winter, 1991). Transcripts of imaginative stories made in response to picture cards from the Thematic Apperception Test have been widely used, although Winter (1991) has developed a system for coding motives from speeches and personal documents, a system which permits motives to be coded from archival material. These indirect approaches to assessing affiliation, achievement and power motives are based on the assumption that people are not always conscious of the degree to which these three motives determine their behaviour. Trait-like motives may operate unconsciously or outside awareness and so self-report inventories have not been the main way of assessing these motives.

In research on state-like motives or personal action constructs, participants list between 10 and 20 current constructs and rate them on appraisal dimensions in the domains of meaning, controllability, social support, efficacy and stress (Little, 1999). To evaluate the meaning of personal action constructs, people are asked to rate how important, enjoyable, value-congruent or expressive of their identity the constructs are. To evaluate the controllability of personal action constructs people are asked to rate the degree of control they have over them and whether projects were initiated more by themselves or others. To evaluate the social support for personal action construct-related projects, people are asked to rate the degree to which projects are visible to members of the social network and supported by them. Efficacy is evaluated by asking people to rate the degree to which they are making progress with their projects and expect to continue to do so. Stress is evaluated by requesting ratings of various personal demands and stress symptoms associated with the personal action constructs.

Implicit and explicit motives

Implicit, trait-like motives, assessed through content analysis of responses to picture cards from the Thematic Apperception Test or personal documents and speeches have been found to differ in a number of important ways from explicit state-like motives or personal action constructs (McClelland *et al.*, 1989; Kihlstrom, 1999). Implicit motives are largely unconscious whereas explicit motives are conscious. Implicit motives are more strongly related to long-term behavioural trends whereas explicit motives are more strongly related to immediate choices. Explicit self-attributed motives are aroused by extrinsic social demands whereas implicit motives are aroused by intrinsic task incentives. Measures of implicit and explicit motives have low correlations with each other, and McClelland *et al.* (1989) argue that this is because there are two distinct motive systems.

This hypothesis of implicit and explicit motive systems is not unlike Schacter's (1987) distinction between implicit and explicit memory. Implicit (or procedural) memory is reflected in a change in the performance of tasks, attributable to information obtained in the past which is not consciously recollected. Implicit memory is involved in skills development, post-hypnotic amnesia and dissociative disorders (Kihlstrom, 1999). Explicit (or declarative) memory, in contrast, involves consciously re-experiencing and/or reporting a past event.

IMPLICATIONS

A summary of self-help strategies for promoting strengths and enhancing subjective well-being based on research on traits, motives and emotions is given in Table 6.3. These can be incorporated into clinical practice.

CONTROVERSIES

The main controversy in the field of trait personality theory concerns the most parsimonious and valid number of personality traits. Eysenck (1990)

Table 6.3 Strategies for promoting strengths and well-being based on research on traits and motives

Domain	Strategy
Motivation-based strategies for increasing subjective well-being	• Pursue projects you initiate rather than those set up by others • Pursue projects over which you have a lot of control • Pursue projects which are supported by important people in your network • Pursue projects which are moderately challenging but not overly demanding • Pursue non-conflicting sets of project goals that are coherently interrelated
Promoting trait-related strengths and altruism in children	• Develop secure attachments to your infants by being attuned to their needs and meeting them in predictable ways • Develop a warm relationship with your children in which you listen to what they say and respect their opinions • Have clear rules and fair non-violent consequences for rule following and rule breaking which you always apply • Be an altruistic, kind role model

has proposed a 3-trait model while Cattell's (1990) model of normal personality contains 16 primary traits (including intelligence). The differences between these extreme positions is due in part to differences in the factor-analytic methods used and the range of items analysed. The Five-Factor Model represents a compromise between the extreme positions of Eysenck and Cattell.

SUMMARY

There are links between certain traits and motives on the one hand and personal strengths or subjective well-being on the other. Traits are relatively enduring personal characteristics which influence behaviour. In recent years trait theory has come to be dominated by the Five-Factor Model of Personality which includes stability (neuroticism), extraversion, openness to experience, agreeableness and conscientiousness, and all are associated with facets that may be considered as personal strengths. These may be reliably assessed with inventories and rating scales. Fifty per cent of the variance in extraversion and neuroticism and 40 per cent of the variance in agreeableness, conscientiousness and openness to experience may be accounted for by genetic factors. Evidence from longitudinal studies supports the link between temperament and personality traits. Overall, personality traits are fairly constant across the lifespan. Typological studies repeatedly identify a resilient profile associated with high scores on all traits within the Five-Factor Model. Distinctions may be made between three neurobiological systems broadly associated with specific personality traits. The behavioural facilitation system or reward system is associated with extraversion. Its function is to energise reward-seeking behaviour. The constraint system modulates impulsive reward-seeking behaviour and corresponds to a combination of the traits of conscientiousness and agreeableness. The third system, which may be referred to as the punishment system, is associated with neuroticism. Its function is to distinguish threatening from non-threatening stimuli and to inhibit behaviour that may lead to punishment.

Trait-like motives – notably altruism, affiliation and achievement motives – constitute personal strengths, while state-like motives can have a significant effect on subjective well-being. Subjective well-being is associated with pursuing projects that are personally meaningful; which are initiated by oneself rather than others and over which one has much control; which are supported by important people in our network; which are progressing well; and which are moderately challenging but not overly stressful or demanding. Subjective well-being is also associated with having non-conflicting sets of personal action constructs that are consistent with each other and coherently interrelated.

QUESTIONS

Personal development questions

1. Complete a copy of a five-factor personality inventory. Score and interpret it following instructions in the manual.
2. What trait-related strengths have you identified in doing this exercise?
3. What steps can you take to use these strengths more frequently in your life?
4. What would be the costs and benefits of taking these steps?
5. Take some of these steps and assess the impact it has on your well-being by assessing yourself before and afterwards on one of the well-being scales contained in Chapter 1.

Research questions

1. Set up a series of hypotheses about possible relationships between the traits in the Five-Factor Model and the 24 strengths assessed by the Values in Action Inventory listed in Table 2.1. Design and conduct a study to test these hypotheses.
2. Conduct PsychInfo searches covering literature published in the past couple of years using the terms relevant to issues covered in this chapter, such as 'Five-Factor', 'Big Five', 'altruism', 'affiliation motive',

'achievement motivation', and 'power motive' combined with terms such as happiness and well-being. Identify a study that interests you and that is feasible to replicate and extend. Conduct the replication.

FURTHER READING

Academic

Hogan, P., Johnson, J. and S. Briggs, S. (1997). *Handbook of Personality Psychology*. New York: Academic Press.
Pervin, L. and John, O. (1999). *Handbook of Personality: Theory and Research*. New York: Guilford.

MEASURES FOR USE IN RESEARCH

Traits

Buss, A. and Plomin, R. (1975). *A Temperament Theory of Personality Development*. New York: Wiley. (Contains the EASI Temperament Survey.)
Clark, L. and Watson, D. (1990). 'The General Temperament Survey'. Unpublished manuscript. University of Iowa, Iowa City, IA.
Costa, P. and McCrae, R. (1992). *Revised NEO Personality Inventory (NEO-PI-R and NEO Five-Factor Inventory (NEO-FFI) Professional Manual*. Odessa, FL: Psychological Assessment Resources.
Eysenck, H. and Eysenck, S. (1975). *Manual of the Eysenck Personality Questionnaire*. San Diego, CA: Educational and Industrial Testing Service.
Goldberg, L. (1992). The development of markers for the Big Five factor structure. *Psychological Assessment* 4: 26–42. (Contains 50 and 100 trait-descriptive adjective checklists.)
John, O. and Srivastava, S. (1999). The big five trait taxonomy: history, measurement and theoretical perspectives. In L. Pervin and O. John (eds), *Handbook of Personality* (2nd edn, pp. 102–38). New York: Guilford. (Contains the 44-item Big Five Inventory.)
Wiggins, J. (1995). *Interpersonal Adjective Scale: Professional Manual*. Odessa, FL: Psychological Assessment Resources.

Motives

Klinger, E. (1987). The interview questionnaire technique: reliability and validity of a mixed ideographic-nomothetic measure of motivation. In J. Butcher and C. Spielberger (eds), *Advances in Personality Assessment* (vol. 6, pp. 31–48). Hillsdale, NJ: Erlbaum.
Smith, C. (1992). *Motivation and Personality: Handbook of Thematic Content Analysis*. New York: Cambridge University Press. (Contains descriptions of a number of systems for coding motives from text.)

Winter, D. (1991). Measuring personality at a distance: development and validation of an integrated system for scoring motives in running text. In A. Stewart, J. Healty, Jr and D. Ozer (eds), *Perspectives in Personality: Approaches to Understanding Lives* (vol. 3, pp. 58–89). London: Jessica Kingsley. (Describes a system for coding motives from transcripts.)

GLOSSARY

Achievement motive.　An implicit, trait-like motive shown by a preference to work hard to reach high standards.

Affiliation motive.　An implicit, trait-like motive shown by a preference to be involved in warm, intimate interpersonal relationships.

Agreeableness.　A trait characterised by trust and altruism.

Altruism.　An implicit, trait-like motive shown by a preference to increase the welfare of another person.

Conscientiousness.　A trait characterised by self-discipline and competence.

Extraversion.　A trait characterised by sociability and seeking excitement.

Motives.　Implicit or explicit dispositions that energise us to pursue particular sets of goals.

Neuroticism.　A trait characterised by anxiety, depression and self-regulation difficulties.

Openness to experience.　A trait characterised by willingness to explore novel thoughts, values, feelings and situations.

Personal action constructs.　Explicit and conscious state-like motives including current concerns, personal projects, life tasks and personal strivings.

Power motive.　An implicit, trait-like motive shown by a preference to have an impact on others through attaining high status.

Temperament.　The characteristic affective response style which is present from infancy and due to predominantly constitutional or hereditary factors.

Traits.　Relatively enduring personal characteristics, which, along with situational variables, influence behaviour, cognition and affect.

Chapter 7

Positive self

Learning objectives

- Be able to distinguish between self as an agent and self as an object.
- Be able to describe the main research findings on the measurement, development and correlates of self-esteem and the concept of defensive self-esteem.
- Understand the sources and outcomes of self-efficacy and how to evaluate it.
- Be able to distinguish between self-efficacy on the one hand and locus of control, general self-efficacy, desirability of control, sense of coherence and hardiness on the other.
- Be able to give an account of the psychology of a variety of coping strategies including problem solving, social support, catharsis, crying, faith, meditation, relaxation, exercise, reframing, humour and distraction.
- Appreciate the variety of assessment instruments for evaluating coping styles including the Coping Inventory for Stressful Situations, the Functional Dimension of Coping Scale, the Ways of Coping Questionnaire, the Coping Responses Inventory, the COPE and the Adolescent Coping Orientation for Problem Experiences, A-COPE.
- Be able to describe the development and correlates of adaptive defences and their assessment.
- Appreciate the variety of assessment instruments for evaluating defence mechanisms including the defence mechanism rating scales, the defence style questionnaire, and the defence mechanisms profile.
- Understand the clinical implications of research on self-esteem, self-efficacy, coping styles and defence mechanisms for facilitating happiness.
- Be able to identify research questions that need to be addressed to advance our understanding of self-esteem, self-efficacy, coping styles and defence mechanisms on the one hand and happiness on the other.

While we currently take the idea of self for granted, this was not always the case (Baumeister, 1997). In the Middle Ages people's identities were linked to their social positions, occupations and family ties and people were not supposed to want to change these. People knew their identities since these were largely dictated by their place in society. Also, the issue of personal development did not arise in the sense in which it is a major issue for many people today. People learned their occupation. Many had their marriages arranged by their families. In western Judeo-Christian society, most people were guided by Christian values and beliefs. They had faith in God and a belief that leading a good and sinless life would lead to salvation in the afterlife. They had faith in their Monarch and a belief that if they fulfilled their duties within society, their Monarch would protect and not punish them. These constraints did not leave a great deal of scope for personal development or to a concern with individual differences in personal growth. During the Early Modern period (1500–1800) an interest developed in differences between people and the uniqueness of the individual. Autobiographical writing and a focus on the detailed differences between people's life experiences began to emerge. This later gave way to focus on the inner life and to the belief that fulfilment might be enhanced by developing a deeper understanding of the inner life of the self through art, culture, contemplation and poetry. This coincided with an emerging questioning of the certainties of religion, monarchies and the values entailed by these. People began to question their faith in their gods, their kings and their values. Democracy also began to supplant monarchies with the idea that people choose their leaders rather than their being appointed by God. At the turn of the nineteenth century the popularisation of the idea of the unconscious through the works of Sigmund Freud (an idea that had a long past but a short history) expanded the popular concept of the inner self and the idea that achieving self-knowledge and personal development were challenging undertakings. Lifecycle theorists such as Erik Erikson (1968) later proposed the idea that at transitional points between the stages of development of the lifecycle, identity crises could occur in which people questioned the way they were living their lives and entertained choices about making major changes in their lifestyles. This idea of an identity crisis entailed the view that the self was separate from the social and religious contexts in which it resided. This way of thinking was facilitated by the rise in geographic, social and occupational mobility. It was also supported by increasing wealth which gave freedom to entertain the idea of choosing different lifestyles. Wealth and mobility in turn were facilitated by huge advances in science and technology which were made as a result of the scientific revolution. While the emergence of the modern conception of self has been liberating on the one hand, it has also entailed a cost. Because it has become increasingly difficult to put all one's faith in the supernatural order or the social order, people are forced to look elsewhere for values and many turn to the self or close personal relationships as a source of value. Relationships will be dealt with in Chapter 8. Here the focus will be on the self. Whereas in the past, a focus on the self was termed selfishness, a pejorative term, there are many positive terms for self-focused concerns in modern psychology, notable self-knowledge, self-esteem, self-efficacy, self-evaluation and self-regulation. Many of these are of concern to positive psychology.

SELF AS OBJECT AND AGENT

This distinction between self-as-object and self-as-subject or agent is a consistent theme throughout the literature on the psychology of self. Some features of these two aspects of the self are presented in Table 7.1 (Robins et al., 1999). The self-as-object theme underpins constructs from social, cognitive, behavioural and narrative psychology such as self-concept, self-schemas, self as a set of learned skills, self as narrative, self as constructed in language and the self as a socially constructed and culturally determined phenomenon. The self-as-agent theme is central to theories in the evolutionary tradition that highlight the biological underpinnings of the self as a conscious agent with the capacity to perceive, learn, communicate and adapt to the environment. The self-as-agent theme also underpins psychoanalytic

Table 7.1 Two aspects of self

Self as agent or subject	Self as object
Self-awareness	Self-representation
Self as 'I'	Self as 'me'
Self as consciousness	Self-concept
Self as collection of states of consciousness	Self-schemas
Self as perceiver	Self as an object of perception
Self as biological organism adapting to environment	Self as a concept socially constructed in a community and culture
Self as organism with capacity to learn	Self as a repertoire of learned skills
Self as speaker	Self constructed in language
Subjective experience	Narrative self and autobiographical memory
Self as organism motivated to achieve (conflicting) goals	Ideal self and possible selves as goals to be pursued
Self-regulation	Self-evaluative beliefs
Self as user of coping strategies and defence mechanisms	Self-esteem and self-efficacy

Source: Adapted from Robins et al. (1999): 448.

conceptions of the self as motivated to achieve conflicting goals such as aggressive self-preservation, sexual self-reproduction and social co-operation. In contrast, the notion of ideal selves or possible selves as goals to be pursued are entailed by a conception of the self as an object rather than an agent.

Research on both aspects of self, particularly research on self-evaluation and self-regulation, have pinpointed strengths of importance to positive psychology. High self-esteem and strong self-efficacy beliefs, entailed by the view of self-as-object, contribute to personal strength and resilience (Mruk, 1999; Bandura,1997). We have better health and well-being when we evaluate ourselves positively (high self-esteem) and believe that we will succeed at tasks we attempt (high self-efficacy). Coping effectively with life challenges and using adaptive defence mechanisms to manage intra-psychic conflict are entailed by the view of self-as-agent. We have better health and well-being when we use certain types of coping strategies to manage life challenges and certain types of defence mechanisms to manage anxiety arising from conflicting sexual, aggressive and social motives (Conte and Plutchik, 1995; Zeidner and Endler, 1996). These issues will be the main focus in the present chapter.

SELF-ESTEEM

William James (1890) defined self-esteem as the feeling of self-worth that derives from the ratio of our actual successes to our pretensions. By pretensions he meant our estimation of our potential successes and this is informed by our values, goals and aspirations. This definition of self-esteem highlights that it is a construct which addresses the way we evaluate ourselves and measure our own sense of self-worth by comparing how we are and how we aspire to be. Self-esteem is not a unitary construct but is hierarchically organised with overall global self-esteem based on general judgements of self-worth and, beneath this, subtypes of self-esteem based on evaluations of self-worth in different contexts, such as within the family, school, work setting, leisure setting, or peer group (Mruk, 1999).

Measures of self-esteem

Multidimensional self-report self-esteem questionnaires are useful for assessing self-esteem profiles across a number of domains. Particularly well-designed, reliable and valid scales are O'Brien and Epstein's (1988) Multi-dimensional Self-Esteem Inventory for adults and Battle's (1992) Culture-Free Self-Esteem Inventories for children and adults. O'Brien and Epstein's (1988) Multidimensional Self Esteem Inventory for adults is very comprehensive and yields scores for global self-esteem, competence, lovability, likability, personal power, self-control, moral self-approval, body appearance, body functioning, identity integration and defensive self-esteem enhancement. Battle's (1992) Culture-Free Self-Esteem Inventory for children yields scores for global self-esteem, parental self-esteem, school-based self-esteem and peer group-related self-esteem. The Culture-Free Self-Esteem Inventory for adults measures global self-esteem, social self-esteem and personal self-esteem. Both versions also contain a lie scale which measures defensive responding.

Unidimensional self-esteem scales useful for screening purposes include Rosenberg's (1979) Self-esteem Inventory for children, Nugent and Thomas's (1993) Self-esteem Rating Scale for adults and children and Coopersmith's (1981) Self-esteem Inventories for adults and children.

Self-concept inventories measure self-perception and some researchers have used them as indices of self-esteem. The Piers–Harris Children's Self-Concept Scale (Piers and Harris, 1969) and the Tennessee Self-Concept Scales (Fitts, 1988) for adults and children are among the more psychometrically robust measures of self-concept.

Development of self-esteem

Reviews of our current knowledge about self-esteem allow a number of conclusions to be drawn concerning the development of self-evaluative beliefs (Baumeister, 1997; Bednar and Peterson, 1995; Brown, 1998; Mruk, 1999; Robins et al., 1999). Children whose parents are accepting of their strengths and limitations and set explicit high, but attainable standards, which they support their children in attaining, develop high self-esteem. High self-esteem is also associated with a consistent authoritative parenting style in which children are treated with warmth and respect and given opportunities to discuss directives and rules about good conduct. In contrast, children whose parents are inconsistent, permissive, strictly authoritarian, rejecting or abusive develop low self-esteem. Parental example and modelling also has an impact on the development of self-esteem, a greater impact than the verbal advice parents give their children. Parents who cope with life challenges by using an active problem-solving coping style are more likely, through their example, to help their children develop high self-esteem. An avoidant parental coping style is associated with the development of low self-esteem in children. Self-esteem is also influenced by wider social factors, notably socio-economic status. Higher socio-economic status is associated with high self-esteem and poverty is associated with lower self-esteem.

Higher self-esteem is associated with achievement (not failure); having the power and skills to influence others (not powerlessness); acting in a way we perceive to be moral (rather than immoral); and being accepted and approved of by others (rather than rejected). Thus, self-esteem derives from our own evaluations of our worth based on an appraisal of our personal accomplishments, virtues and attributes as well as from our perceptions of the way we are evaluated by others.

Self-esteem is relatively stable over time, but may change at lifecycle transition points (Robins *et al.*, 1999). Self-esteem tends to be high in pre-schoolers. It then declines gradually during the pre-adolescent years. This gradual decline may be due to greater reliance on social comparison information and feedback from external sources such as peers and teachers. With the onset of adolescence there is a further drop in self-esteem but then it increases gradually over the course of adolescence. The drop in self-esteem at the onset of adolescence may be due to the child evaluating the physical and social changes that accompany the transition to adolescence negatively. That is, children may find the maturation of their bodies; the transition from primary to secondary school; and alterations in peer relationships particularly challenging and so evaluate themselves less posit-ively. The drop in self-esteem at the onset of adolescence may also be a reflection of the increased capacity of adolescents to imagine how others judge them: an ability that emerges in the formal operational period. Over the course of adolescence, there is considerable variability in changes in self-esteem, but with the onset of adulthood self-esteem gradually increases. There is some evidence that improvements in self-esteem may occur at transitional points in adult life such as graduation from college, marriage, changing jobs, or moving house. In older adulthood there is a decline in self-esteem. Individual differences in self-esteem are relatively stable over time, and longitudinal studies show that stability is greater in adulthood than childhood. Changes in self-esteem in early adulthood are due to many factors, notably optimistic or pessimistic attributional explanations made for success and failure. Optimistic explanatory styles are discussed in Chapter 3.

The stability of self-esteem is in part due to the ways in which people process information about the self. When people are processing information of particular relevance to how they evaluate themselves, the way information is processed appears to be driven by four motives:

1. self-enhancement;
2. maintaining a consistent view of the self;
3. maintaining a socially approved view of the self; and
4. maintaining an accurate view of the self (Robins *et al.*, 1999).

Thus, people tend to be motivated to process information in a biased way that supports a particularly positive view of themselves as noted in Chapter 3 (Taylor and Brown, 1988, 1994). They also interpret available informa-tion in a biased way that is consistent with the views they typically have of themselves (Swann, 1997). In addition, people are motivated to process information and present themselves in ways that increase the approval they receive from significant members of their social networks (Schlenker, 1980). Finally, people are motivated to process information accurately (Kelly, 1955). When faced with new information about the self, people with high self-esteem will process that information in a biased self-enhancing way, consistent with their positive view of the self and their wish to gain the approval of others. People with low self-esteem, in contrast, will selectively attend to new information which confirms their existing negative self-evaluations.

Correlates of self-esteem

A number of factors have been shown to characterise people with high and low levels of self-esteem (Baumeister, 1997; Bednar and Peterson, 1995; Brown, 1998; Mruk, 1999; Robins *et al.*, 1999). High self-esteem is associated with good personal adjustment across the lifespan, positive affectivity, personal autonomy, androgyny, internal locus of control, greater self-knowledge, setting appropriate goals, fulfilling personal commitments, coping well with criticism or negative feedback, managing stress well, and showing low levels of self-criticism and criticism of others. Low self-esteem is associated with poor psychological adjustment, a variety of mental health problems including depression, anxiety, drug abuse, eating disorders, difficulties making and maintaining stable relationships, poor stress management, poor immune system functioning under stress, and suicide. People with high levels of self-esteem are concerned mainly with enhancing their views of themselves and seek opportunities to excel and stand out. If they receive negative feedback on laboratory tasks they persist for a while and then abandon the task if they continue to fail. However, people with low self-esteem are concerned with self-protection and avoiding failure, humiliation or rejection. If they fail on laboratory tasks they tend to persist until they succeed. Thus, people with high self-esteem have the overall goal of enhancing their views of themselves by focusing on their strengths and seeking opportunities to use these to be outstanding, whereas people with low self-esteem aim to find out about their shortcomings so that they can remediate these in order to be adequate and avoid failure.

Defensive self-esteem enhancement

Some people report high self-esteem as a defence against negative social evaluation. O'Brien and Epstein's (1988) Multidimensional Self-Esteem Inventory for adults includes a subscale for assessing defensive self-esteem enhancement. Defensively high self-esteem may be characterised by extreme sensitivity to criticism and bragging and criticising others on the one hand, or immersion in work and responding to criticisms with inappropriate aggression on the other. These profiles are quite different from the depressed, anxious and socially withdrawn person with low self-esteem.

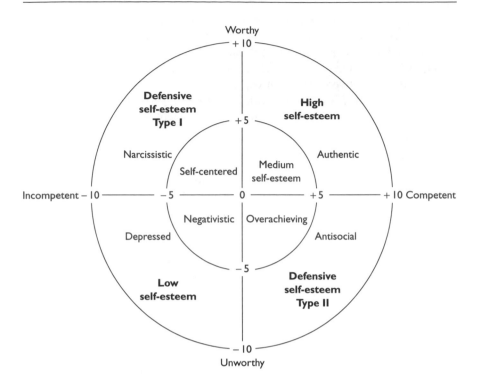

Figure 7.1 Self-esteem and competence
Source: Adapted from Mruk (1999): 164–5.

In Figure 7.1. Professor Chris Mruck's (1999) model of self-esteem is presented as a framework within which to conceptualise defensive self-esteem enhancement. The two axes within the model are competence, which refers to skills for competing tasks, and worthiness, which refers to the affective experience of having a sense of worth and the cognitive judgement that one has worth. Within this model, people with high levels of competence and worth have authentic high self-esteem, while low self-esteem, negativism and depression are associated with low levels of competence and worth.

There are two types of defensive self-esteem. People with these types of self-esteem behave in many contexts like people with high self-esteem. However, when their vulnerabilities are challenged they behave in ways that are not consistent with high self-esteem. The first type of defensive self-esteem is associated with low competence but a high sense of worth. Such people have extreme sensitivity to criticism because of their sense of incompetence and inadequacy. When they feel that their competence is being challenged, to defend against anxiety associated with their sense of inadequacy in this area, they may brag, reflecting the use of the defence mechanism of overcompensation. Or they may criticise and blame others, which reflects the defensive displacement of self-directed criticism onto others. Self-centred people have a moderate level of this type of self-esteem. In its extreme form this type of adaptation is associated with narcissistic personality disorder.

The second type of defensive self-esteem is associated with high competence but a low sense of worth. Such people have extreme sensitivity to criticism of their worth, because of their underlying sense of unworthiness. When they feel that their worth is being challenged, to defend against anxiety associated with a low sense of self-worth, such people may become immersed in their work and produce an exceptional number of competent achievements, thereby using sublimation as a defence. Their workaholic behaviour reflects an attempt to compensate for a low sense of worthiness through overachievement, Alternatively they may respond to criticism and threats to their worthiness with bullying and inappropriate aggression, thereby using antisocial acting-out as a defence.

Improving self-esteem

A number of strategies for improving derive from William James's (1890) definition of self-esteem as the ratio of achievements to aspirations and Chris Mruk's competence and worthiness model of self-esteem. These include: skills training; environmental change; cognitive therapy; and capitalising upon transitions that promote self-esteem.

Skills training may increase competence. This includes training in problem-solving skills, social skills, assertiveness skills, academic skills, and work-related skills, depending on the area of low competence. Where a low sense of worthiness derives from poverty or social disadvantage, environmental changes such as occupational retraining, occupational placement, or social relocation to a less disadvantaged area may be appropriate. Where a low sense of worthiness is due to unrealistically high aspirations, despite a realistic level of achievement, then cognitive therapy may be required to help challenge their very high standards. People with low self-esteem have a cognitive bias to filter-out positive feedback inconsistent with negative self-evaluation, and cognitive therapy helps people re-calibrate this filter (Swann, 1997). Only when skills for challenging unrealistically high standards and screening out positive feedback have been acquired can people accept positive affirming feedback; recognise the value of the achievements that derive from newly learned problem-solving or social skills; or capitalise upon transitional points in their lives that have the potential for fostering self-esteem, such as changing jobs, or relocating, or making a developmental lifecycle transition, such as graduating from college.

While self-esteem is concerned with global evaluations of self-worth and self-efficacy, the next topic to be addressed is concerned with focal evaluations of specific competencies.

SELF-EFFICACY

Professor Albert Bandura at Stanford University is the originator of self-efficacy theory: a set of ideas embedded within his more general social-cognitive theory of personality (Bandura, 1997, 1999). Perceived self-efficacy refers to beliefs which we hold about our capability of organising and performing tasks within a specific domain to effectively lead to specific goals. Efficacy beliefs guide much of our lives, since we generally pursue courses of action which we believe will lead to desired outcomes and have little incentive to act in ways which we believe will involve failure. According to Bandura, in any domain of functioning our efficacy beliefs (or judgements about our capabilities) determine our expectations about the effects or consequences of our actions. If we expect to be successful and achieve desired outcomes, then this acts as an incentive to perform the action. If we expect to be unsuccessful, this acts as a disincentive. These efficacy beliefs and expectations of certain consequences determine our behavioural performance, and this in turn leads to certain outcomes. For example, if I judge myself to be capable of sailing my 14-foot dinghy round a race course in a 25-mile-an-hour wind, this is a self-efficacy belief. The anticipated physical pleasure of coming ashore after the exertion of doing so and winning a sailing race, the social approval of other competitors for winning, and the self-satisfaction are physical, social and self-evaluative positive outcome expectations respectively. The act of sailing around the course is a performance and is distinct from the outcome which follows from successful performance. This theory is diagrammed in Figure 7.2. In any domain of functioning our efficacy beliefs will vary in their level, strength and generality. These beliefs will lead to expectations about the effects or consequences of our behavioural performance. We may hold expectations about the physical and social effects or consequences of our behavioural performance and their effects on how we will evaluate ourselves if we perform well or poorly.

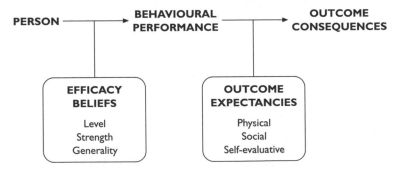

Figure 7.2 Relationship between self-efficacy beliefs and outcome expectations
Source: Adapted from Bandura (1997): 22.

These expectations of the outcomes or consequences of our performance may vary along a set of continua from positive to negative. Performance does not always affect outcome. For example, in many jobs (for example public service jobs in Ireland) the level of remuneration received is not tied to job performance. However, where performance is linked to outcome, efficacy beliefs predict expected and actual outcome in a range of domains including academic and occupational performance and habit control in areas such as eating, drug use, adherence to medical regimes and anxiety management.

Self-efficacy and self-esteem differ insofar as self-esteem is concerned with judgements about personal worth, while self-efficacy is concerned with judgements about personal capabilities. These are independent constructs. Whereas self-esteem effects our general mood, self-efficacy beliefs about our ability to succeed at specific tasks determines how well we perform at these tasks.

With Bandura's model there is a reciprocal interaction between perceived self-efficacy, behaviour and the external environment. Predicting behaviour in a given setting is best done with tailor-made domain-specific measures of self-efficacy, usually single-item 100-point rating scales. Self-efficacy beliefs assessed in this way are far more powerful predictors of behaviour than general measures of self-concept or self-esteem (Bandura, 1997).

Measurement of self-efficacy

Measurements of perceived self-efficacy are indices of beliefs we have about how effectively we can use the skills we possess under particular conditions. Measurements of self-efficacy are by definition domain-specific (Bandura, 1997). Thus, we may measure efficacy beliefs about our capacity to protect ourselves against sexually transmitted diseases or our capacity to sail a dinghy under stormy conditions. Separate measurements are used for these different domains.

Sources of self-efficacy

Self-efficacy beliefs are constructed from four sources of information:

1. mastery experiences;
2. vicarious experiences;
3. social persuasion; and
4. physical and emotional states.

(Bandura, 1997)

Resilient self-efficacy develops from mastery experiences in which goals are achieved through perseverance and overcoming obstacles. Self-efficacy also develops from observing others succeed through sustained effort. People's self-efficacy beliefs may be strengthened if they are persuaded that they can succeed and then given manageable challenges which confirm their coach's persuasive exhortations. Finally, people's self-efficacy beliefs are enhanced by pursuing goals when physically fit and in a positive mood.

Outcomes of self-efficacy

Self-efficacy beliefs regulate functioning through cognitive, motivational, emotional and choice processes (Bandura, 1997). At a cognitive level, people with high perceived self-efficacy show greater cognitive resourcefulness, strategic flexibility and effectiveness in managing environmental challenges. They use a future-time perspective to structure their lives. They focus on potentially beneficial opportunities rather than risks. They visualise successful outcomes and use these to guide their problem-solving efforts.

At a motivational level people with strong self-efficacy beliefs set challenging goals, expect their efforts to produce good results, ascribe failure to controllable factors such as insufficient effort, inadequate strategies or unfavourable circumstances rather than uncontrollable factors such as lack of ability, view obstacles as surmountable and so are motivated to persist in striving to achieve their goals.

Efficacy beliefs regulate emotional states by allowing people to interpret potentially threatening demands as manageable challenges and by reducing worrying and negative thinking about potential threats. Efficacy beliefs also regulate emotional states by facilitating problem-focused coping to alter potentially threatening environmental circumstances; by enabling people to solicit social support to act as a buffer against stress; and by facilitating the use of self-soothing techniques such as humour, relaxation and exercise to reduce arousal associated with potentially threatening situations.

Self-efficacy beliefs enhance the functioning of the immune system and lead to better physical health, greater resilience in the face of stress, and better psychological and social adjustment. Within specific domains such as work, sports, weight-control, smoking cessation, alcohol use and mental health problems, the development of self-efficacy beliefs leads to positive outcomes.

Locus of control, general self-efficacy, desirability of control, sense of coherence and hardiness

There are a number of constructs related to self-efficacy which deserve mention. Julian Rotter (1966) in the 1960s introduced the construct of locus of control, which in some respects was a forerunner of the idea of self-efficacy and optimistic explanatory style mentioned in Chapter 3. According to Rotter individuals differ in the degree to which they expect important sources of reinforcement to be within their control or influenced by external factors such as chance, fate, or the actions of other powerful people. A huge literature has developed which supports the beneficial effects for most people of an internal locus of control on psychological adjustment and physical health (e.g. Lefcourt, 1982). Many instruments have been developed to measure locus of control including Rotter's (1966) original I-E scale and the locus of control scale for children (Nowicki and Strickland, 1973). Factor analyses revealed that locus of control was multidimensional, with different factors tapping beliefs about whether events were controlled by the self, chance, fate or powerful others. This led to the development of multidimensional scales such as the Multidimensional Locus of Control Scale (Levenson, 1973) and the Multidimensional Health Locus of Control Scale (Wallston et al., 1978). The latter reflects the trend for researchers to recognise that beliefs and expectancies about locus of control may be domain-specific, a tenet which finds expression in its most extreme form in Bandura's (1997) self-efficacy theory. Despite Bandura's insistence that efficacy beliefs were highly domain-specific, a general self-efficacy scale was developed which evaluates overall expectations of effectively controlling aspects of the environment (Sherer et al., 1982). Scales were also developed to evaluate individual differences in other belief-systems relevant to control, such as the desirability of control (Burger and Cooper, 1979). The beneficial effects of perceived control are in part determined by the desirability of control. Antonovsky (1993) developed a measure of sense of coherence, a construct associated with resilience in the face of major trauma such as immigration following war. The sense of coherence scale assesses the degree to which life situations are perceived as meaningful, comprehensible and manageable. The manageability aspect of the scale suggests that it shares features with other control-related constructs. Kobasa (1979) developed the hardiness scale which is predictive of continued health and well-being despite increases in life stress. The scale evaluates beliefs that significant aspects of one's life situation are controllable; the expectation that life will entail challenges; and a commitment to finding meaning in life. Overall, evidence from intervention studies which have evaluated the effects of programmes which aim to enhance a sense of personal control over physical and psychological difficulties show that such interventions are beneficial (Thompson, 2002).

A recognition that there are many ways for controlling life challenges is central to the psychology of coping strategies which is the focus of the next section.

COPING STRATEGIES

Coping strategies are used to manage situations in which there is a perceived discrepancy between stressful demands and available resources for meeting these demands (Zeidner and Endler, 1996). Rudolph Moos's conceptual framework of the coping process is presented in Figure 7.3. According to

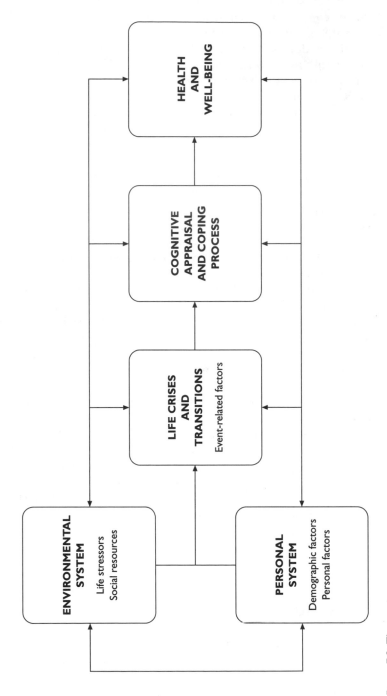

Figure 7.3 The coping process
Source: Adapted from Holahan et al. (1996): 27.

this framework, factors within the individual's environmental system (notable social supports and stresses) and their personal system (such as traits and demographic attributes), all of which are relatively stable, influence changes in life circumstances such as life crises and transitions. All of these factors affect health and well-being both directly and indirectly through cognitive appraisal and coping. The central role that coping plays is highlighted by its central place in this framework. The bi-directional pathways indicate the possibility of reciprocal feedback occurring at any stage of the stress and coping process. Moos's model is one example of complex conceptualisations of the stress and coping process which subsume earlier dispositional and contextual models (Holahan *et al.*, 1996). Dispositional models highlight the role of relative stable personal factors determining the choice and effectiveness of coping strategies. In contextual models the choice and effectiveness of coping strategies is viewed as being largely determined by the nature of the stresses with which the person has to cope and the way these are appraised.

Within the stress and coping literature, there is a growing consensus that distinctions may be made between problem-focused, emotion-focused and avoidant coping strategies (Zeidner and Endler, 1996). Emotion-focused coping strategies are appropriate for managing affective states associated with uncontrollable stresses such as bereavement. For controllable stresses such as college examinations or job interviews, problem-focused coping strategies, which aim to directly modify the source of stress, are more appropriate. In some situations where time out from active coping is required to marshal personal resources before returning to active coping, avoidant coping may be appropriate. For all three coping styles, a distinction may be made between functional and dysfunctional strategies. Some commonly used functional and dysfunctional coping strategies are listed in Table 7.2.

Functional, problem-focused coping strategies include accepting responsibility for solving the problem; seeking accurate information about the problem; seeking dependable advice and help; developing realistic action plans; carrying out plans either alone or with the help of other people; staying focused by postponing competing activities; and maintaining an optimistic view of one's capacity to solve the problem. Optimism has been discussed in Chapter 3. Creativity and wisdom, which are important characteristics for problem-focused coping, were discussed in Chapter 5. It is also probable that certain personality traits such as conscientiousness, discussed in Chapter 6, are important for facilitating problem-focused coping.

Dysfunctional problem-focused coping strategies include accepting little responsibility for solving the problem; seeking inaccurate or irrelevant information; seeking support and advice from inappropriate sources (such as fortune tellers); developing unrealistic plans, such as winning the lotto; not following through on problem-solving plans; procrastination; and holding a pessimistic view of one's capacity to solve the problem.

Table 7.2 Functional and dysfunctional, problem, emotion and avoidance focused coping strategies

Type	Aim	Functional	Dysfunctional
Problem-focused	Problem solving	• Accepting responsibility for solving the problem • Seeking accurate information • Seeking dependable advice and help • Developing a realistic action plan • Following through on the plan • Postponing competing activities • Maintaining an optimistic view of one's capacity to solve the problem	• Taking little responsibility for solving the problem • Seeking inaccurate information • Seeking questionable advice • Developing unrealistic plans • Not following through on plans • Procrastination • Holding a pessimistic view of one's capacity to solve the problem
Emotion-focused	Mood regulation	• Making and maintaining socially supportive and empathic friendships • Seeking meaningful spiritual support • Catharsis and emotional processing • Reframing and cognitive restructuring • Seeing the stress in a humorous way • Relaxation routines • Physical exercise	• Making and maintaining destructive relationships • Seeking meaningless spiritual support • Unproductive wishful thinking • Long-term denial • Taking the stress too seriously • Drug and alcohol abuse • Aggression
Avoidance-focused	Avoiding source of stress	• Temporarily mentally disengaging from the problem • Temporally engaging in distracting activities • Temporally engaging in distracting relationships	• Mentally disengaging from the problem for the long term • Long-term engagement in distracting activities • Long-term engagement in distracting relationships

Source: Based on Zeidner and Endler (1996).

Where stresses are uncontrollable, emotion-focused coping strategies such as making and maintaining socially supportive friendships, particularly those in which it is possible to confide deeply felt emotions and beliefs, are appropriate. Key requirements for developing this coping strategy are internal working models of relationships based on secure attachment and also the capacity to empathise with others (Cassidy and Shaver, 1999). Attachment was discussed in Chapter 4. An emotion-focused coping strategy related to seeking social support is catharsis. That is the process of verbally expressing in detail intense emotional experiences and engaging in processing of emotionally charged thoughts and memories within the context of a confiding relationship. Seeking meaningful spiritual support is another emotion-focused coping strategy. Reframing, cognitive restructuring and looking at stresses from a humorous perspective are emotion-focused coping strategies where the aim is to reduce distress by thinking about a situation in a different way. Such reframing or cognitive restructuring may occur as part of the catharsis process or quite separately from it. Relaxation routines and physical exercise are other functional emotion-focused coping strategies used to regulate mood in a highly deliberate way. Support, catharsis, reframing, humour, relaxation and exercise are coping strategies that do little to alter the source of stress. Rather, they permit the regulation of negative mood states that arise from exposure to stress.

Dysfunctional emotion-focused coping strategies include making destructive rather than supportive relationships; seeking spiritual support which is not personally meaningful; engaging in long-term denial rather than catharsis; engaging in wishful thinking rather than constructive reframing; taking oneself too seriously rather than looking at stresses in a humorous light; abusing drugs and alcohol rather than using relaxation routines; and engaging in aggression rather than physical exercise. Dysfunctional coping strategies may lead to short-term relief but in the long term they tend to maintain rather than resolve stress-related problems.

Psychologically disengaging from a stressful situation and the judicious short-term involvement in distracting activities and relationships are functional avoidant coping strategies. Turning off thoughts about work-related stress when leaving the office, listening to music when waiting to undergo a painful medical procedure, and holding a light conversation with people in the supermarket queue before facing the stress of visiting the bank manager are examples of such coping strategies. Avoidant coping strategies become dysfunctional when they are used as a long-term solution to stress management.

Problem solving

For a wide range of relatively controllable life challenges and stresses, problem-solving approaches to coping have been found to improve physical and mental health and increase personal well-being (Holahan et al., 1996).

In addition, training in problem-solving skills has been shown to enhance psychological adjustment (D'Zurilla and Nezu, 1999).

Problem-solving ability may be assessed with Paul Heppner's (1988) Problem-Solving Inventory, one of the most widely used instruments in the field. There is good evidence from a range of studies that problem-solving appraisal as assessed by this instrument is associated with better physical health, better psychological and social adjustment, lower levels of depression and hopelessness, lower levels of suicidality in at-risk groups, lower levels of substance abuse and less punitive parenting styles (Heppner and Goug-Gwi, 2002).

Problem-solving skills, which are central to problem-focused coping strategies, involve a distinct set of clearly defined steps (D'Zurilla and Nezu, 1999). Problem solving involves breaking big vague problems into many smaller specific problems which are then defined in solvable rather than unsolvable terms. Next, multiple possible solutions are generated without judging the merits of these. The emphasis is on generating a lot of potential solutions representing a wide range of possibilities. The third step involves examining the pros and cons or costs and benefits of each of these before selecting the best course of action to follow. The fourth step is implementing the action plan. Finally, the effectiveness of the plan is evaluated against pre-set goals. If the problem remains unsolved, the process is repeated in light of knowledge about why the attempted solution was ineffective. Conjoint social problem solving is discussed in more detail in Chapter 4.

Social support

From an evolutionary perspective, living co-operatively in groups has conferred many benefits on humans. It has helped us to protect ourselves from more powerful animals and provided a context within which to divide up the various survival tasks such as hunting, gathering and rearing children. However, group living also confers a somewhat unexpected benefit. The quantity and quality of our social relationships strongly affects our health. People with larger social support networks and stronger social bonds with members of their networks have better physical and mental health, fewer illnesses and less depression, recover more rapidly from physical illness and psychological problems, and have a lower risk of death (Taylor, Dickerson and Cousino Klein, 2002; Sarason et al., 1990).

Distinctions are made in the literature between perceived social support, supportive relationships and supportive networks (Pierce et al., 1996). Perceived social support is the perception that others are available to provide emotional or instrumental assistance if it is required. Supportive relationships are dyadic social bonds from which people can derive emotional or instrumental assistance when required. Collectively an individual's complete set of supportive relationships constitute their social network.

Good measures of perceived social support include the long and short forms of the Social Support Questionnaire (Sarason *et al.*, 1983; Sarason *et al.*, 1987) and the Multidimensional Scale of Perceived Social Support (Dahlem *et al.*, 1991). Perceived social support is positively correlated with extraversion and negatively correlated with neuroticism, suggesting it is a trait-like attribute. People with high levels of perceived social support have distinctive personal profiles (Pierce *et al.*, 1996). They structure situations so stresses are less likely to occur, develop more effective coping skills and are more interpersonally effective is seeking help from members of their network when required. It is probable that these characteristics are the adult outcome of early secure attachments. It is ironic that people with high perceived social support, because of their confidence and effective coping skills, probably have less need to draw on their social support network than others.

The quality of individual supportive relationships may be assessed with instruments such as the Quality of Supportive Relationships Inventory (Pierce *et al.*, 1991) which measure a construct related to social support but not identical to it. Compared with perceived social support the quality of supportive relationships is more closely related to the absence of loneliness. For married couples, the quality of support within the marital relationship may render a person less vulnerable to experiencing challenging life events as stressful and determine the availability of assistance in coping with life events once they have occurred. People who have had secure attachments to caregivers in infancy and childhood are better at making and maintaining high-quality supportive relationships in adulthood.

Interventions which target individuals within their social networks, rather than in isolation, are more likely to enhance perceived social support and the quality of supportive relationships. Such interventions include marital and family therapy; multisystemic therapy for children, families and their social networks; and multisystemic prevention programmes that focus on individuals, families and their wider communities (Carr, 2000a, 2000b, 2002).

Catharsis

When we have faced traumas or challenges that outstripped our capacity to cope, and we try to keep these out of our minds or keep them secret from others, our health suffers. People who have been abused as children, victimised as adults or bereaved and who do not address memories of these events have poorer health, attend their doctors more often and suffer from more illnesses (Zeidner and Endler, 1996).

There are many ways to address such memories and all effective ways involve remembering the trauma, holding it in consciousness and tolerating the anxiety associated with this while linking the affect-laden, warded-off memory with our overall view of ourselves in the world (Keane, 1998;

Niederhoffer and Pennebaker, 2002; Pennebaker, 1997; Shapiro, 2001; Stanton *et al.*, 2002). This coping mechanism involves sustained exposure to the traumatic memories, and often this is achieved by telling the story of the trauma in a graphic way that allows the events to be re-experienced. Traditionally the process of gaining relief from trauma by recounting the event within the context of a trusting relationship is referred to as catharsis.

Professor James Pennebaker at the University of Texas at Austin has devoted more than twenty years to the scientific study of the effects of writing about traumatic memories. In these studies he has typically invited individuals from various groups (students, disaster survivors, victims of different types of traumas, people recently made redundant) to participate in writing experiments. These involve visiting a laboratory on 4 consecutive days and writing in total privacy for 15 minutes. Typically half of the participants are randomly assigned to a trauma writing condition and the other half to a control condition in which they write about something other than their trauma, usually trivial details about what they have done in the past 24 hours. Those in the trauma writing condition are asked to write continuously in a detailed and uncensored way about their trauma. They are instructed to write about their deepest thoughts and emotions concerning the trauma and to hold nothing back.

Participants in these studies are then followed up at six-monthly intervals and comparisons made between the health status of participants in the trauma writing condition and the control condition. Results from these studies collectively show that people who write about their traumas show better immune system functioning, better health and fewer visits to the doctor compared with those who write about trivial topics.

The results of these studies have clear implications for our health. We should write regularly about current difficulties that we face. When writing we should write continuously without regard for grammar, spelling or style. We should write about the objective facts of the situation and also about our deepest thoughts and feelings concerning these facts. We should do this writing in privacy where there are no distractions. The writing should be for ourselves alone and not written for a confidant or friend, since we can be fully honest when we are the audience of our own writing. Immediately after writing about troublesome difficulties we may expect to feel sad or gloomy, but in the long term this exercise is good for our health.

How does writing about trauma or telling and retelling traumatic stories work? Probably by allowing the affect-laden memories which are stored in the amygdala to develop less affect-laden counterparts stored in the hippocampus. Thus when cues elicit memories of the events, we have the option of remembering the less affect-laden version of the memories in the hippocampus. This hypothesis entails the view that cathartic coping helps us to develop a bypass around the affect-laden memories. However, it does not eliminate these affect-laden memories which stay stored in the amygdala and can continue to be elicited by strong cues. This hypothesis deserves urgent testing.

Crying

There is strong empirical support to show that crying leads to immediate emotional relief and a short-term reduction in tension particularly when it entails positive relationship changes. There is little support for the popular notion that crying following trauma leads to better long-term psychological adjustment and physical health (Vingerhoets and Cornelius, 2001). This does not mean that crying is bad for us or has a limited long-term positive effect. Rather, currently little good research has been done on this important subject. There are large individual differences in crying proneness which can be measured by scales such as the adult crying inventory (Vingerhoets and Cornelius, 2001). These differences are associated with culture, gender, age, socialisation and personality. Children, females and those socialised to view crying as acceptable are more prone to crying. People who score highly on the traits of neuroticism, extraversion and empathy are more likely to cry. Crying pronenesss also varies with changes in physical and mental health. For example, people are more likely to cry when they are tired, pregnant, pre-menstrual, depressed or frustrated. Situational factors as well as overall level of crying proneness affect crying. The presence of others may either inhibit or stimulate crying depending upon the cultural norms governing the display of emotional behaviour involving crying. Crying has strong effects on others and may elicit sympathy or censure which in turn may affect crying behaviour.

Faith

To cope with external crises and intra-psychic conflict, people may turn to religion as a way of coping. In Chapter 3 it was mentioned that Freud (1928) thought that faith in a benevolent God, who would reward us in the afterlife if we controlled our aggressive and sexual instincts, was a coping style essential for civilisation (although he referred to these beliefs as an illusion). In Chapter 1 it was noted that moderate correlations have been found between happiness and involvement in religious activity. This may be because religion provides a coherent belief-system that allows people to find meaning in life and make sense of the adversities, stresses and inevitable losses which occur over the course of the lifecycle. It may also be due to the fact that involvement in routine attendance at religious services and being part of a religious community provides people with social support. Both of these factors may partly explain the correlation between religious faith and physical health (Sherman and Simonton, 2001; Plante and Sherman, 2001). However, other factors may be involved. In a large North American survey, it was found that dedicated members of churches had up to seven years' greater life expectancy than people who were not members of churches. This longevity was largely due to church members having healthier lifestyles involving less drinking, smoking and promiscuity (Hummer *et al.*, 1999). Prayer and religious coping, where people view God as a partner in coping with life stresses, eases depression and reduces suicide rates (Pargament, 1997).

Professor Michael Argyle at Oxford has found that various aspects of religious experience are correlated with aspects of personality (Argyle, 2000, 2002). Religious experiences involve three factors: a transcendent factor (contact with god); a mystical factor (loss of sense of self and timelessness); and a social factor (being united with others). Religious experiences are more common in people who score high on intrinsic religiosity (a belief that faith is an end in itself). Strength of religious faith is correlated positively with empathy and negatively with Eysenck's psychoticism factor that measures social non-conformity. Religious fundamentalism is correlated with dogmatism. Religious experience is correlated with schizotypy, a personality dimension which assesses subclinical psychotic-like tendencies such as idiosyncratic delusional beliefs and hallucinatory-like experiences. A fuller explanation of the effectiveness of religious faith as a coping strategy will need to take account of these different aspects of religious experience and their personality correlates.

Meditation

Whether we are facing a large uncontrollable stress such as bereavement or just the daily round of hassles and challenges of everyday life, one way of coping is to focus our attention on something other than ruminative stress-related thoughts and to actively disengage from these while not denying their existence. This process is at the heart of westernised adaptations of eastern mystical calming forms of meditation such as Jon Kabat Zinn's (1990, 1994) Mindfulness Based Stress Reduction, Transcendental Meditation, and Herbert Benson's (1975) Relaxation Response. All of these techniques involve sitting quietly without interruption for set periods of time each day. Then, while accepting that a variety of thoughts (positive and negative) may enter consciousness, to focus attention on the present moment or a fixed stimulus such as one's breath or a mantra and simply observe rather than suppress or engage with thoughts as they arise and leave consciousness. In mindfulness-based meditation we take an observer role, and watch our thoughts flow past. In mindfulness-based meditation we recognise that we are not our thoughts, but we are free to observe them. We also recognise that our thoughts are not reality and so we do not have to accept them as true.

There is a large body of scientific evidence to show that meditation, which involves this process, has a positive effect on immediate and long-term psychological well-being for a wide range of healthy people and also those with physical and mental health difficulties (Murphy and Donovan, 1999; Shapiro *et al.*, 2002). In the short term it leads to a reduction in physiological arousal and a positive mental state. In the longer term it leads to better health. Short-term physiological changes include reduced heart rate and respiration rate, reduction in rate of spontaneous skin conductance fluctuations, reductions in cortisol levels and an increase in the rate of EEG alpha waves. In the long term meditation can enhance a range of psychological functions including cognitive functioning, creativity and empathy. In the long term meditation can also be helpful in the management of conditions such as hypertension and chronic pain and psychological conditions such as anxiety and depression. In one important controlled trial of a mindfulness-based programme for people with chronic depression, people who practised mindfulness meditation relapsed at about half the rate of those who did not meditate (Segal *et al.*, 2002).

Relaxation

Muscle-relaxation exercises, breathing exercises, visualisation exercises, autosuggestion and bio-feedback have all been shown to be effective for reducing physiological arousal and inducing a physical and psychologically relaxed state (Davis *et al.*, 1995; Madders, 1997). Thus, these various relaxation procedures may be used to cope with stress responses, particularly those evoked by uncontrollable stressors. Relaxation procedures have been shown to be effective for managing anxiety, pain, essential hypertension and other stress responses (Sarafino, 2002). An example of relaxation, breathing and visualisation exercises is contained in Table 7.3.

Exercise

Regular daily exercise can help us cope with hassles of daily life and has significant psychological and physical benefits (Sarafino, 2002). At a psychological level regular exercise reduces feelings of depression and anxiety; enhances the speed and accuracy of our work; and improves our self-concepts. At a physiological level, in the short term exercise leads to the release of endorphins, which are morphine-like chemical substances produced in the brain, and which lead to a sense of well-being when released. Exercise also promotes fitness. It increases agility and promotes cardiovascular functioning. Regular exercise also slows down or prevents weight gain with ageing. Regular exercise throughout adulthood reduces the risk for heart disease and cancer and is associated with longevity. The ideal exercise programme involves about three hours' exercise a week spread over five sessions. Each session should begin with a warm-up where muscles in the major muscle groups are stretched and some strength and endurance exercises

Table 7.3 Relaxation exercises

RELAXATION EXERCISES

After a couple of weeks daily practice, you will have developed enough skill to use these exercises to get rid of unwanted body tension.

- Set aside 20 minutes a day to do these relaxation exercises.
- Do them at the same time and in the same place every day.
- Before you begin, remove all distractions (by turning off bright lights, the radio etc.) and loosen any tight clothes (like belts, ties or shoes).
- Lie on a bed or recline in a comfortable chair with the eyes lightly closed.
- Before and after each exercise breath in deeply and exhale slowly three times while saying the word relax.
- Repeat each exercise twice.
- Throughout the exercises, if your parent is helping, you ask them to speak in a calm relaxed quiet voice.

Area	Exercise
Hands	Close your hands into fists. Then allow them to open slowly. Notice the change from tension to relaxation in your hands and allow this change to continue further and further still so the muscles of your hands become more and more relaxed.
Arms	Bend your arms at the elbow and touch your shoulders with your hands. Then allow them to return to the resting position. Notice the change from tension to relaxation in your arms and allow this change to continue further and further still so the muscles of your arms become more and more relaxed.
Shoulders	Hunch your shoulders up to your ears. Then allow them to return to the resting position. Notice the change from tension to relaxation in your shoulders and allow this change to continue further and further still so the muscles of your shoulders become more and more relaxed.
Legs	Point your toes downwards. Then allow them to return to the resting position. Notice the change from tension to relaxation in the fronts of your legs and allow this change to continue further and further still so the muscles in the fronts of your legs become more and more relaxed. Point your toes upwards. Then allow them to return to the resting position. Notice the change from tension to relaxation in the backs of your legs and allow this change to continue further and further still so the muscles in the backs of your legs become more and more relaxed.
Stomach	Take a deep breath and hold it for three seconds, tensing the muscles in your stomach as you do so. Then breath out slowly. Notice the change from tension to relaxation in your stomach muscles and allow this change to continue further and further still so your stomach muscles become more and more relaxed.

Face

Clench your teeth tightly together. Then relax. Notice the change from tension to relaxation in your jaw and allow this change to continue further and further still so the muscles in your jaw become more and more relaxed.

Wrinkle your nose up. Then relax. Notice the change from tension to relaxation in the muscles around the front of your face and allow this change to continue further and further still so the muscles of your face become more and more relaxed.

Shut your eyes tightly. Then relax. Notice the change from tension to relaxation in the muscles around your eyes and allow this change to continue further and further still so the muscles around your eyes become more and more relaxed.

All over

Now that you've done all your muscle exercises, check that all areas of your body are as relaxed as can be. Think of your hands and allow them to relax a little more.
Think of your arms and allow them to relax a little more.
Think of your shoulders and allow them to relax a little more.
Think of your legs and allow them to relax a little more.
Think of your stomach and allow it to relax a little more.
Think of your face and allow it to relax a little more.

Breathing

Breath in ...one...two...three....and out slowly..one..two..three..four...five...six ...and again.
Breath in ...one...two..three....and out slowly..one..two..three..four...five...six ...and again.
Breath in ...one...two..three....and out slowly..one..two..three..four...five..six.

Visualising

Imagine you are lying on a beautiful sandy beach and you feel the sun warm your body.
Make a picture in your mind of the golden sand and the warm sun.
As the sun warms your body you feel more and more relaxed.
As the sun warms your body you feel more and more relaxed.
As the sun warms your body you feel more and more relaxed.

The sky is a clear, clear blue. Above you, you can see a small white cloud drifting away into the distance.
As it drifts away you feel more and more relaxed.
It is drifting away and you feel more and more relaxed.
It is drifting away and you feel more and more relaxed.

As the sun warms your body you feel more and more relaxed.
As the cloud drifts away you feel more and more relaxed.

(Wait for 30 seconds)

When you are ready open your eyes to face the rest of the day relaxed and calm.

are done, such as push-ups or pull-ups. The middle phase of each exercise session should include aerobic exercises, i.e. energetic physical activity that requires high levels of oxygen. The cool-down phase should involve less vigorous exercise such as walking. We are more likely to follow-through on exercise plans if we formulate clear goals, set convenient times and locations for exercising, keep a written record of our progress, and arrange for ourselves and others in our families and peer groups to reward adherence to the exercise programme and goal attainment.

Reframing

With reframing we attempt to mentally step out of the old frame and look at our problems within the context of an alternative frame of reference that makes the emotional impact of the problems less severe or finding a solution to the problem easier (Carr, 2000b). For example, if I'm walking down the street and a friend passes by on the other side without saying hello, I may think to myself that he doesn't like me, probably because he has heard some untrue bad rumour about what I said or did recently. All this may leave me feeling quite upset and vowing never to contact him again. I could reframe this same situation by thinking to myself that he must be preoccupied and have a lot on his mind not to notice me, therefore it would be nice to go over and say hello and ask him how he is. This may leave me feeling a lot better and possibly strengthen our friendship. The first framing of the problem is pessimistic and the second is optimistic. Optimistic framings are more conducive to psychological well-being than pessimistic framings as discussed in Chapter 3. Pessimistic framings, particularly those where failures are attributed to oneself, are associated with depression. Anxiety, in contrast, is typically associated with the pessimistic tendency to routinely interpret relatively ambiguous situations as involving potential threats such as infection, injury, or social embarrassment. People with anger-management problems typically see socially ambiguous situations as involving an immediate and intentional interpersonal threat. For example, such a person may ask you in a threatening manner why you are looking at them or what you meant by some benign remark, because they framed it as threatening. Most of us, in turn, are apt to respond to such hostility with defensiveness, because we frame the situation (quite realistically) as threatening. However, some people are gifted at using humour for coping with these and other stressful situations, a coping strategy that will be addressed in the next section.

One important type of reframing is benefit finding and benefit reminding (Nolen-Hoeksema and Davis, 2002; Tennen and Affleck, 2002). When people cope with adversity in this way they reframe a difficult or challenging situation in such a way as to highlight the positive benefits of the apparently adverse situation for them. Usually this takes place some time (months or years) after the adverse event. For example, studies of bereaved people, mothers of acutely ill newborns, heart-attack survivors and survivors of other illnesses and adversities have shown that those who cope through benefit finding report that these adverse events have offered them benefits which fall broadly into three categories: enhanced personal development; formation of a new life perspective; and strengthened relationships with family members and close friends. There is also some evidence to show that benefit finding is associated with positive post-traumatic physical and psychological adjustment.

Humour

Professor Herbert Lefcourt at the University of Waterloo in Canada has shown conclusively in an extensive series of studies that humour is a particularly effective coping strategy (Lefcourt, 2001, 2002). The tendency to see the funny side of situations (rather than their irritating aspects) and the capacity to alter difficult situations by using humour may be evaluated with the Situational Humour Response Questionnaire and the Coping Humour Scale respectively (Lefcourt, 2001). People who obtain high scores on these measures showed less stress-related symptomatology such as depression in response to stressful life events. Humour has been found to aid recovery from illness and surgery. Immune system functioning has also been found to be improved when humour is used to cope with stressful situations. Humour may help us cope by uplifting our sense of well-being through laughter and/ or by increasing social support from our immediate social network, since humour elicits social support from others.

Distraction

For certain individuals in certain circumstances, distraction (rather than monitoring) is an effective coping strategy. Evidence from studies of adults and children shows that distraction can be an effective short-term coping strategy for some individuals dealing with painful medical procedures and coping with painful medical conditions (Carr, 2000b; Katz et al., 1996). Professor Heinz Krohne (1996) at Johannes Gutenburg University in Germany has developed an instrument which measures tolerance for uncertainty and tolerance for arousal, two constructs which factor analysis confirmed were orthogonal. He has shown in a series of studies in health psychology and laboratory experiments that people who are intolerant of arousal but tolerant of uncertainty can effectively use distraction to manage stressful situations. In contrast, people tolerant of arousal but intolerant of uncertainty prefer to obtain preparatory information about the objective characteristics of impending stresses and their subjective sensory impact as a way of coping.

ASSESSING COPING

Measures of coping have been developed for evaluating general coping style or coping with very specific situations (such as undergoing painful medical procedures). The following instruments for assessing general coping style have moderate to good psychometric properties: the Coping Inventory for Stressful Situations (Endler and Parker, 1990); the Functional Dimension of Coping Scale (Ferguson and Cox, 1997); the Ways of Coping Questionnaire (Folkman and Lazarus, 1988); the Coping Responses Inventory (Moos, 1993); the COPE (Carver *et al.*, 1989); and the Adolescent Coping Orientation for Problem Experiences (Patterson and McCubbin, 1987). From Table 7.4 it may be seen that all of these instruments contain subscales to measure strategies for problem-focused coping; emotion-focused coping; and avoidant coping. However, for instruments with more than four or five subscales, factor structures tend to be unstable. This is probably because both personal dispositions and situational factors contribute to variance in coping style.

Coping Inventory for Stressful Situations

This instrument measures general dispositions to cope in particular ways. It yields scores for task-oriented coping, emotion-oriented coping and avoidant coping which is subdivided into distraction and social diversion (Endler and Parker, 1990). For each item respondents indicate the frequency with which they cope with difficult, stressful or upsetting situations in the way specified in the item on five-point Likert scales. This instrument has a stable factor structure.

Functional Dimension of Coping Scale

This instrument measures situation-specific coping styles. To complete the Functional Dimension of Coping Scale participants first name a stressful situation or event and then specify what they did to cope with this stress process (Ferguson and Cox, 1997). They then rate each of 16 statements to indicate the function of their coping response. These 16 statements cover 4 coping functions for which subscale scores may be computed. These four subscales are approach, avoidance, reappraisal and emotional regulation. The 4-factor structure of the 16 items has been replicated in a number of studies.

Ways of Coping Questionnaire

This instrument measures situation-specific coping styles. It yields scores on eight coping dimensions: confrontative coping; distancing; self-controlling;

Table 7.4 Subscales in selected coping style assessment instruments

Coping style category	Endler and Parker (1990) Coping Inventory for Stressful Situations	Ferguson and Cox (1997) Functional Dimensions of Coping Scale	Folkman and Lazarus (1988) Ways of Coping Questionnaire	Moos (1993) Coping Responses Inventory	Carver, Scheier and Weintraub (1989) COPE	Patterson and McCubbin (1987) Adolescent Coping Orientation for Problem Experiences
Problem-focused	Task-oriented coping	Approach-coping	Planned problem solving Confrontative coping Accepting responsibility Self-controlling	Problem solving Logical analysis	Active coping Planning Seeking instrumental social support Restraint coping Suppressing competing activities	Solving family problems Seeking professional support Developing self-reliance and optimism
Emotion-focused	Emotion-oriented coping	Emotional regulation Reappraisal	Seeking social support Positive reappraisal	Acceptance or resignation Seeking guidance and support Positive reappraisal Emotional discharge	Acceptance Seeking emotional social support Turning to religion Positive reinterpretation and growth Joking about the stressor Focusing on and venting emotions Denial Substance use	Developing social support Investing in close friends Seeking spiritual support Being humorous Ventilating feelings Relaxing
Avoidant-coping	Avoidant-coping Social diversion Distraction	Avoidance-coping	Escape avoidance Distancing	Cognitive avoidance Seeking alternative rewards	Behavioural disengagement Mental disengagement	Avoiding problems Seeking diversions Engaging in a demanding activity

seeking social support; accepting responsibility; escape-avoidance; planned problem solving; and positive reappraisal (Folkman and Lazarus, 1988). Responses for each item are given on four-point Likert scales with respect to actual stresses experienced in the preceding week.

Coping Responses Inventory

This set of inventories measures dispositional coping styles. The inventories yield scores on eight coping dimensions: logical analysis; problem solving; positive reappraisal; seeking guidance and support; cognitive avoidance; acceptance or resignation; seeking alternative rewards; and emotional discharge (Moos, 1993). There are adult and adolescent versions of the inventory and actual and ideal versions which yield scores for coping strategies used and preferred coping strategies.

COPE

This inventory measures dispositional coping styles. It contains 15 scales which measure active coping, planning, suppression of competing activities, restraint coping, seeking social support for instrumental reasons, seeking social support for emotional reasons, positive reinterpretation and growth, acceptance, turning to religion, focusing on and venting of emotions, denial, behavioural disengagement, mental disengagement, joking about the stressor, and substance use (Carver *et al.*, 1989).

Adolescent Coping Orientation for Problem Experiences (A-COPE)

This dispositional coping style inventory for adolescents yields scores on 12 dimensions: ventilating feelings; seeking diversions; developing self-reliance and optimism; developing social support; solving family problems; avoiding problems; seeking spiritual support; investing in close friends; seeking professional support; engaging in a demanding activity; being humorous; and relaxing (Patterson and McCubbin, 1987).

DEFENCE MECHANISMS

Defence mechanisms and coping strategies are both constructs which explain how we protect ourselves from being overwhelmed by strong negative feelings of anxiety and frustration. However, there are important differences between the two constructs and the psychological processes to which they refer. The idea of coping strategies was developed within the cognitive-behavioural tradition to explain how we consciously manage situations in which external demands (such as exams) outstrip personal resources (such as our memory of the material being examined) (Zeidner and Endler, 1996). Defence mechanisms, on the other hand, evolved within the psychoanalytic tradition to explain how unconscious processes (such as repression) regulate negative affect associated with intra-psychic factors (such as traumatic memories or unacceptable sexual or aggressive impulses).

The concept of defence mechanism was introduced into modern psychology by Sigmund Freud (1896), the founder of psychoanalysis. The central idea, which was articulated in different ways throughout the development of Freud's various theories, was that a variety of unconscious psychological manoeuvres were used to fend off, distort or disguise unacceptable impulses and ideas and keep them out of consciousness. Freud's daughter, Anna (A. Freud, 1936), summarised and extended her father's list of defence mechanisms in her influential text, *The Ego and the Mechanisms of Defence*. Most of the defences described in her text, along with a number of others which have been introduced by various psychoanalysts over the second half of the twentieth century, are defined in Table 7.5.

Defences have been conceptualised in at least three ways (Conte and Plutchik, 1995; Paulhus *et al.*, 1997). Within Freud's earliest writings, defences were conceptualised as a way of excluding memories of actual traumatic events (such as sexual abuse) from consciousness so as to avoid re-experiencing traumatic pain. Within Freud's later structural model, defences were conceptualised as psychological strategies used to cope with anxiety caused by the conflict between unacceptable impulses (sexual or aggressive urges from the id) and the prohibitions of the conscience (or superego). Thus, if a person experiences an unacceptable sexual or aggressive impulse, anxiety about the consequences of acting on this impulse will be experienced because such actions would violate the prohibitions of the superego. Violating these prohibitions would lead to distress associated with internal processes, such as guilt, and external processes, such as anger and retaliation from the recipients of sexual or aggressive impulse-driven behaviour. Defence mechanisms are used to regulate or reduce anxiety and other negative emotional states that accompany conflict.

A slightly different view of defences is taken by object-relations theory, self-psychology and within the interpersonal psychoanalytic tradition. Here defences are viewed as a way of coping with anxiety that arises from conflict between a wish to express some aspect of the self which is unacceptable to caregivers or significant members of the individual's family or social network and the wish to retain the support of these significant people or their introjected representations by complying with their injunctions. For example, a youngster who is angry with his mother may wish to express his anger directly but fear the mother's retaliation or the personal experience of guilt. If he uses the primitive defence mechanism of passive aggression he may regulate the negative emotions associated with this conflict by agreeing to

Table 7.5 Defence mechanisms at different levels of maturity

Level	Features of defences	Defence	The individual regulates emotional discomfort associated with conflicting wishes and impulses or external stress by:
High adaptive level	Promote an optimal balance among unacceptable impulses and prosocial wishes to maximise gratification and permit conscious awareness of conflicting impulses and wishes	Anticipation	considering emotional reactions and consequences of these before the conflict or stress occurs and exploring the pros and cons of various solutions to these problematic emotional states
		Affiliation	seeking social support from others, sharing problems with them without making them responsible for them or for relieving the distress they entail
		Altruism	dedication to meeting the needs of others and receiving gratification from this (without excessive self-sacrificing)
		Humour	reframing the situation which gives rise to conflict or stress in an ironic or amusing way
		Self-assertion	expressing conflict-related thoughts or feelings in a direct yet non-coercive way
		Self-observation	monitoring how situations lead to conflict or stress and using this new understanding to modify negative affect
		Sublimation	channelling negative emotions arising from conflict or stress into socially acceptable activities such as work or sports
		Suppression	intentionally avoiding thinking about conflict or stress
Mental inhibitions	Keep unacceptable impulses out of awareness	Displacement	transferring negative feelings about one person onto another less threatening person
Compromise formation level		Dissociation	experiencing a breakdown in the integrated functions of consciousness, memory, perception, or motor behaviour
		Intellectualisation	the excessive use of abstract thinking or generalisations to minimise disturbing feelings arising from conflict
		Isolation of affect	losing touch with the feelings associated with descriptive details of the conflict, trauma or stress
		Reaction formation	substituting acceptable behaviours, thoughts or feelings which are the opposite of unacceptable or unwanted behaviours, thoughts or feelings that arise from a conflict
		Repression	expelling unwanted thoughts, emotions or wishes from awareness
		Undoing	using ritualistic or magical words or behaviour to symbolically negate or make amends for unacceptable impulses

Level		Defense	Description
Minor image-distorting level	Distort image of self and others to regulate self-esteem	Devaluation	attributing exaggerated negative characteristics to the self or others
		Idealisation	attributing exaggerated positive characteristics to the others
		Omnipotence	attributing exaggerated positive characteristics or special abilities and powers to the self which make oneself superior to others
Disavowal level	Keep unacceptable impulses and ideas out of consciousness with or without misattribution of these to external causes	Denial	refusing to acknowledge the painful features of the situation or experiences which are apparent to others
		Projection	attributing to others one's own unacceptable thoughts, feelings and wishes
		Rationalisation	providing an elaborate self-serving or self-justifying explanation to conceal unacceptable thoughts, actions or impulses
Major image-distorting level	Gross distortion or misattribution of aspects of the self or others	Autistic fantasy	engaging in excessive daydreaming or wishful thinking as a substitute for using problem solving or social support to deal with emotional distress
		Projective identification	attributing to others one's own unacceptable aggressive impulses; then inducing others to feel these by reacting aggressively to them; then using the other person's aggressive reactions as justification for acting out unacceptable aggressive impulses
		Splitting of self-image or image of others	failing to integrate the positive and negative qualities of self and others and viewing self and others as either all good or all bad
Action level	Action or withdrawal from action	Acting out	acting unacceptably to give expression to the experience of emotional distress associated with conflict or stress
		Apathetic withdrawal	not engaging with others
		Help-rejecting complaining	making repeated requests for help and then rejecting help when offered as a way of expressing unacceptable aggressive impulses
		Passive aggression	unassertively expressing unacceptable aggression towards others in authority by overtly complying with their wishes while covertly resisting these
Level of defensive dysregulation	Failure of defences to regulate conflict-related feelings leading to a breakdown in reality testing	Delusional projection	attributing to others one's own unacceptable thoughts, feelings and wishes to an extreme degree
		Psychotic denial	refusing to acknowledge the painful features of the situation or experiences which are apparent to others to an extreme degree
		Psychotic distortion	viewing reality in an extremely distorted way

Source: Based on American Psychiatric Association (1995): 751–3.

do certain household chores but doing them slowly or inefficiently. If he uses a neurotic defence mechanism, he may deal with the conflict by displacing his anger onto siblings and fighting with them. If he uses a mature defence mechanism like sublimation, he may play football after doing chores to physically release the tension associated with the negative emotional state.

This example shows that some defence mechanisms are more adaptive than others. In Appendix B of DSM IV (APA, 1994), a defensive functioning scale is presented which organises defence mechanisms into seven levels. This scale is summarised in Table 7.5. The scale was developed by Professors George Vaillant, Mardi Horowitz, Bram Fridhandler, S. Cooper and Michael Bond, all of whom are leading researchers in the field. The scale represents the culmination of much of what we know about defence mechanisms and their operation, based on both clinical and experimental investigations. A very broad conceptualisation of defence is entailed by this scale in that it includes both conscious coping mechanisms, such as self-assertion, and unconscious defence mechanisms as traditionally defined, such as repression. It is also clear from this scale that defences allow people to regulate negative affect such as anxiety or depression associated with internal conflict between unacceptable sexual and aggressive urges and prosocial wishes and also associated with confronting external interpersonal stress, threat or trauma. Defences at different levels achieve this regulatory function in different ways.

At the adaptive level defences regulate negative affect by allowing a balance to be achieved between unacceptable impulses and prosocial wishes or between demands and coping resources. This balance maximises the possibilities of gratification. Also, while the balance is being achieved, the conflicting impulses and wishes, demands and personal resources and related emotions are all held in consciousness. Anticipation, affiliation, altruism, humour, self-assertion, self-observation, sublimation and suppression are adaptive defences and these will be considered in detail later after the remaining levels of the scale have been described.

At the second level – the level of mental inhibitions or compromise formation – defences regulate negative affect by keeping unacceptable wishes out of consciousness. Of these, repression is the prototypical defence. Other defences at this level include displacement, dissociation, intellectualisation, isolation of affect, reaction formation and undoing.

Minor image distortion of the self or others, through devaluation, idealisation or omnipotence occurs at the next level. Defences at this level regulate self-esteem by enhancing or exaggerating positive aspects of the image of the self and one's allies and exaggerating negative attributes of others. Traditionally these defences are referred to as narcissistic since they typify the narcissistic personality. Defences at this level are related to optimistic self-evaluation and positive illusions addressed in Chapter 3.

At the next level, negative affect associated with conflict between un-acceptable impulses and prosocial wishes is regulated by disavowal through denial, projection or rationalisation.

Major image distortion to regulate negative affect associated with conflict occurs at the next level. Splitting is the prototypical defence at this level. Here negative affect is regulated by viewing some people as 'all bad' and directing all unacceptable aggressive impulses towards them. Concurrently a subset of people are viewed as 'all good' and revered for this. Traditionally these defences are referred to as borderline since they typify the borderline personality.

At the action level, conflict-related negative affect is regulated by express-ing it through behaviour: either aggressive or promiscuous sexual behaviour or social withdrawal.

Where there is a failure to regulate negative affect associated with conflict the person may struggle to do so by breaking contact with reality and engaging in psychotic denial, distortion or delusional projection.

A model of the way defences operate to reduce anxiety and distress associated with conflict is presented in Figure 7.4. This model presents in diagrammatic form the material presented in the preceding section.

Adaptive defences

Anticipation, affiliation, altruism, humour, self-assertion, self-observation, sublimation and suppression are adaptive defences. To illustrate these, after defining each positive defence an example will be given. For all of these defences unacceptable sexual or aggressive urges, anxiety or depression associated with conflict concerning the expression of these impulses, or emotional distress associated with managing interpersonal threat or trauma are regulated by transforming the affect into positive actions. Positive adapt-ive defences enrich our lives. They do more than allow us to make the best of a bad situation. Valliant uses the metaphor of transforming base metal into gold to characterise the way adaptive defences allow unacceptable impulses to find expression in a way that enriches our lives.

Anticipation involves considering and partially experiencing emotional reactions and the consequences of these before the conflict or stress occurs and exploring the various solutions to these problematic emotional states. Anticipation involves both cognitive planning and allowing oneself to experience some of the affect that may occur in the impending situation and practising regulating it. For example, when I worked as a sailing in-structor I taught children capsize drill on moderately windy days in a rela-tively sheltered creek, so that they would be able to regulate their anxiety better if they capsized in strong winds on unsheltered water. As well as training them in capsize drill, this helped them to use anticipation as a defence mechanism.

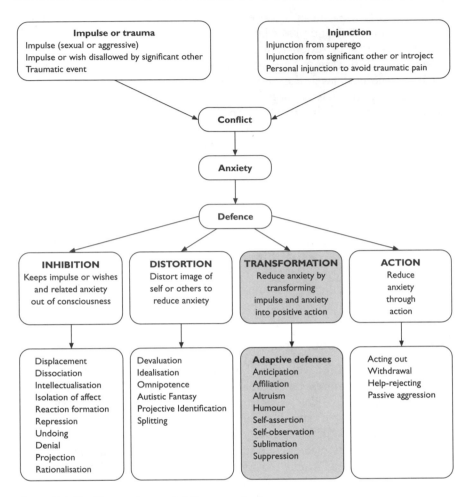

Figure 7.4 Conflict, anxiety and defence mechanisms

Affiliation involves seeking social support from others, sharing problems with them and doing this without making them responsible for the problem or for relieving the distress they entail. For example, a woman who has had a hard day at work may use affiliation as a defence by calling a close friend when she gets home and talking about the conflict entailed by her aggression towards her boss and her wish to behave professionally in her job. The defence mechanism – affiliation or support seeking – tends to deepen friendships, and in this sense is transformative. Social support has been mentioned already as a coping strategy and will be mentioned again in Chapter 8 on positive relationships.

Altruism is dedication to meeting the needs of others and receiving gratification from this without engaging in excessive self-sacrifice. For example, a woman physically abused as a child may cope with the conflict between her feelings of aggression towards herself and her own children, on the one hand, and her wish to behave morally, on the other, by devoting some of her time to helping children at a domestic violence refuge.

When humour is used as a defence, we reframe situations that gives rise to conflict or stress in an ironic or amusing way. For example, in the song 'Alice's Restaurant', Arlo Guthrie is charged by a police officer with littering after a letter addressed to Arlo is found in an illegal rubbish dump. Arlo regulated his anxiety about expressing unacceptable rage towards the arresting officer by saying to Officer Obie, that he could not tell a lie. He said that he put that letter under that mountain of litter. We are all enriched when anxiety and aggression are transformed into humour.

Self-assertion involves expressing conflict-related thoughts or feelings in a direct yet non-coercive way. For example, unacceptable rage at a neighbour for holding a loud party till 4.00 am the night before an exam may be managed assertively by asking the neighbour to turn down the music.

Self-observation involves monitoring how situations lead to conflict or stress and using this new understanding to modify negative affect. For example, noting that pressures to be kind, thoughtful and to do all the shopping and preparation for Christmas can lead to unacceptable aggression may lead a person to pace these demands better in future.

Sublimation is the channelling of negative emotions arising from conflict or stress into socially acceptable activities such as work, sports or art. For example, channelling aggression associated with being vindictively cross-examined as an expert witness in a child protection case into aerobic exercise or an academic description of the process of being an expert witness is sublimation. Sublimation is also the defence mechanism that allows unfulfilled sexual desire to be transformed into music or poetry.

Suppression is the intentional avoidance of thinking about conflict or stress. For example, consciously setting aside thoughts and feelings associated with a conflictual work meeting, when going for a drink with a friend after work, involves suppression. Suppression is the defence entailed in stoicism and the British stiff upper lip.

Correlates of adaptive defences

In a 50-year longitudinal study of three large cohorts, Professor George Vaillant (2000) at Harvard University used rating scales to assess the positive defences of altruism, sublimation, suppression, anticipation and humour from interview transcripts and personal accounts of life events of participants. He found that the use of positive defences was unrelated to gender, years of education, parental socio-economic status and IQ. However the use of positive defences in early adulthood was predictive of midlife psychosocial functioning, social support, subjective well-being, marital satisfaction and income. The use of adaptive defences was also associated with less disability in middle life and greater resilience against developing depression in the face of multiple life stresses.

Development of adaptive defences

From an evolutionary perspective defences serve an important self-preservative function, in that they prevent harm that might come from expression of impulses that would lead to retaliative aggression from others. Highly adaptive defences fulfil this function but also maximise personal gratification within the prevailing social constraints. Over the lifespan, defences follow a developmental trajectory from the less sophisticated to the more sophisticated (Cramer, 1991). Simple defences such as denial appear during the earliest years. Children, incapable of escaping from anxiety-provoking situations, block out noxious sensory experiences by, for example, going to sleep. During the pre-adolescent years, as they develop logical thought, they develop sufficient skills for more complex defences such as projection (blaming others) and rationalisation (giving spurious explanations for expressing unacceptable impulses). In adolescence, with the advent of abstract reasoning skills, complex defences such as intellectualisation evolve. There is good evidence that abusive parent–child relationships lead to the development of major image-distorting defences associated with borderline personality disorder (Clarkin and Lenzenweger, 1996). However, we are currently unsure about how and when adaptive defences develop or the conditions which nurture their development (Vaillant, 2000).

ASSESSING DEFENCES

Both rating scales and self-report scales have been developed to assess adaptive defence mechanisms. The Defence Mechanism Rating Scales (Perry and Kardos, 1995) is the best available method for objectively rating defences from tapes or transcripts. An early version of this was used in Valliant's (2000) longitudinal studies mentioned above and these scales were the forerunners of the DSM IV defensive functioning scale presented in Table 7.5. Strictly speaking, defences cannot be measured by self-report instruments because defences operate out of awareness. However, attempts have been made to measure conscious derivatives of unconscious defence mechanisms using self-report inventories. Many of these, however, only measure maladaptive defence mechanisms. The Defence Style Questionnaire (Bond and Wesley, 1996) and the Defence Mechanisms Profile (Johnson and Gold,

1995) are notable exceptions insofar as both contain subscales which measure adaptive defences.

Defence Mechanism Rating Scales

This instrument contains scales for rating 27 defence mechanisms at 7 levels:

1. Mature defences: affiliation; altruism; anticipation; humour; self-assertion, self-observation, sublimation and suppression.
2. Obsessional defences: isolation; intellectualisation; and undoing.
3. Other neurotic defences: repression; dissociation; reaction formation; and displacement.
4. Minor image-distorting narcissistic defences: omnipotence; idealisation; and devaluation.
5. Disavowal defences: denial; projection; rationalisation; and fantasy.
6. Major image-distorting borderline defences: splitting and projective identification.
7. Action defences: acting out; passive aggression; and hypochondriasis.
(Perry and Kardos, 1995)

The rating scales contain clear criteria for rating the presence or absence of the defences and for distinguishing one defence from another based on data in interview recordings or transcripts. Scores may be computed for each of the 27 scales and an overall index of a person's level of defensive functioning may also be computed. The scales have moderate reliability and good criterion validity. They correlate with measures of adaptive functioning and mental health.

Defence Style Questionnaire

This 88-item self-report inventory yields scores on four styles of defensive functioning: maladaptive action (33 items); image-distorting (15 items); self-sacrificing (8 items); and adaptive (7 items) (Bond and Wesley, 1996). Each defensive style consists of particular defence mechanisms. The maladaptive-action style includes passive-aggression, projection, regression, inhibition, projective identification, acting out, somatisation, withdrawal, fantasy, help-rejecting, complaining and undoing. The image-distorting style includes omnipotence, omnipotence and devaluation, denial, splitting, primitive idealisation, projection and isolation. The self-sacrificing style includes pseudo-altruism, reaction formation and denial. The adaptive style includes suppression, sublimation, humour, anticipation and affiliation. The inventory also contains a social desirability response set scale. Responses to all items are given on nine-point Likert scales ranging from 1 = strongly disagree to 9 = strongly agree. The four defensive styles fall on a continuum from unhealthy to healthy functioning in the following order: maladaptive action; image-distorting; self-sacrificing; and adaptive. Normative data are available for various samples including non-patients, patients with borderline personality disorder, and other groups of psychiatric patients. The subscales have acceptable internal consistency and test–retest reliability. The instrument has good validity. Subscales correlate with clinician's ratings of defences on the defence mechanism rating scale. Patient groups have significantly higher scores on maladaptive defensive style scales than normal controls. Factor analyses of items confirm its four-subscale structure.

Defence Mechanisms Profile

This is a 40-item sentence completion inventory which yields scores on 14 subscales which are grouped into four categories:

1. tension reduction: physical incorporation; indirect incorporation; physical expulsion; and verbal expulsion.
2. early defences: denial; and withdrawal.
3. middle-range defences: undoing; displacement; turning against self; reaction formation; and compensation.
4. Advanced defences: substitution; rationalisation; and intellectualisation.

(Johnson and Gold, 1995)

Each sentence stem in this instrument describes a conflictual or tension-evoking situation and written responses are assigned to one (or more) of the 14-scale categories according to explicit criteria. The test has good interrater and test–retest reliability and there is some evidence for concurrent validity.

IMPLICATIONS

A summary of self-help strategies for promoting strengths and well-being based on research on self-esteem, self-efficacy, positive coping strategies and adaptive defences is given in Table 7.6. These can be incorporated into clinical practice.

CONTROVERSIES

There are many controversies within the domains covered in this chapter. The first concerns the validity of the idea of a self. If we propose a self as a central aspect of personality, are we not open to all the logical difficulties that go with Descartes' problem of separating the material-body and non-material soul, and making the latter the driver of the former even though by

Table 7.6 Strategies for promoting strengths and well-being based on research on self-esteem, self-efficacy, positive coping strategies and adaptive defences

Domain	Strategy
Fostering self-esteem in children	• Accept your children's profile of strengths and limitations • Set explicit high, but attainable standards in their areas of strength • Support children in attaining these standards • Adopt a consistent authoritative parenting style in which you treat your children with warmth and respect and allow them some influence over the way household routines and rules for good conduct are set and enforced • Be a good role model for your children by coping with life challenges using an active problem-solving coping style
Increasing self-esteem	• Identify the domain in which you have low self-esteem • Obtain skills training in the area of low competence (e.g. problem-solving skills, social skills, academic skills, or work-related skills)
Increasing self-efficacy	• In a specific domain set overall goals, along with a series of intermediate small but achievable goals to ensure mastery experiences occur frequently • When you achieve goals, acknowledge your mastery experiences and reflect on how competent you expect to be next time you attempt to achieve a similar goal • Observe other people who have succeeded through sustained effort in working towards goals like yours • Arrange for significant members of your social network or coaches who know the domain in which you wish to excel to persuade you that you can succeed in mastering manageable goals • Pursue goals when you are physically and mentally fit and in a positive mood
Coping	• Develop and use functional coping strategies such as problem solving, social support, spiritual support, catharsis, reframing, humour, relaxation routines, physical exercise and distraction listed in Table 7.2
Defences	• Develop and use adaptive defences such as anticipation, affiliation, altruism, humour, self-assertion, self-observation, sublimation and suppression listed in Table 7.5

Source: Based on Mruk (1999); Bandura (1997); Zeidner and Endler (1996); American Psychiatric Association (1994): 751–3.

definition the immaterial cannot influence the material? In large part we are re-creating this problem, but modern empirical psychologists simply live with this. They define aspects of the self, study their longitudinal development and crossectional bio-psychosocial correlates, and leave the problem of dualism unsolved.

With respect to self-esteem and self-efficacy, there are good arguments that these are distinct constructs, since predictions based on measurements of self-efficacy are far more accurate. However, there is also an argument that self-evaluative beliefs may be hierarchically organised with global beliefs about self-worth at the top of the hierarchy and specific efficacy beliefs beneath this.

With respect to defence mechanisms and coping styles, there is an argument that these are quite distinct phenomena, with coping strategies being conscious and deliberately deployed while defence mechanisms are unconscious and run on automatic pilot. However, there is much overlap between lists of coping strategies and defence mechanisms and little clear conceptual basis for this. There is therefore an argument that perhaps all self-regulatory procedures fall along a number of continua, including the degree to which we are consciously aware of them and the degree to which we deliberately use them, and that an attempt should be made to develop an integrative framework within which to conceptualise defence mechanisms and coping strategies.

SUMMARY

Because it has become increasingly difficult to put faith in the supernatural or social order, since the turn of the last century, people are increasingly forced to look elsewhere for values. Many turn to the self as a source of value and it has become an important focus for modern western psychology. Self-focused concerns of particular relevance to positive psychology include self-evaluation (which underpins self-esteem and self-efficacy) and self-regulation through the use of coping strategies and defence mechanisms. To some extent theoretical and empirical work on self-evaluation has privileged the notion of self-as-object while studies of self-regulation have placed greater emphasis on self-as-subject. Studies of self-evaluation show that high self-esteem and strong self-efficacy beliefs contribute to personal strength and resilience. Self-efficacy and self-esteem differ insofar as self-esteem is concerned with judgements about global personal worth, while self-efficacy is concerned with judgements about specific personal capabilities. Self-esteem develops within a family context in which parents are accepting of children's strengths and limitations and set explicit high, but attainable, standards which they support their children to achieve. Self-efficacy beliefs are probably fostered by a similar family environment but since they are more specific than beliefs about self-worth they are fostered by specific types of mastery experiences, specific vicarious experiences, social persuasion concerning the performance of specific tasks, and conducting these specific tasks in positive physical and emotional states. Studies of self-regulation show that better health and well-being occur when certain types of coping strategies are used to manage life challenges and certain types of defence mechanisms are adopted to manage anxiety arising from conflicting sexual, aggressive and social motives. Emotion-focused coping strategies such as fostering social support are appropriate for uncontrollable stresses such as bereavement. For controllable stresses problem-focused coping strategies such as problem solving are more appropriate. Where time out from active coping is required to marshal personal resources before returning to active coping, avoidant coping such as distraction may be appropriate. For all three coping styles, a distinction may be made between functional and dysfunctional strategies. The idea of coping strategies was developed within the cognitive-behavioural tradition to explain the conscious management of situations in which external demands (such as exams) tax personal resources (such as our memory of the material being examined). The concept of defence mechanisms, on the other hand, evolved within the psychoanalytic tradition to explain how unconscious processes (such as repression) regulate anxiety associated with conflict between unacceptable impulses (sexual or aggressive urges from the id) and the prohibitions of the conscience (or superego). In Appendix B of DSM IV, a defensive functioning scale is presented which organises defence mechanisms into seven levels. Defences at different levels regulate anxiety in different ways. At the adaptive level defences regulate anxiety by allowing a balance to be achieved between unacceptable impulses and prosocial wishes. This balance maximises the possibilities of gratification. Anticipation, affiliation, altruism, humour, self-assertion, self-observation, sublimation and suppression are adaptive defences. Over the lifespan, defences follow a developmental trajectory from less sophisticated to more sophisticated. However, we are currently unsure about how and when adaptive defences develop or the conditions which nurture their development.

QUESTIONS

Personal development questions

1. Describe a situation that occurred within the past month, in which you successfully coped with external stress or internal conflict.
2. What coping strategies or defences did you use?
3. Describe a situation that occurred within the past month, in which it was critical for you to cope with external stress or internal conflict, but you were not successful in doing so.
4. What coping strategies or defences would you like to have had so that you could have coped better?
5. What steps can you take now to develop these coping strategies and defences?
6. What would be the costs and benefits of taking these steps?

7. Take some of these steps and assess the impact it has on your well-being by assessing yourself before and afterwards on one of the well-being scales contained in Chapter 1.

Research questions

1. Design and conduct a study to test the hypothesis that there is a significant correlation between happiness and one or more functional coping strategies or adaptive defence mechanisms.
2. Conduct PsychInfo searches covering literature published in the past couple of years using the terms 'self-esteem', 'self-efficacy', 'coping strategy', and 'defence mechanism' coupled with the term 'well-being'. Identify a study that interests you and that is feasible to replicate and extend. Conduct the replication.

FURTHER READING

Academic

Bandura, A. (1997). *Self-Efficacy*. New York: Freeman.
Conte, H. and Plutchik, R. (1995). *Ego Defences: Theory and Measurement*. New York: Wiley.
Mruk, C. (1999). *Self-esteem* (2nd edn). New York: Springer.
Zeidner, M. and Endler, N. (1996). *Handbook of Coping: Theory, Research, Applications*. New York: Wiley.

Self-help: problem solving

D'Zurilla, T. and Nezu, A. (1999). *Problem Solving Therapy* (2nd edn). New York: Springer Verlag.

Self-help: stress management

Benson, H. (1975). *The Relaxation Response*. New York: William Morrow.
Benson, H. and Stuart, E. (1992). *The Wellness Book: A Comprehensive Guide to Maintaining Health and Treating Stress Related Illness*. This research-based guide shows how a range of techniques can be used to cope with stress-related illness. The techniques include relaxation, nutrition, exercise, body awareness, cognitive restructuring, problem solving and humour.
Davis, M., Eshelman, E. and McKay, M. (1995). *The Relaxation and Stress Workbook* (4th edn). Oakland, CA: New Harbinger. This workbook gives practical advice based on sound evidence and covers nutrition, exercise, relaxation, visualisation, meditation, thought-stopping, time management and managing stress at work.

Kabat Zinn, J. (1990). *Full Catastrophe Living: Using the Wisdom of Your Body and Mind to Face Stress, Pain and Illness.* New York: Delacorte Press.

Kabat Zinn, J. (1994). *Wherever You Go. There You Are: Mindfulness Meditation in Everyday Life.* New York: Hyperion.

Levine, M. (2000). *The Positive Psychology of Buddhism and Yoga.* Mahwah, NJ: Erlbaum.

Lovelace, R. (1990). *Stress Master.* New York: Wiley. This practical and humorous guide gives research-based advice on changing stressful thinking, relaxation, nutrition, exercise, addictions and relaxation.

Madders, J. (1997). *The Stress and Relaxation Handbook: A Practical Guide to Self-Help Techniques.* London: Vermillion. This illustrated guide shows how relaxation exercises can be used to manage stress and pain associated with stress-related conditions.

Self-esteem

Burns, D. (1993a). *Ten Days to Self-esteem.* New York: Quill.

Burns, D. (1993b). *Ten Days to Self-esteem. The Leader's Manual.* New York: Quill.

Assertiveness

Alberti, R. Emmons, M. (1995). *Your Perfect Right: A Guide to Assertive Living* (7th edn). San Luis Obispo, CA: Impact. (A research-based guide to assertiveness.)

Bower, A. and Bower, G. (1991). *Asserting Yourself: A Practical Guide for Positive Change.* Reading: MA: Addison-Wesley. (A research-based guide to assertiveness.)

Bramson, R. (1981). *Coping with Difficult People.* New York: Dell. This is a practical guide to dealing with difficult people at work: the aggressive person, the complainer, the silent person, the negativist, the know-all and the indecisive.

Coping with abuse

Bass, E. and Davis, L. (1992). *The Courage to Heal* (revised 2nd edn). New York: Harper Perennial. (This is a good self-help guide for women who have survived sexual abuse.)

Lew, M. (1990). *Victims no Longer: Men recovering from Incest and other Sexual Child Abuse.* New York: Harper and Row. (This is a good self-help guide for men who have survived sexual abuse.)

Walker, L. (1979). *The Battered Woman.* New York: Harper Row. (This is a good self-help book for women abused by their partners.)

Surviving trauma

Pennebaker, J. (1997). *Opening Up: The Healing Power of Confiding in Others.* New York: Guilford Press. This self-help guide, based on a sound research base, shows how writing about trauma or confiding in others helps to prevent trauma from creating ill-health.

MEASURES FOR USE IN RESEARCH

Self-esteem and self-concept

Battle, J. (1992). *Culture-Free Self-Esteem Inventories: Examiner's Manual* (2nd edn). Austin, TX: Pro-ed. (Measures multiple dimensions of self-esteem across the lifespan.)

Byrne, B. (1995). *Measuring Self-Concept Across the Life Span: Issues and Instrumentation*. Washington, DC: American Psychological Association.

Coopersmith, S. (1981). *Self-esteem Inventories*. Palo Alto, CA: Consulting Psychologists Press. (Measures multiple dimensions of self-esteem across the lifespan.)

Fitts, W. (1988). *Tennessee Self-Concept Scale*. Los Angeles, CA: Western Psychological Services. (Measures multiple dimensions of self-concept across the lifespan.)

Nugent, W. and Thomas, J. (1993). Validation of the Self-Esteem Rating Scale. *Research of Social Work Practice* 3: 191–207. (Describes a reliable and valid 32-item unidimensional self-esteem scale for use with adults.)

O'Brien, E. and Epstein, S. (1988). *Multidimensional Self-Esteem Inventory*. Odessa, FL: Psychological Assessment Resources. (Measures multiple dimensions of self-esteem in adults.)

Piers, E. and Harris, D. (1969). *Piers-Harris Children's Self-Concept Scale*. Los Angeles, CA: Western Psychological Services. (Measures multiple dimensions of self-concept in childhood and adolescence.)

Rosenberg, M. (1979). *Conceiving the Self*. New York: Basic Books. (Contains the 10-item unidimensional Rosenberg Self-Esteem Scale for use with children and adolescents.)

Control-related constructs

Antonovsky, A. (1993). The structure and properties of the sense of coherence scale. *Social Science and Medicine*, 35: 725–33.

Burger, J. and Cooper, H. (1979). The desirability of control. *Motivation and Emotion* 3: 381–93. (Contains the desirability of control scale.)

Kobasa, S. (1979). Stressful life events, personality and health: an inquiry into hardiness. *Journal of Personality and Social Psychology* 37: 1–11.

Levenson, H. (1973). Multidimensional locus of control in psychiatric patients. *Journal of Consulting and Clinical Psychology* 41: 397–404.

Nowicki, S. and Strickland, B. (1973). A locus of control scale for children. *Journal of Consulting and Clinical Psychology* 40: 148–54.

Rotter, J. (1966). Generalised expectancies for internal versus external control of reinforcement. *Psychological Monographs* 90: 1–28. (Contains the original locus of control scale.)

Sherer, M., Maddux, J., Mercandante, B., Prentice-Dunn, S., Jacobs, B. and Rogers, R. (1982). The Self-Efficacy Scale: construction and validation. *Psychological Reports* 51: 663–71.

Wallston, K., Wallston, B. and DeVellis, R. (1978). Development of the Multidimensional Health Locus of Control (MHLC) Scales. *Health Education Monographs* 6: 161–70.

Coping

Carver, C., Scheier, M. and Weintraub, J. (1989). Assessing coping strategies: a theoretically based approach. *Journal of Personality and Social Psychology* 56: 267–83. (Describes the COPE.)

Endler, N. and Parker, J. (1990). *Coping Inventory for Stressful Situations (CISS)*. Toronto, Canada: Multi Health Systems.

Ferguson, E. and Cox, T. (1997). The functional dimensions of coping scale: theory, reliability and validity. *British Journal of Health Psychology* 2: 109–29.

Folkman, S. and Lazarus, R. (1988). *Manual for the Ways of Coping Questionnaire*. Palo Alto, CA: Consulting Psychologists Press.

Moos, R. (1993a). *Coping Responses Inventory: Adolescent Form Manual*. Odessa, FL: Psychological Assessment Resources.

Moos, R. (1993b). *Coping Responses Inventory: Adult Form Manual*. Odessa, FL: Psychological Assessment Resources.

Patterson, J. and McCubbin, H. (1987). Adolescent coping style and behaviours: conceptualisation and measurement. *Journal of Adolescence* 10: 163–86.

Problem-solving

Heppner, P. (1988). *The Problem Solving Inventory*. Palo Alto, CA: Consulting Psychologists Press.

Social support

Dahlem, N., Zimet, G. and Walker, R. (1991). A multidimensional scale of perceived social support. *Journal of Clinical Psychology* 47: 756–61.

Pierce, G., Sarason, I. and Sarason, B. (1991). General and relationship-based perceptions of social support: are two constructs better than one? *Journal of Personality and Social Psychology* 61: 1028–39. (Describes the Quality of Relationship Inventory.)

Sarason, I., Levine, H., Basham, R. and Sarason, B. (1983). Assessing social support: the social support questionnaire. *Journal of Personality and Social Psychology* 44: 127–39.

Sarason, I., Sarason, B., Shearin, E. and Pierce, G. (1987). A brief measure of social support: practical and theoretical considerations. *Journal of Social and Personal Relationships* 4: 497–510.

Religious coping

Sherman, A. and Simonton, S. (2001). Assessment of religiousness and spirituality in health research. In T. Plante and A. Sherman (eds), *Faith and Health: Psychological Perspectives* (pp. 139–66). York: Guilford. (Contains descriptions of a series of scales.)

Coping by catharsis

Stanton, A., Kirk, S., Cameron, C. and Danoff-Burg, S. (2000). Coping through emotional approach: scale construction and validation. *Journal of Personality and Social Psychology* 78: 1150–69.

Humour as a coping strategy

Lefcourt, H. (2001). *Humour: the Psychology of Living Buoyantly*. New York: Kluwer/ Plenum. (Contains the Situational Humour Response Questionnaire and the Coping Humour Scale.)

Disposition to cry

Vingerhoets, A. and Cornelius, R. (2001). *Adult Crying: A Biopsychosocial Approach*. Hove, UK: Brunner-Routledge. (Contains the Adult Crying Scale.)

Defence mechanisms

Bauer, S. and Rockland, L. (1995). The inventory of defence-related behaviours: an approach to measuring defence mechanisms in psychotherapy. In H. Conte and R. Plutchik (eds), *Ego Defences: Theory and Measurement* (pp. 300–14). New York: Wiley. (Available from Dr Stephen Bauer, North Shore University Hospital, Cornell University Medical College, Manhasset, New York.)

Bond, M. and Wesley, S. (1996). Manual for the Defence Style Questionnaire. Montreal Quebec: McGill University. (Write to Dr Michael Bond, Dept of Psychiatry, Sir Mortimer B. Davis – Jewish General Hospital, 4333 Chemin De la Cote Ste-Catherine, Montreal, Quebec, Canada, H3T 1E4, Phone 514-3408210).

Conte, H. and Apter, A. (1995). The Life Style Index: a self-report measure of ego defences. In H. Conte and R. Plutchik (eds), *Ego Defences: Theory and Measurement* (pp. 179–201). New York: Wiley. (Write to Dr Hope Conte and Dr Robert Plutchik, Albert Einstein College on Medicine, Bronx, New York, USA for the lifestyle index.)

Ihilevich, D. and Gleser, G. (1986a). *Defence Mechanisms: Their Classification, Correlates and Measurement with the Defence Mechanisms Inventory*. Odessa, Florida: Psychological Assessment Resources. Available from www.parinc.com

Ihilevich, D. and Gleser, G. (1986b). *Defence in Psychotherapy: Their Clinical Application of the Defence Mechanisms Inventory*. Odessa, Florida: Psychological Assessment Resources. www.parinc.com

Johnson, N. and Gold, S. (1995). Defence Mechanisms Profile: a sentence completion test. In H. Conte and R. Plutchik (eds), *Ego Defences: Theory and Measurement* (pp. 247–62). New York: Wiley. (Dr Stephen Gold, Nova University, Community Mental Health Centre, Fort Lauderdale, Florida, USA.)

Perry, C. and Kardos, M. (1995). A review of defence mechanism rating scales. In H. Conte and R. Plutchik (eds), *Ego Defences: Theory and Measurement* (pp. 283–99). New York: Wiley. (Contains a description of the Defence Mechanism Rating Scale available from Sir Mortimer B. Davis – Jewish General Hospital, 4333 Chemin De la Cote Ste-Catherine, Montreal, Quebec, Canada, H3T 1E4.)

Plutchik, R., Kellerman, H. and Conte, H. (1979). The structural theory of ego defences and emotions. In C. Izard (ed.). *Emotions in Personality and Psychopathology* (pp. 229–57). New York: Plenum Press. (Describes the early version of the Life Style Index.)

GLOSSARY

Adaptive defences.   Anticipation, affiliation, altruism, humour, self-assertion, self-observation, sublimation and suppression.

Coping strategies.   Consciously selected routines for managing situations in which there is a perceived discrepancy between stressful demands and available resources for meeting these demands.

Defence mechanisms.   Unconscious processes which regulate negative affect associated with intra-psychic factors by excluding memories of actual traumatic events from consciousness; by attenuating anxiety caused by the conflict between unacceptable impulses and the prohibitions of the conscience; or by modifying anxiety that arises from conflict between a wish to express some aspect of the self which is unacceptable to caregivers or significant members of the family or social network and the wish to retain the support of these significant people or their introjected representations by complying with their injunctions.

Hardiness.   Kobasa's term for beliefs that significant aspects of one's life situation are controllable; the expectation that life will entail challenges; and a commitment to finding meaning in life.

Locus of control.   Rotter's term for the degree to which we expect important sources of reinforcement to be within our control or influenced by external factors such as chance, fate, or the actions of other powerful people.

Self-efficacy.   Bandura's term for beliefs which we hold about our capability to organise and perform tasks within a specific domain to effectively lead to specific goals.

Self-esteem.   James's term for the feeling of self-worth that derives from the ratio of our actual successes to our pretensions.

Sense of coherence.   Antonovsky's term for the degree to which life situations are perceived as meaningful, comprehensible and manageable.

Chapter 8

Positive relationships

Learning objectives

- Be able to define the stages of the family lifecycle and the tasks entailed by each stage.
- Be able to describe the main research findings on friendship, trust and betrayal, forgiveness and atonement, and gratitude.
- Be able to give an account of psychosocial factors associated with marriage and marital satisfaction.
- Be able to describe optimal parenting roles and grandparenting roles; and day-care, pre-school, school, and peer group settings.
- Understand factors that facilitate the growth of adolescent autonomy and resilience in adolescence.
- Appreciate key psychological factors associated with midlife re-evaluation and the challenges of later life.
- Be able to define the additional stages of the family lifecycle associated with divorce and remarriage and the tasks entailed by each stage.
- Be able to give an account of attachment theory and the circumplex model of interpersonal behaviour.
- Appreciate important empirically based marital and family systems models of assessment.
- Understand the clinical implications of research on the family lifecycle and marital and family systems for facilitating happiness.
- Be able to identify research questions that need to be addressed to advance our understanding of giftedness, creativity and wisdom on the one hand and happiness on the other.

The importance of friendship and family relationships for happiness was noted in Chapter 1. In this chapter, a fuller exploration of positive relationships is the central concern. The family lifecycle is a particularly useful

framework within which to conceptualise the development of positive relationships. Families are unique social systems insofar as membership is based
on combinations of biological, legal, affectional, geographic and historical
ties. In contrast to other social systems, entry into family systems is through
birth, adoption, fostering or marriage and members can leave only by death.
Severing all family connections is never possible. Furthermore, while family
members fulfil certain roles which entail specific definable tasks such as the
provision of food and shelter, it is the relationships within families which
are primary and irreplaceable. With single-parenthood, divorce, separation
and remarriage as common events, a narrow and traditional definition of
the family is no longer useful (Walsh, 1993).

THE FAMILY LIFECYCLE

Having noted the limitations of a traditional model of the family structure,
we find, paradoxically, the most useful available models of the family lifecycle
are based upon the norm of the traditional nuclear family, with other family
forms being conceptualised as deviations from this norm (Carter and
McGoldrick, 1989). One such model is presented in Table 8.1. This model
delineates the main developmental tasks to be completed by the family at
each stage of development.

Leaving home

In the first two stages of family development, the principal concerns
are with differentiating from the family of origin by completing school,
developing relationships outside the family, completing one's education and
beginning a career. In developing relationships outside the family young
adults must address such issues as friendship; trust and betrayal; atonement
and forgiveness; and gratitude.

Friendship

Close friendships are an important source of well-being (Argyle, 2001).
People choose friends who are broadly similar to themselves in terms of
attributes, skills and values (Swann, 1983). People choose friends with similar values to theirs so that their friends will reinforce their positive view of
themselves. On highly valued attributes and skills central to their self-
conceptions, people choose friends who are slightly less good than themselves, so as to avoid rivalry. In contrast, on attributes and skills that are
less central to their self-conceptions, people choose friends who are slightly
better than themselves to create a context in which they and others can
value their friends highly for these positive qualities (Tesser and Phalus,

Table 8.1 Stages of the family lifecycle

Stage	Tasks
1. Family of origin experiences	• Maintaining relationships with parents, siblings and peers • Completing school
2. Leaving home	• Differentiation of self from family of origin and developing adult-to-adult relationship with parents • Developing intimate peer relationships • Beginning a career
3. Premarriage stage	• Selecting partners • Developing a relationship • Deciding to marry
4. Childless couple stage	• Developing a way to live together based on reality rather than mutual projection • Realigning relationships with families of origin and peers to include spouses
5. Family with young children	• Adjusting marital system to make space for children • Adopting parenting roles • Realigning relationships with families of origin to include parenting and grandparenting roles • Children developing peer relationships
6. Family with adolescents	• Adjusting parent–child relationships to allow adolescents more autonomy • Adjusting marital relationships to focus on midlife marital and career issues • Taking on responsibility of caring for families of origin
7. Launching children	• Resolving mid-life issues • Negotiating adult-to-adult relationships with children • Adjusting to living as a couple again • Adjusting to including in-laws and grandchildren within the family circle • Dealing with disabilities and death in the family of origin
8. Later life	• Coping with physiological decline • Adjusting to the children taking a more central role in family maintenance • Making room for the wisdom and experience of the elderly • Dealing with loss of spouse and peers • Preparation for death, life review and integration

Source: Adapted from Carter and McGoldrick (1989).

1983). The capacity to make and maintain stable, supportive and satisfying friendships is determined by many historical, personal and environmental factors. Adult attachment style is particularly important, and this has its roots in childhood attachment experiences. People with a secure attachment style tend to develop better-quality peer relationships which hold up under stress than those with anxious attachment styles (Allen and Land, 1999). Attachment styles have been discussed in Chapter 4. With respect to personality traits, extraversion, agreeableness and stability (as opposed to neuroticism) facilitate the development of friendships. Personality traits have been discussed in Chapter 6. At an environmental level, opportunities in school, leisure activities, the family and the community to meet with peers, at least some of whom have similar attributes, skills and values, are important for the development of friendships.

Trust and betrayal

Trust and betrayal are important features of close relationships. Positive benefits, including happiness, derive from trusting and being trustworthy and also from not betraying others or being betrayed. In research on trust, a distinction may be made between generalised and relational trust (Jones et al., 1997). Generalised trust refers to our expectations about social motives of other people in general, whereas relational trust refers to our expectations of trust within close relationships.

People with high generalised trust, as measured by instruments such as Rotter's (1967) trust scale, expect others to behave honourably in most situations. Comparative studies of people with high and low levels of generalised trust have shown that high levels of trust are associated with being personally trustworthy, being more ethical, reporting greater subjective well-being, being perceived by the opposite sex as more attractive and being viewed as more desirable as a close friend (Rotter, 1980). People with high generalised trust are no more gullible than others. Low levels of trust are associated with alienation and low socio-economic status.

People with high levels of relational trust expect another person with whom they have a close or intimate relationship (such as a spouse, romantic partner, friend or colleague) to act honourably (Holmes and Rempel, 1989). By definition, relational trust involves risking rejection and betrayal in intimate relationships. Relational trust involves the expectation that a relational partner is predictable and dependable, and faith that they will continue to be so. Relational trust develops over time and the rate of development is influenced by the level of attachment or love for the relational partner. High levels of relational trust are associated with better personal adjustment and relationship development.

Betrayal, by violating relational trust, is fairly commonplace and typically occurs within the context of important close relationships (Jones et al., 1997). Studies of narrative accounts of acts of betrayal and being betrayed show that people attribute their own acts of betrayal to intentional but transitory factors such as anger, depression, momentary impulsivity, or intoxication. In contrast, they attribute the actions of those who betray them to intentional and stable factors such as having a mean streak or lack of principles. The Interpersonal Betrayal Scale evaluates the general tendency to betray others by lying, breaking promises or other acts of deceit (Jones *et al.*, 1997). Compared with trustworthy people, those who score high on the Interpersonal Betrayal Scale tend to be younger, less well-educated, to have had more unhappy childhoods, to have been married for a shorter duration or to be divorced, to have lower levels of social support and to have more psychological problems and disorders. In contrast, people who score in the trustworthy range of this scale tend to be better adjusted on all of these parameters and also to show better self-control, subjective well-being, responsibility, tolerance, and psychological mindedness.

Forgiveness and atonement

Betrayal, breaches of trust, acts of physical or psychological hostility all occur within friendships and other relationships. A friend breaks a promise. One partner lies to another about an extramarital affair. A parent in frustration hits a child. In some instances, these transgressions are met with retaliation or a quest for retribution. The quest for retribution may in turn elicit reciprocal retaliation. Spirals of retribution and retaliation which culminate in the destruction of relationships may follow. Forgiveness and atonement are important ways for curbing such escalating spirals (McCullough, Pargament and Thoresen, 2000; McCullough and Witvliet, 2002). Forgiveness is a personal prosocial response to an acknowledged transgression for which the transgressor was clearly responsible. With forgiveness, we say to the transgressor, 'I acknowledge that you made a transgression against me, but I am not going to seek retribution, because I forgive you'. With forgiveness, the debt created by the transgression is cancelled. Forgiveness is distinct from legal pardoning, since it is a personal response to a breach in a relationship rather than the result of a legal process. Forgiveness is distinct from condoning or justifying the transgression, rationalising or excusing the transgression as arising from extenuating circumstances, denying the seriousness of the transgression, or forgetting that the transgression occurred, since all of these do not involve an acknowledged transgression for which the other party was clearly responsible. Atonement, in contrast, is the contrite acknowledgement of wrongdoing by a transgressor and making reparation for wrongdoing or injury to another person. With atonement we say, 'I acknowledge that I have hurt you, I'm sorry for that, and I will make amends for my transgression'. Together, forgiveness and atonement are ways of repairing relationships that have been damaged by transgressions.

At an experiential level there are benefits and barriers to forgiveness and atonement (Exline and Baumeister, 2000). Where grudges are held for a long time, these can be experienced as an ongoing psychological weight to carry. When we forgive others, there is a sense of a burden being lifted.

Forgiveness can also elicit repentance on the part of the transgressor. Forgiveness can lead to improved psychological and physical well-being and
to a deepening of the relationship with the transgressor. Alongside these
benefits, there are barriers to the expression of forgiveness. We may feel that
our forgiveness will be interpreted as a sign of weakness and that this will
lead to repeated transgressions. Also, when we forgive others, we give up
our position as an aggrieved victim and lose the power to induce guilt and
the luxury of experiencing and expressing righteous indignation.

Atonement, too, has its benefits. When we atone for transgressions we
reduce our feelings of guilt and may also elicit forgiveness from those against
whom we have transgressed. Atonement and repentance may also improve
psychological and physical well-being. However, there are barriers to
atonement. Atonement entails acknowledging personal responsibility for
wrongdoing, experiencing the feelings of guilt and shame that go with this
acknowledgement, and accepting the punishment associated with the transgression. For violent transgression (including domestic violence and child
abuse) this may involve legal penalties such as imprisonment.

Both forgiveness and atonement require us to put pride aside and be
humble. Humility involves seeing oneself as no better or no worse than
others. Both forgiveness and atonement require us to empathise with the
other person's position (be they transgressor or victim) and understand how
the situation looks from their perspective. Setting pride aside, humility and
empathy – all extremely challenging processes since they render us vulnerable to attack – are major obstacles to engaging in forgiveness or atonement.

Trait and state measurements of forgiveness have been developed
(McCullough, Hoyt and Rachel, 2000). Trait measures evaluate the general
disposition to forgive others, while state measures evaluate the degree to
which forgiveness has occurred in a particular situation. Research using
such measures has thrown light on correlates of forgiveness (McCullough,
Pargament and Thoresen, 2000; McCullough and Witvliet, 2002). People
become more forgiving with age and this is related to moral development.
The higher the level of moral development the more forgiving people
are. Forgiving people have distinctive personalities characterised by greater
stability and less neuroticism on the one hand and greater agreeableness on
the other. Unforgiving people obtain high scores on measures of narcissism
(e.g. Raskin and Hall, 1979). Certain situations are more conducive to
forgiveness. People find it easier to forgive transgressions that are less
intentional, less severe, entail fewer negative consequences and for which the
transgressor apologises. All of these conditions reduce victims' negative
affect towards transgressors and so make it easier for victims to empathise
with transgressors and this in turn makes forgiveness easier. Within intimate
relationships, people find it easier to forgive their partners if they have
a high level of relationship satisfaction, a high level of commitment to

the relationship and a high level of psychological intimacy with their partners.

Forgiveness is associated with better psychological and physical well-being, greater marital satisfaction, less criminality and better adjustment to bereavement (McCullough, Pargament and Thoresen, 2000; McCullough and Witvliet, 2002; Oyen et al., 2001). More forgiving people have fewer mental and physical health problems. Laboratory studies also support the link between forgiveness and well-being. In an experimental analogue study Witvliet et al. (2001) found that participants showed far greater arousal as indexed by heart-rate, blood pressure and skin conductance in situations where they mentally rehearsed non-forgiving responses to transgressors compared with situations where they mentally rehearsed forgiving responses. Interventions that increase forgiveness enhance psychological and physical well-being. For example, Friedman et al. (1986) found that, compared with controls, hostile heart-attack survivors who learned how to adopt a forgiving attitude showed a reduction in hostility and heart problems after an intervention programme which aimed to promote relaxation, forgiveness and a balanced lifestyle.

Forgiveness has an important role to play in individual and marital psychotherapy. In individual psychotherapy adults who have 'unfinished business' from childhood, in which their parents or carers abused them or transgressed against them, may benefit from resolving this unfinished business and forgiving their transgressor (Malcolm and Greenberg, 2000). Such therapy involves engaging in an imaginal dialogue with the transgressor using the Gestalt therapy empty-chair technique. During this dialogue there is an acceptance into awareness of strong feelings of anger and sadness associated with the transgression; a letting go of unmet interpersonal needs arising from the transgression; the development of empathy for the transgressor; and the construction of a new way of conceptualising the self and the transgressor. In marital therapy where partners have hurt each other, facilitating forgiveness and atonement may be central to helping couples break out of destructive repetitive patterns of interaction which maintain their marital distress (Coop-Gordon et al., 2000). In marital therapy, unlike individual therapy, the dialogue is not imaginal and often both partners have experienced transgressions. Thus both partners initially express strong feelings of anger and sadness associated with the transgression and a letting go of unmet interpersonal needs arising from the transgression. This creates a context within which a detailed understanding of the many historical, situational, relational and personal factors that contributed to the transgression can be explored. This quest for meaning allows partners to gradually develop empathy for each other; and finally partners' construction of a new way of conceptualising each other and their relationship that allows them to move on.

Reconciliation is distinct from forgiveness and atonement (Exline and Baumeister, 2000). Reconciliation entails a willingness to form a contract to come together to live or work in an atmosphere of trust on an ongoing basis. It is possible after a transgression for forgiveness and atonement to occur, without any progression to reconciliation or relationship re-building occurring. It is also possible for people to agree to reconciliation, without forgiveness and atonement having occurred, and for the process of reconciliation to create a context within which forgiveness and atonement can happen.

Gratitude

Gratitude occurs in relationships when we acknowledge that we are the recipients of the prosocial behaviour of others. McCullough *et al.* (2001) argue, on the basis of a thorough review of available empirical evidence, that gratitude is a moral emotion for three reasons. First, the experience of gratitude lets us know that we have been behaving in a prosocial way towards others. Second, it motivates us to engage in prosocial behaviour and inhibits antisocial behaviour. Third, it reinforces moral behaviour in the person who has acted in a benevolent way to whom we have expressed our gratitude. Gratitude is also good for our health. Emmons and Shelton (2002) have shown in a series of studies that people who kept diaries of events for which they were grateful show improved health and subjective well-being compared with people who kept diaries of stresses or other types of events within their day-to-day lives. McCullough *et al.* (2002) have developed a self-report measure of the disposition to be grateful which may be used to investigate the role of gratitude in relationships.

Forming a couple

From Table 8.1 it may be seen that in the third stage of the family lifecycle model, the principal tasks are those associated with selecting a partner and deciding to marry or cohabit. In the following discussion, the term marriage is used to cover both traditional marriage or the more modern arrangement of long-term cohabitation. Marriage may be conceptualised as the joining together of two families and traditions, rather than the joining of two individuals. B. Adams (1986) views mate selection as a complex process that involves four stages. In the first phase partners are selected from among those available for interaction. At this stage, people select mates who are physically attractive and similar to themselves in interests, intelligence, personality and other valued behaviours and attributes. In the second phase there is a comparison of values following revelation of identities through self-disclosing conversations. If this leads to a deepening of the original attraction then the relationship will persist. In the third phase, there is an exploration of role compatibility and the degree to which mutual empathy is possible. Once interlocking roles and mutual empathy have developed, the costs of separation begin to outweigh the difficulties and tensions associated with staying together. If the attraction has deepened sufficiently and the barriers to separation are strong enough, consolidation of the relationship occurs. In the fourth and final phase a decision is made about long-term compatibility and commitment. If a positive decision is reached about both of these issues, then marriage or long-term cohabitation may occur. When partners come together they are effectively bringing two family traditions together, and setting the stage for the integration of these traditions, with their norms and values, rules, roles and routines, into a new tradition. Couple formation and marriage entail the development of a series of important relationships: the marital relationship, kinship relationships and later parent–child relationships, all of which have the potential to contribute to happiness and well-being (Argyle, 2001).

Marriage

In the fourth stage of the family lifecycle model, the childless couple must develop routines for living together which are based on a realistic appraisal of the other's strengths, weaknesses and idiosyncrasies rather than on the idealised views which formed the basis of their relationship during the initial period of infatuation.

Marital satisfaction

The following demographic factors are associated with marital satisfaction (Newman and Newman, 1991):

- High level of education;
- High socio-economic status;
- Similarity of spouses interests, intelligence and personality;
- Early or late stage of family lifecycle;
- Sexual compatibility;
- For women, later marriage.

The precise mechanisms linking these factors to marital satisfaction are not fully understood. However, the following speculations seem plausible. Higher educational level and higher socio-economic status probably lead to greater marital satisfaction because where these factors are present people probably have better problem-solving skills and fewer chronic life stresses such as crowding. Although there is a cultural belief that opposites attract, the research results show that similarity is associated with marital satisfaction, probably because of the greater ease with which similar people can empathise with each other and pursue shared interests. Marital satisfaction drops during the child-rearing years and satisfaction is highest before children are born and when they leave home. During these periods, it may be that greater satisfaction occurs because partners can devote more time and energy to joint pursuits and there are fewer opportunities for conflict involving child management. Most surveys find wide variability in the frequency with which couples engage in sexual activity but confirm that it is sexual compatibility rather than frequency of sexual activity that is associated with marital satisfaction.

Studies of belief systems and interaction patterns of happy couples show that they have distinctive features (Harvey *et al.*, 2002; Gottman, 1993; Jacobson and Gurman, 1995; Carr, 2000b). These include:

- Respect;
- Acceptance;
- Dispositional attributions for positive behaviour;
- More positive than negative interactions;
- Focusing conflicts on specific issues;
- Rapidly repairing relationship ruptures;
- Managing differing male and female conversational styles;
- Addressing needs for intimacy and power.

Happy couples attribute their partners' positive behaviours to dispositional rather than situational factors. For example, 'She helped me because she is such a kind person', not 'She helped me because it was convenient at the time.' The ratio of positive to negative exchanges has been found to be about five to one in happy couples (Gottman, 1993). So even though happy couples have disagreements, this is balanced out by five times as many positive interactions. When happy couples disagree, they focus their disagreement on a specific issue, rather than globally criticising or insulting their partner. This type of behaviour is a reflection of a general attitude of respect which characterises happy couples. Happy couples tend to rapidly repair their relationship ruptures arising from conflict and they do not allow long episodes of non-communication, sulking or stonewalling to occur. Sometimes happy couples resolve conflicts by agreeing to differ. The specific process of agreeing to differ reflects a general attitude of acceptance. There is good evidence that men and women have different conversational styles. Men use conversation predominantly to convey task-focused information and to resolve task-related problems. Women use conversation predominantly to make and maintain relationships (Tannen, 1990). In their communication with each other, happy couples find ways to manage these differing conversational styles so that psychological intimacy may be fostered rather than compromised. So males in such relationships make efforts to use conversation to make and maintain their relationship with their partner and females are tolerant of the challenge that this poses. Difficulties and disagreements about communication and intimacy on the one hand and the power balance or role structure of the relationship on the other are central themes for distressed couples (Jacobson and Gurman, 1995). With respect to intimacy, usually males demand greater psychological distance and females insist on greater psychological intimacy. With respect to power, males commonly wish to retain the power and benefits of traditional gender roles while females wish to evolve more egalitarian relationships. In happy couples, partners' needs for intimacy and power within the relationship are adequately met, and partners have the capacity to negotiate with each other about modifying the relationship if they feel that these needs are being thwarted. A brief measure of marital satisfaction is presented in Table 8.2.

Types of marriages

Fitzpatrick (1988) and Gottman (1993) have both identified three types of stable satisfactory marriages in questionnaire and observational studies. I have termed these traditional, androgynous and avoidant couples. Characteristics of these types of marriage are summarised in the first part of Table 8.3. Traditional couples adopt traditional sex-roles and lifestyles and take a low-key approach to conflict management. Androgynous couples strive to create egalitarian roles and take a fiery approach to conflict resolution. Avoidant couples adopt traditional sex-roles but live parallel lives and avoid conflict. Two types of unstable couples were identified in Gottman's (1993) study. In Table 8.3 I have labelled these conflictual and disengaged couples. The former engaged in conflict but without resolution and the latter avoided conflict much of the time. Gottman found that in all three stable types of couples the ratio of positive to negative verbal exchanges during conflict resolution was 5:1. For both unstable types of couples the ratio of positive to negative exchanges was approximately 1:1. Gottman and Fitzpatrick's work highlights the fact that there are a number of possible models for a stable marital relationship. Their work also underlines the importance of couples engaging in conflict with a view to resolving it rather than avoiding conflict. Negativity is only destructive if it is not balanced out by five times as much positivity. Indeed, negativity may have a prosocial role in balancing the needs for intimacy and autonomy and in keeping attraction alive over long periods.

Families with children

In the fifth stage of the family lifecycle model, given in Table 8.1, the main tasks are for couples to adjust their roles as marital partners to make space for young children, for couples' parents to develop grandparental roles, and for children as they move into middle childhood to develop peer relationships.

Table 8.2 Kansas Marital Satisfaction Scale

For these three questions circle the answer that best gives your opinion of your marriage.

	Extremely dissatisfied	Very dissatisfied	Somewhat dissatisfied	Mixed	Somewhat satisfied	Very satisfied	Extremely satisfied
How satisfied are you with your marriage?	1	2	3	4	5	6	7
How satisfied are you with your husband or wife as a spouse?	1	2	3	4	5	6	7
How satisfied are you with your relationship with your husband or wife?	1	2	3	4	5	6	7

Source: Adapted from Schumm et al. (1986).

Table 8.3 Five types of couples

Stability	Type	Characteristics
Stable	Traditional couples	• They adopt traditional sex roles • They privilege family goals over individual goals • They have regular daily schedules • They share the living space in the family home • They express moderate levels of both positive and negative emotions • They tend to avoid conflict about all but major issues • They engage in conflict and try to resolve it • At the outset of an episode of conflict resolution, each partner listens to the other and empathises with their position • In the later part there is considerable persuasion
	Androgynous couples	• They adopt androgynous egalitarian roles • They privilege individual goals over family goals • They have chaotic daily schedules • They have separate living spaces in their homes • They express high levels of positive and negative emotions • They tend to engage in continual negotiation about many issues • Partners disagree and try to persuade one another from the very beginning of episodes of conflict resolution
	Avoidant couples	• They adopt traditional sex roles • They have separate living space in their homes • They avoid all conflict • They have few conflict-resolution skills • Partners state their case when a conflict occurs but there is no attempt at persuasion or compromise • They accept differences about specific conflicts as unimportant compared with their shared common ground and values • Conflict-related discussions are unemotional
Unstable	Conflictual couples	• They engage in conflict without any constructive attempt to resolve it • Continual blaming, mind-reading and defensiveness characterise their interactions • High levels of negative emotion and little positive emotion are expressed • Attack-withdraw interaction pattern
	Disengaged couples	• They avoid conflict and have few conflict resolution skills • Brief episodes of blaming, mind-reading and defensiveness characterise their interactions • Low levels of negative emotion and almost no positive emotion is expressed • Withdraw-withdraw interaction pattern

Source: Based on Gottman (1993) and Fitzpatrick (1988).

Parenting roles

The development of positive parenting roles involves couples establishing routines for meeting children's needs for

- safety
- care
- control, and
- intellectual stimulation.

Developing these routines is a complex process. Routines for meeting children's needs for safety include protecting children from accidents by, for example, not leaving young children unsupervised and also developing skills for managing frustration and anger that the demands of parenting young children often elicit. Routines for providing children with food and shelter, attachment, empathy, understanding and emotional support need to be developed to meet children's needs for care in these various areas. Routines for setting clear rules and limits, for providing supervision to ensure that children conform to these expectations, and for offering appropriate rewards and sanctions for rule following and rule violations meet children's need for control. Parent–child play and communication routines for meeting children's needs for age-appropriate intellectual stimulation also need to be developed, if the child is to show optimal emotional and intellectual development.

In Chapter 4 (on emotional intelligence) it was noted that children develop secure emotional attachments to their parents if their parents are attuned to their needs for safety, security and being physically cared for and if their parents are responsive to children's signals that they require their needs to be met (Bowlby, 1988). When this occurs, children learn that their parents are a secure base from which they can explore the world. When this does not occur, children develop insecure attachments which may compromise their capacity to form secure intimate relationships in later life.

Reviews of the extensive literature on parenting suggest that by combining the two orthogonal dimensions of warmth or acceptance and control, four parenting styles may be identified and each of these is associated with particular developmental outcomes for the child (Darling and Steinberg, 1993). These four styles are presented in Figure 8.1. *Authoritative parents* who adopt a warm, accepting child-centred approach coupled with a moderate degree of control which allows children to take age-appropriate responsibility, provide a context which is maximally beneficial for children's development as autonomous confident individuals. Children of parents who use an authoritative style learn that conflicts are most effectively managed by taking the other person's viewpoint into account within the context of an amicable negotiation. This set of skills is conducive to efficient joint

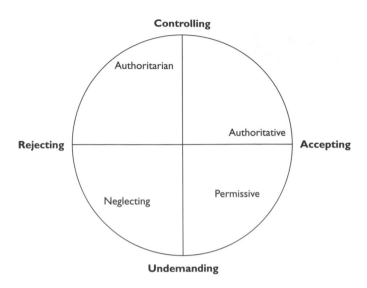

Figure 8.1 Patterns of parenting
Source: Based on Darling and Steinberg (1993): 487–96.

problem solving and the development of good peer relationships and consequently the development of a good social support network. This parenting style is also conducive to good moral development (Kagan and Lamb, 1987). Children of *authoritarian parents* who are warm and accepting but controlling tend to develop into shy adults who are reluctant to take initiative. The parents' disciplinary style teaches them that unquestioning obedience is the best way to manage interpersonal differences and to solve problems. Children of *permissive parents* who are warm and accepting but lax in discipline, in later life lack the competence to follow through on plans and show poor impulse-control. Children who have experienced little warmth or acceptance from their parents and who have been either harshly disciplined or had little or inconsistent supervision develop adjustment problems. A brief measure of parenting satisfaction is presented in Table 8.4.

Grandparenting roles

In addition to developing parental roles and routines for meeting children's needs, a further task of this stage is the development of positive grandparental roles and the realignment of family relationships that this entails. Neugarten and Weinstein (1964) identified a number of types of grandparental roles. First, there were those that adopted a formal role and were not involved in child care but loving and emotionally involved with the grandchildren. The second role was essentially fun seeking and these grandparents acted as

Table 8.4 Kansas Parental Satisfaction Scale

For these three questions circle the answer that best gives your opinion of your relationship with your child or children.

	Extremely dissatisfied 1	Very dissatisfied 2	Somewhat dissatisfied 3	Mixed 4	Somewhat satisfied 5	Very satisfied 6	Extremely satisfied 7
How satisfied are you with your child or children's behaviour?	Extremely dissatisfied 1	Very dissatisfied 2	Somewhat dissatisfied 3	Mixed 4	Somewhat satisfied 5	Very satisfied 6	Extremely satisfied 7
How satisfied are you with yourself as a parent?	Extremely dissatisfied 1	Very dissatisfied 2	Somewhat dissatisfied 3	Mixed 4	Somewhat satisfied 5	Very satisfied 6	Extremely satisfied 7
How satisfied are you with your relationship(s) with your child or children?	Extremely dissatisfied 1	Very dissatisfied 2	Somewhat dissatisfied 3	Mixed 4	Somewhat satisfied 5	Very satisfied 6	Extremely satisfied 7

Source: Adapted from James et al. (1985): 163–9.

playmates for the grandchildren. The third type of grandparental role was that of a distant figure who had little contact with grandchildren. The fourth role-type was that of parental surrogate and these grandparents assumed the role of parent to the grandchildren so that the mother could work outside the home. The final grandparental role was that of a reservoir of family wisdom who occupied a powerful patriarchal or matriarchal position within the extended family. Where grandparents adopt roles that are supportive of parents and grandchildren, they contribute to family resilience. Where they adopt roles that greatly increase the demands on parents and grandchildren, without offering support, then they may contribute to the development of adjustment problems.

Day-care

Families with children may involve their offspring in day-care. High quality day care is characterised by a continuity in the relationship between the infant and the staff; a responsivity in staffs' reactions to infants' signals and needs; a low ratio of infants to staff; and a safe, spacious and well-equipped physical facility (McGurk et al., 1993). Children who receive high-quality day-care and whose parents adopt a responsive style in their interactions with them develop secure attachments to their parents. Where parents have difficulty in meeting their youngsters' needs, high quality day-care may be an important source of social support for the children. Furthermore, such day-care placements may provide parents with an opportunity to work outside the home and receive the social support that work-based relationships can provide.

Pre-school

Many families with young children place their children in pre-schools. Pre-school placement is particularly important for disadvantaged children. Pre-school early intervention educational programmes for socially disadvantaged or low-birth weight children can have beneficial long-lasting effects on psychosocial adjustment, cognitive development and school attainment particularly if certain conditions prevail (Carr, 2002; Sylva, 1994). In effective early intervention programmes families are engaged very early in the child's life. Effective programmes involve long-term supportive and educational home visiting in addition to pre-school-placement. Child-stimulation; parent training and support; and conjoint parent–child sessions to promote secure attachment all typify good pre-school programmes. Effective programmes extend right up to the start of primary school. A central factor is a good working relationship between the parents and the pre-school staff. Children and parents must also have access to positive role models who, by their example and success, show the value of schooling. Finally, a teaching method which incorporates the elements of planning activities, doing these activities and reviewing performance is vital to success. Four life skills, the foundations of which are laid by successful pre-school programmes, distinguish those children who have positive outcomes. The first is the development of a goal-oriented and planned approach to solving scholastic and social problems. The second is the development of aspirations for education and employment. The third is the development of a sense of responsibility for one's own actions. The fourth is a sense of duty and responsibility towards others.

School

Particular types of schools are especially conducive to positive child development. In their study of secondary schools, Rutter *et al.* (1979) found that a series of features of the secondary school environment had a favourable influence on behaviour and attainment and these factors were independent of child and family characteristics. These features are:

- Firm authoritative leadership of the staff team by the principal;
- Firm authoritative management of classes by teachers with high expectations of success, clear rules and regular homework which is graded routinely;
- A participative approach to decision making among the staff about curriculum planning and school management which fosters cohesion among the staff and the principal;
- Many opportunities for pupils to participate in the running of the school which fosters pupil loyalty to the school;
- A balance of emphasis on both academic attainment and excellence in other fields such as sport;
- Teachers model good behaviour;
- Teachers regularly appreciate, reward and praise academic and non-academic achievements;
- A balance between intellectually able and less able pupils;
- An attractive, comfortable and pleasant school environment.

Subsequent research on both primary and secondary schools has supported and extended Rutter's original findings and shown that the following attributes are also associated with high attainment: presenting pupils with clear predetermined goals or standards, creating an expectation of success, structuring material so that it is easily interpretable, using sufficient repetition to keep the pupils on task, presenting information clearly, providing extra help if necessary to ensure that goals are reached and providing feedback. This type of approach to teaching requires moderate class sizes, a variable which has been consistently associated with pupil performance (Sylva, 1994).

Children's peer group roles

Peer group membership is a source of social support and relationships which enhance well-being and so has an important bearing on the optimal development of children (Dunn and McGuire, 1992; Malik and Furman, 1993; Williams and Gilmore, 1994). Over the first five years, with increasing opportunities for interaction with others and the development of language, interaction with other children increases. Co-operative play premised on an empathic understanding of other children's viewpoints gradually emerges and is usually fully established by middle childhood. Competitive rivalry (often involving physical or verbal aggression or joking) is an important part of peer interactions, particularly among boys. This allows youngsters to establish their position of dominance within the peer group hierarchy. There are important sex differences in styles of play adopted, with girls being more co-operative and relationship-focused and boys being more competitive and activity-focused. Boys tend to play in larger peer groups whereas girls tend to play within small groups characterised by emotionally intimate exclusive friendships. Sex-segregated play is almost universal in middle childhood.

Peer friendships are noteworthy because they constitute a significant source of social support, a context within which to learn about the management of networks of relationships and how important friendship is for happiness. Children who are unable to make and maintain friendships, particularly during middle childhood and early adolescence, are at risk for the development of psychological difficulties. Children who have developed secure attachments to their parents are more likely to develop good peer friendships. This is probably because their experience with their parents provides them with a useful cognitive model on which to base their interactions with their peers. Children reared in institutions have particular difficulty with peer relationships in their teens.

Popular children are described by their peers as helpful, friendly, considerate and capable of following rules in games and imaginative play. They also tend to be more intelligent and physically attractive than average. They accurately interpret social situations and have the social skills necessary for engaging in peer group activities. About 10 per cent–15 per cent of children are rejected by their peer group. In middle childhood two main types of unpopular child may be distinguished: the aggressive youngster and the victim. Victims tend to be sensitive, anxious, have low self-esteem and lack the skills required to defend themselves and establish dominance within the peer group hierarchy. They are often the targets for bullies (Olweus, 1993). Unpopular aggressive children are described by peers as disruptive, hyperactive, impulsive and unable to follow rules in games and play. Their aggression tends to be used less for establishing dominance or a hierarchical position in the peer group and more for achieving certain instrumental goals, for example taking a toy from another child.

Popular children are effective in joining in peer group activities. They hover on the edge, tune-in to the group's activities and carefully select a time to become integrated into the group's activities. Unpopular children, particularly the aggressive type, do not tune-in to group activities. They tend to criticise other children and talk about themselves rather than listening to others. Warmth, a sense of humour and sensitivity to social cues are important features of socially skilled children. Unpopular children, particularly the aggressive type, are predisposed to interpreting ambiguous social cues negatively and becoming involved in escalating spirals of negative social interaction.

Unpopularity is relatively stable over time. A child who is unpopular this year is likely to remain so next year and this unpopularity is not wholly based on reputation. For the aggressive unpopular child, inadequate cognitive models for relationships, difficulties in interpreting ambiguous social situations and poor social skills appear to be the main factors underpinning this stability of unpopularity. For the unpopular victim the continued unpopularity is probably mediated by low self-esteem, avoidance of opportunities for social interaction and a lack of prosocial skills. Also, both types of unpopular children miss out on important opportunities for learning about co-operation, teamwork and the management of networks of friendships. While unpopularity is not uniformly associated with long-term difficulties, it appears to put such youngsters at risk for developing academic problems, dropping out of school, conduct problems in adolescence, mental health problems in adulthood and criminality.

Families with adolescents

In the sixth stage of the family lifecycle model presented in Table 8.1, which is marked by children's entry into adolescence, parent–child relationships require realignment to allow adolescents to develop more autonomy. Concurrently, demands of caring for ageing grandparents may occur. This is an extremely complex and demanding stage of the family lifecycle, particularly for parents.

Facilitating the growth of adolescent autonomy

Good parent–child communication and joint problem-solving skills facilitate the renegotiation of parent–child relationships and the growth of adolescent autonomy. Results of empirical studies of adolescent relationships with parents, peers and partners contradict many commonly held misconceptions (Hill, 1993; Papalia and Wendkos-Olds, 1995). Psychoanalytic writers, on the basis of clinical observations of distressed adolescents, argued that parent–child conflict is the norm in adolescence. Epidemiological studies of adolescents show that this is not the case. While one in five families experience some parent–child conflict, only one in twenty experience extreme conflict. A traditional view of adolescence is one where a visionary adolescent confronts conservative parental values. Epidemiological studies show that in most families parent–adolescent quarrels are about mundane topics like untidiness, music, clothing and curfew-time. They are rarely about values or ethics. A traditional view of adolescence posits a gradual erosion of the quality of parent–adolescent relationships with a complementary increase in the quality of the adolescent–peer relationships. Studies of attachment suggest that this is not the case. Secure attachments to parents are correlated with secure attachments to peers.

Promiscuity in adolescence is not the norm. Most surveys show that a majority of older teenagers view premarital sex between committed partners as acceptable. Premarital sex with multiple partners is viewed as unacceptable. Teenage pregnancy is a risk factor for later adjustment primarily because it may interfere with education and compromise the career prospects of the teenager. Adolescent marriages resulting from unplanned pregnancies run a high risk of dissolution, and these young families often develop multiple life problems and require particularly intensive multisystemic intervention (Brunk et al., 1987).

Resilience in adolescence

Adolescence is a risky period (Hill, 1993). Opportunities for developing a wide variety of psychological problems abound. A central concern for many parents is knowing the degree to which the dice is loaded in favour of the adolescent emerging from adolescence relatively unscathed. Factors which have been found in longitudinal studies to characterise adolescents and children who are resilient in the face of adversity are summarised in Table 8.5 (Rolf et al., 1990; Rutter, 1999). Adolescents are more likely to show good adjustment if they have an easy temperament and a high level of intellectual ability. A high level of self-esteem, and optimistic attributional style, a general belief in control over one's life and a specific belief that factors related to specific stresses may be controlled (high self-efficacy) are all associated with good adjustment. These traits (high IQ and easy temperament) and positive belief-systems probably render youngsters less vulnerable to becoming overly physiologically aroused and aggressive or demoralised and depressed when faced with life stresses. Adolescents are less adversely affected by life stresses if they have good planning skills, a sense of humour and the capacity to empathise with others. All of these coping skills can help youngsters detach from deviant or incapacitated attachment figures (such as criminal or incapacitated parents) and deviant peers and seek out more resourceful and prosocial attachment figures and peers. Selecting or creating a positive social network (through marriage, positive school experiences, good friendships, or talented performance in sports or arts) can halt negative chain reactions or start positive chain reactions that facilitate personal development. Better adjustment to life stress occurs when adolescents come

Table 8.5 Factors associated with resilience in adolescence

Domain	Factors
Family factors	• Absence of early separation or losses • Secure attachment • Authoritative parenting • Father involvement
Community factors	• Positive educational experience • Good social support network (including good peer relationships, and involvement in organised religious activity) • High socio-economic status
Psychological traits	• High ability level • Easy temperament
Self-evaluative beliefs	• High self-esteem • Internal locus of control • Task-related self-efficacy • Optimistic attributional style
Coping skills	• Planning skills • Sense of humour • Empathy skills • Skill in detaching from deviant attachment figures and peer groups • Skill in finding or creating a social supportive network • Skill in using unique talents (e.g. sport or music) to create social supportive network and avoid deviant network

Source: Based on Rolf *et al.* (1990) and Rutter (1999): 119–44.

from higher socio-economic groups, have good social support networks comprising family members and peers and attend schools that provide a supportive yet challenging educational environment. Secure attachment relationships to primary caregivers who adopt an authoritative parenting style and the involvement of both mothers and fathers in parenting are the major positive family factors associated with adolescents' adjustment to life stress. The absence of childhood separations, losses, bereavements, parental mental health problems, criminality and marital discord also characterise the families of children who are resilient in the face of stress.

Grandparental care

Increasingly, with the lengthening of the average lifespan, the responsibility of caring for ageing parents is becoming a routine responsibility for men and women in midlife. The stress associated with this role and the impending death of the ageing parent tends to be most acutely felt by daughters of ageing parents. Social support from family and friends and periodic relief-custodial-care are important coping resources for such daughters to employ in managing the stresses of caring for ageing parents.

Launching

The seventh stage of the family lifecycle model in Table 8.1 is concerned with the transition of young adult children out of the parental home. Ideally this transition entails the development of a less hierarchical relationship between parents and children. During this stage, the parents are faced with the task of adjusting to living as a couple again, to dealing with disabilities and death in their families of origin and of adjusting to the expansion of the family if their children marry and procreate.

Midlife re-evaluation

As adolescents grow up and begin to leave home, parents must contend not only with changes in their relationships with their maturing children but also with a midlife re-evaluation of their marital relationship and career aspirations. This process which may have begun in the previous lifecycle stage takes on considerable momentum as the family home empties. Just as the notion of the universality of adolescent rebellion has not been supported by the results of carefully conducted community-based surveys, so also the popular conception of the midlife crisis has been found to be a relatively rare phenomenon (Papalia and Wendkos-Olds, 1995; Santrock, 1995). Longitudinal studies show that many men and women in their 40s become more introspective and re-evaluate their roles within the family and the world of work. For men there may be a shift in values with an increased valuing of family-life over work-life. For women there may be an increased emphasis on work over family. However, these changes in values rarely lead to changes that assume crisis proportions.

Gould (1981) has shown in an extensive study of clinical and non-clinical populations that the assumptions and belief systems learned within the family of origin are challenged in a gradual way over the course of adulthood and this process reaches a resolution in midlife. Gould's findings are summarised in Table 8.6. The assumptions of childhood give a sense of safety and security. They include a belief in omnipotent thought; a belief in omnipotent protective parents; a belief in the absoluteness of the parent's world view; and defences against a rage reaction to separation. Adult consciousness on the other hand is governed by an acceptance that we create our own lives according to beliefs and values that are different from those internalised in childhood.

In the late teens, if the adolescent is to be liberated from the family, the parent's world view must be appraised. Their parents' roles as protectors must be evaluated and their command over the youth's sexuality and body

Table 8.6 False assumptions challenged in adulthood

Period	False assumption	Belief systems
Late teens	I will always belong to my parents and believe in their world	• If I get any more independent it will be a disaster • I can only see the world through my parents' assumptions • Only they can guarantee my safety • They must be my only family • I don't own my body
20s	Doing it their way will bring results and they will guide me through difficulties	• If I follow the rules, I will be rewarded • There is only one right way to do things • Rationality, commitment and effort will always prevail over other forces • My partner will do those things for me that I cannot do for my self (i.e. give me a love-cure)
30s	Life is simple and controllable. There are no significant co-existing contradictory forces within me	• What I know intellectually, I know emotionally • I am not like my parents in ways that I don't want to be • I can see the reality of those close to me clearly • I can realistically identify and deal with threats to my security
40s	There is no evil in me or death in the world. The sinister has been expelled	• My work or my relationships grant me immunity from death and danger • There is no life beyond this family • I am innocent

Source: Based on Gould (1981).

must be challenged. The conflict is between retaining a childhood role and trying out new roles.

In the 20s, within the work arena, the idea that life is fair and if you stick to the rules you will win, is challenged. With relationships, the idea that our partners can make up for our deficiencies and we can make up for theirs is also challenged here. The idea that love can cure personal deficiencies must be given up during the 20s. For example, a talkative partner can't make up for a quiet partner's style nor can a nurturing partner fulfil all their partner's dependency needs. When these assumptions have been challenged the person is in a position to differentiate sufficiently to establish a family separate from the family of origin.

The assumptions that are challenged up to the 20s relate to the outer world. In the 30s, assumptions about our inner selves or our relationships with ourselves are challenged. The person realises that one can know something intellectually such as 'this row with my partner can be resolved through patient negotiation' and yet lack the emotional knowledge to work through the process of negotiation. In the 30s people realise that they have many characteristics of their parents which they dislike. For example, they may treat their children unfairly. This has to be recognised if patterns are not to be repeated across generations. There must be an acceptance of a partner's evolution and growth and the fact that we cannot assume that we see their point of view today just because we saw it a year ago. There are many threats to security in midlife both within marriage and the workplace. Perceived threats within marriage are often projections, rather than realistic threats.

People in their 30s assume that the feelings of being mistreated or taken for granted are real threats from their partners rather than projections onto their partners of ways in which they were treated as children by their parents or significant others. The belief that we can always identify and deal with threats accurately must be challenged in midlife.

In the 40s illusions of safety are challenged. For men, the most common illusion is 'If I am successful I will never be frightened again.' For women the most widespread illusion is 'I cannot be safe without a man to protect me.' When these illusions are challenged, both men and women are freed from slavish adherence to career or marital roles to make the best use of their remaining years with an awareness of their mortality in mind. Within marriage both husbands and wives must challenge the belief that there is no life outside the marriage. This may lead to them choosing to separate or choosing consciously to live together. The choice to remain married enriches the marriage. In midlife there must be a reappraisal of the idea that we are innocent, since this is usually a defence against the childhood tendency to label certain emotional states as bad or unacceptable. There is an examination of how we label these emotional experiences rather than a continued attempt to try to deny them.

For example:

- Anger need not be labelled as destructiveness;
- Pleasure need not be labelled as irresponsibility;
- Sensuality need not be labelled as sinfulness;
- Wicked thoughts need not entail wicked actions;
- Dissatisfaction need not be labelled as greed;
- Love need not be labelled as weakness;
- Self-concern need not be labelled as selfishness.

When these aspects of the self are relabelled rather than denied and integrated into the conscious self, a process of liberation and increased psychological vitality occurs. For Gould (1981), at the end of the midlife period the adult experiences a consciousness where the guiding belief is 'I own myself' rather than 'I am theirs'. The sense of self-ownership gives life meaning.

Later life, illness and death

In the final stage of the family lifecycle model in Table 8.1, the family must cope with the parents' physiological decline, and approaching death, while at the same time developing routines for benefiting from the wisdom and experience of the elderly. A central issue for all family members in this stage as parents move into later life is coping with their approaching death, possible terminal illness and the inevitability of death and ultimately bereavement. These losses involve the following grief processes:

- shock
- denial or disbelief
- yearning and searching
- sadness
- anger
- anxiety
- guilt and bargaining
- acceptance.

There is not a clear-cut progression through these processes from one to the next (Stroebe et al., 1993; Walsh and McGoldrick, 1991). Rather, at different points in time, one or other process predominates when a family member has experienced a loss or faces death. There may also be movement back and forth between processes.

Shock and denial

Shock is the most common initial reaction; it can take the form of physical pain, numbness, apathy or withdrawal. The person may appear to be stunned and unable to think clearly. This may be accompanied by denial, disbelief or avoidance of the reality of the bereavement, a process which can last minutes, days, even months. During denial people may behave as if the dead family member is still living, albeit elsewhere. Thus, the bereaved may speak about future plans that involve the deceased. Terminally ill people may talk about themselves and their future as if they were going to live indefinitely.

Yearning and searching

A yearning to be with the deceased, coupled with disbelief about their death, may lead younger family members to engage in frantic searches for the dead person, wandering or running away from the home in a quest for the person who has died. Children or grandchildren within the family may phone relatives or friends trying to trace the person who has died. During this process those who have lost family members may report seeing them or being visited by them. Some children carry on full conversations with what presumably are hallucinations of the deceased person. Mistaking other people for the deceased is also a common experience during the denial process. With terminal illness, the yearning for health may lead to a frantic search for a miracle cure and to involvement in alternative medicine.

Sadness

When denial gives way to a realisation of the reality of death, family members may experience profound sadness, despair, hopelessness and depression. The experience of sadness may be accompanied by low energy, sleep disruption, a disturbance of appetite, tearfulness, an inability to concentrate and a retreat from social interaction. Young children or grandchildren experiencing the despair process may regress and begin to behave as if they were a baby again, wetting their beds and sucking their thumbs, hoping that by becoming a baby, the dead person may return to comfort them. With terminal illness, despair, hopelessness and depression finds expression in an unwillingness to fight the illness.

Anger

Complementing the despair process, there is an anger process associated with the sense of having been abandoned. Aggression, conflict within the family and the wider social system, and drug and alcohol abuse are some of the common ways that grief-related anger finds expression. With terminal illness, the anger may be projected onto family members or members of the medical team. Destructive conflicts within these relationships may occur, such as refusal to adhere to medical regimes, to take medication or to participate in physiotherapy.

Anxiety

The expression of such anger may often be followed by remorse or fear of retribution. Young children or grandchildren may fear that the deceased family member will punish them for their anger and so it is not surprising that they may want to leave the light on at night and may be afraid to go to bed alone. In adolescents and adults anxiety is attached to reality-based threats. So, where a family member has been lost through illness or accident, those grieving may worry that they too will die from similar causes. This can lead to a belief that one is seriously ill and to a variety of somatic complains such as stomach aches and headaches. It may also lead to a refusal to leave home lest a fatal accident occur.

Guilt and bargaining

The guilt process is marked by self-blame for causing or not preventing the death of the deceased. Family members may also find themselves thinking that if they died this might magically bring back the deceased. Thus, the guilt process may underpin suicidal ideation or self-injury which invariably leads to referral for mental health assessment. With terminal illness, the illness may be experienced as a punishment for having done something wrong. This sense of guilt underpins the bargaining process in which people facing death engage. The bargaining process may be carried out as imagined conversations with a deity, where the dying person makes promises to live a better life if they are permitted to live longer.

Acceptance

The final grief process is acceptance. With bereavement, the surviving family members reconstruct their view of the world so that the deceased person is construed as no longer living in this world, but a benign and accessible representation of them is constructed which is consistent with the family's belief system. For example, a Christian may imagine that the deceased is in heaven. Atheists may experience the deceased as living on in their memory or in projects or photographs left behind. In terminal illness, acceptance involves a modification of the world view so that the future is foreshortened and therefore the time remaining is highly valued and is spent living life to the full rather than searching in vain for a miracle cure. For bereaved families, new lifestyle routines are evolved as part of the process of accepting the death of a family member and the family is re-organised to take account of the absence of the deceased person. With terminal illness, once the family accept the inevitability of imminent death, routines which enhance the quality of life of the dying person may be evolved. A summary of the grief processes is presented in Table 8.7.

Table 8.7 Behavioural expressions of themes underlying grief processes following bereavement or facing terminal illness

Grief Process	Bereavement		Terminal illness	
	Underlying theme	Adjustment problems arising from grief processes that may lead to referral	Underlying theme	Adjustment problems arising from grief processes that may lead to referral
Shock	• I am stunned by the loss of this person	• Complete lack of affect and difficulty engaging emotionally with others • Poor concentration	• I am stunned by my prognosis and loss of health	• Complete lack of affect and difficulty engaging emotionally with others • Poor concentration
Denial	• The person is not dead	• Reporting seeing or hearing the deceased • Carrying on conversations with the deceased	• I am not terminally ill	• Non-compliance with medical regime
Yearning and searching	• I must find the deceased	• Wandering or running away • Phoning relatives	• I will find a miracle cure	• Experimentation with alternative medicine
Sadness	• I am sad, hopeless and lonely because I have lost someone on whom I depended	• Persistent low mood, tearfulness, low energy and lack of activity • Appetite and sleep disruption • Poor concentration and poor school work	• I am sad and hopeless because I know I will die	• Giving up the fight against illness • Persistent low mood, tearfulness, low energy and lack of activity • Appetite and sleep disruption • Poor concentration and poor school work

Anger	• I am angry because the person I needed has abandoned me	• Aggression • Conflict with family members and others • Drug or alcohol abuse • Poor concentration	• I am angry because it's not fair. I should be allowed to live	• Non-compliance with medical regime • Aggression • Conflict with medical staff, family members and peers • Drug or alcohol abuse • Poor concentration
Anxiety	• I am frightened that the deceased will punish me for causing their death or being angry with them. I am afraid that I too may die of an illness or fatal accident	• Separation anxiety, agoraphobia and panic • Somatic complaints, and hypochondriasis • Poor concentration	• I am frightened that death will be painful or terrifying	• Separation anxiety and regressed behaviour • Agoraphobia and panic
Guilt and bargaining	• It is my fault that the person died so I should die	• Suicidal behaviour	• I will be good if I am allowed to live	• Overcompliance with medical regime
Acceptance	• I loved and lost the person who died and now I must carry on without them while cherishing their memory	• Return to normal behavioural routines	• I know that I have only a short time left to live	• Attempts to live life to the full for the remaining time

Source: Adapted from Carr (1999).

Positive reaction to necessary losses

Reviews of empirical studies of bereavement confirm that there is extraordinary variation in grief processes and that for some people in certain circumstances bereavement and grieving lead to personal growth (Shackleton, 1983; Stroebe, 1993; Wortman and Silver, 1989). Depression following bereavement is not universal. Only about a third of people suffer depression following bereavement. Failure to show emotional distress initially does not necessarily mean that later adjustment problems are inevitable. Also, contrary to the popular myth that grief counselling is the panacea for loss, not everyone needs to work through their sense of loss by immediate intensive conversation about it. Different people use different coping strategies to cope with loss. Some use distraction or avoidance, while others use confrontation of the grief experience and working through. Those that effectively use the former coping strategy may not show emotional distress. The quality of family relationships may improve in response to bereavement or terminal illness, with supportive relationships being strengthened.

Negative reactions to loss

Results of empirical studies confirm that for some people bereavement is a particularly destructive experience which does not lead to personal growth and development (Shackleton, 1983; Stroebe, 1993; Wortman and Silver, 1989). A return to normal functioning following bereavement does not always occur rapidly. While the majority of people approximate normal functioning within two years, a substantial minority of bereaved people continue to show adjustment difficulties even seven years after bereavement. Extreme distress following bereavement commonly occurs in those who show protracted grief reactions. Resolution and acceptance of death does not always occur. For example, parents who lose children or those who lose a loved one in an untimely fatal accident show protracted patterns of grief. Grief may have a marked effect on physical functioning. Infections and other illnesses are more common among bereaved people and this is probably due to the effect of loss-related stress on the functioning of the immune system. However, with the passage of time immune system functioning returns to normal. Just as bereavement may strengthen supportive family relationships, it may also weaken already discordant relationships and lead to family breakdown. While children's grief reactions tend to be briefer than those of adults, loss of a parent leaves young children vulnerable to depression in adult life. Adults bereaved as children have double the risk of developing depression when faced with a loss experience in adult life compared with their non-bereaved counterparts. Bereaved children most at risk for depression in adulthood are girls who were young when their parents died a violent or sudden death and who subsequently received inadequate care associated with the surviving parent experiencing a prolonged grief reaction.

We have considered a family lifecycle model which assumes lifelong monogamy, we will now look at lifecycle models that address other types of family arrangements, particularly those which evolve when separation, divorce and remarriage occurs.

LIFECYCLE STAGES ASSOCIATED WITH SEPARATION AND DIVORCE

Divorce is no longer considered to be an aberration in the normal family life-cycle, but a normative transition for a substantial minority of families (Bray and Hetherington, 1993; Brody et al., 1988; Hetherington and Stanley-Hagan, 1999). Family transformation through separation, divorce and re-marriage may be conceptualised as a process involving a series of stages. Carter and McGoldrick's (1989) model of the stages of adjustment to divorce is presented in Table 8.8. This model outlines tasks that must be completed during various stages of the transformation process that involves separation and remarriage. Failure to complete tasks at one stage may lead to adjustment problems for family members at later stages and referrals for family therapy.

Decision to divorce

In the first stage the decision to divorce occurs and accepting one's own part in marital failure is the central task. However, it is useful to keep in mind that many contextual factors contribute to divorce, including socio-economic status, urban/rural geographical location, age at marriage, premarital pregnancy, psychological adjustment and parental divorce (Raschke, 1987). Divorce is more common among those from lower socio-economic groups with psychological problems who live in urban areas and who have married before the age of 20. It is also common where premarital pregnancy has occurred and where parental divorce has occurred. Divorce is less common among those from higher socio-economic groupings without psychological problems who live in rural areas and who have married after the age of 30. Where premarital pregnancy has not occurred and where the couples' parents are still in their first marriage, divorce is also less common. The economic resources associated with high socio-economic status (SES), the community integration associated with rural living, the psychological resources associated with maturity and the model of marital stability offered by non-divorced parents are the more common explanations given for the associations among these factors associated with divorce. The relationship between these various factors and divorce, while consistent, are moderate to weak. That is, there are significant subgroups of people who show some or all of these risk factors but do not divorce.

Table 8.8 Extra stages in the family lifecycle entailed by separation or divorce and remarriage

Stage	Task
1. Decision to divorce	• Accepting one's own part in marital failure
2. Planning separation	• Co-operatively developing a plan for custody of the children, visitation and finances • Dealing with the families of origin's response to the plan to separate
3. Separation	• Mourning the loss of the intact family • Adjusting to the change in parent–child and parent–parent relationships • Avoiding letting marital arguments interfere with parent-to-parent co-operation • Staying connected to the extended family • Managing doubts about separation and becoming committed to divorce
4. Post-divorce period	• Maintaining flexible arrangements about custody, access and finances without detouring conflict through the children • Ensuring both parents retain strong relationships with the children • Re-establishing peer relationships and a social network
5. Entering a new relationship	• Completing emotional divorce from the previous relationship • Developing commitment to a new marriage
6. Planning a new marriage	• Planning for co-operative co-parental relationships with ex-spouses • Planning to deal with children's loyalty conflicts involving natural and step-parents • Adjust to widening of extended family
7. Establishing a new family	• Realigning relationships within the family to allow space for new members • Sharing memories and histories to allow for integration of all new members

Source: Adapted from Carter and McGoldrick (1989).

Separation

In the second stage of the lifecycle model of divorce, plans for separation are made. A co-operative plan for custody of the children, visitation, finances and dealing with families of origin's response to the plan to separate must be made if positive adjustment is to occur. The third stage of the model is separation. Mourning the loss of the intact family; adjusting to the change in parent–child and parent–parent relationships; preventing marital arguments from interfering with interparental co-operation; staying connected to the extended family; and managing doubts about separation are the principal tasks at this stage.

Divorce leads to multiple life changes which affect parental well-being and the impact of these changes on parental well-being is mediated by a range of personal and contextual factors (Raschke, 1987; Bray and Hetherington, 1993). Divorce leads custodial parents to experience major changes in their lives including a change in residential arrangements, economic disadvantage, loneliness associated with social network changes and role-strain associated with the task overload that results from having to care for children and work outside the home. Non-custodial parents experience all of these changes with the exception of role-strain. Changes in divorced couples' residential arrangements, economic status, social networks and role demands lead to a deterioration in physical and mental health for the majority of individuals immediately following separation. Mood swings, depression, identity problems, vulnerability to common infections and exacerbation of previous health problems are all common sequelae for adults who have separated or divorced. However, for most people these health problems abate within two years of the separation.

Post-divorce period

The fourth stage of the lifecycle model of divorce is the post-divorce period. Here couples must maintain flexible arrangements about custody, access and finances without detouring conflict through the children; and retain strong relationships with the children; and re-establish peer relationships. The stresses and strains of residential changes, economic hardship, role changes and consequent physical and psychological difficulties associated with the immediate aftermath of separation may compromise parents' capacity to co-operate in meeting their children's needs for safety, care, control, education and relationships with each parent (Amato, 1993). Authoritarian-punitive parenting, lax laissez-faire or neglectful parenting and chaotic parenting, which involves oscillating between both of these extreme styles, are not uncommon among both custodial and non-custodial parents who have divorced. Couples vary in the ways in which they co-ordinate their efforts to parent their children following divorce. Three distinct co-parenting styles have been identified in studies of divorced families (Bray and Hetherington, 1993). With *co-operative parenting* a unified and integrated set of rules and routines about managing the children in both the custodial and non-custodial households is developed. This is the optimal arrangement but only occurs in about one in five cases. With *parallel parenting* each parent has his or her own set of rules for the children and no attempt is made to integrate these. Most children show few adjustment problems when parallel parenting occurs and this is the most common pattern. When *conflictual parenting* occurs, the couple do not communicate directly with each other. All messages are passed through the child and this go-between role, forced upon the child, is highly stressful and entails sustained adjustment problems (Hetherington, 1989).

Parental separation and divorce are major life stressors for all family members. For children, the experiences of separation and divorce may lead to short- and longer-term adjustment reactions (Amato, 1993; Amato and Keith, 1991a; Amato and Keith, 1991b; Wallerstein, 1991). During the two-year period immediately following divorce, most children show some adjustment problems. Boys tend to display conduct or externalising behaviour problems and girls tend to experience emotional or internalising behaviour problems. Both boys and girls may experience educational problems and relationship difficulties within the family, school and peer group. The mean level of maladjustment has consistently been found to be worse for children of divorce in comparison with those from intact families on a variety of measures of adjustment including conduct difficulties, emotional problems, academic performance, self-esteem and relationships with parents. This has led to the erroneous conclusion by some interpreters of the literature that divorce always has a negative effect on children. When the impact of divorce on children is expressed in terms of the percentages of maladjusted children, it is clear that divorce leads to maladjustment for only a minority of youngsters. A small proportion of individuals from families where divorce has occurred have difficulty making and maintaining stable marital relationships, have psychological adjustment difficulties and attain a lower socio-economic level in comparison with adults who have grown up in intact families.

Certain characteristics of children and certain features of their social contexts mediate the effects of parental divorce on their adjustment (Amato, 1993; Amato and Keith, 1991a; Hetherington, 1989; Hetherington and Stanley-Hagan, 1999; Raschke, 1987; Wallerstein, 1991; Walker, 1993). In terms of personal characteristics, males between the ages of 3 and 18 are particularly at risk for post-divorce adjustment problems, especially if they have biological or psychological vulnerabilities. Biological vulnerabilities may result from genetic factors, prenatal and perinatal difficulties, or a history of serious illness or injury. Psychological vulnerabilities may be entailed by low intelligence, a difficult temperament, low self-esteem, an external locus of control, or a history of previous psychological adjustment problems. Specific features of children's families and social networks may render them vulnerable to adjustment difficulties following parental separation or divorce. Children are more likely to develop post-separation difficulties if there have been serious difficulties with the parent–child relationship prior to the separation. Included here are insecure attachment, inconsistent discipline and authoritarian, permissive or neglectful parenting. Exposure to chronic family problems including parental adjustment problems, marital discord, domestic violence, family disorganisation, and a history of previous separations and reunions also place children at risk for post-separation adjustment problems. Early life stresses, such as abuse or bereavement, may also compromise children's capacity to deal with stresses entailed by parental separation. In contrast to these factors that predispose children to post-separation adjustment difficulties, better post-separation adjustment occurs where youngsters have a history of good physical and psychological adjustment and where their families have offered a stable parenting environment.

Following parental separation, adjustment difficulties may be maintained by a variety of psychological factors within the child and a range of psychosocial factors within the child's family and social network (Amato, 1993; Amato and Keith, 1991a; Hetherington, 1989; Raschke, 1987; Wallerstein, 1991; Walker, 1993). At a personal level, adjustment problems may be maintained by rigid sets of negative beliefs related to parental separation. These beliefs may include the view that the child caused the separation and has the power to influence parental reunification, or a belief that abandonment by parents and rejection by peers is inevitable. Within the child's family and social network, adjustment problems following separation may be maintained by sustained parental conflict and routine involvement of the child in this ongoing parental acrimony. The use of non-optimal parenting styles, a lack of consistency in parental rules and routines across custodial and non-custodial households, a lack of clarity about new family roles and routines within each household, and confused family communication may all maintain children's post-separation adjustment problems. These parenting and co-parenting problems which maintain children's adjustment difficulties are in turn often a spin-off from parents' personal post-separation adjustment problems. The degree to which parental post-separation problems compromise their capacity to provide a co-parenting environment that minimises rather than maintains their children's adjustment reactions is partially determined by the stresses parents face in the aftermath of separation. These include the loss of support, financial hardship and social disadvantage.

In contrast to these factors that maintain post-separation adjustment difficulties, better post-separation adjustment occurs in youngsters who have psychological strengths such as high self-esteem, an internal locus of control, realistic beliefs about their parents' separation and divorce, good problem-solving skills and good social skills. In terms of the child's family and social network, better adjustment occurs usually after a two-year period has elapsed, where parental conflict is minimal and not channelled through the child, and where an authoritative parenting style is employed. Where parents cope well with post-separation grief, have good personal psychological resources, and a high level of satisfaction within their new relationships, children show better post-separation adjustment. Parental commitment to resolving child-management difficulties and a track record of coping well with transitions in family life may be viewed as protective factors. The availability of social support for both parents and children from the extended family and peers and the absence of financial hardship are also protective factors for post-separation adjustment. Where the school provides a concerned student-centred, achievement-oriented ethos with a high level of student contact and supervision, children are more likely to show positive adjustment following separation. The factors discussed above have a cumulative effect, with more predisposing and maintaining factors being associated with worse adjustment and more protective factors being associated with better adjustment.

New relationships

Establishing a new relationship occurs in the fifth stage of the divorce lifecycle model. For this to occur emotional divorce from the previous relationship must be completed and a commitment to a new marriage must be developed. The sixth stage of the model is planning a new marriage. This entails planning for co-operative co-parental relationships with ex-spouses and planning to deal with children's loyalty conflicts involving natural and step-parents. It is also important to adjust to the widening of the extended family. In the final stage of the model establishing a new family is the central theme. Realigning relationships within the family to allow space for new members and sharing memories and histories to allow for integration of all new members are the principal tasks of this stage.

Step-families have unique characteristics which are, in part, affected by the conditions under which they are formed (Hetherington, 1989; Raschke, 1987). On the positive side, surveys of step-families have found them to be more open in communication, more willing to deal with conflict, more pragmatic and less romantic and more egalitarian with respect to child care and housekeeping tasks. On the negative side, compared with intact first marriages, step-families are less cohesive and more stressful. Step-parent–child relationships on average tend to be more conflictual than parent–child relationships in intact families. This is particularly true of step-father–daughter relationships and may be due to the daughter's perception of the step-father encroaching on a close mother–daughter relationship.

Children's adjustment following remarriage is associated with age, gender and parents' satisfaction with the new marriage (Hetherington and

Stanley-Hagan, 1999). Good adjustment occurs when the custodial parent remarries while children are pre-adolescent or in their late adolescence or early adulthood. All children in divorced families resist the entry of a step-parent. But during the early teenage years (10–15) this resistance is at a maximum. Divorced adults with children in middle childhood and early adolescence who wish to remarry should try to wait until after the children have reached about 16–18 years, if they want their new relationship to have a fair chance of survival. Remarriage is more disruptive for girls than for boys. Marital satisfaction in the new relationship has a protective effect for young boys and it is a risk factor for pre-adolescent girls. Young boys benefit from their custodial mothers forming a satisfying relationship with a new partner. Such satisfying relationships lead step-fathers to behave in a warm, child-centred way towards their step-sons and to help them learn sports and academic skills. These skills help young boys become psychologically robust. Pre-adolescent girls feel that the close supportive relationship they have with their divorced mothers is threatened by the development of a new and satisfying marital relationship. They usually respond with increased conduct problems and psychological difficulties. In adolescence, when the remarriage has occurred while the children were pre-adolescent, a high level of marital satisfaction is associated with good adjustment and a high level of acceptance of the step-parent for both boys and girls.

ASSESSING RELATIONSHIPS

The most useful measures for assessing positive relationships and interpersonal behaviour are grounded in sound theoretical models. These include attachment theory, interpersonal theory and a number of systemic models of family functioning.

Attachment theory

Within attachment theory it is assumed that children's early experiences with their primary caregivers lead them to become either securely or insecurely attached (Bowlby, 1988; Cassidy and Shaver, 1999). Where caregivers are attuned to infants' needs and meet them reliably, infants develop an internal working model of their caregiver as a secure base from which to explore the world and so show considerable confidence in doing so. Where caregivers fail to meet their infants' needs in a reliable way, infants develop internal working models of their caregivers as unreliable and view themselves as insecure. This may find expression as ambivalent (clingy) or avoidant (sulky) attachment, or as disorganised attachment which involves alternating between anxious and avoidant attachment patterns.

A variety of ways of assessing attachment style in infants have been developed (Solomon and George, 1999). The gold standard for assessing the attachment style of infants is a laboratory-based observational procedure referred to as the Strange Situation (Ainsworth *et al.*, 1978). Extensive training is required to administer and score this. A promising alternative requiring no training is the Attachment Q-Set (Waters, 1987) which is based on parental home observations. Attachment style in adults may also be measured in a variety of ways (Crowell *et al.*, 1999). Of these the Adult Attachment Interview and its rating scales is the gold standard (George *et al.*, 1984; Main and Goldwyn, 1994). As in the Strange Situation, extensive training is required to administer and score this. A good self-report measure of adult romantic attachment which is based on an integration of other available self-report measures of adult attachment in romantic relationships is the Experiences of Close Relationships Inventory (Brennan *et al.*, 1998).

Circumplex model of interpersonal behaviour

In the circumplex model of interpersonal behaviour, each person is assumed in childhood to learn a dominant interpersonal style which characterises their way of interacting with others, and which serves the function of reducing insecurity and maximising self-esteem. The model is an empirically testable refinement of Harry Stack Sullivan's Interpersonal Psychiatry (Kiesler, 1996). Within the circumplex model of interpersonal behaviour, dispositions to engage in particular types of interpersonal interactions with others are construed as falling within a two-dimensional space defined by a vertical axis that extends from dominance to submission and a horizontal axis that extends from cold hostility to warm friendliness (Wiggins and Trapnell, 1997). From Figure 8.2 it may be seen that the interpersonal dispositions in the octants of the interpersonal space are defined by combinations of the two dominance and nurturance axes. These eight dispositions are assured–dominant, gregarious–extraverted, warm–agreeable, unassuming–ingenuous, unassured–submissive, aloof–introverted, cold-hearted, arrogant–calculating. Dimensions of the circumplex model of interpersonal behaviour may be measured using a variety of instruments (Kiesler, 1996). These include the Interpersonal Adjective Scale (Wiggins, 1995) and the Inventory of Interpersonal Problems (Horowitz *et al.*, 2000). Correlational studies show that the dominance and nurturance axes of the circumplex model of interpersonal behaviour correspond to the extraversion and agreeableness factors of the five-factor personality theory (Wiggins and Trapnell, 1997). Measures derived from the circumplex model of interpersonal behaviour may be used to test hypotheses about the development of interpersonal strengths, such as having styles in the north-east quadrant of the model (assured–dominant, gregarious–extraverted, and warm–agreeable) and these relationships between these styles and subjective well-being.

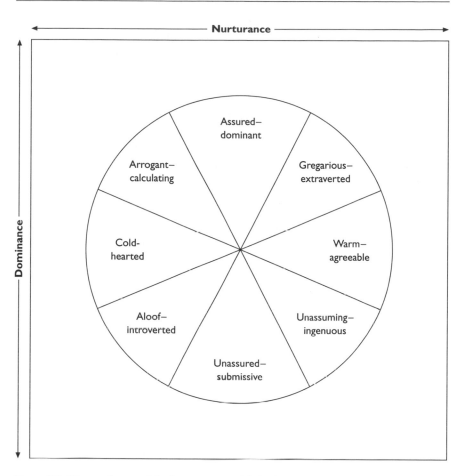

Figure 8.2 Circumplex model of Interpersonal behaviour
Source: Adapted from Wiggins and Trapnell (1997): 749.

Family systems models

In family systems models individual differences in the functioning of whole families are conceptualised as varying along a number of dimensions. Models which have led to the development of widely used and psychometric-ally sound assessment instruments include the McMaster Model of Family Functioning (Miller *et al.*, 2000), the Beavers Family Systems Model (Beavers and Hampson, 2000), the Circumplex Model of Marital and Family Systems, (Olson, 2000), and the Process Model of Family Functioning (Skinner *et al.*, 2000).

The McMaster Model of Family Functioning (Miller *et al.*, 2000) describes families along six interrelated dimensions: problem solving, communication, roles, affective responsiveness, affective expression and behaviour control. Functional families display adaptive levels of all of these processes whereas families who have difficulties in managing tasks and lifecycle transitions show less adaptive levels of these processes. The status of families on these dimensions may be evaluated with the self-report McMaster Family Assessment Device (Epstein *et al.*, 1983) or with the McMaster Structured Interview of Family Functioning (Bishop *et al.*, 1980) and the McMaster Clinical Rating Scale (Miller *et al.*, 1994).

The Beavers Family Systems Model (Beavers and Hampson, 2000) contains two dimensions: family competence and family style. Family competence, conceptualised as a horizontal axis, ranges from optimal functioning to severely dysfunctional. Family competence progresses from chaotic functioning, through extreme rigidity and marked dominance submission patterns, to equality and flexibility in family relationships. Family style, conceptualised as a vertical axis, ranges from highly centripetal to highly centrifugal. An extremely centripetal style compromises children's opportunities to develop autonomy from the nuclear family. A highly centrifugal family style expels children from the security of the family prematurely. Extreme styles are hypothesised to occur in more dysfunctional families and a more blended and flexible style is expected to occur in healthier families. In this sense the family style dimension is curvilinear. The two main dimensions of the model may be evaluated with the Beavers Interactional Competence Scale and the Beavers Interactional Style Scale (Beavers and Hampson, 1990). The Self-Report Family Inventory may be used to evaluate the competence dimension of the model (Beavers and Hampson, 1990).

The Circumplex Model of Family Functioning (Olson, 2000) describes families along three dimensions: cohesion, adaptability and communication. The cohesion dimension ranges from enmeshed to disengaged. The adaptability dimension ranges from rigid to chaotic. Extreme scores on each dimension are associated with family difficulties. Moderate levels of cohesion and adaptability are hypothesised to typify well-functioning families. Thus, both cohesion and adaptability are conceptualised as bearing a curvilinear relationship to the health and well-being of family members. The third dimension, communication, ranges from problematic to highly functional and a family's status on this dimension is hypothesised to determine the ease with which changes on the other two dimensions may occur. All three dimensions of the model may be evaluated by observation with the Clinical Rating Scale for the Circumplex Model (Olson, 1990). The self-report Family Adaptability and Cohesion Evaluation Scales (FACES) may be used to assess adaptability and cohesion (Olson *et al.*, 1986).

The Family Process Model is a conceptual framework for conducting family assessments according to seven key dimensions: task accomplishment; role performance; communication; affective expression; involvement; control; values and norms (Skinner *et al.*, 2000). The set of self-report instruments derived from the model – The Family Assessment Measures – provide scores on these dimensions at three levels for the family system, various dyadic family relationships and individual functioning (Skinner *et al.*, 1995).

A focus on strengths and competence is central to all models. The dimensions of family functioning in each of the models are conceptualised in terms of family resources and competencies rather than deficits and problems.

Marital systems models

Marital systems models are premised on the idea that for couples to function co-operatively and experience marital satisfaction they must show optimal functioning on dimensions such as affective communication, problem-solving communication and role compatibility. The Marital Satisfaction Inventory–Revised is a self-report measure which assesses marital system functioning and marital satisfaction (Snyder, 1997). It yields scores for each member of a couple on the following scales: affective communication; role orientation; problem-solving communication; aggression; family history of distress; time together; dissatisfaction with children; disagreement about finances; conflict over child-rearing; sexual dissatisfaction; and global distress.

IMPLICATIONS

A summary of self-help strategies for promoting strengths and well-being based on research on the family lifecycle is given in Table 8.9. These can be incorporated into clinical practice.

CONTROVERSIES

There is potential for a debate about the appropriateness of including the study of relationships under the umbrella of positive psychology (Ryff and Singer, 2000). On the one hand it may be argued that the study of relationships belongs within the field of developmental or lifespan psychology. On the other, it is universally accepted that significant social relationships are central to well-being and happiness. Furthermore, studies of marriage and parenting only occasionally address issues such as health and physiological functioning. On the other hand, studies of health and social support rarely address optimal relational functioning within the family context. Professor Carol Ryff has argued that a worthy goal for the new millennium is promoting interaction between these two traditions by evolving a joint focus on the

Table 8.9 Strategies for promoting strengths and well-being based on research on the family lifecycle

Domain	Strategy
Managing transitions	• Accept that all lifecycle transitions involve both gains and losses • Use problem-solving and communication skills described in Chapter 9 to negotiate lifecycle transitions with members of your social network • Acknowledge that you will find your own way to grieve the necessary losses that go with lifecycle transitions, and this may involve a variety of processing including shock, denial, yearning and searching, sadness, anger, anxiety, guilt and bargaining, and acceptance
Friendship and forgiveness	• Choose friends with similar values to your own • Choose friends who are better than you are on attributes and skills that are not central to your self-concept so you can value your friend highly for these positive qualities • Choose friends who are slightly less good than you are on attributes and skills central to your self-conception so as to avoid rivalry • When breaches of trust occur in friendships acknowledge strong feelings of anger and sadness associated with the transgression • Let go of unmet interpersonal needs arising from the transgression • Develop empathy for the transgressor • Construct a new way of seeing yourself and the transgressor
Enhancing marital satisfaction	• Accept and respect your partner as he or she is, rather than trying to change them • Attribute their positive behaviour to internal stable positive dispositions • Set aside time every day to listen and talk about your experiences using the communication skills described in Chapter 9. • Try to engage in five times as many positive interactions as negative ones • When conflicts occur focus on jointly resolving the issue using the problem-solving skills described in Chapter 9 rather than finding fault with your partner • If you get overly physiologically aroused during joint problem solving, take time out to relax using the skills in Table 7.3 before recommencing • When conflicts occur, try to resolve them quickly rather than delaying conflict resolution • Jointly accept that some misunderstandings occur because men use conversation predominantly to resolve task-related problems, while women use conversation predominantly to make and maintain relationships • Jointly accept that some disagreements occur because males demand greater psychological distance and females insist on greater psychological intimacy • Jointly accept that some disagreements occur because males commonly wish to retain the power and benefits of traditional gender roles while females wish to evolve more egalitarian relationships
Optimal parenting	• Help children develop secure attachment by being attuned to their needs for physical and emotional care; control and intellectual stimulation and try to meet them reliably and predictably • Help children develop emotional intelligence by following the guidelines in Table 4.6 • Help children develop self-esteem by following the guidelines in Table 7.6 • Help children develop the capacity for flow experiences by following the guidelines in Table 2.4

positive health implications of interpersonal flourishing. Studies in this area should focus on the physiological correlates of optimal family relationships.

SUMMARY

Friendship, kinship, relationships and marriage are all-important sources of happiness. The family lifecycle is a useful framework within which to conceptualise the development of positive relationships. Families are unique social systems insofar as membership is based on combinations of biological, legal, affectional, geographic and historical ties. In contrast to other social systems, entry into family systems is through birth, adoption, fostering or marriage and members can leave only by death. The family lifecycle may be conceptualised as a series of stages, each characterised by a sct of tasks family members must complete to progress to the next stage. Failure to complete tasks may lead to adjustment problems. In the first two stages of family development, the principal concerns are with differentiating from the family of origin by completing school, developing relationships outside the family, completing one's education and beginning a career. In developing relationships outside the family young adults must address such issues as friendship, trust, betrayal, atonement and forgiveness. In the third stage, the principal tasks are those associated with selecting a partner and deciding to marry. In the fourth stage, the childless couple must develop routines for living together which are based on a realistic appraisal of the other's strengths, weaknesses and idiosyncrasies. In the fifth stage, the main task is for couples to adjust their roles as marital partners to make space for young children. In the sixth stage, which is marked by children's entry into adolescence, parent–child relationships require realignment to allow adolescents to develop more autonomy. The demands of grandparental dependency and midlife re-evaluation may compromise parents' abilities to meet their adolescents' needs for the negotiation of increasing autonomy. The seventh stage is concerned with the transition of young adult children out of the parental home. During this stage, the parents are faced with the task of adjusting to living as a couple again, to dealing with disabilities and death in their families of origin and of adjusting to the expansion of the family if their children marry and procreate. In the final stage of this lifecycle model, the family must cope with the parents' physiological decline, and approaching death, while at the same time developing routines for benefiting from the wisdom and experience of the elderly.

Family transformation through separation, divorce and remarriage may also be viewed as a staged process. In the first stage the decision to divorce occurs and accepting one's own part in marital failure is the central task. In the second stage, plans for separation are made. A co-operative plan for custody of the children, visitation, finances and dealing with families of origin's response to the plan to separate must be made if positive adjustment is to occur. The third stage of the model is separation. Mourning the loss of the intact family; adjusting to the change in parent–child and parent–parent relationships; preventing marital arguments from interfering with interparental co-operation; staying connected to the extended family; and managing doubts about separation are the principal tasks at this stage. The fourth stage is the post-divorce period. Here couples must maintain flexible arrangements about custody, access and finances without detouring conflict through the children; and retain strong relationships with the children; and re-establish peer relationships. Establishing a new relationship occurs in the fifth stage. For this to occur emotional divorce from the previous relationship must be completed and a commitment to a new marriage must be developed. The sixth stage of the model is planning a new marriage. This entails planning for co-operative co-parental relationships with ex-spouses and planning to deal with children's loyalty conflicts involving natural and step-parents. It is also important to adjust to the widening of the extended family. In the final stage of the model establishing a new family is the central theme. Realigning relationships within the family to allow space for new members and sharing memories and histories to allow for integration of all new members are the principal tasks of this stage.

The most useful measures for assessing relationships and interpersonal behaviour are grounded in sound theoretical models such as attachment theory, interpersonal theory and a number of systemic models of marital and family functioning.

QUESTIONS

Personal development questions

1. At what stage are you in the family lifecycle?
2. What have you learned from this chapter about the stage in which you currently find yourself?
3. What steps can you take now to enhance your life by applying some of this new knowledge to your current situation?
4. What would be the costs and benefits of taking these steps?
5. Take some of these steps and assess the impact it has on your well-being by assessing yourself before and afterwards on one of the well-being scales contained in Chapter 1.

Research questions

1. Design and conduct a study to test the hypothesis that there is a significant correlation between happiness and the dimensions of family functioning assessed by the McMaster Family Assessment Device.

2. Conduct PsychInfo searches covering literature published in the past couple of years using the terms 'friendship', 'marriage', and 'parenting' coupled with the term 'well-being'. Identify a study that interests you and that is feasible to replicate and extend. Conduct the replication.

FURTHER READING

Academic reading

Carr, A. (2000b). *Family Therapy: Concepts, Process and Practice.* Chichester: Wiley.

Self-help: forgiveness

Worthington, E. (2001). *Five Steps to Forgiveness.* New York: Crown.

Self-help: communication

Bolton, R. (1986). *People Skills.* New York: Touchstone. (A practical guide for developing communication, negotiation and assertiveness skills.)

McKay, M., Davis, M. and Fanning, P. (1997). *How to Communicate: The Ultimate Guide to Improving Your Personal and Professional Relationships.* New York: Fine. (Practical exercises for developing communication, negotiation and assertiveness skills.)

Self-help: coping with living single

Broder, M. (1988). *The Art of Living Single.* New York: Avon. (Gives practical advice on managing loneliness, and building social and romantic relationships.)

Burns, D. (1985). *Intimate Connections: New Clinically Tested Programme for Overcoming Loneliness.* New York: Morrow. (Practical and proven strategies for developing relationships.)

Zimbardo, P. (1987). *Shyness.* Reading, MA: Addison-Wesley. (Outlines factors contributing to shyness and practical strategies for overcoming them.)

Self-help: enhancing marital intimacy and coping with marital distress

Gottman, J. and Silver, N. (1999). *The Seven Principles for Making Marriage Work.* London: Weidenfeld and Nicolson. (This guide is based on years of research by Gottman.)

Markman, H., Stanley, S. and Blumberg, S. (1994). *Fighting for Your Marriage.* San Francisco, CA: Jossey Bass. (This guide is based on a scientifically evaluated premarital programme.)

Sternberg, R. (1987). *The Triangle of Love.* New York: Basic Books. (This book is based on the author's research.)

Tannen, D. (1990). *You Just Don't Understand: Women and Men in Conversation.* New York: Ballentine. (Outlines different conversational styles used by men and women and how a knowledge of these can help enhance communication in intimate relationships.)

Self-help: enhancing sexual experience and coping with sexual difficulties

Kaplan, H. (1987). *Illustrated Manual of Sexual Therapy.* New York: Brunner/Mazel. (This practical therapist's manual of scientifically validated treatment techniques and exercises can be used as a self-help guide by couples with problems such as premature ejaculation or anorgasmia.)

McCarthy, B. and McCarthy, E. (1993). *Sexual Awareness: Enhancing Sexual Pleasure.* New York: Carroll and Graf. (This guide to enhancing sexual experience is based on sound research and principles of social learning theory.)

Self-help: pregnancy

Brott, A. and Ash, J. (1995). *The Expectant Father.* New York: Abbeville. (A good guide for men whose wives are pregnant.)

Eisenberg, A., Eisenberg-Murkoff, H. and Hathaway, S. (1996). *What to Expect When You're Expecting* (revised edn). New York: Workman. (An authoritative guide to common concerns during pregnancy.)

Kitzinger, S. (1996). *The Complete Book of Pregnancy and Childbirth.* New York: Knopf. (A very thorough and practical guide to pregnancy and the process of childbirth.)

Self-help: parenting

Brazelton, T. (1983). *Infants and Mothers* (revised 3rd edn). New York: Delta Seymor Lawrence. (This book describes the developmental milestones for the first year of babies with active, average and quiet temperaments.)

Brazelton, T. (1989). *Toddlers and Parents* (revised 2nd edn). New York: Delacorte. (This book describes the developmental milestones for the toddler years.)

Forehand, R. and Long, N. (1996). *Parenting the Strong-Willed Child: The Clinically Proven Five Week Programme for Parents of Two to Six Year Olds.* Chicago: Contemporary Books. (A research-based programme for managing childhood behaviour problems.)

Leach, P. (1997). *Your Baby and Child from Birth to Age Five* (revised edn). New York: Knopf. (An authoritative guide to parenting.)

Self-help: coping with divorce

Brown, L. and Brown, M. (1986). *Dinosaurs Divorce: A Guide for Changing Families.* Boston, MA: Little Brown. (This small illustrated guide is for young children whose parents are divorcing.)

Gardner, R. (1985). *The Boys and Girls Book about Divorce.* New York: Bantam. (This guide is for 10–12-year-old children.)

Kalter, N. (1990). *Growing up with Divorce.* New York: Free Press. (This book is for parents who are divorcing to help them deal with their children's needs during the process.)

Neuman, G. and Romanowski, P. (1998). *Helping Your Kids Cope with Divorce.* New York: Times Books. (This book is for parents who are divorcing to help them deal with their children's needs during the process.)

Self-help: living in stepfamilies

Eckler, J. (1993). *Step by Step-Parenting: A Guide to Successful Living with a Blended Family* (2nd edn). White Hall, VA: Betterway Publications.

Visher, E. and Visher, J. (1982). *How to Win as a Step-Family.* New York: Dembner.

Self-help: coping with developmental challenges of adult life and ageing

Levinson, D. (1986). *Seasons of a Man's Life.* New York: Ballantine. (A good research-based account of male developmental stages of adult life, especially middle life.)

Osterkamp, L. (1992). *How to Deal with Your Parents When They Still Treat You Like a Child.* New York: Berkeley. (A good guide to help young adults manage family of origin relationships more effectively.)

Sheehy, G. (1976). *Passages: Predictable Crises of Adult Life.* New York: Dutton. (A good intuitive account of developmental stages in adult life.)

Skinner, B. and Vaughan, M. (1993). *Enjoy Old Age: A Programme of Self-Management.* New York: Norton. (This guide to later life was written by two old professors from Harvard University.)

Self-help: coping with loss

Colgrove, M., Bloomfield, H. and McWilliams, P. (1991). *How to Survive the Loss of Love* (Second Edition). Los Angeles, CA: Prelude Press. (A good guide for dealing with loss through separation and bereavement.)

James, J. and Cherry, F. (1988). *The Grief Recovery Handbook. A Step-by-Step Program for Moving beyond Loss.* New York: Harper Row. (A good practical workbook.)

Rando, T. (1991). *How to Go on Living When Someone You Love Dies.* New York: Bantam. (A guide to the variety of different ways that people grieve and the impact of grief on the family.)

Viorst, J. (1986). *Necessary Losses.* New York: Simon and Schuster. (This outstanding book shows how growth and maturity may be achieved by dealing with the inevitable losses and separations associated with transitions in adult life.)

MEASURES FOR USE IN RESEARCH

Interpersonal behaviour

Horowitz, L., Alden, L., Wiggins, J. and Pincus, A. (2000). *Inventory of Interpersonal Problems.* San Antonio, TX: Psychological Corporation. (Available at www.psychcorp.com)

Wiggins, J. (1995). *Interpersonal Adjective Scale: Professional Manual.* Odessa, FL: Psychological Assessment Resources.

Attachment

Ainsworth, M., Blehar, M., Waters, E. and Wass, S. (1978). *Patterns of Attachment: A Psychological Study of the Strange Situation.* Hillsdale, NJ: Erlbaum.

Brennan, K., Clark, C. and Shaver, P. (1998). Self-report measurement of adult attachment: An integrative overview. In J. Simpson and W. Rholes (eds), *Attachment Theory and Close Relationships* (pp. 46–76). (Contains a self-report measure of adult romantic attachment also available at http://psychology.ucdavis.edu/Shaver/ecl.html)

George, G., Kaplan, N. and Main, M. (1984). Adult Attachment Interview. Unpublished manuscript. University of California at Berkeley.

Main, M. and Goldwyn, R. (1994). The Adult Attachment Rating and Classification System: Manual in Draft (Version 6.0). Unpublished manuscript, University of California at Berkeley.

Waters, E. (1987). The Attachment Q-Set. (Revision 3.0). Unpublished manuscript. State University of New York at Stonybrook.

Family functioning

Beavers, W.R. and Hampson, R.B. (1990) *Successful Families: Assessment and Intervention.* New York: W.W. Norton.

Bishop, D., Epstein, N., Keitner, G., Miller, I. and Zlotnick, C. (1980). *The McMaster Structured Interview for Family Functioning.* Providence, Rhode Island: Brown University Family Research Program.

Epstein, N., Baldwin, L. and Bishop, D. (1983). The McMaster Family Assessment Device. *Journal of Marital and Family Therapy* 9: 171–80.

Miller, I., Kabacoff, R., Bishop, D., Epstein, N. and Keitner, G. (1994). The development of the McMaster Clinical Rating Scale. *Family Process* 33: 53–69.

Olson, D.H. (1990). *Clinical Rating Scale for the Circumplex Model.* St Paul, MN: Family Social Science, University of Minnesota.

Olson, D.H., McCubbin, H.I., Barnes, H., Larsen, A., Muxen, M. and Wilson, M. (1986). *Family Inventories.* St Paul, MN: Family Social Science, University of Minnesota.

Skinner, H.A., Steinhauer, P.D. and Santa-Barbara, J. (1995). *Family Assessment Measure – III Manual.* Toronto, Canada: Multi Health Systems.

Marital adjustment

Snyder, D. (1997). *Marital Satisfaction Inventory – Revised.* Los Angeles, CA: Western Psychological Services.
Spanier, G.B. (1976). Measuring dyadic adjustment: new scales for assessing the quality of marriage and similar dyads. *Journal of Marriage and the Family* 38: 15–28.

Gratitude, trust, forgiveness and narcissism

Berry, J., Worthington, E., Parrott, L., O'Connor, L. and Wade, N. (In Press). Dispositional forgiveness: Construct validity and development of the transgression narrative test of forgiveness (TNTF). *Personality and Social Psychology Bulletin.* (Describes a measure of trait forgiveness.)
Berry, J., Worthington, E., Parrott, L., O'Connor, L. and Wade, N. (In Press). The measurement of trait forgiveness. (Describes a measure of trait forgiveness.)
McCullough, M., Emmons, R. and Tsang, J. (2002). The grateful dispositions: a conceptual and empirical topography. *Journal of Personality and Social Psychology* 82: 112–27.
McCullough, M. and Witvliet, C. (2002). The psychology of forgiveness. In C.R. Snyder and S. Lopez (eds), *Handbook of Positive Psychology* (pp. 446–58). New York: Oxford University Press. (Contains a transgression specific measure of forgiveness – the Transgression Related Interpersonal Motivations Inventory (TRIM).)
Raskin, R. and Hall, C. (1979). A narcissistic personality inventory. *Psychological Reports* 45: 590.
Rotter, J. (1967). A new scale for the measurement of interpersonal trust. *Journal of Personality* 23: 651–65.
Subcoviak, M., Enright, R., Wu, C., Gassin, E., Freedman, S., Olson, L. and Sarinopoulos, I. (1995). Measuring interpersonal forgiveness in late adolescence and middle childhood. *Journal of Adolescence,* 18, 641–655. (Describes a transgression specific measure of forgiveness – the Enright Forgiveness Inventory.)

GLOSSARY

Beavers Family Systems Model.   A model which describes families along two dimensions: family competence and family style. These dimensions may be evaluated with the Beavers Interactional Competence Scale and the Beavers Interactional Style Scale.

Circumplex Model of Family Functioning.   A model which describes families along three dimensions: cohesion; adaptability; and communication. These dimensions may be evaluated by observation with the Clinical Rating Scale.

Circumplex Model of Interpersonal Behaviour.   A model within which dispositions to engage in particular types of interpersonal interactions with others are construed as falling within a two-dimensional space defined by a vertical axis that extends from dominance to submission and a horizontal axis that extends from cold hostility to warm friendliness.

Resilience.   The capacity to withstand exceptional stresses and demands without developing stress-related problems.

The family lifecycle.   A model of the stages through which families progress over the lifetime of family members which specifies the tasks associated with each stage.

The Family Process Model.   A model which describes family functioning on seven key dimensions: task accomplishment; role performance; communication; affective expression; involvement; control; values and norms. These may be assessed with the Family Assessment Measure.

McMaster Model of Family Functioning.   A model which describes families along six interrelated dimensions: problem solving; communication; roles; affective responsiveness; affective expression; and behaviour control. The dimensions may be evaluated with the self-report McMaster Family Assessment Device.

Chapter 9

Positive change

Learning objectives

- Be able to describe a model of how strengths can be brought to bear on opportunities and challenges to promote well-being.
- Be able to describe the stages of change model with reference to precontemplation, contemplation, planning, action, maintenance and termination.
- Give an account of the change process and techniques involved in making transitions between the various stages of change.
- Understand important research findings on informal and formal helping relationships.
- Be able to summarise the main conclusions that can be drawn about the effectiveness of psychological therapy for children, adolescents and adults.
- Be able to summarise the main conclusions that can be drawn about the effectiveness of psychological prevention programmes for children, adolescents and their families.
- Understand the clinical implications of research on the stages of change model for facilitating subjective well-being.
- Be able to identify research questions that need to be addressed to advance our understanding of the stages of change and the enhancement of subjective well-being.

Throughout the lifecycle we all develop psychologically. We develop new skills, competencies and strengths. We confront opportunities for growth and development and challenges that place demands on our capacity for coping. For example, at transitional points between stages of the lifecycle presented in Table 8.1 in the previous chapter, we face such events as leaving home, marriage, having children, and so forth. Each of these transitions offers an opportunity to develop new skills, but they may also challenge our coping skills to the limit. For example, leaving the security of the family and living alone or with friends offers the opportunity to develop confidence and independence but we may also face the challenges of rejection by others, loneliness, poverty, and so forth. We may cope well with these challenges by finding ways to connect with other people and ways to carefully manage a small budget. Alternatively, we may use dysfunctional coping strategies such as self-isolation, confrontation, excessive drinking and over-eating. These in turn can lead to the development of bad habits such as depression, aggression, addiction and obesity, which themselves are further opportunities and challenges. In this chapter, the focus will be on addressing opportunities and challenges in ways that promote positive change, personal growth and development.

BRINGING STRENGTHS TO BEAR ON OPPORTUNITIES AND CHALLENGES

Opportunities for change and challenges to our coping resources fall into the following categories. First, there are those specific to the completion of a particular stage of the lifecycle. For example, for teenagers in Ireland completing secondary school is an opportunity and challenge associated with adolescence. Second, there are opportunities and challenges associated with transitions from one stage of the lifecycle to the next, an example of which was given in the first paragraph. Third, there are challenges associated with making and breaking long-standing habits. Long-standing habits we may wish to break include smoking and poor weight control. On the other hand, better mood management or greater altruism are long-standing habits we may wish to cultivate. Fourth, there are opportunities and challenges which arise on a day-to-day basis: the normal hassles of everyday life such as coping with traffic, dealing with interpersonal conflict, working to deadlines, or boredom. Finally there are unusual opportunities and challenges such as bereavement, robbery, moving house or financial problems including poverty. Events within each of these categories may challenge our coping resources to their limits, but they may also provide opportunities for personal growth and development.

When faced with opportunities or challenges, we bring our strengths to bear on the situation. These include historical, personal and contextual strengths. Historical strengths are those early experiences that equip us as adults to cope with demanding situations. These include early secure attachment, the childhood experience of authoritative parenting, positive school placement experiences, and past experiences of coping successfully with adversity (all of which have been discussed in Chapter 8). Personal strengths are those attributes which help us to solve complex problems. These include personal character strengths, intelligence, creativity, wisdom, emotional intelligence, easy temperament, positive personality traits, positive motives, self-esteem, self-efficacy, positive defences, positive coping strategies and immunocompetence (all of which have been discussed in Chapters 2 through 8). Contextual strengths are positive features of our current social network and lifestyle. They include positive family relationships within our current family, our family of origin and our social support network as well as fulfilling leisure activities, and fulfilling occupational roles that constitute our lifestyle.

In addressing opportunities and challenges, we use our strengths to help us match our strategy for managing the situation to its demands and to our readiness to engage with the challenge or opportunity. Sometimes we deny that there is an opportunity or challenge to be faced and are not yet ready to deal with it. At other times, we accept the challenge and face it head on. This issue of readiness to change, and the stages of change, will be addressed in more detail below.

There may be a range of positive outcomes after dealing effectively with opportunities and challenges. These include improvements in physical health and psychological well-being, flow experiences and an overall enhancement of our personal strengths.

A diagrammatic summary of this process of bringing strengths to bear on opportunities and challenges is presented in Figure 9.1. This model shares many features with the formulation model presented in the *Handbook of Child and Adolescent Clinical Psychology* (Carr, 1999) and the strengths model for working with people who have severe and chronic psychological difficulties (Rapp, 1998).

STAGES OF CHANGE

While it often feels that coping with the challenges of life is too difficult and we experience ourselves as being 'stuck', change and growth are inevitable. Not only that, but change and growth follow a predictable course from precontemplation, through contemplation, planning, action, maintenance and termination (Prochaska, 1999). Change can be accelerated by understanding the change process and matching our strategies for change to the stage of change in which we find ourselves. If we do not match our change strategies to the stage in which we are, then we may slow down the process of change.

The six stages of change – precontemplation, contemplation, planning, action, maintenance and termination – were first proposed by Professors James Prochaska, Carlo DiClemente and John Norcross – based on their analysis of 24 schools of psychotherapy and their later study of personal growth and change both inside and outside psychotherapy (Prochaska and DiClemente, 1992; Prochaska and Norcross, 1994; Prochaska *et al.*, 1994).

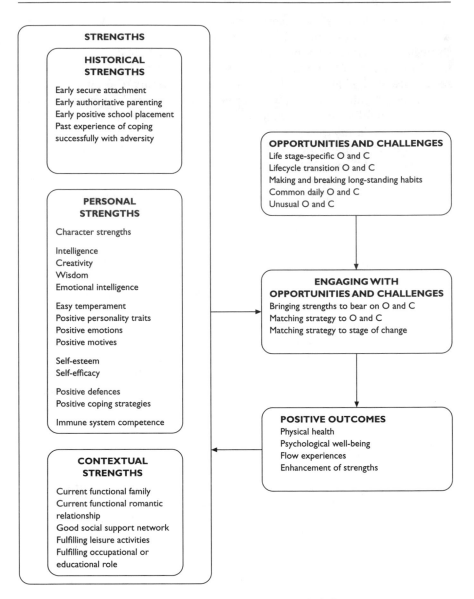

Figure 9.1 Bringing strengths to bear on opportunities and challenges

They found that the stages are common to all forms of psychotherapy and all self-change processes that occur outside psychotherapy. They also found that certain change processes are maximally effective in helping people progress from one stage to the next. A diagram of the stages of change and change process is presented in Figure 9.2. Prochaska *et al.* were inspired to

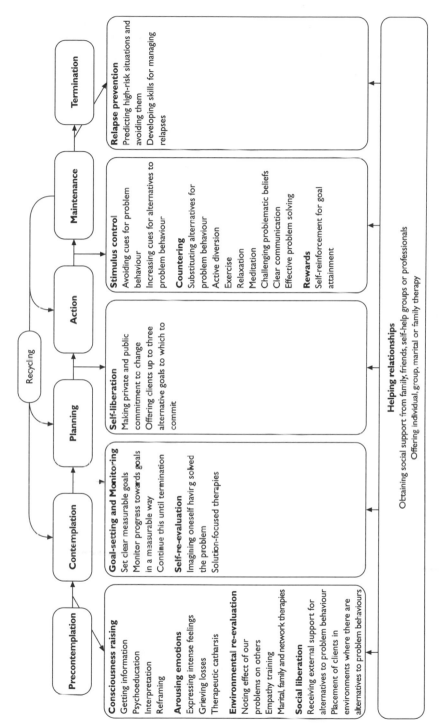

Figure 9.2 Change processes, self-change techniques and therapeutic interventions associated with transition through stages of change
Source: Based on Prochaska et al. (1994) and Prochaska (1999).

search for the change processes and stages common to all psychotherapies, by the finding from the first major meta-analysis of hundreds of treatment outcome studies which showed that different types of psychotherapies for a variety of problems have similar outcomes (Smith *et al.*, 1980). Each of the stages of change has distinct features. Let us look at each of these in turn.

Precontemplation

In the precontemplation stage, we deny that we have a problem. For example, we may say 'Smoking is not a problem for me. I don't to wish to give it up. It does no harm at all.' In the precontemplation we avoid getting information about our problem. We overestimate the costs of resolving our difficulties and underestimate the costs of not addressing our problems. We remain in the precontemplation stage by using some of the defence mechanisms described in Table 7.5. notably the relatively primitive defences of denial, projection and rationalisation. Through denial, we filter out information that lets us know we have a problem and simply say no problem exists. Through projection we blame difficulties on others so that, for example, we may say I don't have a drink problem, but I have a problem with everyone nagging me about drinking. When we provide plausible excuses for not resolving our difficulties, we are using the defence of rationalisation.

Contemplation

In the contemplation stage, we move from denying that we have a problem in a particular area to accepting that there may be a problem, which we may address within the foreseeable future (the next six months). However, there is also an experience of ambivalence arising from balancing the costs and benefits of changing. So we might say, 'Smoking is a problem for me, sometimes I'm short of breath and worry about my long-term health. There are pros and cons to stopping smoking. I enjoy it but it may be harming my health.' However, difficulties arise in this stage of change if we become chronic contemplators and substitute thinking about the problem for action. Often the fear of change and the implications of giving up our familiar ways and replacing these with new and unfamiliar possibilities keep us trapped in chronic contemplation marked by intense ambivalence. When we become trapped in chronic contemplation we use certain defences to avoid progressing from thinking to action. We may become locked into a search for absolute certainty, and say, 'When I'm certain that I have the right solution, I will solve the problem.' We may find ourselves waiting for the magic moment and say, 'I will solve the problem when the magic moment arrives.' We may lapse into wishful thinking and say 'I wish there was cure for cancer' or 'I wish tomorrow all these difficulties would be gone.' With premature action we act impulsively by starting crash diets, going cold turkey with nicotine or alcohol, trying to cheer up with depression and then fail. The experience of failure confirms our belief that change is not possible.

Planning

In the planning stage, a commitment to change in the next month is made. We say things like, 'I'm going to give up cigarettes very soon. I must get some nicotine patches and set a date for my last cigarette.' During the planning stage we transform the global decision to change made during the contemplation stage into specific steps in a well-articulated action plan. We also shift our focus from gathering information about the problem to thinking in detail about possible solutions. A precondition for moving from the planing to the action stage is that the balance of the pros and cons of changing the problem behaviour must change in the following way. Extensive research based on surveys of thousands of effective self-changers has allowed Professor James Prochaska to quantify the magnitude of changes in pros and cons essential for effective change (Prochaska, 1999). From the precontemplation stage to the action stage, the pros must increase by one standard deviation and the cons must decrease by half a standard deviation in order to move safely into the action stage with a good chance of success. This is illustrated by graphs of the scores of successful self-changers on the pros and cons of change for four health behaviours in Figure 9.3. In these graphs, pros and cons are quantified as T scores which have a mean of 50 and a standard deviation of 10. You can use the decisional balance scale in Table 9.1 to find out if you are ready to take action to solve any particular problem. For the pros and cons scales in Table 9.1 the means are 21 and the standard deviation of the scales are 7 for the pros scale and 8 for the cons scale. To progress from the planning to the action stage you must obtain a total pros score of 28 and a total cons score below 17.

Action

In the action stage, we actually change our behaviour by putting our plan into action. However, there are pitfalls to avoid. For example, sometimes we do insufficient planning or proceed from contemplation to action without any real planning. Planning is essential to set a useful course of action and to translate a decision into a logical sequence of steps that will lead to a solution. In other instances we want to change but are unwilling to put in the effort and make the sacrifices that are required to solve the problem. All change demands effort and sacrifice. Sometimes action plans fail because they are based on the idea that there is 'a magic bullet' which on its own can solve our problems. This is not true. Complex human problems typically require complex solutions with many different components. A final impediment to effective action is doing 'more of the same', that is endlessly repeating

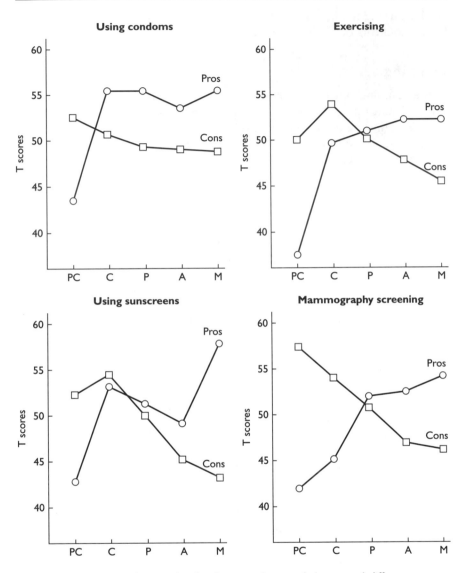

Figure 9.3 Relationship betwen levels of pros and cons of change and different stages of change

Source: Adapted from Prochaska *et al.* (1994): 163.

a partially effective solution which may actually maintain or exacerbate the problem. For example, crash diets are partially effective in the short term, but lead to weight gain in the long term. Repeatedly going on crash diets actually makes you gain weight.

Table 9.1 The decisional balance questionnaire for assessing the pros and cons of change

<table>
<tr><td colspan="3">Put a number between 1 and 5 in the box opposite each
statement to indicate your current belief.
1 = Not important
2 = Slightly important
3 = Somewhat important
4 = Quite important
5 = Very important</td></tr>
<tr><td></td><td>*Pros*</td><td>*Cons*</td></tr>
<tr><td>1. Some people would think less of me if I change</td><td></td><td>☐</td></tr>
<tr><td>2. I would be healthier if I change</td><td>☐</td><td></td></tr>
<tr><td>3. Changing takes a lot of time</td><td></td><td>☐</td></tr>
<tr><td>4. Some people would feel better about me if I change</td><td>☐</td><td></td></tr>
<tr><td>5. I'm concerned I might fail if I try to change</td><td></td><td>☐</td></tr>
<tr><td>6. Changing would make me feel better about myself</td><td>☐</td><td></td></tr>
<tr><td>7. Changing takes a lot of effort and energy</td><td></td><td>☐</td></tr>
<tr><td>8. I would function better if I change</td><td>☐</td><td></td></tr>
<tr><td>9. I would have to give up some things I enjoy</td><td></td><td>☐</td></tr>
<tr><td>10. I would be happier if I change</td><td>☐</td><td></td></tr>
<tr><td>11. I get some benefits from my current behaviour</td><td></td><td>☐</td></tr>
<tr><td>12. Some people could be better off if I change</td><td>☐</td><td></td></tr>
<tr><td>13. Some people benefit from my current behaviour</td><td></td><td>☐</td></tr>
<tr><td>14. I would worry less if I change</td><td>☐</td><td></td></tr>
<tr><td>15. Some people would be uncomfortable if I change</td><td></td><td>☐</td></tr>
<tr><td>16. Some people would be happier if I change</td><td>☐</td><td></td></tr>
<tr><td>**Total pros**</td><td>☐</td><td></td></tr>
<tr><td>**Total cons**</td><td></td><td>☐</td></tr>
<tr><td colspan="3">To progress to the action stage you must obtain
a total pros score of 28 and
a total cons score below 17.</td></tr>
</table>

Source: Adapted from Prochaska *et al.* (1994): 169–79.

Maintenance

In the maintenance stage, we take active steps to make sure we don't relapse or slip back into old habits. Social pressure, internal challenges, special situations and testing our willpower can all lead to relapse. With social pressure, friends and family may urge us to return to old patterns of behaviour suggesting that this will not do any harm if we return to old habits briefly. Internal challenges involve thinking in overconfident ways about our problem or using primitive defences such as denial or rationalisation to allow us to relapse into old ways. Special situations are those that include opportunities and cues to return to old problem behaviours. Sometimes we pose tests for our willpower, for example keeping cigars in the house after we have given up smoking just to remind us that we have the willpower to avoid them.

Termination

In the termination stage we experience no wish to relapse and complete confidence that we can manage our difficulties. For many life challenges this rarely occurs and we commit to a lifetime of maintenance. Also, a process of recycling is not uncommon, where we return periodically to earlier stages of change and then progress through some of the stages again. For example, when attempting to maintain behaviour change, we may relapse and return to the contemplation stage and have to progress through the planning and action stages again before returning to the maintenance stage.

Most self-changers relapse and recycle, so it is realistic when we try to solve a problem or face a challenge to expect to relapse a few times and have to revisit the contemplation, planning, action and maintenance stages of change. It is not helpful to expect to get it right first time, since this way of thinking can lead to demoralisation. If we expect relapses, we avoid a pattern of thinking that Professor Alan Marlatt calls the Abstinence Violation Effect (AVE) (Marlatt and Gordon, 1985). He found that many abstinent problem drinkers who relapsed told themselves things like this: 'I've had one drink. So I know now I'm completely out of control and so will become completely drunk. One drink-Drunk.' This AVE thinking pattern is not unique to people with alcohol problems. It can occur when we are trying to overcome any life challenge. The key to managing AVE thinking patterns is to recognise them, realise that they are irrational and develop alternatives to them. A relapse is in fact a sign of progress. We have to relapse a few times before we go into long-term maintenance and termination. Relapse is an opportunity for learning about situations, relationships and ways of thinking, behaving and feeling that put at us at risk for relapse. For example, if our problem is marital conflict we may find that we become embroiled in arguments with our partners when we are tired, when we are driving, when we are intoxicated, or depressed and demoralised. Relapses also teach us that a great deal more effort, time and thought is necessary for us to solve our problems than we initially thought. Relapses may let us know that we have been using the wrong set of strategies for maintaining change. For example, it may not be appropriate to remain silent to avoid conflict with our partners each time we disagree with them. Rather, it may be more appropriate to communicate our views clearly and kindly.

CHANGE PROCESSES

Transition through the stages of change is facilitated by engaging in a limited number of change processes. Professor James Prochaska and his team have identified the small number of change processes listed in bold in the lower half of Figure 9.2 by reviewing change techniques used in the main approaches to psychotherapy and integrating these into a transtheoretical model (Prochaska and Norcross, 1994). Subsequent research on people who changed behaviour, such as smoking and weight control, either through their own efforts or through therapy showed that specific change techniques are uniquely effective in facilitating specific transitions through the stages of change.

Consciousness raising, arousing emotions, environmental re-evaluation and social liberation are particularly helpful in facilitating movement from precontemplation to contemplation. In making the transition from contemplation to planning, self-re-evaluation was the most important change process. Self-liberation through making a commitment to change is critical for the transition from planning to action and this may be coupled with goal-setting and monitoring: processes that should be continued throughout the stages of change until termination. In moving from the action to the maintenance stages, contingency management, stimulus control, countering and engaging in helping relationships are maximally beneficial. Finally, in making the transition from maintenance to termination, relapse prevention is the most important change process. The goals of each of these change processes will now be described along with self-help techniques and therapeutic interventions associated with each of them.

From precontemplation to contemplation

In making the transition from precontemplation to contemplation, consciousness raising, arousing emotions, environmental re-evaluation and social liberation are particularly helpful change processes.

Consciousness raising

This involves increasing awareness about the defences that prevent us from recognising the problem along with obtaining information about the problem, its causes, consequences and possible solutions. So during consciousness raising we become aware that we use denial, rationalisation, projection or other defences as a way of avoiding recognising our problem. We identify factors that may have predisposed us to developing the problem; factors that may have precipitated the onset of the problem; factors that maintain the problem; the negative impact of the problem on our own well-being and that of our family and friends; the strengths and resources that we may bring to bear on the problem to resolve it; and the benefits for ourselves, our friends and our family of resolving the problem.

Self-change strategies for promoting consciousness raising include personal reflection, listening to personal feedback from family and friends about our behaviour, and getting information from the TV, magazines, books and the internet about our problems. Personal reflection and feedback from close friends and family are particularly important in alerting us to the defences we are using to avoid taking responsibility for our problems and the specific effects of the problem on our life situation. Information from the media and books can give us more general information about the problem, possible solutions, the costs of not resolving the problem, and the benefits of resolving our difficulties.

Therapists can facilitate consciousness raising through general psycho-education about the problem and by inviting clients to reflect on the costs of not resolving the problem for themselves and their families and the benefits of resolving their difficulties. Interpreting defences such as denial, rationalisation and projection and confronting clients with the destructive impact of their behaviour on themselves and others in individual, group, marital or family therapy are all consciousness raising interventions. However, they tend to promote disengagement from therapy rather than retention and so are more appropriately reserved for clients who have moved into the contemplation stage of change.

Arousing emotions

If consciousness raising promotes change by helping us to get factual information about our challenges and problems, emotional arousal promotes change by connecting us with important emotions associated with our difficulties. This involves experiencing and expressing strong emotions about the problems or challenges that we face, and then using the experience of these strong emotions as a basis for recognising that we have difficulties that can no longer be denied and must be addressed. When we, or members of our families, suffer lifestyle-related illnesses, for example having a heart-attack, this can arouse intense fear which may serve as a stimulus for changing our lifestyles so that we modify our diet, substance use and exercise patterns to maximise our health. In other instances, hope for the future and a wish to live long enough to see dreams come true can move us from precontemplation to contemplation. When my daughter was born, the emotional impact of that helped me to start the process of giving up smoking. I had been smoking for over twenty years and was smoking more than twenty a day. I knew that if I wanted to see my girl grow to adulthood, I would have to stop smoking to reduce the risk of lung cancer. Guilt is another emotion that can help us break out of denial. Many people with substance use and alcohol problems are moved to accept that they have a problem when they experience intense guilt (when sober) for hurt they have caused their family and friends when intoxicated. The experience of grief that follows bereavement or loss can lead us to dramatically change our lives for the better. So also can joy and inspiration. Indeed, charismatic figures in business, sports and religious cults use inspiration and the intense emotions that go with it to lead people to strive to reach particular standards of behaviour.

Watching dramatic films about people who face the challenges you face is one of the most powerful self-change strategies for promoting emotional arousal. Dramas generally arouse more intense emotions than documentaries. They offer us an opportunity to identify with the main protagonists and the struggles they undergo in changing their life situation.

Therapists can facilitate emotional arousal by encouraging catharsis, a process which is particularly useful where people have suffered losses and need to work through their grief before changing their lives. Psychodrama and role playing are particularly useful techniques for promoting catharsis.

Environmental re-evaluation

With environmental re-evaluation, we consider and assess how our problem behaviour, or the way we are avoiding facing the challenges and opportunities in our lives, affects others such as our family, friends or members of our community. We also consider how changing our behaviour would affect these people. We are moved to change by noting the negative effects of not changing on others and the positive effects on others of changing our behaviour for the better.

Self-reflection and listening to feedback from others about how our behaviour affects them are important self-change techniques for promoting environmental re-evaluation.

Marital and family therapy and therapies that involve people's social networks are particularly useful in helping people become aware of how their behaviour affects other members of their social environment. Empathy training is also useful to promote environmental re-evaluation and is often a key feature of treatment programmes for sex-offenders.

Social liberation

Social liberation is a change process in which society offers opportunities for us to choose alternatives to our problem behaviours and we become aware that these alternatives are available and use them to help us change.

For example, the creation of no-smoking zones; the enforcement of speed limits; offering media support for the idea of a designated driver when people go drinking; the development of ecologically supportive transport and waste disposal systems; and the development of self-help programmes for various life difficulties are all alternatives that society has created and which we may choose in order to modify our lifestyles for the better. Unfortunately we live in a society where commercial interests, including producers of tobacco, alcohol, automobiles, and so forth, create many opportunities to undermine healthy alternatives and wage a media-based propaganda war against those that promote healthy alternatives.

Successful self-changers are vigilant for alternatives to problem behaviours and choose these alternatives that society has put in place to facilitate the process of change. In the move from precontemplation to contemplation, self-changers become aware of the alternative available within society that can support the process of personal change.

Therapeutic techniques that facilitate social liberation include placement of clients in environments where there are alternatives to problem behaviours such as treatment foster care for delinquent youngsters, supportive educational environments for children with learning difficulties, and therapeutic communities for people with substance use or mental health problems.

From contemplation to planning

In making the transition from contemplation to planning, goal setting, monitoring and self-re-evaluation are the most important change processes.

Goal setting and monitoring

With goal setting define clear, unambiguous, visualisable, measurable goals for problem resolution. These goals allow us to know in a concrete way when our problems are solved and when we have successfully managed the challenges we have faced. Monitoring progress involves routinely assessing progress towards goals in a concrete measurable way and then recording this. This process is continued until termination. With consumption problems like smoking, drinking, eating or spending, it is appropriate to measure the amount consumed per day (e.g. number of cigarettes, calories, drinks, pounds or dollars) as well as weekly changes in health and well-being (ratings of breathlessness on a 10-point scale, weight, number of hangovers, bank balance). With relationship difficulties, mood problems and pain it is appropriate to measure the frequency, duration and intensity on a 10-point scale of episodes of relationship conflict, depression, anxiety, anger or pain. For each specific episode it is very useful to also routinely record what happened just before the episode; what you were doing and thinking about during the episode, and what happened immediately afterwards. This information may throw light on things that triggered problematic episodes and factors that maintain or reinforce these episodes. This information is useful to use when progressing from the stages of action to maintenance, since it allows us to carefully develop stimulus control, countering and contingency management strategies to address our problems. This will be elaborated below. The cognitive-behaviour therapy tradition, more than any other, has developed the most sophisticated methods for goal setting and monitoring progress.

Self-re-evaluation

With self-re-evaluation we compare our views of ourselves with our problems unresolved and our problems resolved and ask ourselves which version of ourselves is more consistent with our core values. We also explore the costs of not changing and the benefits of changing. So if our problem is frequent angry fights with our partners we ask ourselves the following sequence of questions:

- What does it say about me as a person if I deal with differences in our relationship by frequently becoming very angry? Does it say that I am a cruel person?
- What would it say about me as a person if I could deal with differences in our relationship in a less aggressive way? Does it say that I am a kind person?
- Which type of person do I want to be: a cruel person or a kind person?
- What would I lose by becoming less angry?
- What would I gain by becoming kinder?

A similar sequence of questions may be asked of any problem and these are the types of questions that successful self-changers ask themselves. Self-evaluation involves giving up the search for the miracle cure, the magic moment, wishful thinking and impulsive urges to solve our problems without carefully thinking through our plans for change. It involves accepting that while change has its benefits for how we view ourselves, our behaviour and our values, all change involves costs. Self-re-evaluation involves living with ambivalence about change and tolerating the distress that this entails.

Offering clients a warm and empathic helping relationship within which they can explore the pros and cons of change and a containing environment within which they can explore their ambivalence is the main therapeutic technique for facilitating self-re-evaluation. Solution-focused approaches, such as inviting clients to imagine themselves having solved the problem and helping them to build a mental image of themselves as having mastered the challenges of their lives, is another important way to promote self-re-evaluation.

From planning to action

Self-liberation through making a commitment to change is critical for the transition from planning to action.

Self-liberation

The process of self-liberation involves making a choice to address the challenges in our lives and making a commitment to change our problematic behaviour. We transform the global decision to change made during the contemplation stage into a decision to take specific steps to solve the problem. This involves a shift from focusing on the causes of the problem to thinking in detail about problem-solving strategies. So big difficulties need to be broken down into small steps. For example, if we want to manage anxiety better, we need to list those situations that make us anxious and rank order them from the least to the most anxiety-provoking and plan to tackle them one at a time starting with the least threatening.

A precondition for moving from the planning to the action stage is that the pros must increase and the cons must decrease. When the correct decisional balance of pros and cons has been reached according to the questionnaire results in Table 9.1, it is time to set a date some time within the next month to enter the action stage of change. We need to be careful to select a time that favours change rather than one that makes change difficult when setting dates to start action programmes. For example, it's probably easier to tackle difficulties like anxiety or depression during the summer months, if that is a time when demands on us are low and the mood of others around us is buoyant. However, summer and Christmas are often times of indulgence and so they are difficult times to change diets or alcohol use.

A final strategy for self-liberation is making a declaration to family, friends and others that we are planning to make a change in our lives. It takes courage to make a public commitment because we risk losing face if we do not follow through and this motivates us to stick to our plans.

Including family members or close friends in therapy; inviting clients and their families to brainstorm all the forces that promote resistance and prevent a commitment to change being made; inviting clients and their families to evaluate the pros and cons of change; and creating opportunities where clients can make a self-initiated public commitment to change are the most important therapeutic strategies for facilitating self-liberation. In exploring pros and cons of change, greater commitment is generated if clients are invited to personalise the costs of the problem and the benefits of change. There is a big difference between saying 'smoking can cause cancer' and 'I might never see my daughter graduate from college and sail to Greece with me because of cancer caused by smoking.' Exploring personal vulnerabilities to problems can also increase commitment. For example, one of my clients with a mood disorder used an acceptance of his vulnerability to bouts of depression evidenced by a strong family history of mood disorders to help him make a commitment to a strict treatment programme. This involved regular daily exercise, adherence to a regime of antidepressant medication, and regular relapse-prevention monthly psychotherapy sessions. Self-initiated commitments to change are far more powerful motivators than imposed commitments. If clients are given two or three possible courses of action for solving their problems from which to choose, then this is effectively creating an opportunity for them to make a self-initiated choice about changing, and so they are more likely to be motivated to stick to the action plans they choose (Miller, 1985).

From a therapeutic perspective, a useful way to address the issue of commitment is to distinguish clearly between the phases of assessment and treatment. The assessment stage may be spread over a number of sessions, during which clients (and their families in the case of marital and family therapy) move through the stages of precontemplation, contemplation and planning. At the end of the assessment phase, clients may be invited to form a contract for treatment. In agreeing to such a contract, they are making a commitment to change their problem behaviour (Carr, 1999, 2000b).

From action to maintenance

In moving from the action to the maintenance stage stimulus control, countering, rewards and engaging in helping relationships are the most useful change processes. Briefly, stimulus control involves changing situations that trigger the onset of problematic episodes; countering involves replacing problem behaviours with alternatives; and reward entails arranging for the successful avoidance of problem episodes to be positively acknowledged. More detailed descriptions of these processes will be given below. However, an important issue concerns exactly how 'deeply do we dig' in replacing the antecedents, correlates and consequences of episodes of problematic behaviour. Prochaska and Norcross (1994) argue that a range of factors are involved in maintaining long-standing problems which pose ongoing opportunities and challenges to personal development. These are:

- situational maintaining factors
- negative beliefs
- interpersonal and family conflicts
- unconscious conflicts.

These factors are hierarchically organised, with earlier factors being more responsive to change than later factors. Situational maintaining factors include things like environmental triggers or signals for us to engage in a problem behaviour. For example, many smokers find that having a cup of coffee is a trigger for making them want to light a cigarette. Negative beliefs are stories that we tell ourselves, which keep our problem behaviour going. For example, when smokers relapse they often tell themselves things like, 'I deserve a puff on a cigarette after all I've been through . . . and now that I've had one puff, I'm out of control, I just have to finish the pack.' Interpersonal and family conflicts maintain problem behaviours by either triggering them or reinforcing them. Thus smokers may find that when they get into conflict with friends or family members they smoke or when they smoke, they get attention from friends and family in the form of arguments and conflict. While situational factors and cognitions can be changed without the commitment of others to change, when conflict with family and friends maintains problem behaviours, then often family and friends have to make a commitment to change too if the problem is to be solved. Finally, problem behaviours can be maintained by intra-psychic conflict which may be unconscious. For example, each time a person feels the anxiety that goes with a preconscious sense that they may have unacceptable sexual or aggressive urges towards an important person in their social network which stems from a similar feeling they had towards a parent, they may cope with this by smoking. As a rule, when developing an action plan for change we should try strategies that address situational factors first, cognitions second, relationships third, and finally unconscious conflicts. This rule helps us to avoid using a sledgehammer to crack a nut by, for example, embarking on intensive psychoanalytic exploration when a simple situational intervention might be all that is needed. It also allows us to know how to proceed when situational interventions are ineffective.

Stimulus control

Stimulus control involves changing our environment so that it contains fewer cues for problem behaviour and more cues for productive alternatives. For example, noise, heat and intoxication all increase the probability that distressed couples will have aggressive arguments if they attempt to discuss contentious issues. A stimulus control strategy for reducing the frequency for arguments would be to avoid discussing contentious issues in noisy, hot places when drunk. People who are attempting to stop smoking, drinking or drug use may initially use the stimulus control strategy of avoiding situations that increase cravings for these substances and not keep these substances in their homes. However, while avoidance of cues that trigger problem behaviours is a useful initial stimulus-control strategy, in the long term a useful goal is to become capable of tolerating situations that trigger problem behaviours. Tolerance for these trigger situations may be developed in the following way. List all cues for problem behaviour and assign each a number between 1 and 100 to indicate the strength with which it elicits an urge to engage in problem behaviour. These cues may be real (for example standing in a bar) or imaginal (fantasising being at a cocktail party). Then start with the least powerful cue and carefully practise for designated time periods (such as an hour a day) tolerating being in the presence of progressively more powerful cues. Various coping strategies may be used to promote tolerance, such as listening to music, doing relaxation exercises, or enlisting the aid of family members to provide support and encouragement throughout the challenge. As well as avoiding cues for problem behaviour and developing tolerance for them, an important stimulus-control strategy is increasing the number and salience of cues for alternatives to problem behaviour. For example, for people wanting to increase their fitness, put a reminder note on the fridge door and beside the TV to take a 30-minute walk every day. For couples wanting to increase their intimacy, set the timer on the TV to go off at 10.30 pm each evening to remind them to spend time before going to bed talking to each other about their day.

For problematic behaviour patterns triggered or maintained by complex family relationship dynamics or intra-psychic conflicts, family therapy or psychodynamic therapy are useful in identifying these triggers, developing tolerance to them and identifying alternative triggers for alternatives to problem behaviour.

Countering

Countering is a change process in which we substitute alternatives for problem behaviours. Countering strategies include diversion of energies into other enjoyable activities; regular physical exercise; regular practising of relaxation routines or meditation; countering negative beliefs; replacing submissiveness or confused communication with clear assertive communication; and replacing passivity, ineffective activity or impulsivity with goal-directed problem solving. Exercise routines, relaxation and meditation are described in Chapter 7. Countering negative beliefs, communication and problem solving have been mentioned in Chapter 4 as ways of enhancing emotional intelligence in adults, but will be recapped below also.

Countering negative beliefs

To counter negative beliefs with positive ones, the first step is to keep a diary of mood or urge change episodes containing the following three columns:

- the activity that led to the change in mood or urge;
- the beliefs that led to the change in mood or urge;
- the consequent mood or urge rating after the activity on a 10-point scale.

Reviewing this type of diary allows us to see that it is our interpretation of events that contributes to negative mood or changes in our urges. This provides a rationale for learning the Challenge Test Reward (CTR) routine for challenging negative beliefs. Challenging negative beliefs involves generating alternative positive beliefs that could have been held in a specific situation in which a negative belief occurred and then looking for evidence to test the validity of these alternatives. When the negative belief has been shown to be invalid we self-reward ourselves. So, for example, one alternative to the automatic thought, *He didn't talk to me so he doesn't like me* is *He didn't talk to me because he is shy.* If there is evidence that the person in question never injured me before and on a couple of occasions smiled at me, then the more valid statement is that the person is shy. I may reward myself for challenging and testing this negative belief by telling myself that I have done a good job of testing my negative belief. Through the consistent use of the CTR routine, we can gradually train ourselves to give up negative beliefs that underpin depression, anxiety and anger and replace these beliefs with positive alternatives. The CTR routine is a way of coaching ourselves in the skills of reframing which was discussed in Chapter 7. Cognitive therapy and attributional retraining, discussed in Chapter 3, are a well-developed and highly effective way for helping people to counter negative belief systems.

Countering confused communication

To counter confused communication we need to schedule episodes for clear communication and during these episodes use clear communication and listening skills. This is particularly appropriate for couples, families or work groups who have problems with conflict and clear communication. To set up an episode of clear communication, schedule a specific time and place for the conversation. This should be a time when there is no pressure to be elsewhere and a place in which there are no distractions. Issues and problems should be discussed one problem at a time. Take turns fairly and make the speaking turns brief. When speaking, decide the exact points you want to say. Organise them logically. Say them clearly and then check that you have been understood. When you are certain the other person has understood you accurately, allow space for a reply. Listen without interruption and when the other person has finished speaking, summarise their key points. Check that you have understood what they said accurately before you reply. Here are some ways of avoiding the obstacle to clear communication. When you are speaking, state your points without attacking or blaming the other person or sulking. When you are listening, focus on accurately remembering what the other person is saying rather than interrupting, composing your reply, defending yourself, or attacking the other person. Try to listen without judging what is being said and avoid negative mind-reading where you attribute bad intentions to the other person. It is helpful when speaking to try to frame your points as congruent *I statements*, for example, 'I feel angry about what happened between you and me earlier today.' This *I statement* is more conducive to clear communication than the following accusatory negative mind-reading statement: 'You started attacking me again earlier today like you always do just to get at me.' Marital and family therapy is a well-developed and highly effective way for helping couples and families improve communication skills.

Countering confused problem solving

To counter confused problem solving we need to schedule episodes for clear problem solving and during these episodes to use problem-solving skills. For most life difficulties problem solving is a joint task we undertake with family members, friends or colleagues. To set up an episode of problem solving schedule a specific time and place where there are no distractions. Break big vague problems into many smaller specific problems. Define these in solvable rather than unsolvable terms. Generate many possible solutions without judging the merits of these, examining the pros and cons or costs and benefits of each of these before selecting the best course of action to follow. Agree to implement the action plan after the problem-solving session and schedule a time to meet and review progress. When you meet, evaluate the effectiveness of the plan against preset goals. If the problem remains unsolved, repeat the process in light of knowledge about why the attempted solution was ineffective. To avoid obstacles to clear joint problem solving show the people with whom you are trying to solve the problem that it is the problem (not the person) that makes you feel bad. Acknowledge your share of responsibility for causing the problem (if that is the case) and finding the solution. Do not explore pros and cons of all of the solutions until you have finished brainstorming. When you solve the problem, celebrate success. Problem solving is included in a wide variety of individual, marital and family approaches to therapy.

Reward

While stimulus control is a change process concerned with addressing factors that trigger problem behaviours and alternatives to these, reward is a change process that focuses on the consequences of behaviours. The consequences of behaviour affect the probability that the behaviour will recur. Often problem behaviours are maintained because they bring rewards. For example, people with panic attacks and agoraphobia develop a housebound lifestyle, because by doing so they avoid the intense anxiety they would experience if they had a panic attack while away from their homes. Often family members, friends and work colleagues inadvertently reinforce problem behaviour. For example, families of people with agoraphobia often inadvertently reward adopting a constricted lifestyle by running errands for the housebound person, making excuses for them and arranging for people to come and visit rather than encouraging the agoraphobic person to go out. Similarly, families of people with alcohol or drug problems inadvertently reinforce drug abuse by making excuses on behalf of the person with the drug problem when they cannot attend school or work.

Successful self-changers arrange for rewards that maintain problem behaviours to cease and for alternatives to problem behaviours to be rewarded. This is done by arranging to reward ourselves or arranging to have members of our family, close friends or close work colleagues reward us for alternatives to problem behaviours. It also involves blocking all self-rewards or rewards or attention from others for engaging in problem behaviour. To use the reward-change process, list your overall goal and break this down into many small subgoals. List personal prizes or rewards that you could give yourself for succeeding. Assign a reward or prize to each subgoal. Always reward positive changes, however small, with immediate personal verbal praise by saying to yourself, for example, 'Well done. You did that well.' Then follow through and reward yourself for achieving subgoals by assigning yourself a designated prize. Tell a close friend or family member your plan and keep them briefed on your progress. Keep a written record of your achievements. To avoid some of the obstacles to implementing reward routines make the subgoals very small and the prizes or rewards moderately large and very attractive to you. Select friends or family members who will stick with you throughout the change process. Regularly tell your friend or family member how confident you feel about using self-reward.

From maintenance to termination

Finally, in making the transition from maintenance to termination, relapse prevention and management is the most important change process.

Relapse prevention and management

Because most of us who attempt to change our behaviour to meet the challenges of life relapse and recycle, relapse prevention and management is an important change process. There are clearly defined strategies for relapse prevention and management. Anticipate situations where there will be pressure for relapse. Develop step-by-step plans to delay relapse or avoid or escape from these situations initially by brainstorming many alternatives. Involve a close friend or a family member in planning relapse management. Role-play risky relapse situations using modelling rehearsal, shaping and reinforcement to develop relapse-management skills. Tell your close friend or family members how confident you feel (on a 10-point scale) about using your plans for delaying relapse or avoiding or escaping from each of five specific fairly risky situations, that is tell them about your level of self-efficacy, a concept described in Chapter 7 (Bandura, 1997). Then imagine how you would feel if you relapsed. Verbalise the way you would experience the Abstinence Violation Effect (AVE) (Marlatt and Gordon, 1985), that is the beliefs and feelings of disappointment, fear, or powerlessness that you would expect to have when you relapse. Brainstorm ways that you could effectively cope with these thoughts and feelings. Tell your close friends and family what strategies you will use for coping with relapses and how confident you feel (on a 10-point scale) about using these strategies.

IMPLICATIONS

A summary of self-help strategies for moving through the stages of change when addressing opportunities and challenges is given in Table 9.2. These can be incorporated into clinical practice.

INFORMAL HELPING RELATIONSHIPS

Helping relationships are useful throughout the stages of change (Prochaska, 1999; Prochaska *et al.*, 1994). Successful self-changers use trusting, accepting, socially supportive relationships with family, friends and self-help groups during attempts to change the problem behaviour. During the precontemplation stage effective self-changers ask a trusted person to help them acknowledge the reality of their problem and the defences they use to deny its reality. During the precontemplation stage effective helpers don't nag, don't give up, don't push for premature action and don't inadvertently reinforce the problem behaviour. Ineffective helpers do all of these things and may reinforce the problem by minimising it, making excuses for the person with the problem, avoiding discussing the reality of the problem and avoid recommending the problem be addressed in a careful planned way. During the contemplation stage successful self-changers use their relationship with a trusted person to explore their understanding of their problem and the pros and cons of change, and effective helpers facilitate this through warmly empathising with the person who wants to change, letting them know that their complex ambivalent position about changing their behaviour is understood. During the planning and action stages successful self-changers let their close family and friends know their plans. They also ask for help with removing triggers for problem behaviours from the home or workplace. They ask other family members or friends to exercise, relax, meditate, clearly communicate, effectively problem solve and share other countering routines with them. They also ask close family and friends to stop inadvertently rewarding problem behaviour and start praising them for

Table 9.2 Summary of strategies for making transitions from one stage of change to the next when using strengths to manage challenges and opportunities for change

Transition	Strategy	
From precontemplation to contemplation	Consciousness raising	• Identify defences that prevent you from seeing you have a challenge to face • Get information from the media about this challenge • Get feedback from friends about how you manage this challenge
	Arousing emotions	• Use reflection, talking with friends, reading literature and watching films to identify and express strong emotions associated with the area of life you wish to change
	Environmental re-evaluation	• Consider how changing and not changing will affect others in your social network
	Social liberation	• Identify and choose alternatives to problem behaviours that society has put in place to facilitate the process of change in managing your particular challenge
From contemplation to planning	Goal setting and monitoring	• Define clear, unambiguous, visualisable, measurable goals for problem resolution
	Self-re-evaluation	• Compare your view of yourself with and without your problems resolved and state which version is more consistent with your core values • Explore the costs of not changing and the benefits of changing
From planning to action	Self-liberation	• Explore costs and benefits of changing or maintaining the status quo • Personalise the vulnerability to the problem and its consequences • Personalise the costs of the problem • Personalise the benefits of the solution • Develop positive future expectations • Acknowledge the reality of resistance to change • Break big challenges into a series of smaller challenges • Make a declaration to significant members of your social network that you are planning to make a change in your life
From action to maintenance	Stimulus control	• Keep a diary of episodes in which negative moods, urges or behaviours occur and for each episode note antecedent triggers, negative beliefs and consequent problematic moods, urges or behaviours • Triggers may be stimulus situations or interpersonal transactions which give rise to negative beliefs or activate unconscious conflicts

	• Initially avoid all triggers for problem behaviour • Later develop tolerance to triggers by systematically learning to cope with increasingly stronger triggers
Countering negative beliefs	• Use the CTR routine to counter negative beliefs identified by stimulus control and diary keeping • Challenge negative beliefs by generating alternative positive beliefs that could have been held in a situation in which a negative belief occurred • Test the validity of this alternative by looking for evidence to support it • Reward yourself for when you show the negative belief is not valid
Countering confused communication	• When listening, listen without judging • Put your own opinions and emotions on hold • Summarise what you have heard the other person say • Check that your summary is accurate • When speaking, decide on the points you want to make • Organise them logically • Say them clearly • Check that you have been understood • State your points without attacking, blaming or sulking • Repeat as necessary
Countering confused problem-solving	• Break big vague problems into many smaller specific problems • Define these in solvable terms • Focus on the problem, not the person • Generate many possible solutions • When all solutions are generated, examine the pros and cons of each • Select the best solution • Implement the solution • Review progress • Repeat as necessary • Celebrate success
Rewards	• Arrange for rewards that maintain problem behaviours to cease and for alternatives to problem behaviours to be rewarded
Relapse prevention	• Anticipate situations where there will be pressure for relapse • Develop step-by-step plans to delay relapse or avoid or escape from these situations
From maintenance to termination	

Source: Based on Prochaska (1999): 227–55 and Prochaska et al. (1994).

alternatives to problem behaviours. During the planning and action stages effective helpers develop a clear understanding of the change plan and wholeheartedly support the person through it as requested. During the maintenance stage effective self-changers contact their close friend or family member periodically to let them know how they are doing, and also during times when they are at risk of relapse, and ask for support. Effective helpers maintain long-term contact and both praise the self-changer for maintaining behaviour change and give support when there is a risk of relapse.

PSYCHOTHERAPEUTIC RELATIONSHIPS

Most people manage the opportunities and challenges with which life presents them without professional psychological therapy. However, some people participate in psychotherapy to facilitate the change process. The process of change within psychotherapy is no different from the process of change that occurs without therapy. Psychological therapies are designed to help people identify their current stage of change and to find strategies to help us move from one stage of change to the next. All psychological therapies involve therapists and clients developing a therapeutic relationship on the one hand, and the therapist using specific technical skills on the other, to help clients draw on their personal strengths and move from one stage of change to the next.

From Figure 9.4, which is adapted from Lambert's (1992) literature review, it may be seen that 40 per cent of change during therapy may be

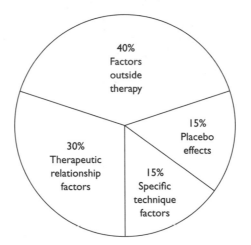

Figure 9.4 Factors which contribute to the improvement of clients during psychotherapy
Source: Based on Lambert and Barley (2002).

attributed to factors outside treatment and the remainder to features of the therapy situation. While specific therapeutic techniques and clients' expectations of improvement (or the placebo effect as it is sometimes called) each account for about 15 per cent of change, the therapeutic relationship is by far the most important determinant of therapeutic change and accounts for about 30 per cent of improvement during therapy.

The growth of a therapeutic relationship follows distinct stages involving planning, contracting, assessment, therapy, managing resistance or ambivalence about change and disengagement (Carr, 1999, 2000b). These stages of therapy closely parallel Prochaska's (1999) stages of change. Research on common factors that contribute to a positive therapeutic outcome and principles of good clinical practice point to a number of key features of the working alliance (Norcross, 2002; Sprenkle et al., 1999; Bergin and Garfield, 1994). The therapeutic relationship is characterised by warmth, empathy and genuineness. The therapist should form a collaborative partnership in which clients are experts on the specific features of their own situation and therapists are experts on general scientific and clinical information relevant to psychological development and the broad class of problems of which the presenting problem is a specific instance. Assessment should be conducted from a position of respectful curiosity in which therapists continually strive to uncover new information about the problem and potential solutions and invite the clients to consider the implications of viewing their difficulties from multiple perspectives (Cecchin, 1987). An invitational approach should be adopted in which clients are invited (not directed) to participate in assessment and treatment (Kelly, 1955). There should be a balanced focus on strengths and resilience on the one hand and on problems and constraints on the other. A focus on strengths promotes hope and mobilises clients to use their own resources to solve their problems (Hubble et al., 1999). However, a focus on understanding why the problem persists and the factors that maintain it is also important, since this information informs more efficient problem solving. There should be an acknowledgement that clients and therapists inadvertently bring to the working alliance attitudes, expectations, emotional responses and interactional routines from early significant caregiving and care-receiving relationships. These transference and countertransference reactions, if unrecognised, may compromise therapeutic progress and so should be openly and skilfully addressed when resistance to therapeutic change occurs.

THE EFFECTIVENESS OF PSYCHOLOGICAL THERAPIES

For most common psychological problems, between two-thirds and three-quarters of clients improve following psychological therapy (Bergin and Garfield, 1994; Carr, 2000a, 2000b, 2000c; Christophersen and Mortweet,

2001; Fonagy *et al.*, 2002; Nathan and Gorman, 2002; Pinsof and Wynne, 1995; Roth and Fonagy, 1996). Most adult and child clients attend therapy for only 6–10 sessions for individual and family or marital therapy (Garfield, 1994; Weisz and Weiss, 1993). This is not surprising given that by 8 sessions 50 per cent of adult clients have shown improvement and by 26 sessions 75 per cent have made significant gains (Lambert and Bergin, 1994). Thus, it is clear that earlier sessions (the first 8–10) make a major contribution to improvement and thereafter the contribution of each session to improvement decreases. Approximately 10 per cent of patients are harmed by therapy (Lambert and Bergin, 1994). Clients with severe long-standing problems, such as borderline personality disorder, are particularly susceptible to deterioration. For clients with these problems, deterioration is more likely to occur in therapy which focuses on breaking down habitual coping strategies and defences. Coldness, disrespect and lack of empathy on the part of the therapist have been shown consistently to lead to deterioration.

Psychological treatments that work for adult problems

While global meta-analytic reviews have concluded that approaches to therapy based on different models yield similar results, focused reviews of well-controlled studies point to the effectiveness of specific techniques for particular problems. For adult psychological problems the conclusions outlined below and summarised in Table 9.3 concerning the effectiveness of psychological treatments may be drawn (Carr, 2000b, Chapter 17, 2000c; Nathan and Gorman, 2002; Roth and Fonagy, 1996). For marital difficulties behavioural marital therapy involving coaching in developing exchange contracts, communication and problem-solving skills training has been found to be effective. So too has insight-oriented marital therapy which facilitates understanding the impact of unresolved family-of-origin issues on current marital conflict and emotionally focused couples therapy which facilitates expressing sadness associated with unmet attachment needs. For psychosexual problems sex therapy involving behavioural exercises to develop control over sexual arousal and orgasm is effective.

Cognitive therapy involving learning to challenge depressive thinking styles; social skills training to modify depression-maintaining social environments; and interpersonal therapy and marital therapy involving modifying depression-maintaining interaction patterns within close relationships are all effective treatments for depression with or without adjunctive antidepressant medication. To prevent relapse in bipolar disorder when people are being maintained on mood-stabilising medication such as lithium carbonate or carbamezapine, cognitive-behaviour therapy which focuses on learning to challenge depressive or elated thinking styles and family therapy to reduce family stress and enhance family communication and problem solving are particularly effective.

Table 9.3 Summary of research on psychological treatments that work for problems in adulthood

Problem area	Psychological treatments that work for problems in adulthood
Relationship problems	Behavioural marital therapy involving exchange contracts, communication and problem-solving skills training Insight-oriented marital therapy which facilitates understanding the impact of unresolved family of origin issues on current marital conflict Emotionally focused couples therapy which facilitates expressing sadness associated with unmet attachment needs
Psychosexual problems	Sex therapy involving behavioural exercises to develop control over sexual arousal and orgasm
Depression	Cognitive therapy involving learning to challenge depressive thinking styles Social-skills training to modify depression-maintaining social environments Interpersonal therapy and marital therapy which modifies depression-maintaining interaction patterns within close relationships
Relapse prevention in bipolar disorder	Multimodal treatment involving mood-stabilising medication (e.g. lithium carbonate) and cognitive behaviour therapy to learn to challenge depressive or elated thinking styles and family therapy to reduce family stress and enhance family communication and problem solving
Simple phobias	Behaviour therapy involving gradual or intensive exposure to feared stimuli coupled with relaxation and coping-skills training
Social phobias	Cognitive-behaviour therapy involving learning to challenge threat-oriented thinking styles and behavioural exercises to counter social avoidance behaviour coupled with relaxation and coping-skills training
Panic disorder and agoraphobia	Cognitive-behaviour therapy with family support involving exposure to increasing anxiety-provoking situations; relaxation and coping-skills training; and learning to challenge threat-oriented thinking styles
Obsessive compulsive disorder	Behaviour therapy with family support involving exposure to cues which elicit obsessions (such as dirt) and prevention from engaging in compulsive anxiety-reducing responses (such as repeated hand-washing) coupled with relaxation and coping-skills training
Post-traumatic stress disorder	Behaviour therapy involving exposure to trauma-related cues and memories and concurrent relaxation and coping-skills training including use of repeated distraction during exposure (for example in the eye movement desensitisation reprocessing protocol)
Generalised anxiety disorders	Cognitive-behaviour therapy with coaching in challenging threat-oriented thinking styles and exposure to feared situations coupled with relaxation and coping-skills training
Relapse prevention in schizophrenia	Multimodal treatment involving antipsychotic medication; family therapy to reduce family stress and improve family communication and problem-solving skills; cognitive therapy to reduce the negative impact of hallucinations and delusions; and social-skills training to reduce negative symptoms of schizophrenia
Alcohol problems	Family supported multimodal treatment with family-based engagement of client in treatment; detoxification; self-control training for controlled drinking or AA attendance for abstinence; social-skills training; stress-management training; and medication (disulfiram/antibuse)

Table 9.3 (Cont'd)

Problem area	Psychological treatments that work for problems in adulthood
Smoking cessation	Spouse-supported cognitive-behaviour therapy with psychoeducation; stimulus-control techniques such as removing ashtrays; setting a quit date; moving from urge-cued smoking to scheduled smoking; reducing the frequency of smoking and the potency of cigarettes smoked; coping-skills training for managing withdrawal; and relapse prevention
Bulimia	Cognitive-behaviour therapy involving psychoeducation; self-monitoring; mapping the antecedents and consequences of the binge–purge cycle; challenging the thinking style that underpins the bingeing-and-purging cycle; using stimulus control techniques to regularise eating routines; and problem-solving skills training
Anorexia	Refeeding followed by psychodynamic psychotherapy to give insight into a formulation which links (1) client's early relationships with parents, (2) current life symptomatology and relationship difficulties, and (3) relationship with the therapist; and developing less destructive ways to assert autonomy and achieve a stronger sense of personal identity
Insomnia	Multimodal treatment with the gradual withdrawal of medication once client shows proficiency in using stimulus-control techniques; sleep restriction; relaxation training; and challenging thinking styles which perpetuate insomnia
Surgical recovery	Pre-operative cognitive-behaviour therapy involving giving procedural and sensory information; relaxation training; relaxation and cognitive coping-skills training; and the provision of emotional support
Chronic pain management	Family-supported operant pain management involving scheduled increases in physical exercise; reduction in pain medication usage; and arranging for hospital staff and family members to avoid reinforcing pain- and sick-role behaviour, while concurrently offering positive reinforcement to the client for engaging in adaptive behaviour
	Cognitive behavioural treatment involving psychoeducation; training in relaxation, guided imagery, activity pacing, and pleasant event scheduling; and cognitive coping-skills training
Chronic neurological disease management in older adults	Psychoeducation to empower carers of older adults with disabilities to manage their disabled relatives more effectively
Adjustment to heart disease	Family-supported cognitive-behaviour therapy with psychoeducation; relaxation and cognitive coping-skills training; communication-skills training; and advice on diet, drugs and exercise
Adjustment to cancer	Cognitive-behaviour therapy with relaxation training and guided imagery to control anxiety, nausea and vomiting associated with chemotherapy; and supportive-expressive group therapy to increase quality of life, mood, and immune system functioning
Relapse prevention in sexual offending	Cognitive-behaviour therapy to challenge denial of responsibility for offending and cognitive distortions and to promote victim empathy and understanding the cycle of sexual offending coupled with covert sensitisation to alter deviant sexual arousal patterns and social-skills training

Source: This table is based on material reviewed in Carr (2000b): ch. 17; Carr (2000c) ch. 1: 1–52; Nathan and Gorman (1998); Roth and Fonagy (1996).

For anxiety disorders all effective treatments involve exposure to the feared stimulus and the use of relaxation and coping strategies to deal with such exposure and such psychological treatments may be offered with or without adjunctive antidepressant medication. For phobias gradual or intensive exposure to feared stimuli coupled with relaxation and coping-skills training is highly effective. Cognitive-behaviour therapy, involving learning to challenge threat-oriented thinking styles, and behavioural exercises to counter social avoidance behaviour coupled with relaxation and coping-skills training, is effective for social phobias. For panic disorder with agoraphobia, cognitive-behaviour therapy with family support, which involves exposure (*in vivo*) to increasing anxiety-provoking situations, relaxation and coping-skills training and learning to challenge threat-oriented thinking styles, is an effective treatment package. Exposure to cues which elicit obsessions (such as dirt) and prevention from engaging in compulsive anxiety-reducing responses (such as repeated hand-washing) coupled with relaxation and coping-skills training is an effective treatment for obsessive compulsive disorder. For post-traumatic stress disorder exposure to trauma-related cues and memories and concurrent relaxation and coping-skills training, including use of repeated distraction during exposure (for example in the eye movement desensitisation reprocessing protocol), have been shown to be effective. Cognitive-behaviour therapy where the focus is on challenging threat-oriented thinking styles and exposure to feared situations coupled with relaxation and coping-skills training is effective for generalised anxiety disorders.

To prevent relapse in schizophrenia, where people have been stabilised on antipsychotic medication, psychoeducational family therapy to reduce family stress and improve family communication and problem-solving skills; cognitive therapy to reduce the negative impact of hallucinations and delusions; and social-skills training to reduce negative symptoms of schizophrenia have all been shown to be effective and collectively are an empirically supported intervention package.

Psychological treatments can be effective in managing alcohol and smoking problems. Effective treatment programmes for alcohol problems include some combination of the following components: family-based engagement of clients in treatment, detoxification, self-control training for controlled drinking or AA attendance for abstinence; social-skills training; stress-management training; and medication (disulfiram/antibuse) which renders alcohol consumption nauseating. Spouse-supported cognitive behaviour therapy with psychoeducation; stimulus-control techniques such as removing ashtrays; setting a quit date; moving from urge-cued smoking to scheduled smoking; reducing the frequency of smoking and the potency of cigarettes smoked; coping-skills training for managing withdrawal; and relapse prevention are the core elements of effective smoking cessation programmes.

Cognitive behaviour therapy for bulimia is particularly effective and involves psychoeducation; self-monitoring; mapping the antecedents and consequences of the binge–purge cycle; challenging the thinking style that underpins the bingeing-and-purging cycle; using stimulus-control techniques to regularise eating routines; and problem-solving training. For anorexia, refeeding followed by psychodynamic psychotherapy has been shown to be effective in young adult women. This therapy facilitates insight into a uniquely constructed psychodynamic formulation which draws parallels between:

1. the client's early relationship experiences with parents;
2. current life symptomatology and relationship difficulties; and
3. the client's relationship with the therapist.

Clients use their insight to develop less destructive ways to assert autonomy and achieve a stronger sense of personal identity.

For medical problems such as insomnia, anxiety about surgical procedures, coping with chronic pain, managing sick relatives, and coping with heart disease and cancer, psychological interventions have been shown to improve adjustment. Multimodal treatment with the gradual withdrawal of medication once clients show proficiency in using stimulus-control techniques; sleep restriction; relaxation training; and challenging thinking styles which perpetuate insomnia are key elements in effective treatment programmes for insomnia. Pre-operative cognitive-behaviour therapy involving giving procedural and sensory information; relaxation training; relaxation and cognitive coping-skills training; and the provision of emotional support are effective ways of improving the rate of recovery from surgery. Where people develop a constricted lifestyle due to chronic pain, family-supported operant pain management is effective in improving quality of life. This involves scheduled increases in physical exercise; reduction in pain-medication usage; and arranging for hospital staff and family members to avoid reinforcing pain- and sick-role behaviour, while concurrently offering positive reinforcement to the client for engaging in adaptive behaviour. Cognitive-behavioural treatment involving psychoeducation; training in relaxation, guided imagery, activity pacing and pleasant event scheduling; and coaching in the development of cognitive coping skills are an effective treatment package for alleviating chronic pain. Where families are caring for older relatives with chronic neurological disease, psychoeducation empowers such carers to manage their disabled relatives more effectively and reduces the burden of care. Family-supported cognitive-behaviour therapy with psychoeducation; relaxation and cognitive coping-skills training; communication-skills training; and advice on diet, drugs and exercise are core elements of effective programmes for people recovering from myocardial infarctions and at risk of further heart-attacks. Effective psychological interventions for people with cancer include cognitive-behaviour therapy with relaxation training and guided imagery to control anxiety, nausea and vomiting associated with chemotherapy; and supportive-expressive group therapy to increase quality of life, mood and immune system functioning.

To prevent relapse in sexual offenders, cognitive-behaviour therapy is particularly effective. Effective programmes challenge denial of responsibility for offending and cognitive distortions while also promoting victim empathy and understanding of the cycle of sexual offending. In addition, such programmes involve covert sensitisation to alter deviant sexual-arousal patterns and social-skills training.

Psychological treatments that work for child and adolescent problems

Research on effective psychological treatments for problems in childhood and adolescence allow the conclusions set out here and summarised in Table 9.4 to be drawn (Carr, 2000a, 2000b, Chapter 17, 2002; Christophersen and Mortweet, 2001; Fonagy et al., 2002). Pre-school feeding, sleeping and toileting difficulties may all be effectively addressed with psychological interventions. For infants who show non-organic failure to thrive, multidisciplinary assessment and intensive child-focused refeeding and parent training to help the mother and child develop regular and appropriate feeding patterns is particularly effective. Family-based behaviour therapy, which entails the use of stimulus-control techniques (setting bedtime routines) and daytime sleep restriction and nap reduction, is an effective treatment for children with night waking difficulties. The frequency of nightmares may be reduced by challenging thinking styles which perpetuate anxiety and offering relaxation and coping-skills training. Parents are trained to prompt children to use these anxiety-management skills and reward them for doing so, and avoid inadvertently reinforcing anxious behaviour. Effective treatment for nocturnal enuresis involves parent-supported urine-alarm-based programmes in which children learn bladder control by being awakened each time they bedwet by a urine-activated alarm system and receive rewards for avoiding bedwetting from their parents. Family-based programmes that involve children using laxatives and increasing the intake of dietary fibre and parents rewarding children for engaging in regular toileting routines have been shown to improve encopresis.

Relaxation and coping-skills training have been shown to effectively reduce the frequency and intensity of headaches and recurrent abdominal pain. Effective programmes are family-based, and parents are trained to prompt children to use these pain-control skills and reward them for doing so. For painful surgical procedures, preparatory programmes have been shown to be effective. These involve psychoeducation, observing a model coping with the medical procedure, relaxation and cognitive coping-skills training, behavioural rehearsal and receiving incentives for coping with the painful procedures. During painful procedures distraction either alone or enhanced through hypnosis is also effective.

For childhood anxiety disorders, effective treatments involve exposure to the feared stimulus and the use of relaxation and coping strategies to deal

Table 9.4 Summary of research on psychological treatments that work for problems in childhood and adolescence

Problem area	Psychological treatments that work for problems in childhood and adolescence
Non-organic failure to thrive	Multidisciplinary assessment and intensive child-focused refeeding and parent training to help the mother and child develop regular and appropriate feeding patterns
Sleep problems	For night waking, family-based behaviour therapy involving the use of stimulus-control techniques (setting bedtime routines), night time sleep restriction and daytime nap reduction. For nightmares, challenging thinking styles which perpetuate anxiety, coupled with relaxation and coping-skills training. Parents are trained to prompt and reward children for using anxiety-management skills and avoid inadvertently reinforcing anxious behaviour
Enuresis	Parent-supported urine-alarm-based programmes in which children learn bladder control by being awakened by a urine-activated alarm system each time they bedwet, and receive rewards for avoiding bedwetting from their parents
Encopresis	Family-based programmes that involve children using laxatives and increasing the intake of dietary fibre, and parents rewarding children for engaging in regular toileting routines
Headaches	Family-based programmes in which children receive relaxation and coping-skills training and parents are trained to prompt children to use these pain-control skills and reward them for doing so
Recurrent abdominal pain	Family-based programmes in which children receive relaxation and coping-skills training and parents are trained to prompt children to use these pain-control skills and reward them for doing so
Painful surgical procedures	Preparatory programmes involving psychoeducation, observing a model coping with the medical procedure, relaxation and cognitive coping-skills training, behavioural rehearsal and receiving incentives for coping with the painful procedures. During painful procedures distraction either alone or enhanced through hypnosis is effective
Phobias	Family-based behaviour therapy in which children are gradually or intensively exposed to feared stimuli and also learn to use relaxation and coping skills. Parents are trained to prompt and reward children for using anxiety management skills and avoid inadvertently reinforcing anxious behaviour
School refusal	Family-based behaviour therapy involving home–school liaison, exposure to feared situations where the child is helped to return to school either gradually or immediately, and relaxation and coping-skills training. Parents and school staff are trained to prompt children to use these anxiety-management skills and reward them for doing so, and to avoid inadvertently reinforcing avoidant behaviour
Obsessive compulsive disorder	Behaviour therapy with family support involving exposure to cues which elicit obsessions (such as dirt) and prevention from engaging in compulsive anxiety-reducing responses (such as repeated hand-washing) coupled with relaxation and coping-skills training. Parents are trained to prompt and reward children for using anxiety-management skills and avoid inadvertently reinforcing compulsions by actively participating in them

Problem	Description
Post-traumatic stress disorder following sexual abuse or disasters	Cognitive-behaviour therapy involving graded exposure coupled with relaxation and coping-skills training in cases of child sexual abuse. Parents are trained to prompt children to use these anxiety-management and safety skills and reward them for doing so, and avoid inadvertently reinforcing anxious or risky behaviour
Depression	Cognitive therapy involving learning to challenge depressive thinking styles. Social-skills training to modify depression-maintaining social environments. Interpersonal therapy and family therapy involving modifying depression-maintaining interaction patterns within close relationships
Paediatric anorexia	Family-based treatment involving intensive engagement of the adolescent and parents in treatment; psychoeducation about the nature of anorexia and risks associated with starvation; weight restoration and monitoring; shifting the focus from the nutritional intake to normal psychosocial developmental tasks of adolescence; facilitating the adolescent's individuation and increasing autonomy within the family; and relapse prevention
Adjustment problems after physical child abuse	Multisystemic intervention involving behavioural parent training in child-management skills; parent-focused cognitive-behaviour therapy to help parents cope with anger, anxiety and depression; and peer-assisted, child-focused, group-based therapy to foster self-regulation, social skills and cognitive development. Well-adjusted peers should assist with such groups
Post-divorce adjustment problems	Multisystemic intervention with group-based therapy for children involving supportive psychoeducation, problem-solving skills training, social-skills training and stress-management training; and parent training focusing on communication and child-management skills
ADHD	Multimodal, multisystemic programmes involving behavioural parent training or family therapy where the goal is to enhance child-management skills; training in self-regulation skills for children; school-based behavioural therapy where teachers shape and reinforce appropriate classroom behaviour; and stimulant medication (e.g. methylphenidate)
Pre-adolescent oppositional defiant disorder	Multisystemic intervention involving video-modelling-supported behavioural parent training in child-management skills and concurrent video-modelling-supported, child-focused, social problem-solving skills training
Adolescent conduct disorder	Family therapy, multisystemic therapy and treatment fostercare may be offered on a continuum of care for increasingly treatment resistant conduct-disordered adolescents. Such family therapy focuses on facilitating high levels of parental co-operation in problem solving around the management of teenagers' conduct problems. Multisystemic therapy entails interventions that target conduct problem-maintaining factors within the multiple social systems of which the youngster is a member (peer group, family, school and community). In treatment fostercare trained foster parents use the principles of social learning theory to resocialise adolescents with extremely antisocial behaviour patterns.
Adolescent drug abuse	Intensive family engagement procedures followed by detoxification and either family therapy or multisystemic therapy similar to that for adolescent conduct disorder

Source: This table is based on material reviewed in Carr (2000a); Carr (2002); Carr (2000b, ch. 17); Christophersen and Mortweet (2001); Fonagy et al. (2002).

with such exposure coupled with prompting and reinforcement of children by parents for effective coping. These procedures are used for phobias including school phobia which in addition requires close home–school liaison. For obsessive compulsive disorder children are exposed to cues which elicit obsessions (such as dirt) and prevented from engaging in compulsive anxiety-reducing responses (such as repeated hand-washing) while parents prompt and reward the used of relaxation and coping-skills training. For post-traumatic stress disorder following sexual abuse or disasters, children undergo graded exposure and this is coupled with relaxation and coping-skills training as well as safety-skills training.

Cognitive therapy involving learning to challenge depressive thinking styles; social-skills training to modify depression-maintaining social environments; and interpersonal therapy and family therapy involving modifying depression-maintaining interaction patterns within close relationships have all been shown to be effective for childhood depression.

For paediatric anorexia, family-based treatment has been shown to be particularly effective. This involves intensive engagement of the adolescent and parents in treatment; psychoeducation about the nature of anorexia and risks associated with starvation; weight restoration and monitoring; shifting the focus from the nutritional intake to normal psychosocial developmental tasks of adolescence; facilitating the adolescent's individuation and increasing autonomy within the family; and relapse prevention.

For adjustment problems after physical child abuse, multisystemic intervention programmes are effective. Such intervention involves behavioural parent training in child-management skills; parent-focused cognitive-behaviour therapy to help parents cope with anger, anxiety and depression; and child-focused group-based therapy to foster self-regulation, social skills and cognitive development. Well-adjusted peers should be included in such group therapy or pre-school groups for abused children.

Multisystemic programmes are also effective for children who show post-divorce adjustment problems. These entail group-based therapy in which children participated in supportive psychoeducation, problem-solving skills training, social-skills training and stress-management training; and parent training focusing on communication and parenting skills.

For attention deficit hyperactivity disorders, multimodal multisystemic programmes are effective. These involve behavioural parent training or family therapy; training in self-regulation skills for children; school-based behavioural therapy; and stimulant medication (e.g. methylphenidate). For pre-adolescent oppositional defiant disorder, effective multisystemic programmes involve video-modelling-supported behavioural parent training and concurrent video-modelling-supported, child-focused, social problem-solving skills training. For adolescent conduct disorder, family therapy, multisystemic therapy and treatment fostercare may be offered on a continuum of care. Family therapy focuses on facilitating high levels of parental co-operation in problem solving around the management of teenagers' problem behaviour. Multisystemic therapy entails interventions that target conduct problem-maintaining factors within the multiple social systems of which the youngster is a member (i.e. child, family, school and community). In treatment fostercare trained foster parents use the principles of social learning theory to resocialise adolescents with extremely antisocial behaviour patterns. Intensive family engagement procedures followed by detoxification and either family therapy or multisystemic therapy similar to that for adolescent conduct disorder are effective treatments for adolescent drug abuse.

PREVENTION OF PSYCHOLOGICAL PROBLEMS

A growing body of evidence from controlled trials of prevention programmes supports the view that psychological interventions can prevent the development of a wide variety of psychological problems (Carr, 2002; Guralnick, 1997). Some of these results are presented in Table 9.5. For the prevention of developmental delay in low birth weight infants, multisystemic programmes which begin in neonatal intensive care units and involve home-visiting, community-based outpatient and pre-school follow-up sessions are effective. Such programmes should include child stimulation; parent training and support; and conjoint parent–child sessions to promote secure attachment. Effective programmes are continued throughout the pre-school years until the child's development falls within normal limits. Multisystemic programmes are also effective in the prevention of cognitive delays in socially disadvantaged children. These family-based early intervention programmes involve home-visiting, family support and pre-school or school-based intensive input which extends into middle childhood. Multisystemic family-based early intervention programmes are also effective in preventing adjustment problems in children with sensory disabilities. These programmes include child-focused and parent-focused components and these components should be offered flexibly on a home-visiting basis and at local health, social service or educational centres.

For the prevention of adjustment problems in children with autism, intensive long-term, structured programmes are the most effective. Such programmes are grounded in applied behavioural analysis; structured learning principles, and speech and language remedial therapy. To prevent challenging behaviour in children with intellectual disabilities, interventions that focus on antecedents of challenging behaviour, such as functional communication training and instructional manipulation, should be used first and procedures which focus on altering the consequences of challenging behaviour, such as overcorrection and restraint, should be used when the other procedures are ineffective.

Table 9.5 Summary of research on psychological prevention programmes that work for problems in childhood and adolescence

Problem area	Psychological prevention programmes that work
Prevention of developmental delay in low birth weight infants	Multisystemic programmes which begin in neonatal intensive care units and involve home-visiting, community-based, outpatient parent-focused and pre-school child-focused follow-up sessions. Such programmes should include child stimulation; parent training and support; and conjoint parent–child sessions to promote secure attachment. They should be continued until the child's development falls within normal limits
Prevention of cognitive delays in socially disadvantaged children	Multisystemic, family-based early intervention programmes involving home-visiting, family support and pre-school programmes which extend into middle childhood. Such programmes should include child stimulation; parent training and support; conjoint parent–child sessions to promote secure attachment. They should be continued until the child's development falls within normal limits
Prevention of adjustment problems in children with sensory disabilities	Multisystemic family-based early intervention programmes which include child-focused and parent-focused components and these components should be offered flexibly on a home-visiting basis and at local health, social service or educational centres
Prevention of adjustment problems in children with autism	Intensive, home, pre-school and school-based, long-term structured programmes grounded in applied behavioural analysis; structured learning principles, and speech and language remedial therapy
Prevention of challenging behaviour in children with intellectual disabilities	Behavioural interventions, based on functional analysis of challenging behaviour that focus on antecedents of the target behaviour, such as functional communication training and instructional manipulation should be used first and procedures which focus on altering the consequences of challenging behaviour such as overcorrection, restraint and punishment should be used when the other procedures are ineffective
Prevention of physical abuse	Multisystemic community-based programmes which begin prenatally and which include home-visiting conducted by nurses or paraprofessionals, behavioural parent training focusing on childcare skills, stress-management and life-skills training until assessment indicates that the risk of physical abuse has been substantially reduced

Prevention of sexual abuse	Multisystemic school-based primary prevention safety-skills training programmes which equip pre-adolescent children with the skills necessary for preventing child sexual abuse (CSA) and offer psychoeducation on CSA to parents, teachers and community-based health, social services and law enforcement professionals. These programmes should be developmentally staged with different programme materials for younger and older children; be of relatively long duration spanning a school term; be taught using multimedia materials and active skills-training methods.
Prevention of bullying	Whole school bullying prevention programmes which incorporate a wide range of strategies at school, class and individual levels within the context of an overall school policy in which the administration of the school, including the board of management, the principal, teachers and other staff along with the pupils take responsibility for preventing bullying
Prevention of adjustment problems in children with asthma	Family-based, psychoeducational programmes which include relaxation and coping-skills training for children and behavioural-skills training for children and parents in asthma management. Initially parents prompt and reinforce youngsters for managing asthma, but gradually youngsters take increasing responsibility for self-management
Prevention of adjustment problems in children with diabetes	Family-based, psychoeducational programmes which include relaxation and coping-skills training for children and behavioural-skills training for children and parents in diabetes management. Initially parents prompt and reinforce youngsters for managing diabetes, but gradually youngsters take increasing responsibility for self-management. School liaison meetings; home-visiting; and peer counselling should be offered for newly diagnosed patients
Prevention of teenage smoking, alcohol use and drug abuse	Peer-led, school-based programmes spanning an academic year in which young teenagers receive accurate information about the immediate effects of drugs; conservative normative information about drug use; and learn drug-refusal skills and general social problem-solving skills
Prevention of teenage pregnancy, sexually transmitted diseases and HIV infection	School-based programmes for younger adolescents should focus on delaying sexual intercourse and those for older teenagers should focus on the avoidance of unprotected sexual intercourse. Skills training for both groups should include anticipating and avoiding or escaping from sexually risky situations. Skills training for older teenagers should include buying carrying and using condoms.
Prevention of suicide in adolescence	Multisystemic prevention programmes which include school-based didactic instruction and discussion, bibliotherapy, and behavioural-coping skills training for adolescents and other members of their social networks. Such programmes should form part of an overall prevention plan which also includes screening programmes for students at risk; crisis services and hotlines for students at risk; and postvention programmes for families following suicide attempts

Source: Carr (2002); Guralnick (1997).

Multisystemic community-based programmes are effective in preventing physical abuse. Such programmes begin prenatally and include home-visiting conducted by nurses or paraprofessionals, behavioural parent training, stress management and life-skills training.

For the prevention of sexual abuse, multisystemic school-based primary prevention safety-skills training programmes are effective. These programmes equip pre-adolescent children with the skills necessary for preventing child sexual abuse (CSA) and offer psychoeducation on CSA to parents, teachers and community-based health, social services and law enforcement professionals. These programmes should be developmentally staged with different programme materials for younger and older children; be of relatively long duration spanning a school term; be taught using multimedia materials and active skills training methods.

For the effective prevention of bullying, whole school bullying prevention programmes are effective. These incorporate a wide range of strategies at school, class and individual levels within the context of an overall school policy in which the administration of the school, including the board of management, the principal, teachers and other staff along with the pupils take responsibility for preventing bullying.

For preventing adjustment problems in children with chronic illnesses such as asthma and diabetes, family-based psychoeducational programmes which include relaxation training for children and behavioural skills training for children and parents in illness management are particularly effective. Initially parents prompt and reinforce youngsters for managing their illness, but gradually youngsters take increasing responsibility for self-management.

For the prevention of teenage smoking, alcohol use and drug abuse, peer-led, school-based programmes targeting young teenagers are effective. These should be of long duration (up to 30 sessions) and give accurate information about the immediate effects of drugs; conservative normative information about drug use; and offer coaching in drug-refusal skills and general social problem-solving skills.

For the prevention of teenage pregnancy, sexually transmitted diseases and HIV infection, school-based programmes are effective. For younger adolescents these should focus on delaying the onset of sexual intercourse and for older teenagers they should focus on the avoidance of unprotected sex. Skills training for both groups should focus on anticipating and avoiding or escaping from sexually risky situations. Skills training for older teenagers should include learning skills for buying, carrying and using condoms.

For the prevention of suicide in adolescence, multisystemic school-based prevention programmes are effective. These programmes include didactic instruction and discussion, bibliotherapy, and behavioural coping-skills training for adolescents and other members of their social networks. Such programmes should be included as part of an overall prevention plan which also includes: screening programmes for students at risk; crisis services and hotlines for students at risk; and postvention programmes for families following suicide attempts.

CONTROVERSIES

In the field of psychological change historically there have been many controversies. For example, the humanistic and behavioural traditions disagreed over the relative importance of the quality of the therapeutic relationship and therapeutic techniques. This matter has now been empirically resolved and most accept the resolution presented in Figure 9.4.

There has also been debate over the relative efficacy of different therapeutic approaches. Many comparative studies and meta-analyses have shown that most psychotherapeutic techniques are equally effective. This has been referred to as the dodo bird verdict (Luborsky et al., 1975). The allusion is to the pronouncement of the dodo bird in Lewis Caroll's *Alice in Wonderland* that 'Everybody has won and so all must have prizes.' As comparative treatment outcome studies become more tightly designed and change processes become more clearly specified and measured, there is a growing understanding as to why different approaches may be equally effective for the same class of problems (Nathan and Gorman, 2002).

There was potential for a debate about whether there were clear differences between people who made changes in their lives with and without professional help. However, research on the stages of change model has shown that change processes are similar for self-changers and for those who seek professional help (Prochaska, 1999).

One of the most important areas of potential controversy concerns the position clinical psychology as a profession should adopt with respect to changing behaviour. The predominant style of practice is for psychologists to devote the lion's share of their time and effort to individual, group, couples and family therapy with clients and patients who have been referred with a wide variety of psychological problems and disabilities. A strong argument cam be made that psychologists should devote their time to prevention programmes which target particularly dangerous or costly problems, such as AIDS, cancer or child abuse, in entire communities rather than a ragbag of difficulties in individuals, small groups or families (Prochaska, 1999).

SUMMARY

Positive change, personal growth and development may occur in response to opportunities for change and challenges to our coping resources. These include those specific to the completion of a particular stage of the lifecycle; those associated with transitions from one stage of the lifecycle to the next;

those associated with making and breaking long-standing habits; those that arise on a day-to-day basis; and unusual events such as bereavement, or robbery. In addressing opportunities and challenges, we use our strengths to help us match our strategy for managing the situation to its demands and to our readiness to engage with the challenge or opportunity. Positive outcomes from the effective management of opportunities and challenges include positive changes in physical health and psychological well-being and an overall enhancement of our personal strengths. Change and growth follow a predictable course from precontemplation, through contemplation, planning, action, maintenance and termination. Change can be accelerated by understanding the change process and matching the strategies for change to the stage of change in which we find ourselves. Consciousness raising, arousing emotions, environmental re-evaluation and social liberation are particularly helpful in facilitating movement from precontemplation to contemplation. In making the transition from contemplation to planning, self-re-evaluation is the most important change process. Self-liberation through making a commitment to change is critical for the transition from planning to action and this may be coupled with goal setting and monitoring, processes that should be continued throughout the stages of change until termination. In moving from the action to the maintenance stage, stimulus control, countering and reward are maximally beneficial. Finally, in making the transition from maintenance to termination, relapse prevention and management is the most important change process. Helping-relationships facilitate progress through the stages of change. Such relationships may be informal and involve close friends or family members. Alternatively they may be formal and involve a professional such as a clinical psychologist. While specific therapeutic techniques account for about 15 per cent of change in psychotherapy, the therapeutic relationship accounts for about 30 per cent of therapeutic improvement. The growth of a therapeutic relationship follows distinct stages involving planning, contracting, assessment, therapy, managing resistance or ambivalence about change and disengagement and these parallel the stages of change. For most common psychological problems, between two-thirds and three-quarters of clients improve following psychological therapy. Most adult and child clients attend therapy for only 6–10 sessions for individual and family or marital therapy and by 8 sessions 50 per cent of adult clients have shown improvement. Approximately 10 per cent of patients are harmed by therapy. While global meta-analytic reviews have concluded that approaches to therapy based on different models yield similar results, focused reviews of well-controlled studies point to the effectiveness of specific techniques for particular problems in children, adolescents and adults. Psychological interventions can also prevent the development of a wide variety of psychological problems. A client satisfaction questionnaire which can be used to evaluate any type of change-oriented service is presented in Table 9.6.

Table 9.6 Client Satisfaction Questionnaire

Please help us improve our programme by answering some questions about the service you have received. We are interested in your opinions, whether they are positive or negative. Please circle your answer to each of the following questions. We also welcome your comments and suggestions which you can write on the back of this page.

1. How would you rate the quality of the service you have received?	4 Excellent	3 Good	2 Fair	1 Poor
2. Did you get the kind of service you wanted?	1 No, definitely	2 No, not really	3 Yes, generally	4 Yes, definitely
3. To what extent has our programme met your needs?	4 Almost all of my needs have been met	3 Most of my needs have been met	2 Only a few of my needs have been met	1 None of my needs have been met
4. If a friend were in need of similar help, would you recommend our programme to him or her?	1 No, definitely	2 No, I don't think so	3 Yes, I think so	4 Yes, definitely
5. How satisfied are you with the kind of help you have received?	1 Quite satisfied	2 Indifferent or mildly dissatisfied	3 Mostly satisfied	4 Very satisfied
6. Have the services you received helped you to deal more effectively with your problems?	4 Yes, they helped a great deal	3 Yes, they helped somewhat	2 No, they didn't really help	1 No, they seemed to make things worse
7. In an overall, general sense, how satisfied are you with the service you have received?	4 Very satisfied	3 Mostly satisfied	2 Indifferent or mildly dissatisfied	1 Quite dissatisfied
8. If you were to seek help again, would you come back to our programme?	1 No, definitely	2 No, I don't think so	3 Yes, I think so	4 Yes, definitely

Source: Adapted from Larsen (1979): 197–207.

QUESTIONS

Personal development questions

1. Describe one thing you would like to change about your lifestyle so you could be healthier or happier.
2. From the information in the chapter, what stage of change are you in today?
3. What steps can you take now to move from the stage you are in today towards the next stage of change?
4. What would be the costs and benefits of taking these steps?
5. Take some of these steps and assess the impact it has on your well-being by assessing yourself before and afterwards on one of the well-being scales contained in Chapter 1.

Research questions

1. Design and conduct a study to test the hypothesis that there is a significant correlation between happiness and the stage of change that people are in concerning weight reduction.
2. Find a chapter in this book on a prevention topic that interests you and that contains studies which might be feasible for you to conduct for a postgraduate thesis: A. Carr (2002). *Prevention: What Works with Children and Adolescents? A Critical Review of Psychological Prevention Programmes for Children, Adolescents and their Families.* London: Routledge. Now, using the bibliography at the back of the book, find references to some of the papers describing the studies reviewed in the chapter that interests you. Find these studies in the journals in your university's library. Or order them on interlibrary loan. Or look up the author's name on the net, find their current e-mail address and write to them asking for reprints of their articles. Choose a well-designed study as a model and design a new study which would replicate and extend this study.

FURTHER READING

Academic books on effective treatments

Carr, A. (2000a). *What Works with Children and Adolescents? A Critical Review of Research on Psychological Interventions with Children, Adolescents and Their Families.* London: Routledge.

Carr, A. (2000b). *Family Therapy: Concepts, Process and Practice.* (Chapter 17). Chichester: Wiley.

Carr, A. (2002). *Prevention: What Works with Children and Adolescents? A Critical Review of Psychological Prevention Programmes for Children, Adolescents and their Families.* Hove: Brunner-Routledge.

Christophersen, E. and Mortweet, S. (2001). *Treatments that Work with Children. Empirically Supported Strategies for Managing Childhood Problems.* Washington, DC: APA.

Fonagy, P., Target, M., Cottrell, D. Phillips, J. and Kurtz, A. (2002), *What Works for Whom: A Critical Review of Treatments for Children and Adolescents.* New York: Guilford.

Hubble, M., Duncan, B. and Miller, S. (1999). *The Heart and Soul of Change: What Works in Therapy.* Washington, DC: American Psychological Association.

Nathan, P. and Gorman, J. (2002). *A Guide to Treatments that Work (Second Edition).* New York: Oxford University Press.

Norcross, J. (2002). *Psychotherapy Relationships that Work.* New York: Oxford University Press.

Prochaska, J. and Norcross, J. (1994). *Systems of Psychotherapy: A Transtheoretical Analysis* (3rd edn). Pacific Grove, CA: Brooks/Cole.

Rapp, C. (1998). *The Strengths Model: Case Management with People Suffering from Severe Persistent Mental Illness.* New York: Oxford.

Roth, A. and Fonagy, P. (1996), *What Works for Whom: A Critical Review of Psychotherapy Research.* New York: Guilford.

Self-help: general books on personal change

Butler, G. and Hope, T. (1995). *Manage Your Mind.* New York: Oxford University Press. (This guide based on a bedrock of research shows how seven skills may be used to solve life problems. These are time-management, acknowledging problems, self-care, problem solving, keeping things in perspective, building confidence, and relaxation.)

Prochaska, J., Norcross, J. and DiClemente, C. (1994). *Changing for Good.* New York: Avon.

Self-help: undereating and bingeing

Cooper, P. (1993). *Bulimia Nervosa: A Guide to Recovery.* London: Robinson Publishing.

Fairburn, C. (1995). *Overcoming Binge Eating.* New York: Guilford.

Crisp, A., Joughin, N. Halek, C. and Bower, C. (1996). *Anorexia Nervosa: The Wish to Change. Self-help and Discovery, the Thirty Steps* (2nd edn). Hove: Psychology Press.

Treasure, J. (1997). *Anorexia Nervosa: A Survival Guide for Families, Friends and Sufferers.* Hove: Psychology Press.

Treasure, J. and Schmidt, U. (1993). *Getting Better Bit(e) by Bit(e): A Survival Kit for Sufferers of Bulimia Nervosa and Binge Eating.* Hove, UK: Lawrence Erlbaum.

Self-help: weight control

Bailey, C. (1991). *The New Fit or Fat* (Revised Edition). Boston: Houghton Mifflin. (This research-based guide shows how to use a low fat diet and a lifestyle involving aerobic exercise to lose weight.)

Browness, K. (1990). *The LEARN Programme for Weight Control.* Dallas, TX: American Health Publication/Brownell and Hager. (This guide describes an empirically validated weight loss programme LEARN [Lifestyle, Exercise, Attitudes, Relationships and Nutrition].)

Orinish, D. (1993). *Eat More, Weigh Less.* New York: Harper Collins. (The research-based weight loss programme described in this book focuses on lifestyle change.)

Self-help: alcohol

Alcoholics Anonymous (1976). *Alcoholics Anonymous* (3rd edn). New York: AA. The original AA handbook.

Alcoholics Anonymous (1995). *Twelve Steps and Twelve Traditions.* New York: AA. (A more elaborate statement of the original AA programme.)

Colclough, B. (1993). *Tomorrow I'll Be Different: The Effective Way to Stop Drinking.* London: Viking. (A good self-help book by an abstinent drinker.)

Ellis, A. and Velton, E. (1992). *When AA Doesn't Work for You.* Fort Lee, NJ: Barricade Books. (An alternative self-help guide for people who cannot accept AA's insistence on spiritual commitment, based on the principles of cognitive therapy.)

Self-help: drugs

Trickett, S. (1986). *Coming off Tranquilizers.* New York: Thorsons.

Tyrer, P. (1986). *How to Stop Taking Tranquilizers.* London: Sheldon Press.

MEASURES FOR USE IN RESEARCH

Larsen, D., Attkinson, C., Hargreaves, W. and Nguyen, T. (1979). Assessment of client/patient satisfaction: development of a general scale. *Evaluation and Programme Planning* 2: 197–207.

Willoughby. F., and Edens, J. (1996). The construct validity and predictive validity of the Stages of Change Scale for alcoholics. *Journal of Substance Abuse* 8: 275–99 (The Rhode Island Change Assessment is described in this article and is available at http://www.uri.edu/research/cprc/Measures/urica.htm. Other stages of change measures are available at http://www.uri.edu/research/cprc/measures.htm.)

GLOSSARY

Abstinence Violation Effect.   Marlatt's term for demoralisation which occurs during a relapse, for example, 'I've had one slip. So I know now I'm completely out of control and so will fall completely back into my old ways, so there is nothing I can do now but continue to slip.'

Action.   We actually change our behaviour by putting our plan into action during this stage.

Consciousness raising.   This involves increasing awareness about the defences that prevent us from recognising the problem along with obtaining information about the problem, its causes, consequences and possible solutions.

Contemplation.   In the contemplation stage, we move from denying that we have a problem in a particular area to accepting that there may be a problem, which we may address within the foreseeable future.

Countering.   Countering is a change process in which we substitute alternatives for problem behaviours.

Environmental re-evaluation.   With environmental re-evaluation, we consider and assess how our problem behaviour or the way we are avoiding facing the challenges and opportunities in our lives affects others, such as our family friends or members of our community.

Maintenance.   We take active steps to make sure we don't relapse or slip back into old habits in the maintenance stage.

Planning.   In the planning stage a commitment to change in the next month.

Precontemplation.   In the precontemplation stage, we deny that we have a problem.

Self-liberation.   Transforming the global decision to change made during the contemplation stage into a decision to take specific steps to solve the problem.

Social liberation.   Social liberation is a change process in which society offers opportunities for us to choose alternatives to our problem behaviours and we become aware that these alternatives are available and use them to help us change.

Stages of change theory.   Prochaska, DiClemente and Norcross's view that enduring changes in well-established patterns of behaviour involve progression through the stages of precontemplation, contemplation, planning, action, maintenance, and termination.

Stimulus control.   Changing our environment so that it contains fewer cues for problem behaviour and more cues for productive alternatives.

Termination.   We experience no wish to relapse and have complete confidence that we can manage our difficulties in the termination stage. For many life challenges this rarely occurs and we commit to a lifetime of maintenance.

Afterword

If you have made it this far and read all 9 chapters, my guess is that you might be asking: what does all this mean? Fair question. This book's message is an optimistic one. The results of scientific research point to three reliable ways to find happiness:

- Cultivate relationships which involve deep attachment and commitment;
- Involve yourself in absorbing work and leisure activities in which you exercise your strengths, talents and interests;
- Cultivate an optimistic, future-oriented perspective on life in which you expect the best and value the future more than the present.

If you have enough money to buy this book, then it is unlikely that winning the lottery will have any lasting impact on your overall long-term level of happiness. Do not work exclusively for material gain because this will probably make you unhappy.

Because the set-point for happiness is largely genetically determined, it is unrealistic and indeed may be depressing to continually expect that some-day you will be ecstatically happy. So aim to cruise along just above your happiness set-point.

These simple conclusions have huge implications for government policy. Governments should make it attractive for people to do the following:

- To make and maintain long-term friendships and family relationships including marriages, parent–child relationships, and kinship relationships;
- To work in jobs that fit with people's strengths, talents and interests;
- To pursue absorbing leisure activities where people's strengths, talents and interests can find expression;
- To value the future more than the present.

Governments should not create policies which encourage an excessive focus on working long hours to increase wealth at the expense of important family relationships. They should develop flexible policies which support and reward people for maintaining high-quality long-term marriages, looking after children and older members of the extended family, and fostering long-term friendships, which are often eroded by social mobility and pressure of work.

Governments should develop policies relevant to educational, occupational and leisure settings that promote an ongoing life-long matching of people's strengths and talents to their educational, occupational and leisure roles.

Governments should legislate against advertisements which inaccurately convey that long-term happiness will come from acquiring more and more material products.

Governments should develop national incentive systems which encourage valuing the future as a way of reducing accidents, rather than putting limited resources into trying to engineer a safer environment.

From a clinical perspective, positive psychology offers a strengths-based approach from which to practise. This will complement the deficit-oriented models in which most clinicians have been trained and give patients and clients access to services in which their resilience is privileged rather than their shortcomings.

From a scientific perspective, positive psychology is a field full of possibilities for future research. There are huge opportunities for young scientists to modify old and build new complex biopsychosocial theories about aspects of well-being. There are endless opportunities to empirically test hypotheses derived from these theories about the relationships between large sets of variables and well-being. For the young scientists, in the field of positive psychology, here are Nobel prizes waiting to be won.

Let us close as we began with a few well-chosen words from James Joyce: this book is an invitation to all of us to exchange 'new worlds for old'.

Bibliography

Abramson, L., Alloy, L., Hankin, B., Clements, C., Zhu, L., Hogan, M. and Whitehouse, W. (2000). Optimistic cognitive style and invulnerability to depression. In J. Gillham (ed.) *The Science of Optimism and Hope* (pp. 75–98). Philadelphia, PA: Templeton Foundation Press.

Achenbach, T. (1991). *Integrative Guide for the 1991 CBCL/4–18, YSR and TRF Profiles*. Burlington, VT: University of Vermont Department of Psychiatry.

Ackerman, B., Izard, C., Schoff, K., Youngstrom, E. and Kogos, J. (1999). Contextual risk, caregiver emotionality, and the problem behaviours of six- and seven-year-old children from economically disadvantaged families. *Child Development* 70: 1415–27.

Ackerman, R. and Derubeis, R. (1991). Is depressive realism real? *Clinical Psychology Review* 11: 234–45.

Adams, B. (1986). *The Family: A Sociological Interpretation*. (4th edn) San Diego: Harcourt Brace and Janovich.

Adams, M. (1986). *Odyssey: A Curriculum for Thinking*. Watertown, MA: Mastery Education Corporation.

Ainsworth, M., Blehar, M., Waters, E. and Wass, S. (1978). *Patterns of Attachment: A Psychological Study of the Strange Situation*. Hillsdale, NJ: Erlbaum.

Alfonso,V., Allinson, D., Rader, D. and Gorman, B. (1996). The Extended Satisfaction with Life Scale: development and psychometric properties. *Social Indicators Research* 38: 275–301.

Allen, J. and Land, D. (1999). Attachment in adolescence. In J. Cassidy and P. Shaver (eds), *Handbook of Attachment* (pp. 319–35). New York: Guilford.

Amato, P. (1993). Children's adjustment to divorce: theories, hypotheses and empirical support. *Journal of Marriage and the Family* 55: 23–38.

Amato, P. and Keith, B. (1991a). Parental divorce and the well-being of children: a meta-analysis. *Psychological Bulletin* 110: 26–46.

Amato, P. and Keith, B. (1991b). Consequences of parental divorce for adult well-being: a meta-analysis. *Journal of Marriage and the Family* 53: 43–58.

American Dialect Society (1999). Words of the year. http://www.smericandialect.org/woty

American Psychiatric Association (APA) (1994). *Diagnostic and Statistical Manual of the Mental Disorders (Fourth Edition) DSM-IV*. Washington, DC: APA.

Anderson, E. and Cohler, B. (1987). *The Invulnerable Child*. New York: Guilford.

Andrews, F. and McKennell, A. (1980). Measures of self-reported well-being: their affective, cognitive and other components. *Social Indicators Research* 8: 127–55.

Andrews, F. and Withey, S. (1976). *Social Indicators of Well-being*. New York: Plenum.

Antonovsky, A. (1993). The structure and properties of the sense of coherence scale. *Social Science and Medicine* 35: 725–33.

Apter International (1999). Apter Motivational Style Profile, Manual and Workbook. Uppingham, UK: Author. http://www.apterinternational.com/main.htm. e-mail: <Marieshelton@apterinternational.com>. Apter International Limited, Glaston Road, Uppingham, Rutland LE15 9EU England. Phone: (+44) 01572 821111 Fax: (+44) 01572 813113.

Apter, M. (2001). *Motivational Style in Everyday Life: A Guide to Reversal Theory*. Washington, DC: APA.

Argyle, M. (2000). *Psychology and Religion: An Introduction*. London: Routledge.

Argyle, M. (2001). *The Psychology of Happiness* (2nd edn). London: Routledge.

Argyle, M. (2002). Religion. *The Psychologist* 15 (1): 22–26.

Aspinwall, L., Richter, L. and Hoffman, R. (2001). Understanding how optimism works: an examination of optimists' adaptive moderation of belief and behaviour. In E. Chang, *Optimism and Pessimism: Implications for Theory, Research and Practice* (pp. 217–38). Washington, DC: APA.

Aspinwall, L. and Staudinger, U. (2003). *A Psychology of Human Strengths. Fundamental Questions and Future Directions for a Positive Psychology*. Washington, DC: American Psychological Association.

Averill, J. (1997). The emotions: an integrative approach. In R. Hogan, J. Johnson, J. and S. Briggs (eds), *Handbook of Personality Psychology* (pp. 513–41). New York: Academic Press.

Averill, J. (1999). Individual differences in emotional creativity: structure and correlates. *Journal of Personality* 67: 331–71.

Averill, J. (2000). Intelligence, emotion, and creativity: from trichotomy to trinity. In R. Bar-On and J. Parker (eds), *The Handbook of Emotional Intelligence* (pp. 277–98). San Francisco, CA: Jossey-Bass.

Averill, J. (2002) Emotional creativity: towards spiritualizing the passions, In C.R. Snyder and S. Lopez (eds), *Handbook of Positive Psychology*. New York: Oxford University Press.

Averill, J. and Nunley, E. (1992). *Voyages of the Heart: Living an Emotionally Creative Life*. New York: Free Press.

Axelrod, R. (1984). *The Evolution of Co-operation*. New York: Basic Books.

Ayd, F. and Blackwell, H. (1970). *Discoveries in Biological Psychiatry*. Philadelphia, PA: Lippincott.

Bagby, R., Parker, J. and Taylor, G. (1994). The twenty item Toronto Alexithymia Scale: Part 1. Item selection and cross validation of the factor structure. *Journal of Psychosomatic Research* 38: 23–32.

Baltes, P. and Staudinger, U. (2000). Wisdom: a metaheuristic (pragmatic) to orchestrate mind and virtue towards excellence. *American Psychologist* 55: 122–36.

Bandura, A. (1997). *Self-Efficacy*. New York: Freeman.

Bandura, A. (1999). Social cognitive theory of personality. In L. Pervin and O. John (eds), *Handbook of Personality: Theory and Research* (pp. 154–96). New York: Guilford.

Barlow, D. and Craske, M. (1994). *Master Your Anxiety and Panic II*. Albany, NY: Graywind.

Bar-On, R. (1997). *BarOn Emotional Quotient Inventory (EQ-I): Technical Manual*. Toronto: Multi-Health Systems.

Bar-On, R. (2000). Emotional and social intelligence: insights from the Emotional Quotient Inventory. In R. Bar-On and J. Parker (eds), *The Handbook of Emotional Intelligence* (pp. 363–88). San Francisco, CA: Jossey-Bass.

Bar-On, R. and Parker, J. (2000). *The Handbook of Emotional Intelligence*. San Francisco, CA: Jossey-Bass.

Barton, C. and Alexander, J. (1981). Functional family therapy. In A. Gurman and D. Kniskern (eds), *Handbook of Family Therapy* (pp. 403–43). New York: Brunner/ Mazel.

Basseches, M. (1984). *Dialectical Thinking and Adult Development*. Norwood, NJ: Ablex.

Batson, C. (1991). *The Altruism Question: Towards a Social Psychological Answer*. Hillsdale, NJ: Erlbaum.

Batson, C., Ahmad, N., Lishner, D. and Tsang, J. (2002). Empathy and altruism. In C.R. Snyder and S. Lopez (eds), *Handbook of Positive Psychology* (pp. 485–98). New York: Oxford University Press.

Battle, J. (1992). *Culture-Free Self-Esteem Inventories: Examiner's Manual* (2nd edn). Austin, TX: Pro-ed.

Bauer, S. and Rockland, L. (1995). The inventory of defence related behaviours: an approach to measuring defence mechanisms in psychotherapy. In H. Conte and R. Plutchik (eds), *Ego Defences: Theory and Measurement* (pp. 300–14). New York: Wiley.

Baumeister, R. (1997). Identity, self-concept and self-esteem: the self lost and found. In R. Hogan, J. Johnson and S. Briggs (eds), *Handbook of Personality Psychology* (pp. 681–710). New York: Academic Press.

Beavers, W. and Hampson, R. (1990) *Successful Families: Assessment and Intervention*. New York: W.W. Norton.

Beavers, W. and Hampson, R. (2000). The Beavers Systems Model of Family Functioning. *Journal of Family Therapy* 22: 128–43.

Bechara, A., Tranel, D. and Damasio, A. (2000). Poor judgement in spite of high intellect. Neurological evidence for emotional intelligence. In R. Bar-On and J. Parker (eds), *The Handbook of Emotional Intelligence* (pp. 192–214). San Francisco, CA: Jossey-Bass.

Beck, A. (1976). *Cognitive Therapy and the Emotional Disorders*. New York: International Universities Press.

Beck, A. (1999). *Prisoners of Hate*. New York: HarperCollins.

Becker, E. (1973). *Denial of Death*. New York: Free Press.

Bednar, R. and Peterson, S. (1995). *Self-Esteem: Paradoxes and Innovations in Clinical Theory and Practice* (2nd edn) Washington, DC: American Psychological Association.

Benson, H. (1975). *The Relaxation Response*. New York: William Morrow.

Bergin, A. and Garfield, S. (1994). *Handbook of Psychotherapy and Behaviour Change*. New York: Wiley.

Berry, J., Worthington, E., Parrott, L., O'Connor, L. and Wade, N. (In press). Dispositional forgiveness: construct validity and development of the transgression narrative test of forgiveness (TNTF). *Personality and Social Psychology Bulletin*.

Bilodeau, L. (1992). *The Anger Workbook*. Minneapolis, MN: Compcare.

Bishop, D., Epstein, N., Keitner, G., Miller, I. and Zlotnick, C. (1980). The McMaster Structured Interview for Family Functioning, Providence, Rhode Island: Brown University Family Research Program.

Björgvinsson, T. and Wilde, G. (1995). Risk homeostasis and individual differences in health and safety habits. In Accidents, safety and risk taking. Symposium conducted at the Annual Convention of the Canadian Psychological Association, Charlottetown, Prince Edward Island, Canada, 15–17 June, 1995.

Block, J. and Block, J. (1980). The role of ego-control and ego resilience in the organization of behaviour. In W. Collins (ed.), *The Minnesota Symposium on Child Psychology* (vol. 13, pp. 33–101). Hillsdale, NJ: Erlbaum.

Block, J. and Kremen, A. (1996). IQ and ego-resilience: conceptual and empirical connections and separateness. *Journal of Personality and Social Psychology* 70: 349–61.

Bolton, R. (1986). *People Skills*. New York: Touchstone.

Bond, F. and Dryden, W. (2002). *Handbook of Brief Cognitive Behaviour Therapy*. New York: Wiley.

Bond, M. and Wesley, S. (1996). Manual for the Defence Style Questionnaire. Montreal: McGill University.

Bouhard, T., Lykken, D., McGue, M., Segal, N. and Tellegen, A. (1990). The sources of human psychological differences: the Minnesota Study of Twins Reared Apart, *Science* 250: 223–8.

Bourne, E. (1995). *The Anxiety and Phobia Workbook*. Oakland, CA: New Harbinger.

Bowlby, J. (1988). *A Secure Base: Clinical Implications of Attachment Theory*. London: Routledge.

Boyatzis, R., Goleman, D. and Hay/McBer. (1999). *Emotional Competence Inventory*. Boston, MA: HayGroup.

Boyatzis, R., Goleman, D. and Rhee, K. (2000). Clustering competence in emotional intelligence: insights from the Emotional Competence Inventory. In R. Bar-On and J. Parker (eds), *The Handbook of Emotional Intelligence* (pp. 343–62). San Francisco, CA: Jossey-Bass.

Boyle, M. (1990). *Schizophrenia: A Scientific Delusion*. London: Routledge.

Bray, J. and Hetherington, M. (1993). Special section: families in transition. *Journal of Family Psychology* 7: 3–103.

Brazelton, T. (1983). *Infants and Mothers* (revised 3rd edn). New York: Delta Seymor Lawrence.

Brazelton, T. (1989). *Toddlers and Parents* (revised 2nd edn). New York: Delacorte.

Brennan, K., Clark, C. and Shaver, P. (1998). Self-report measurement of adult attachment: an integrative overview. In J. Simpson and W. Rholes (eds), *Attachment Theory and Close Relationships* (pp. 46–76). New York: Guilford.

Brickman, P. and Campbell, D. (1971). Hedonic relativism and planning the good society. In M. Appley (ed.), *Adaptation-level Theory* (pp. 287–305). New York: Academic Press.

Brody, G., Neubaum, E. and Forehand, R. (1988). Serial marriage: a heuristic analysis of an emerging family form. *Psychological Bulletin* 103: 211–22.

Brown, J. (1998). *The Self*. New York: McGraw-Hill.

Brown, L. and Brown, M. (1986). *Dinosaurs Divorce: A Guide for Changing Families*. Boston, MA: Little Brown.

Brunk, M., Henggeler, S. and Whelan, J. (1987). Comparison of multisystemic therapy and parent training in the brief treatment of child abuse and neglect. *Journal of Consulting and Clinical Psychology* 55: 171–8.

Burger, J. and Cooper, H. (1979). The desirability of control. *Motivation and Emotion* 3: 381–93.

Burns, D. (1980). *Feeling Good: The New Mood Therapy*. New York: Morrow.

Burns, D. (1989). *The Feeling Good Handbook: Using the New Mood Therapy in Everyday Life*. New York: Harper Row (later published by Penguin as a Plume book).

Buss, A. and Plomin, R. (1975). *A Temperament Theory of Personality Development*. New York: Wiley.

Buss, D. (1999). *Evolutionary Psychology: The New Science of the Mind*. Boston, MA: Allyn and Bacon.

Buss, D. (2000). The Evolution of Happiness. *American Psychologist* 55: 15–23.

Butler, G. and Hope, T. (1995). *Manage Your Mind*. New York: Oxford University Press.

Byrne, B. (1995). *Measuring Self-Concept across the Life Span: Issues and Instrumentation*. Washington, DC: American Psychological Association.

Callahan, C. (2000) Intelligence and giftedness. In R. Sternberg (ed.), *Handbook of Intelligence* (pp. 159–75). Cambridge: Cambridge University Press.

Campbell, A., Converse, P. and Rogers, W. (1976). *The Quality of American Life*. New York: Sage.

Campbell, D., Draper, R. and Crutchley, E. (1991). The Milan systemic approach to family therapy. In A. Gurman and D. Kniskern (eds), *Handbook of Family Therapy. Volume II* (pp. 325–62). New York: Brunner/Mazel.

Cantor, N. (1990). From thought to behaviour: 'having' and 'doing' in the study of personality and cognition. *American Psychologist* 45: 735–50.

Cantwell, D. and Rutter, M. (1994). Classification: conceptual issues and substantive findings. In M. Rutter, E. Taylor and L. Hersov (eds), *Child and Adolescent Psychiatry: Modern Approaches* (3rd edn, pp. 3–21). Oxford: Blackwell.

Carr, A. (1999). *Handbook of Child and Adolescent Clinical Psychology: A Contextual Approach*. London: Routledge.

Carr, A. (2000a). *What Works with Children and Adolescents? A Critical Review of Research on Psychological Interventions with Children, Adolescents and Their Families*. London: Routledge.

Carr, A. (2000b). *Family Therapy: Concepts, Process and Practice*. Chichester: Wiley.

Carr, A. (2000c). Chapter 1, Evidence based practice in counselling and psychotherapy. In A. Carr (ed.), *Clinical Psychology in Ireland, Volume 2: Empirical Studies of Problems and Treatment Processes in Adults* (pp. 1–52). Wales: Edwin Mellen Press.

Carr, A. (2001). *Abnormal Psychology*. London: Psychology Press.

Carr, A. (2002). *Prevention: What Works with Children and Adolescents? A Critical Review of Psychological Prevention Programmes for Children, Adolescents and their Families*. Hove: Brunner-Routledge.

Carr, A. and Wilde, G. (1988). Effects of actual and potential stressor control on physiological and self-reported stress responses. *Journal of Social and Clinical Psychology* 6 (3/4): 371–87.

Carter, B. and McGoldrick, M. (1989). *The Changing Family Lifecycle: A Framework for Family Therapy* (2nd edn). New York: Gardner Press.

Carver, C., Scheier, M. and Weintraub, J. (1989). Assessing coping strategies: a theoretically based approach. *Journal of Personality and Social Psychology* 56: 267–83.

Cassidy, J. and Shaver, P. (1999). *Handbook of Attachment*. New York: Guilford.

Cattell, R. (1990). Advances in Cattellian personality theory. In L. Pervin and O. John (eds), *Handbook of Personality: Theory and Research* (pp. 101–10). New York: Guilford.

Cecchin, G. (1987). Hypothesizing, circularity and neutrality revisited: an invitation to curiosity. *Family Process* 26: 405–13.

Chen, Z. and Siegler, R. (2000). Intellectual development in childhood. In R. Sternberg (ed.), *Handbook of Intelligence* (pp. 92–116). Cambridge: Cambridge University Press.

Cherniss, C. (2000). Social and emotional competence in the workplace. In R. Bar-On and J. Parker (eds), *The Handbook of Emotional Intelligence* (pp. 433–58). San Francisco, CA: Jossey-Bass.

Christophersen, E. and Mortweet, S. (2001). *Treatments that Work with Children: Empirically Supported Strategies for Managing Childhood Problems*. Washington, DC: APA.

Clark, L. and Watson, D. (1990). 'The General Temperament Survey'. Unpublished manuscript. University of Iowa, Iowa City, IA.

Clark, L. and Watson, D. (1999). Temperament. In L. Pervin and O. John (eds), *Handbook of Personality: Theory and Research* (pp. 399–423). New York: Guilford.

Clarkin, J. and Lenzenweger, M. (1996). *Major Theories of Personality Disorder*. New York: Guilford.

Clayton, V. and Birren, J. (1980). The development of wisdom across the lifespan: a reexamination of an ancient topic. In P. Baltes and J. Brim (eds), *Lifespan Development and Behaviour* (pp. 103–35). New York: Academic Press.

Cohen, D. and Volkmar, F. (1997). *Handbook of Autism and Pervasive Developmental Disorders* (2nd edn). New York: Wiley.

Colapinto, J. (1991). Structural family therapy. In A. Gurman and D. Kniskern (eds), *Handbook of Family Therapy. Volume II* (pp. 417–43). New York: Brunner/ Mazel.

Colgrove, M., Bloomfield, H. and McWilliams, P. (1991). *How to Survive the Loss of Love* (2nd edn) Los Angeles, CA: Prelude Press.

Collins, M. and Amabile, T. (1999). Motivation and creativity. In R. Sternberg, R. (ed.), *Handbook of Creativity* (pp. 297–312). Cambridge: Cambridge University Press.

Compton, W., Smith, M., Cornish, K. and Qualls, D. (1996). Factor structure of mental health measures. *Journal of Personality and Social Psychology* 76: 406–13.

Conte, H. and Apter, A. (1995). The Life Style Index: a self-report measure of ego defences. In H. Conte and R. Plutchik (eds), *Ego Defences: Theory and Measurement* (pp. 179–201). New York: Wiley.

Conte, H. and Plutchik, R. (1995). *Ego Defences: Theory and Measurement*. New York: Wiley.

Cooper, C. (1999). *Intelligence and Abilities*. London: Routledge.

Cooper, R. (1996/1997). *EQ Map*. San Francisco, CA: AIT and Essi Systems.

Coopersmith, S. (1981). *Self-esteem Inventories*. Palo Alto, CA: Consulting Psychologist Press.

Coop-Gordon, K., Baucom, D. and Snyder, D. (2000). The use of forgiveness in marital therapy. In M. McCullough, K. Pargament and C. Thoresen (eds), *Forgiveness: Theory, Research and Practice* (pp. 203–27). New York: Guilford.

Coppock, V. and Hopton, J. (2000). *Critical Perspectives on Mental Health*. London: Routledge.

Costa, P. and McCrae, R. (1992). *Revised NEO Personality Inventory (NEO-PI-R and NEO Five-Factor Inventory (NEO-FFI) Professional Manual*. Odessa, FL: Psychological Assessment Resources.

Covinton, M., Crutchfield, R., Davies, L. and Olton, R. (1974). *The Productive Thinking Program: A Course in Learning to Think*. Columbus, OH: Merrill.

Cowart, V. (1988). The Ritalin Controversy: what made this drug's opponents hyperactive. *Journal of the American Medical Association* 259: 2521–23.

Cramer, P. (1991). *The Development of Defence Mechanisms: Theory, Research, and Assessment*. New York: Springer-Verlag.

Cropley, A. (1992). *More Ways than One: Fostering Creativity*. Norwood, NY: Ablex.

Crowell, J., Fraley, R. and Shaver, P. (1999). Measurement of individual differences in adolescent and adult attachment. In J. Cassidy and P. Shaver (eds), *Handbook of Attachment: Theory, Research and Clinical Applications* (pp. 287–316). New York: Guilford.

Csikszentmihalyi, M. (1990). *Flow: The Psychology of Optimal Experience*. New York: Harper Row.

Csikszentmihalyi, M. (1993). *The Evolving Self*. New York: HarperCollins.

Csikszentmihalyi, M. (1996). *Creativity: Flow and the Psychology of Discovery and Invention*. New York: Harper Perennial.

Csikszentmihalyi, M. (1997). *Finding Flow: The Psychology of Engagement with Everyday Life*. New York: Basic Books.

Csikszentmihalyi, M. (1999). Implications of a systems perspective for the study of creativity. In R. Sternberg (ed.), *Handbook of Creativity* (pp. 313–35). Cambridge: Cambridge University Press.

Csikszentmihalyi, M. and Csikszentmihalyi, I. (1988). *Optimal Experience: Psychological Studies of Flow in Consciousness*. Cambridge: Cambridge University Press.

Cunningham, M. (1979). Weather, mood and helping behaviour: quasi-experiments with the sunshine Samaritans. *Journal of Personality and Social Psychology* 37: 1947–56.

D'Zurilla, T. and Nezu, A. (1999). *Problem Solving Therapy* (2nd edn). New York: Springer Verlag.

Dahlem, N., Zimet, G. and Walker, R. (1991). A multidimensional scale of perceived social support. *Journal of Clinical Psychology* 47: 756–61.

Dalsgaard, K. (2002) Values in Action Inventory of Strengths for Youth (VIA-Y). Cincinnati, OH: Values in Action Institute. For information, contact dahlsgaa@ CATTELL.psych.upenn.edu Department of Psychology, University of Pennsylvania, 3815 Walnut Street, Philadelphia, PA 19104 215-898-7173.

Damasio, A. (1994). *Descartes' Error*. New York: Grosset/Putnam.

Danner, D., Snowdon, D. and Friesen, W. (2001). Positive emotions early in life and the longevity: findings from the nun study. *Journal of Personality and Social Psychology* 80: 804–13.

Darling, N., and Steinberg, L. (1993). Parenting styles as context: an integrative model. *Psychological Bulletin* 113: 487–96.

Darwin, C. (1872/1998). *The Expression of Emotions in Man and Animals* (3rd edn). New York: Oxford University Press.

Davidson, J. and Downing, C. (2000). Contemporary models of intelligence. In R. Sternberg (ed.), *Handbook of Intelligence* (pp. 34–49). Cambridge: Cambridge University Press.

Davies, M., Stankov, L. and Roberts, R. (1998). Emotional intelligence: in search of an elusive construct. *Journal of Personality and Social Psychology* 75: 989–1015.

Davis, M., Eshelman, E. and McKay, M. (1995). *The Relaxation and Stress Workbook* (4th edn). Oakland, CA: New Harbinger.

De Bono, E. (1971). *Lateral Thinking for Management*. New York: McGraw-Hill.

De Bono, E. (1973). *CoRT Thinking*. Blandford, UK: Direct Educational Services.

De Bono, E. (1985). *Six Thinking Hats*. Boston: Little Brown.

De Bono, E. (1992). *Serious Creativity: Using the Poser of Lateral Thinking to Create New Ideas*. New York: Harper Collins.

Deci, R., Koestner, R. and Ryan, R. (1999). A meta-analytic review of experiments examining the effects of extrinsic rewards on intrinsic motivation. *Psychological Bulletin* 125: 627–68.

Deci, R. and Ryan, R. (1985). *Intrinsic Motivation and Self-determination in Human Behaviour*. New York: Plenum.

DeNeve, K. and Cooper, H. (1998). The happy personality: a meta-analysis of 137 personality traits and subjective well-being. *Psychological Bulletin* 124: 197–229.

Depue, R. (1996). A neurobiological framework for the structure of personality and emotion: implications for personality disorder. In J. Clarkin and M. Lenzenweger (eds), *Major Theories of Personality* (pp. 347–90). New York: Guilford.

Diener, E. (2000). Subjective well-being: the science of happiness and a proposal for a national index. *American Psychologist* 55: 34–43.

Diener, E., Emmons, R., Larsen, R. and Griffin, S. (1985). The Satisfaction with Life Scale. *Journal of Personality Assessment* 49: 71–5.

Diener, E. and Lucas, R. (1999). Personality and subjective well-being. In E. Kahneman, E. Diener and N. Schwartz (eds), *Well-being: The Foundations of Hedonic Psychology* (pp. 213–29). New York: Russell Sage Foundation.

Diener, F., Lucas, R. and Oishi, S. (2002) Subjective well-being. In C.R. Snyder and S. Lopez (eds), *Handbook of Positive Psychology* (pp. 63–73). New York: Oxford University Press.

Diener, E. and Seligman, M. (2002). Very happy people. *Psychological Science* 13: 81–4.

Diener, E., Suh, E., Lucas, R. and Smith, H. (1999). Subjective well-being: three decades of progress. *Psychological Bulletin* 125: 273–302.

Drugan, R. (2000). The neurochemistry of stress resilience and coping: a quest for nature's own antidote to illness. In J. Gillham (ed.) *The Science of Optimism and Hope* (pp. 57–71). Philadelphia, PA: Templeton Foundation Press.

Dunn, J. and McGuire, S. (1992). Sibling and peer relationships in childhood. *Journal of Child Psychology and Psychiatry* 33: 67–105.

Dykema, K., Bergbower, K., Doctora, J. and Peterson, C. (1996). An Attributional Style Questionnaire for general use. *Journal of Psychoeducational Assessment* 14: 100–08.

Eckler, J. (1993). *Step by Step-Parenting: A Guide to Successful Living with a Blended Family* (2nd edn). Whitehall, VA: Betterway Publications.

Eibl-Eibesfeldt, I. (1975). *Ethology: The Science of Behaviour*. New York: Holt, Rinehart and Winston.

Eiser, C. and Morse, R. (2001). The measurement of quality of life in children: past and future perspectives. *Journal of Developmental and Behavioral Pediatrics* 22: 248–56. C.Eiser@sheffield.ac.uk

Ellenberger, H. (1970). *The Discovery of the Unconscious*. New York: Basic Books.

Ellis, A. and Harper, R. (1975). *A New Guide to Rational Living*. North Hollywood, CA: Wiltshire.

Emmons, R. (1997). Motives and life goals. In R. Hogan, J. Johnson and S. Briggs (eds), *Handbook of Personality Psychology* (pp. 485–512). New York: Academic Press.

Emmons, R. and Shelton, C. (2002). Gratitude and the science of positive psychology. In C.R. Snyder and S. Lopez (eds), *Handbook of Positive Psychology* (pp. 459–84). New York: Oxford University Press.

Endler, N. and Parker, J. (1990). *Coping Inventory for Stressful Situations (CISS)*. Toronto: Multi Health Systems.

Epstein, N., Baldwin, L. and Bishop, D. (1983). The McMaster Family Assessment Device. *Journal of Marital and Family Therapy* 9: 171–80.

Epstein, S. (1998). *Constructive Thinking: The Key to Emotional Intelligence*. Westport, CT: Praeger.

Erikson, E. (1959) *Identity and the Life Cycle*. New York: International University Press.

Erikson, E. (1968). *Identity, Youth and Crisis*. New York: Norton.

Erikson, E., Erikson, J. and Kivnick, H. (1986). *Vital Involvement in Old Age*. New York: Norton.

Exline, J. and Baumeister, R. (2000). Expression, forgiveness and repentance; benefits and barriers. In M. McCullough, K. Pargament and C. Thoresen (eds), *Forgiveness: Theory, Research and Practice* (pp. 133–55). New York: Guilford.

Eysenck, H. (1967). *The Biological Basis for Personality*. Baltimore, MD: University Park Press.

Eysenck, H. (1979). The conditioning model of neurosis. *The Behavioural and Brain Sciences* 2: 155–99.

Eysenck, H. (1990). Biological dimensions of personality. In L. Pervin and O. John (eds), *Handbook of Personality: Theory and Research* (pp. 244–76). New York: Guilford.

Eysenck, H. and Eysenck, M. (1985). *Personality and Individual Differences: A Natural Science Approach*. New York: Plenum Press.

Eysenck, H. and Eysenck, S. (1975). *Manual of the Eysenck Personality Questionnaire*. San Diego, CA: Educational and Industrial Testing service.

Falloon, I., Laporta, M., Fadden, G. and Graham-Hole, V. (1993). *Managing Stress in Families*. London: Routledge.

Fava, G., Fafenelli, C., Cazzaro, M., Conti, S. and Grandi, S. (1998). Well-being therapy: a novel psychotherapeutic approach for residual symptoms of affective disorders. *Psychological Medicine* 28: 475 80.

Feeney, J. and Noller, P. (1996). *Adult Attachment*. Thousand Oaks, CA: Sage.

Feist, G. (1999). The influence of personality on artistic and scientific creativity. In R. Sternberg (ed.), *Handbook of Creativity* (pp. 273–96). Cambridge: Cambridge University Press.

Ferguson, E. and Cox, T. (1997). The functional dimensions of coping scale: theory, reliability and validity. *British Journal of Health Psychology* 2: 109–29.

Fincham, F. (2000) Optimism and the family. In J. Gillham (ed.), *The Science of Optimism and Hope* (pp. 271–98). Philadelphia, PA: Templeton Foundation Press.

Finchman, F.D. and Bradbury, T.N. (1992). Assessing Attributions in Marriage: the Relationship Attribution Measure. *Journal of Personality and Social Psychology* 62 (3): 457–68.

Fishman, D. and Franks, C. (1997). The conceptual evolution of behaviour therapy. In P. Watchel and S. Messer (eds), *Theories of Psychotherapy: Origins and Evolution* (pp. 131–80). Washington, DC: APA.

Fitts, W. (1988). *Tennessee Self-Concept Scale*. Los Angeles, CA: Western Psychological Services.

Fitzpatrick, M. (1988). *Between Husbands and Wives: Communication in Marriage*. Newbury Park, CA: Sage.

Foa, E. and Wilson, R. (1991). *STOP Obsessing: How to Overcome your Obsessions and Compulsions*. New York: Bantam.

Folkman, S. and Lazarus, R. (1988). *Manual for the Ways of Coping Questionnaire*. Palo Alto, CA: Consulting Psychologists Press.

Fonagy, P., Target, M., Cottrell, D., Phillips, J. and Kurtz, A. (2002). *What Works for Whom. A Critical Review of Treatments for Children and Adolescents*. New York: Guilford.

Fordyce, M. (1977) Development of a programme to increase personal happiness. *Journal of Counseling Psychology* 24: 511–20.

Fordyce, M. (1983). A programme to increase personal happiness: further studies. *Journal of Counseling Psychology* 30: 483–98.

Fordyce, M. (1988). A review of research on the happiness measure: a sixty second index of happiness and mental health. *Social Indicators Research* 20: 355–81.

Forehand, R. and Long, N. (1996). *Parenting the Strong-Willed Child: The Clinically Proven Five Week Programme for Parents of Two to Six Year Olds*. Chicago: Contemporary Books.

Frederick, S. and Lowenstein, G. (1999) Hedonic adaptation. In E. Kahneman, E. Diener and N. Schwartz (eds), *Well-being: The Foundations of Hedonic Psychology* (pp. 302–29). New York: Russell Sage Foundation.

Fredrickson, B. (2002). Positive emotions. In C.R. Snyder and S. Lopez (eds), *Handbook of Positive Psychology* (pp. 120–34). New York: Oxford University Press.

Freedman, J. and Combs, G. (1996). *Narrative Therapy: The Social Construction of Preferred Realities*. New York: Norton.

Freud, A. (1936). *The Ego and the Mechanisms of Defence*. New York: International University Press.

Freud, S. (1896). Further remarks on the neuropsychoses of defence. In J. Strachey (ed. and trans., 1955). *The Standard Edition of the Complete Works of Sigmund Freud* (vol. 3). London: Hogarth.

Freud, S. (1908). The relation of the poet to day dreaming. In *Collected Papers* (vol. 3, pp. 173–83). London: Hogarth.

Freud, S. (1928). *The Future of an Illusion*. London: Hogarth.

Friedman, E. (1991). Bowen theory and therapy. In A. Gurman and D. Kniskern (eds), *Handbook of Family Therapy. Volume II* (pp. 134–70). New York: Brunner/Mazel.

Friedman, H., Tucker, J., Schwartz, J., Tomlinson-Keasey, C., Martin, L., Wingard, D. and Criqui, M. (1995). Psychosocial and behavioural predictors of longevity: the aging and death of the termites. *American Psychologist* 50: 69–78.

Friedman, M., Thoresen, C., Gill, J. *et al.* (1986). Alteration of Type A behaviour and its effect on cardiac recurrences, in post-myocardial infarction patients: summary results of the Recurrent Coronary Prevention Project. *American Heart Journal* 112: 653–65.

Frisch, M.B. (1994). *Manual and Treatment Guide for the Quality of Life Inventory.* Minneapolis, MN: National Computer Systems.

Galton, F. (1869). *Hereditary Genius.* London: Macmillan.

Gardner, H. (1983/1993). *Frames of Mind: Theory of Multiple Intelligences.* New York: Basic Books.

Gardner, H. (1998). Are there additonal intelligences? The case for natural, spiritual and existential intelligence. In J. Kane (ed.), *Education, Information and Transformation* (pp. 111–32). Englewood Cliffs, NJ: Prentice Hall.

Gardner, R. (1985). *The Boys and Girls Book about Divorce.* New York: Bantam.

Garfield, S. (1994). Research on client variables in psychotherapy. In A. Bergin and S. Garfield (eds), *Handbook of Psychotherapy and Behaviour Change* (pp. 190–228). New York: Wiley.

George, G., Kaplan, N. and Main, M. (1984). Adult Attachment Interview. Unpublished manuscript. University of California at Berkeley.

Gergen, K. (1994). *Realities and Relationships.* Cambridge, MA: Harvard University Press.

Gill, T. and Feinstein, A. (1994). A critical appraisal of the quality of quality-of-life measurements. *Journal of the American Medical Association* 272: 619–26.

Gillham, J. (2000) *The Science of Optimism and Hope.* Philadelphia, PA: Templeton Foundation Press.

Gillham, J., Reivich, K., Jaycox, L. and Seligman, M. (1995). Prevention of depressive symptoms in school children: two year follow-up. *Psychological Science* 6: 343–51.

Goldberg, L. (1992). The development of markers for the Big Five factor structure. *Psychological Assessment* 4: 26–42.

Goleman, D. (1995). *Emotional Intelligence. Why It Can Matter More than IQ.* New York: Bantam.

Goleman, D. (1998). *Working with Emotional Intelligence.* New York: Bantam.

Gordon, W. (1981). *The New Art of the Possible: The Basic Course in Synectics.* Cambridge, MA: Porpoise Books.

Gottman, J. (1993). The roles of conflict engagement, escalation and avoidance in marital interaction: a longitudinal view of five types of couples. *Journal of Consulting and Clinical Psychology* 61: 6–15.

Gottman, J. and Silver, N. (1999). *The Seven Principles for Making Marriage Work.* London: Weidenfeld and Nicolson.

Gottschalk, L. and Lolas, F. (1992). The measurement of quality of life through the content analysis of verbal behavior. *Psychotherapy and Psychosomatics* 58(2): 69–78. http://www.gb-software.com/develop.htm

Gould, S. (1981). *Transformations: Growth and Change in Adult Life.* New York: Simon & Schuster.

Gray, J. (1987). *The Psychology of Fear and Stress* (2nd edn). Cambridge: Cambridge University Press.

Graziano, W. and Eisenberg, N. (1997). Agreeableness: a dimension of personality. In R. Hogan, J. Johnson and S. Briggs (eds), *Handbook of Personality Psychology* (pp. 795–824). New York: Academic Press.

Greenberg, L. and Rice, L. (1997). Humanistic approaches to psychotherapy. In P. Watchel and S. Messer (eds), *Theories of Psychotherapy: Origins and Evolution* (pp. 97–129). Washington, DC: APA.

Greenberger, D. and Padesky, C. (1995). *Mind Over Mood: A Cognitive Therapy Treatment Manual for Clients.* New York: Guilford.

Greening, T. (2001). *Journal of Humanistic Psychology: Special Issue on Positive Psychology, Volume 41 Number 1.* Thousand Oaks, CA: Sage.

Grigorenco, E. (2000). Heritability and intelligence. In R. Sternberg (ed.), *Handbook of Intelligence* (pp. 53–91). Cambridge: Cambridge University Press.

Gross, J. (1999). Emotion and emotion regulation. In L. Pervin and O. John (eds), *Handbook of Personality* (2nd edn, pp. 525–52). New York: Guilford.

Gruber, H. and Wallace, D. (1999). The case study method and evolving systems approach for understanding unique creative people at work. In R. Sternberg (ed.), *Handbook of Creativity* (pp. 93–116). Cambridge: Cambridge University Press.

Guilford, J. (1950). Creativity. *American Psychologist* 5: 444–54.

Guilford, J. (1967). *The Nature of Human Intelligence.* Chicago: University of Chicago Press.

Gur, R. and Sackeim, H. (1979). Self deception: a concept in search of a phenomenon. *Journal of Personality and Social Psychology* 37: 147–69.

Guralnick, M. (1997). *The Effectiveness of Early Intervention.* Baltimore: Brookes.

Haggerty, R., Sherrod, L., Garmezy, N. and Rutter, M. (1994). *Stress, Risk and Resilience in Children and Adolescents: Processes, Mechanisms and Interventions.* Cambridge: Cambridge University Press.

Hankin, B., Abramson, L., Moffitt, T., Silva, P. and McGee, R. (1998). Development of depression from preadolescence to young adulthood: emerging gender differences in a 10 year longitudinal study. *Journal of Abnormal Psychology* 107: 128–40.

Harker, L. and Keltner, D. (2001). Expressions of positve emotion in women's college yearbook pictures and their relationship to personality and life outcomes across adulthood. *Journal of Personality and Social Psychology* 80: 112–24.

Harvey, J., Pauwels, B. and Zickmund, S. (2002). Relationship connection: the role of minding in the enhancement of closeness. In C.R. Snyder and S. Lopez (eds), *Handbook of Positive Psychology* (pp. 423–34). New York: Oxford University Press.

Hayes, J. (1989). *The Complete Problem Solver* (2nd edn). Hillsdale, NJ: Erlbaum.

Headey, B. and Wearing, A. (1991). Subjective well-being: a stocks and flows framework. In F. Strack, M. Argyle and N. Schwartz (eds), *Subjective well-being: An Interdisciplinary Perspective* (pp. 49–73). New York: Pergamon.

Henggeler, S., Schoenwald, S., Bordin, C., Rowland, M. and Cunningham, P. (1998). *Multisystemic Treatment of Antisocial Behaviour in Children and Adolescents.* New York: Guilford.

Heppner, P. (1988). *The Problem Solving Inventory.* Palo Alto, CA: Consulting Psychologists Press.

Heppner, P. and Goug-Gwi, L. (2002). Problem-solving appraisal and psychological adjustment. In C.R. Snyder and S. Lopez (eds), *Handbook of Positive Psychology* (pp. 288–98). New York: Oxford University Press.

Herrnstein, R. and Murray, C. (1994). *The Bell Curve: Intelligence and Class in American Life*. New York: Free Press.

Hetherington, M. (1989). Coping with family transitions: winners, losers and survivors. *Child Development* 60: 1–14.

Hetherington, M. and Stanley-Hagan, M. (1999). The adjustment of children with divorced parents: a risk and resiliency perspective. *Journal of Child Psychology and Psychiatry* 40: 129–40.

Hill, P. (1993). Recent advances in selected aspects of adolescent development. *Journal of Child Psychology and Psychiatry* 34: 69–99.

Hills, P. and Argyle, M. (1998). Musical and religious experiences and their relationship to happiness. *Personality and Individual Difference* 25: 91–102.

Hinshaw, S. (1994). *Attention Deficits and Hyperactivity in Children*. Thousand Oaks: Sage.

Hogan, P., Johnson, J. and Briggs, S. (1997). *Handbook of Personality Psychology*. New York: Academic Press.

Holahan, C., Moos, R. and Schaefer, J. (1996). Coping, stress, resistance, and growth: conceptualising adaptive functioning. In M. Zeidner and N. Endler (eds), *Handbook of Coping. Theory, Research, Applications* (pp. 24–43). New York: Wiley.

Holmes, J. (1999). Brief psychodynamic psychotherapy. In A. Lee (ed.), *Affective and Non-psychotic Disorders: Recent Topics from Advances in Psychiatric Treatment. Volume 2* (pp. 84–9). London: Gaskell.

Holmes, J. and Rempel, J. (1989). Trust in close relationships. In C. Hendrick (ed.), *Close Relationships* (pp. 187–220). Newbury Park, CA: Sage.

Horowitz, L., Alden, L., Wiggins, J. and Pincus, A. (2000). *Inventory of Interpersonal Problems*. San Antonio, TX: Psychological Corporation. (Available at www.psychcorp.com)

Howe, M. (1999). Prodigies and creativity. In R. Sternberg (ed.), Handbook of Creativity (pp. 431–48). New York: Cambridge University Press.

Hubble, M., Duncan, B. and Miller, S. (1999). *The Heart and Soul of Change: What Works in Therapy*. Washington, DC: American Psychological Association.

Hughes, C., Hwang, B., Kim, J. and Eisenman, L. (1995). Quality of life in applied research: a review and analysis of empirical measures. *American Journal on Mental Retardation* 99: 623–41.

Hummer, R., Rogers, G., Nam, C. and Ellison, C. (1999). Religious involvement and US adult mortality. *Demography* 36: 273–85.

Ihilevich, D. and Gleser, G. (1986). *Defence in Psychotherapy. Their Clinical Application of the Defence Mechanisms Inventory*. Odessa, FL: Psychological Assessment Resources. www.parinc.com

Ingham, C. (1993). *Panic Attacks: What They Are, Why They Happen, and What You Can Do about Them*. London: Thorsens (Harper Collins).

Isaksen, S. and Treffinger, D. (1985). *Creative Problem Solving: The Basic Course*. Buffalo, NY: Bearly.

Isen, A. (2000). Positive affect and decision making. In M. Lewis and J. Haviland Jones (eds), *Handbook of Emotions* (2nd edn, pp. 417–36). New York: Guilford.

Izard, C., Libero, D., Putnam, P. and Hayes, O. (1993). Stability of emotion experiences and their relations to states of personality. *Journal of Personality and Social Psychology* 64: 847–60.

Jacobson, N. and Gurman, A. (1995). *Clinical Handbook of Couple Therapy*. New York: Guilford.

James, D.E., Schumm, W.R., Kennedy, C.E., Grigsby, C.C., Shectman, K.L. and Nichols, C.W. (1985). Characteristics of the Kansas Parental Satisfaction Scale among two samples of married parents. *Psychological Reports* 57: 163–9.

James, J. and Cherry, F. (1988). *The Grief Recovery Handbook. A Step-by-Step Program for Moving beyond Loss*. New York: Harper Row.

James, W. (1890). *The Principles of Psychology*. New York: Holt.

Jaycox, L., Reivich, K., Gillham, J. and Seligman, M. (1994). Prevention of depressive symptoms in school children. *Behaviour research and therapy* 32: 374–60.

Jemmott, J. (1987). Social motives and susceptibility to disease: stalking individual differences in health risks. *Journal of Personality* 55: 267–98.

John, O. and Srivastava, S. (1999). The big five trait taxonomy: history, measurement and theoretical perspectives. In L. Pervin and O. John (eds), *Handbook of Personality* (2nd edn, pp. 102–38). New York: Guilford.

Johnson, N. and Gold, S. (1995). Defence Mechanisms Profile: a sentence completion test. In H. Conte and R. Plutchik (eds), *Ego Defences: Theory and Measurement* (pp. 247–62). New York: Wiley.

Johnson, S. and Greenberg, L. (1995). The emotionally focused approach to problems in adult attachment. In N. Jacobson and A. Gurman (eds), *Clinical Handbook of Couple Therapy* (pp. 121–42). New York: Guilford.

Johnstone, L. (2000). *Users and Abusers of Psychiatry: A Critical Look at Psychiatric Practice* (2nd edn). London: Routledge.

Jones, W., Couch, L. and Scott, S. (1997). Trust and betrayal: the psychology of getting along and getting ahead. In R. Hogan, J. Johnson and S. Briggs (eds), *Handbook of Personality Psychology* (pp. 466–85). New York: Academic Press.

Joseph, S. and Lewis, C. (1998). The Depression-Happiness Scale: reliability and validity of a bipolar self-report scale. *Journal of Clinical Psychology* 54: 537–44.

Kabat Zinn, J. (1990). *Full Catastrophe Living: Using the Wisdom of Your Body and Mind to Face Stress, Pain and Illness*. New York: Delacorte Press.

Kabat Zinn, J. (1994). *Wherever You Go, There You Are: Mindfulness Meditation in Everyday Life*. New York: Hyperion.

Kagan, J. and Lamb, S. (1987). *The Emergence of Moral Concepts in Young Children*. Chicago: University of Chicago Press.

Kahneman, D., Diener, E. and Schwartz, N. (1999). *Well-being: The Foundations of Hedonic Psychology*. New York: Russell Sage Foundation.

Kalter, N. (1990). *Growing up with Divorce*. New York: Free Press.

Kamen-Siegel, L., Rodin, J., Seligman, M. and Dwyer, C. (1991). Explanatory style and cell mediated immunity. *Health Psychology* 10: 229–35.

Kane, J. (1995). Current problems with the pharmacotherapy of schizophrenia. *Clinical Neuropharmacology* 18 (Supplement): S154–S180.

Katz, J., Ritvo, P., Irivine, M. and Jackson, M. (1996). Coping with chronic pain. In M. Zeidner and N. Endler (eds), *Handbook of Coping. Theory, Research, Applications* (pp. 252–78). New York: Wiley.

Kazdin, A. (1995). *Conduct Disorders in Childhood and Adolescence*. (2nd edn). Thousand Oaks, CA: Sage.

Keane, T. (1998). Psychological and behavioural treatments for post-traumatic stress disorder. In P. Nathan and J. Gorman (eds), *A Guide to Treatments that Work* (pp. 398–407). New York: Oxford University Press.

Kelly, G. (1955). *The Psychology of Personal Constructs.* Vols 1 and 2. New York: Norton.

Kerr, J. (1997). *Motivation and Emotion in Sport: Reversal Theory.* Hove, England: Psychology Press.

Kerr, J. (1999). *Experiencing Sport: Reversal Theory.* Chichester, England: Wiley.

Keyes, C.L. (1998). Social well-being. *Social Psychology Quarterly* 61: 121–40.

Keyes, C. and Haidt, J. (2001). *Flourishing: The Positive Person and the Good Life.* Washington, DC: APA.

Keyes, C., Shmotkin, D. and Ryff, C. (2000). Optimizing well-being: the empirical encounter of two traditions. *Journal of Personality and Social Psychology* 82(6): 1007–22.

Kiesler, D. (1996). *Contemporary Interpersonal Theory and Research.* New York: Wiley.

Kihlstrom, J. (1999). The psychological unconscious. In L. Pervin and O. John (eds), *Handbook of Personality: Theory and Research* (pp. 424–42). New York: Guilford.

Kirton, M. (1981). A reanalysis of two scales of tolerance to ambiguity. *Journal of Personality Assessment* 45: 407–14.

Klinger, E. (1987). The interview questionnaire technique: reliability and validity of a mixed ideographic-nomothetic measure of motivation. In J. Butcher and C. Spielberger (eds), *Advances in Personality Assessment* (vol. 6, pp. 31–48). Hillsdale, NJ: Erlbaum.

Klinger, E. (1989). Emotional mediation of motivational influences on cognitive processes. In F. Halisch and J. van den Bercken (eds), *International Perspectives on Achievement and Task Motivation* (pp. 317–26). Nisse, Netherlands: Swets and Zeitlinger.

Kobasa, S. (1979). Stressful life events, personality and health: an inquiry into hardiness. *Journal of Personality and Social Psychology* 37: 1–11.

Kohlberg, L. (1976). Moral stages and moralization: the cognitive-developmental approach. In T. Lickona (ed.), *Moral Development and Behaviour: Theory, Research and Social Issues* (pp. 31–53). New York: Holt, Rinehart and Winston.

Kraepelin, E. (1896). *Psychiatrie.* (5th edn). Leipzig: Barth.

Krohne, H. (1996). Individual differences in coping. In M. Zeidner and N. Endler (eds), *Handbook of Coping: Theory, Research, Applications* (pp. 381–409). New York: Wiley.

Kutchins, H. and Kirk, S. (1997). *Making Us Crazy: DSM: The Psychiatric Bible and the Creation of Mental Disorders.* New York: Free Press.

Laing, R.D. (1961). *Self and Others.* Harmondsworth: Penguin.

Laing, R.D. (1965). *The Divided Self.* Harmondsworth: Penguin.

Lambert, M. (1992). Psychotherapy outcome research: implications for integrative and eclectic therapists. In J. Norcross and M. Goldfried (eds), *Handbook of Psychotherapy Integration* (pp. 94–129). New York: Basic Books.

Lambert, M. and Barley, D. (2002). Research summary on the therapeutic relationship and psychotherapy outcome. In J. Norcross (ed.), *Psychotherapy Relationships that Work* (pp. 17–32). New York: Oxford University Press.

Lambert, M. and Bergin, A. (1994). The effectiveness of psychotherapy. In A. Bergin and S. Garfield (eds), *Handbook of Psychotherapy and Behaviour Change* (pp. 143–90). New York: Wiley.

Lane, R. (2000). Levels of emotional awareness. In R. Bar-On and J. Parker (eds), *The Handbook of Emotional Intelligence* (pp. 171–91). San Francisco, CA: Jossey-Bass.

Lane, R., Quinlan, D., Schwartz, G., Walker, P. and Seitlin, S. (1990). Levels of Emotional Awareness Scale: a cognitive developmental measure of emotion. *Journal of Personality Assessment* 55: 124–34.

Lange, G. and Carr, A. (2002). Chapter 3. Prevention of cognitive delays in socially disadvantaged children. In A. Carr (ed.), *Prevention: What Works with Children and Adolescents? A Critical Review of Psychological Prevention Programmes for Children, Adolescents and their Families*. London: Routledge.

Langer, E. (1975). The illusion of control. *Journal of Personality and Social Psychology* 32: 311–28.

Larsen, D., Attkinson, C., Hargreaves, W. and Nguyen, T. (1979). Assessment of client/patient satisfaction: development of a general scale. *Evaluation and Programme Planning* 2: 197–207.

Larsen, R. and Deiner, E. (1992). Promises and problems with the circumplex model of emotion. In M. Clark (ed.), *Emotion: Review of Personality and Social Psychology* (vol. 13, pp. 25–59). Newbury Park, CA: Sage.

Leach, P. (1997). *Your Baby and Child from Birth to Age Five* (revised edn). New York: Knopf.

LeDoux, J. (1996). *The Emotional Brain: The Mysterious Underpinnings of Emotional Life*. New York: Simon Schuster.

Lefcourt, H. (1982). *Locus of Control* (2nd edn). Hillsdale, NJ: Erlbaum.

Lefcourt, H. (2001). *Humour: The Psychology of Living Buoyantly*. New York: Kluwer/Plenum.

Lefcourt, H. (2002). Humour. In C.R. Snyder and S. Lopez (eds), *Handbook of Positive Psychology* (pp. 619–31). New York: Oxford University Press.

Lehman, A. (1999). A review of instruments for measuring quality-of-life outcomes in mental health. In N. Miller and K. Magruder (eds), *Cost-effectiveness of Psychotherapy: A Guide for Practitioners, Researchers, and Policymakers* (pp. 174–81). New York: Oxford University Press.

Levenson, H. (1973). Multidimensional locus of control in psychiatric patients. *Journal of Consulting and Clinical Psychology* 41: 397–404. (Contains a multidimensional locus of control scale.)

Levine, M. (2000). *The Positive Psychology of Buddhism and Yoga*. Mahwah, NJ: Erlbaum.

Levinson, D. (1986). *Seasons of a Man's Life*. New York: Ballantine.

Lewinsohn, P. and Gotlib, I. (1995). Behavioural theory and treatment of depression. In E. Becker and W. Leber (eds), *Handbook of Depression* (pp. 352–75). New York: Guilford.

Lewinsohn, P., Munoz, R., Youngren, M. and Zeiss, A. (1996). *Control Your Depression*. Englewood Cliffs, NJ: Prentice Hall.

Lichter, S., Haye, K. and Kammann, R. (1980). Increasing happiness through cognitive training, *New Zealand Psychologist* 9: 57–64.

Liddle, P. (2001). *Disordered Mind and Brain*. London: Gaskell.

Little, B. (1999). Personality and motivation: personal action and the conative evolution. In L. Pervin and O. John (eds), *Handbook of Personality* (2nd edn, pp. 501–24). New York: Guilford.

Lock, T. (1999). Advances in the practice of electro-convulsive therapy. In A. Lee (ed.), *Affective and Non-psychotic Disorders. Recent Topics from Advances in Psychiatric Treatment*. vol. 2 (pp. 66–75). London: Gaskell.

Lopez, S., Ciarlelli, R., Coffman, L., Stone, M. and Wyatt, L. (2000). Diagnosis for strength: on measuring hope building blocks. In C.R. Snyder (ed.), *Handbook of Hope* (pp. 57–88). Orlando, FL: Academic Press.

Luborsky, L., Singer, B. and Luborsky, L. (1975). Comparative studies of psychotherapies: is it true that 'Everybody has won and so all must have prizes'. *Archives of General Psychiatry* 32: 995–1008.

Luthar, S., Doernaberger, C. and Ziegler, E. (1993). Resilience is not a unidimensional construct: insights from a prospective study on inner city adolescents. *Development and Psychopathology* 5: 703–17.

Lykken, D. (1999). *Happiness: The Nature and Nurture of Joy and Contentment*. New York: St Martin's Press.

Macmillan, M. (1986). A wonderful journey through skull and brains: the travels of Mr Gage's tamping iron. *Brain and Cognition* 5: 67–107.

Madanes, C. (1991). Strategic Family Therapy. In A. Gurman and D. Kniskern (eds), *Handbook of Family Therapy* (vol. 2, pp. 396–416). New York: Brunner/Mazel.

Madders, J. (1997). *The Stress and Relaxation Handbook: A Practical Guide to Self-Help Techniques*. London: Vermillion.

Maddux, J. (2002). Stopping the 'madness': positive psychology and the deconstruction of the illness ideology of the DSM. In C.R. Snyder and S. Lopez (eds), *Handbook of Positive Psychology* (pp. 13–25). New York: Oxford University Press.

Maddux, J. and Mundell, C. (1999). Disorders of personality: diseases or individual differences. In V. Derlega, B. Winstead and W. Jones (eds), *Personality: Contemporary Theory and Research* (pp. 541–71). Chicago: Nelson-Hall.

Mahoney, M. (1991). *Human Change Processes: The Scientific Foundations of Psychotherapy*. New York: Basic Books.

Main, M. and Goldwyn, R. (1994). The Adult Attachment Rating and Classification System: Manual in Draft (Version 6.0). Unpublished manuscript, University of California at Berkeley.

Malcolm, W. and Greenberg, L. (2000). Forgiveness as a process of change in individual psychotherapy. In M. McCullough, K. Pargament and C. Thoresen (eds), *Forgiveness: Theory, Research and Practice* (pp. 179–202). New York: Guilford.

Malik, N. and Furman, W. (1993). Practitioner review: problem in children's peer relations: What can the clinician do? *Journal of Child Psychology and Psychiatry* 34: 1303–26.

Markman, H., Stanley, S. and Blumberg, S. (1994). *Fighting for Your Marriage*. San Francisco, CA: Jossey-Bass.

Marlatt, G. and Gordon, J. (1985). *Relapse Prevention*. New York: Guilford.

Martindale, C. (1999). Biological bases of creativity. In R. Sternberg (ed.), *Handbook of Creativity* (pp. 137–52). Cambridge: Cambridge University Press.

Maruuta, T., Colligan, R., Malinchoc, M. and Offord, K. (2000). Optimists vs pessimists: survival rate among medical patients over a 30 year period. *Mayo Clinic Proceedings* 75: 140–3.

Maslow, A. (1970). *Towards a Psychology of Being* (2nd edn). Princeton, NJ: Van Nostrand.

Masson. J. (1984). *Freud's Suppression of Seduction Theory*. New York: Farrar Strauss and University Press.

Masten, A. and Coatsworth, J. (1998). The development of competence in favorable and unfavorable environments: lessons from research on successful children. *American Psychologist* 53: 205–20.

Matlin, M. and Stang, D. (1978). *The Pollyanna Principle*. Cambridge, MA: Schenkman.

Mayer, J., Caruso, D. and Salovey P. (2000). Selecting a measure of emotional intelligence: the case for ability scales. In R. Bar-On and J. Parker (eds), *The Handbook of Emotional Intelligence* (pp. 320–42). San Francisco, CA: Jossey-Bass.

Mayer, J., DiPaola, M. and Salovey, P. (1990). Perceiving affective content in ambiguous visual stimuli: a component of emotional intelligence. *Journal of Personality Assessment* 54: 772–81.

Mayer, J., Salovey, P. and Caruso, D. (1997). *The Emotional IQ Test (CD-Rom)*. Needham, MA: Virtual Knowledge.

Mayer, J., Salovey, P. and Caruso, D. (1999). *Mayer, Salovey and Caruso Emotional Intelligence Test Item Booklet (Research Version 1.1)*. Toronto: Multi-Health Systems.

Mayer, J., Salovey, P. and Caruso, D. (2000a). Emotional intelligence as zeitgeist, as personality and as a mental ability. In R. Bar-On and J. Parker (eds), *The Handbook of Emotional Intelligence* (pp. 92–117). San Francisco, CA: Jossey-Bass.

Mayer, J., Salovey, P. and Caruso, D. (2000b). Models of emotional intelligence. In R. Sternberg (ed.), *Handbook of Intelligence* (pp. 396–423). Cambridge: Cambridge University Press.

McAdams, D. and de St Aubin, E. (1998). *Generativity and Adult Development*. Washington, DC: American Psychological Association.

McCallum, M. and Piper, W. (1997). *Psychological Mindedness: A Contemporary Understanding*. MahWah, NJ: Erlbaum.

McCallum, M. and Piper, W. (2000). Psychological mindedness and emotional intelligence. In R. Bar-On and J. Parker (eds), *The Handbook of Emotional Intelligence* (pp. 118–35). San Francisco, CA: Jossey-Bass.

McClelland, D. (1985). *Human Motivation*. Glenview, Il.: Scott, Foresman.

McClelland, D., Koestner, R. and Weinberger, J. (1989) How do self-attributed and implicit motives differ? *Psychological Review* 96: 690–702.

McCrae, R. (2000). Emotional intelligence from the perspective of the Five Factor Model. In R. Bar On and J. Parker (eds), *The Handbook of Emotional Intelligence* (pp. 263–77). San Francisco, CA: Jossey-Bass.

McCrae, R. and Costa, P. (1999). A five factor theory of personality. In L. Pervin and O. John (eds), *Handbook of Personality* (2nd edn, pp. 139–53). New York: Guilford.

McCrae, R., Costa, P., Lima, M., Simeos, A., Ostendorf, F., Angleitner, A., Mauri, I., Bratko, D., Caprara, G., Barbaranelli, C., Chae, J. and Piedmont, R. (1999). Age differences in personality across the adult lifespan: parallels in five cultures. *Developmental Psychology* 35: 466–77.

McCullough, M., Emmons, R. and Tsang, J. (2002). The grateful dispositons: a conceptual and empirical topography. *Journal of Personality and Social Psychology* 82: 112–27.

McCullough, M., Hoyt, W. and Rachel, K. (2000). What we know (and need to know) about assessing forgiveness constructs. In M. McCullough, K. Pargament and C. Thoresen (eds), *Forgiveness: Theory, Research and Practice* (pp. 65–8). New York: Guilford.

McCullough, M., Kilpatrick, S., Emmons, R. and Larson, D. (2001). Gratitude as moral affect. *Psychological Bulletin* 127: 249–266.

McCullough, M., Pargament, K. and C. Thoresen, C. (2000). *Forgiveness: Theory, Research and Practice*. New York: Guilford.

McCullough, M. and Witvliet, C. (2002). The psychology of forgiveness. In C.R. Snyder and S. Lopez (eds), *Handbook of Positive Psychology* (pp. 446–58). New York: Oxford University Press.

McFarlane, W. (1991). Family psychoeducational treatment. In A. Gurman and D. Kniskern (eds), *Handbook of Family Therapy. Volume II* (pp. 363–95). New York: Brunner/Mazel.

McGurk, H., Caplan, M., Hennessy, E. and Moss, P. (1993). Controversy, theory and social context in contemporary day care research. *Journal of Child Psychology and Psychiatry* 34: 3–23.

McKay, M., Davis, M. and Fanning, P. (1997). *How to Communicate: The Ultimate Guide to Improving Your Personal and Professional Relationships*. New York: Fine.

McNair, D., Lorr, M. and Doppleman, L. (1971). *Manual for the Profile of Mood States*. San Diego, CA: Educational and Industrial Testing Service.

Messer, S. and Warren, C. (1995). *Models of Brief Psychodynamic Therapy*. New York: Guilford Press.

Michalos, A. (1985). Multiple discrepancies theory (MDT). *Social Indicators Research* 16: 347–413.

Miller, I., Kabacoff, R., Bishop, D., Epstein, N. and Keitner, G. (1994). The development of the McMaster Clinical Rating Scale. *Family Process* 33: 53–69.

Miller, I., Ryan, C., Keitner, G., Bishop, D. and Epstein, N. (2000). The McMaster approach to families: theory, assessment, treatment and research. *Journal of Family Therapy* 22: 168–89.

Miller, N., Luborsky, J., Barber, J. and Docherty, J. (1993). *Psychodynamic Treatment Research*. New York: Basic Books.

Miller, W. (1985). Motivation for treatment: a review with special emphasis on alcoholism. *Psychological Bulletin* 98: 84–107.

Moos, R. (1993a). *Coping Responses Inventory: Adolescent Form Manual*. Odessa, FL: Psychological Assessment Resources.

Moos, R. (1993b). *Coping Responses Inventory: Adult Form Manual*. Odessa, FL: Psychological Assessment Resources.

Morelock, M. and Feldman, D. (1997). High IQ, extreme precocity and savant syndrome. In N. Colangelo and G. Davis (eds), *Handbook of Gifted Eduation* (2nd edn, pp. 439–59). Boston, MA: Allyn and Bacon.

Mruk, C. (1999). *Self-esteem* (2nd edn). New York: Springer.

Murphy, L. and Moriarity, A. (1976). *Vulnerability, Coping and Growth*. New Haven, CT: Yale University Press.

Murphy, M. and Donovan, S. (1999). *The Physical and Psychological Effects of Meditation: A Review of Contemporary Research with a Comprehensive Bibliography 1931–1996* (2nd edn). Sausalito, CA: Institute of Noetic Sciences.

Murray, D. (1983). *A History of Western Psychology*. Englewood Cliffs, NJ: Prentice-Hall.

Myers, D. (1992). *The Pursuit of Happiness*. New York: Morrow.

Myers, D. (2000). The funds, friends and faith of happy people. *American Psychologist* 55: 56–67.

Myers, D. and Diener, E. (1996). The pursuit of happiness. *Scientific American* 274 (May): 54–6.

Nakamura, J. and Csikszentmihalyi, M. (2002). The concept of flow. In C.R. Snyder and S. Lopez (eds), *Handbook of Positive Psychology* (pp. 89–105). New York: Oxford University Press.

Nathan, P. and Gorman, J. (1998). *A Guide to Treatments that Work*. New York: Oxford University Press.

Nathan, P. and Gorman, J. (2002). *A Guide to Treatments that Work (Second Edition)*. New York: Oxford University Press.

Neugarten, B. and Weinstein, R. (1964). The changing American grandparent. *Journal of Marriage and the Family* 26: 199–204.

Neuman, G. and Romanowski, P. (1998). *Helping Your Kids Cope with Divorce*. New York: Times Books.

Newman, B. and Newman, P. (1991). *Development through Life (Fifth edition)*. Pacific Grove, CA: Brooks/Cole.

Newnes, C., Holmes, G. and Dunn, C. (1999). *This is Madness: A Critical look at Psychiatry and the Future of Mental Health Services*. Ross on Wye: PCCS Books. maggie@pccsbks.globalnet.co.uk +44-1989-770707.

Newnes, C., Holmes, G. and Dunn, C. (2001). *This is Madness Too: Critical Perspectives on Mental Health Services*. Ross on Wye: PCCS Books. maggie@ pccsbks.globalnet.co.uk +44-1989-770707.

Nickerson, R. (1999). Enhancing creativity. In R. Sternberg (ed.), *Handbook of Creativity* (pp. 392–429). Cambridge: Cambridge University Press.

Niederhoffer, K. and Pennebaker, J. (2002). Sharing one's story: on the benefits of writing or talking about emotional experience. In C.R. Snyder and S. Lopez (eds), *Handbook of Positive Psychology* (pp. 573–83). New York: Oxford University Press.

Nolen-Hoeksema, S. (2000). Growth and resilience among bereaved people. In J. Gillham (ed.) *The Science of Optimism and Hope* (pp. 107–27). Philadelphia, PA: Templeton Foundation Press.

Nolen-Hoeksema, S. and Davis, C. (2002). Positive responses to loss: perceiving benefits and growth. In C.R. Snyder and S. Lopez (eds), *Handbook of Positive Psychology* (pp. 598–607). New York: Oxford University Press.

Norcross, J. (2002). *Psychotherapy Relationships that Work*. New York: Oxford University Press.

Norcross, J., Santrock, J., Campbell, L., Smith, T., Sommer, R. and Zuckerman, E. (2000). *Authoritative Guide to Self-Help Resources in Mental Health*. New York: Guilford.

Nowicki, S. and Strickland, B. (1973). A locus of control scale for children. *Journal of Consulting and Clinical Psychology* 40: 148–54.

Nugent, W. and Thomas, J. (1993). Validation of the Self-Esteem Rating Scale. *Research of Social Work Practice* 3: 191–207.

Nunn, K., Nicholls, D. and Lask, B. (2000). A new taxonomy: the Uluru Personal Experiential Profile. *Clinical Child Psychology and Psychiatry* 5(3): 313–27.

O'Brien, E. and Epstein, S. (1988). *Multidimensional Self-Esteem Inventory*. Odessa, FL: Psychological Assessment Resources.

O'Connell, K., Potocky, M., Cook, M. and Gerkovich, M (1991). *Metamotivational State Interview and Coding Schedule Instruction Manual*. Kansas City, MO: Midwest Research Institute.

Oliner, S. and Oliner, P. (1988). *The Altruistic Personality: Rescuers of Jews in Nazi Europe*. New York: Free Press.

Olson, D. (2000). Circumplex Model of Marital and Family Systems. *Journal of Family Therapy* 22: 144–67.

Olson, D.H. (1990). *Clinical Rating Scale for the Circumplex Model*. St Paul, MN: Family Social Science, University of Minnesota.

Olson, D.H., McCubbin, H.I., Barnes, H., Larsen, A., Muxen, M. and Wilson, M. (1986). *Family Inventories*. St Paul, MN: Family Social Science, University of Minnesota.

Olweus, D. (1993). *Bullying at School: What We Know and What We Can Do*. Oxford: Blackwell.

Osborn, A. (1963). *Applied Imagination: Principles and Procedures of Creative Thinking*. New York: Scribner's.

Osterkamp, L. (1992). *How to Deal with Your Parents When They Still Treat You Like a Child*. New York: Berkeley.

Ostir, G., Markides, K., Black, S. and Goodwin, J. (2000). Emotional well-being predicts subsequent functional independence and survival. *Journal of the American Geriatrics Society* 48: 473–8.

Oyen, C., Ludwig, T. and VanderLaan, K. (2001). Granting forgiveness and harbouring grudges: implications for emotion, physiology and health. *Psychological Science* 12: 117–23.

Papalia, D. and Wendkos-Olds, S. (1995). *Human Development (Sixth edition)*. New York: McGraw-Hill.

Pargament, K. (1997). *The Psychology of Religion and Coping*. New York: Guilford.

Paris, J. (1996). *Social Factors in the Personality Disorders: A Biopsychosocial Approach to Etiology and Treatment*. Cambridge: Cambridge University Press.

Parker, I., Georgaca, E., Harper, D., McLaughlin, T. and Stowell-Smith, M. (1995). *Deconstructing Psychopathology*. London: Sage.

Parker, J. (2000). Emotional intelligence: clinical and therapeutic implications. In R. Bar-On and J. Parker (eds), *The Handbook of Emotional Intelligence* (pp. 490–504). San Francisco, CA: Jossey-Bass.

Parnes, B. (1981). *Magic of your Mind*. Bufalo, NY: Bearly.

Patterson, J. and McCubbin, H. (1987). Adolescent coping style and behaviours: conceptualisation and measurement. *Journal of Adolescence* 10: 163–86.

Paulhus, D., Fridhandler, B. and Hayes, S. (1997). Psychological defence: contemporary theory and research. In R. Hogan, J. Johnson and S. Briggs (eds), *Handbook of Personality Psychology* (pp. 544–80). New York: Academic Press.

Pavot, W. and Diener, E. (1993). Review of the Satisfaction with Life Scale. *Psychological Assessment* 5: 164–72.

Pennebaker, J. (1997). *Opening Up: The Healing Power of Confiding in Others*. New York: Guilford Press.

Perls, F. (1973). *Gestalt Therapy Verbatim*. Moab, UT: Real People Press.

Perry, C. and Kardos, M. (1995). A review of defence mechanism rating scales. In H. Conte and R. Plutchik (eds), *Ego Defences: Theory and Measurement* (pp. 283–99). New York: Wiley.

Pervin, L. and John, O. (1999). *Handbook of Personality: Theory and Research.* New York: Guilford.

Peterson, C. (2000a). The future of optimism. *American Psychologist* 55: 44–55.

Peterson, C. (2000b). Optimistic explanatory style and health. In J. Gillham (ed.) *The Science of Optimism and Hope* (pp. 245–261). Philadelphia, PA: Templeton Foundation Press.

Peterson, C. and Barrett, L. (1987). Explanatory style and academic performance among university freshmen. *Journal of Personality and Social Psychology* 53: 603–7.

Peterson, C., Schulman, P., Castellon, C. and Seligman, M. (1992). CAVE: Content Analysis of Verbal Explanations. In C. Smith (ed.), *Motivation and Personality: Handbook of Thematic Content Analysis* (pp. 383–92). New York: Cambridge University Press.

Peterson, C. and Seligman, M. (2001a) Values in Action (VIA) Classification of Strengths. http://www.positivepsychology.org/taxonomy.htm

Peterson, C. and Seligman, M. (2001b). Values in Action Inventory of Strengths (VIA-IS) Manual. Department of Psychology, University of Pennsylvania, 3815 Walnut Street, Philadelphia, PA 19104 215-898-7173, chrispet@umich.edu, http://www.positivepsychology.org/viastrengthsinventory.htm

Peterson, C., Seligman, M. and Valliant, G. (1988). Pessimistic explanatory style as a risk factor for physical illness: a thirty-five year longitudinal study. *Journal of Personality and Social Psychology* 55: 23–7.

Peterson, C., Semmel, A., vonBaeyer, C., Abramson, L., Metalsky, G. and Seligman, M. (1982). The Attributional Style Questionnaire. *Cognitive Therapy and Research* 6: 287–99.

Peterson, C. and Villanova, P. (1988). An expanded Attributional Style Questionnaire. *Journal of Abnormal Psychology* 97: 87–9.

Piaget, J. (1976). *The Psychology of Intelligence.* Totowa, NJ: Littlefield, Adams and Co.

Pickering, A. and Gray, J. (1999). The neuroscience of personality. In L. Pervin and O. John (eds), *Handbook of Personality* (2nd edn, pp. 277–99). New York: Guilford.

Pierce, G., Sarason, I. and Sarason, B. (1991). General and relationship-based perceptions of social support: are two constructs better than one? *Journal of Personality and Social Psychology* 61: 1028–39.

Pierce, G., Sarason, I. and Sarason, B. (1996). Coping and social support. In M. Zeidner and N. Endler (eds), *Handbook of Coping. Theory, Research, Applications* (pp. 434–51). New York: Wiley.

Piers, E. and Harris, D. (1969). *Piers-Harris Children's Self-Concept Scale.* Los Angeles, CA: Western Psychological Services.

Pinker, S. (1997). *How the Mind Works.* New York: Norton.

Pinsof, W. and Wynne, L. (1995). *The Effectiveness of Marital and Family Therapies. Journal of Marital and Family Therapy Volume 2. Special Edition.* Washington, DC: AAMFT.

Plante, T. and Sherman, A. (2001). *Faith and Health: Psychological Perspectives.* New York: Guilford.

Plomin, R. and Caspi, A. (1999). Behavioural genetics and personality. In L. Pervin and O. John (eds), *Handbook of Personality* (2nd edn, pp. 251–76). New York: Guilford.

Plucker, J. and Renzulli, J. (1999). Psychometric approaches to the study of human creativity. In R. Sternberg (ed.), *Handbook of Creativity* (pp. 35–61). Cambridge: Cambridge University Press.

Plutchik, R., Kellerman, H. and Conte, H. (1979). The structural theory of ego defences and emotions. In C. Izard (ed.), *Emotions in Personality and Psychopathology* (pp. 229–57). New York: Plenum Press.

Poicastro, E. and Gardner, H. (1999). In R. Sternberg (ed.), *Handbook of Creativity* (pp. 213–25). Cambridge: Cambridge University Press.

Porter, E. (1913). *Pollyanna*. London: Harrap.

Potter-Efron, R. and Potter-Efron, R. (1995). *The Ten Most Common Anger Styles and What to Do about Them*. Oakland, CA: New Harbinger.

Pretzer, J. and Beck, A. (1996). A cognitive theory of personality disorders. In J. Clarkin and M. Lenzenweger (eds), *Major Theories of Personality Disorder* (pp. 36–105). New York: Guilford.

Prochaska, J. (1999). How do people change and how can we change to help many more people? In M. Hubble, B. Duncan and S. Miller (eds), *The Heart and Soul of Change* (pp. 227–55). Washington, DC: American Psychological Association.

Prochaska, J. and DiClemente, C. (1992). The transtheoretical approach. In J. Norcross and M. Goldfried (eds), *Handbook of Psychotherapy Integration* (pp. 300–34). New York: Basic Books.

Prochaska, J. and Norcross, J. (1994). *Systems of Psychotherapy: A Transtheoretical Analysis* (3rd edn). Pacific Grove, CA: Brooks/Cole.

Prochaska, J., Norcross, J. and DiClemente, C. (1994). *Changing for Good*. New York: Avon.

Rando, T. (1991). *How to Go on Living When Someone You Love Dies*. New York: Bantam.

Rapp, C. (1998). *The Strengths Model: Case Management with People Suffering from Severe Persistent Mental Illness*. New York: Oxford.

Raschke, H. (1987). Divorce. In M. Sussman and S. Steinmetz (eds), *Handbook of Marriage and the Family* (pp. 348–99). New York: Plenum.

Raskin, R. and Hall, C. (1979). A narcissistic personality inventory. *Psychological Reports* 45: 590.

Rathunde, K. (1988). Optimal experience and the family context. In M. Csikszentmihalyi and I. Csikszentmihalyi (eds), *Optimal Experience: Psychological Studies of Flow in Consciousness* (pp. 342–63). Cambridge: Cambridge University Press.

Renzulli, J. (1986). A three ring conception of giftedness: a developmental model of creative productivity. In R. Sternberg and J. Davidson (eds), *Conceptions of Giftedness* (pp. 53–92). New York: Cambridge University Press.

Riegel, K. (1973). Dialectic operations: the final period of cognitive development. *Human Development* 16: 346–70.

Riemann, R., Angleitner, A. and Strelau, J. (1997). Genetic and environmental influences on personality: a study of twins reared together using self and peer report NEO-FFI scales. *Journal of Personality* 66: 525–54.

Robins, R., Norem, J. and Cheek, J. (1999). Naturalising the self. In L. Pervin and O. John (eds), *Handbook of Personality: Theory and Research* (pp. 443–47). New York: Guilford.

Rogers, C. (1961). *On Becoming a Person*. Boston, MA: Houghton Mifflin.

Rolf, J., Masten, A., Cicchetti, D., *et al.* (1990). *Risk And Protective Factors in the Development of Psychopathology*. New York: Cambridge University Press.

Rosenberg, M. (1979). *Conceiving the Self*. New York: Basic Books.

Rosenhan, D. (1973). On being sane in insane places. *Science* 179: 250–8.

Roth, A. and Fonagy, P. (1996). *What Works for Whom: A Critical Review of Psychotherapy Research*. New York: Guilford.

Rothbart, M. and Ahadi, A. (1994). Temperament and the development of personality. *Journal of Abnormal Psychology* 103: 55–66.

Rotter, J. (1966). Generalised expectancies for internal versus external control of reinforcement. *Psychological Monographs* 90: 1–28.

Rotter, J. (1967). A new scale for the measurement of interpersonal trust. *Journal of Personality* 23: 651–65.

Rotter, J. (1980). Interpersonal trust, trustworthiness and gullibility. *American Psychologist* 35: 1–7.

Rowe, D. (1997). Genetics, temperament, and personality. In R. Hogan, J. Johnson and S. Briggs (eds), *Handbook of Personality Psychology* (pp. 367–86). New York: Academic Press.

Runco, M. and Sakamoto, S. (1999). Experimental studies of creativity. In R. Sternberg (ed.), *Handbook of Creativity* (pp. 62–92). Cambridge: Cambridge University Press.

Rutter, M. (1994). Resilience: some conceptual considerations. *Contemporary Paediatrics* 11: 36–48.

Rutter, M. (1999). Resilience concepts and findings: implications for family therapy. *Journal of Family Therapy* 21: 119–44.

Rutter, M., Maughan, N., Mortimore, P. and Ouston, J. (1979). *Fifteen Thousand Hours*. London: Open Books.

Ryan, R. and Deci, E. (2000). Self-determination theory and the facilitation of intrinsic motivation, social development and well-being. *American Psychologist* 55: 68–78.

Ryan, R. and Deci, E. (2001). On happiness and human potential. *Annual Review of Psychology* 51: 141–66.

Ryff, C. (1989). Happiness is everything, or is it? Explorations on the meaning of psychological well-being. *Journal of Personality and Social Psychology* 57: 1069–81.

Ryff, C. and Keyes, C. (1995). The structure of psychological well-being revisited. *Journal of Personality and Social Psychology* 69: 719–27.

Ryff, C. and Singer, B. (2000). Interpersonal flourishing: a positive health agenda for the new millennium. *Personality and Social Psychology Review* 4(1): 30–44.

Saarni, C. (1999). *Developing Emotional Competence*. New York: Guilford.

Saarni, C. (2000). Emotional competence: a developmental perspective. In R. Bar-On and J. Parker (eds), *The Handbook of Emotional Intelligence* (pp. 68–91). San Francisco, CA: Jossey-Bass.

Salovey, P. and Mayer, J. (1990). Emotional intelligence. *Imagination, Cognition and Personality* 9: 185–211.

Salovey, P., Mayer, J. and Caruso, D. (2002).The positive psychology of emotional intelligence. In C.R. Snyder and S. Lopez (eds), *Handbook of Positive Psychology* (pp. 159–71). New York: Oxford University Press.

Sanders, D. and Sanders, J. (1984). *Teaching Creativity through Metaphor*. New York: Longman.

Santrock, J. (1995). *Lifespan Development*. (*Fifth edition*.) Madison, WC: WBC Brown and Benchmark.

Sarafino, E. (2002). *Health Psychology* (4th edn). New York: Wiley.

Sarason, B., Sarason, I. and Pierce, G. (1990). *Social Support: An International Review*. New York: Wiley.

Sarason, I., Levine, H., Basham, R. and Sarason, B. (1983). Assessing social support: the social support questionnaire. *Journal of Personality and Social Psychology* 44: 127–39.

Sarason, I., Sarason, B., Shearin, E. and Pierce, G. (1987). A brief measure of social support: practical and theoretical considerations. *Journal of Social and Personal Relationships* 4: 497–510.

Satterfield, J. (2000). Optimism, culture, and history: the roles of explanatory style, integrative complexity, and pessimistic rumination. In J. Gillham (ed.) *The Science of Optimism and Hope* (pp. 349–78). Philadelphia, PA: Templeton Foundation Press.

Schacter, D. (1987). Implicit memory: history and current status. *Journal of Experimental Psychology: Learning, Memory and Cognition* 13: 501–18.

Scharff, J. (1995). Psychoanalytic marital therapy. In N. Jacobson and A. Gurman (eds), *Clinical Handbook of Couple Therapy* (pp. 164–96). New York: Guilford.

Scheier, M. and Carver, C. (1985). Optimism, coping and health: assessment and implications of generalized outcome expectancies. *Health Psychology* 4: 219–47.

Scheier, M., Carver, C. and Bridges, M. (1994). Distinguishing optimism from neuroticism (and trait anxiety, self-mastery and self-esteem): a re-evaluation of the Life Orientation Test, *Journal of Personality and Social Psychology* 67: 1063–78.

Scheier, M., Carver, C. and Bridges, M. (2000). Optimism, pessimism and psychological well-being. In E. Chang (ed.), *Optimism and Pessimism: Theory, Research and Practice*. Washington, DC: American Psychological Association.

Schlenker, B. (1980). *Impression Management: The Self-Concept, Social Identity, and Interpersonal Relations*. Monterey, CA: Brooks/Cole.

Schmutte, P. and Ryff, C. (1997). Personality and well-being: re-examining methods and meanings. *Journal of Personality and Social Psychology* 73: 549–59.

Schulman, M. (2002). How we become moral: the sources of moral motivation. In C.R. Snyder and S. Lopez (eds), *Handbook of Positive Psychology* (pp. 499–514). New York: Oxford University Press.

Schumm, W.R., Paff-Bergen, L.A., Hatch, R.C., Obiorah, F.C., Copeland, J.M., Meens, L.D. and Bugaighis, M.A. (1986). Concurrent and discriminant validity of the Kansas Marital Satisfaction Scale. *Journal of Marriage and the Family* 48: 381–7.

Schutte, D., Malouff, J., Hall, L., Haggerty, D., Copper, J., Golden, C. and Dornhcim, L. (1998). Development and validation of a measure of emotional intelligence. *Personality and Individual Differences* 25: 167–77.

Schwartz, B. (2000). Self determination: the tyranny of freedom. *American Psychologist* 55: 79–88.

Segal, L. (1991). Brief therapy: the MRI approach. In A. Gurman and D. Kniskern (eds), *Handbook of Family Therapy* (vol. 2, pp. 17–199). New York: Brunner/ Mazel.

Segal, Z., Williams, M. and Teasdale, J. (2002). *Mindfulness-Based Cognitive Therapy for Depression*. New York: Guildford.

Segerstrom, S., Taylor, S., Kemeny, M. and Fahey, J. (1998). Optimism is associated with mood, coping, and immune change in response to stress. *Journal of Personality and Social Psychology* 74: 1646–55.

Seligman, M. (1998). *Learned Optimism: How to Change Your Mind and Your Life* (2nd edn). New York: Pocket Books.

Seligman, M. (2002). *Authentic Happiness: Using the New Positive Psychology to Realise your Potential for Lasting Fulfilment*. New York: Free Press.

Seligman, M. and Csikszentmihalyi, M. (2000a). Positive psychology: An introduction. *American Psychologist* 55: 5–14.

Seligman, M. and Csikszentmihalyi, M. (2000b). *Special issue of American Psychologist on Happiness, Excellence and Optimal Human Functioning* (vol. 55, No. 1). Washington, DC: APA.

Seligman, M., Nolen-Hoeksema, S., Thornton, N. and Thorton, K. (1988). Explanatory style as a mechanism of dissappointing athletic performance. *Psychological Science* 1: 143–6.

Seligman, M., Peterson, C., Kaslow, N., Tanenbaum, R., Alloy, L. and Abramson, L. (1984). Attributional style and depressive symptoms among children. *Journal of Abnormal Psychology* 93: 235–8.

Seligman, M. and Schulman, P. (1986). Explanatory style as a predictor of performance as a life insurance agent. *Journal of Personality and Social Psychology* 50: 832–8.

Shackleton, C. (1983). The psychology of grief: a review. *Behaviour Research and Therapy* 6: 153–205.

Shapiro, F. (2001). *Eye Movement Desensitisation and Reprocessing: Basic Principles, Protocols and Procedures* (2nd edn). New York: Guilford Press.

Shapiro, S., Schwartz, G. and Santerre, C. (2002). Meditation and positive psychology. In C.R. Snyder and S. Lopez (eds), *Handbook of Positive Psychology* (pp. 632–45). New York: Oxford University Press.

Sheehy, G. (1976). *Passages: Predictable Crises of Adult Life*. New York: Dutton.

Sherer, M., Maddux, J., Mercandante, B., Prentice-Dunn, S., Jacobs, B. and Rogers, R. (1982). The Self-Efficacy Scale: construction and validation. *Psychological Reports* 51: 663–71.

Sherman, A. and Simonton, S. (2001). Assessment of religiousness and spirituality in health research. In T. Plante and A. Sherman (eds), *Faith and Health: Psychological Perspectives* (pp. 139–66). York: Guilford.

Shizgal, P. (1997). Neural basis of utility estimation. *Current Opinion in Neurobiology* 7: 198–208.

Shorter, E. (1997). *A History of Psychiatry. From the Era of the Asylum to the Age of Prozac*. Chichester: Wiley.

Sifneos, P. (1973). The prevalence of alexithymic characteristics in psychosomatic patients. *Psychotherapy and Psychosomatics* 22: 255–62.

Simonton, K. (2000). Creativity: cognitive, personal, developmental and social aspects. *American Psychologist* 55: 151–8.

Sirgy, M. (1998). Materialism and quality of life. *Social Indicators Research* 43: 227–60.

Skinner, B. and Vaughan, M. (1993). *Enjoy Old Age: A Programme of Self-Management*. New York: Norton.

Skinner, H., Steinhauer, P. and Santa-Barbara, J. (1995). *Family Assessment Measure – III Manual*. Toronto: Multi Health Systems.

Skinner, H., Steinhauer, P. and Sitarenios, G. (2000). Family Assessment Measure (FAM) and Process Model of Family Functioning. *Journal of Family Therapy* 22: 190–210.

Smith, C. (1992). *Motivation and Personality: Handbook of Thematic Content Analysis*. New York: Cambridge University Press.

Smith, M., Glass, G. and Miller, T. (1980). *The Benefits of Psychotherapy*. Baltimore: Johns Hopkins University Press.

Snyder, C.R. (2000). *Handbook of Hope*. Orlando FL: Academic Press.

Snyder, C.R. and Lopez, S. (2002). *Handbook of Positive Psychology*. New York: Oxford University Press.

Snyder, D. (1997). *Marital Satisfaction Inventory – Revised*. Los Angeles, CA: Western Psychological Services.

Solomon, J. and George, C. (1999). The measurement of attachment security in infancy and childhood. In J. Cassidy and P. Shaver (eds), *Handbook of Attachment: Theory, Research and Clinical Applications* (pp. 287–316). New York: Guilford.

Spanier, G.B. (1976). Measuring dyadic adjustment: new scales for assessing the quality of marriage and similar dyads. *Journal of Marriage and the Family* 38: 15–28.

Spearman, C. (1927). *The Abilities of Man*. New York: Macmillan.

Sprenkle, D., Blow, A. and Dickey, M. (1999). Common factors and other non-technique variables in marriage and family therapy. In M. Hubble, B. Duncan and S. Miller (eds), *The Heart and Soul of Change* (pp. 329–60). Washington, DC: American Psychological Association.

Stanton, A., Kirk, S., Cameron, C. and Danoff-Burg, S. (2000). Coping through emotional approach: scale construction and validation. *Journal of Personality and Social Psychology* 78: 1150–69.

Stanton, A., Parsa, A. and Austenfeld, J. (2002). The adaptive potential of coping through emotional approach. In C.R. Snyder and S. Lopez (eds), *Handbook of Positive Psychology* (pp. 148–58). New York: Oxford University Press.

Staub, E. (1974). Helping a person in distress: social, personality and stimulus determinants. In L. Berkowitz (ed.), *Advances in Experimental Social Psychology* (vol. 7, pp. 293–341). New York: Academic Press.

Staw, B., Sutton, R. and Pelled, L. (1994). Employee, positive emotion and favourable outcomes at the workplace. *Organization Science* 5: 51–71.

Steketee, G. and White, K. (1990). *When Once Is Not Enough: Help for Obsessive Compulsives*. Oakland, CA: New Harbinger.

Sternberg, R. (1987). *The Triangle of Love*. New York: Basic Books.

Sternberg, R. (1993). Sternberg Triarchic Abilities Test. Unpublished Manuscript, available from Dr Robert Sternberg, Department of Psychology, Yale University. PO Box 208205, New Haven, CT 06520-8205, USA. email: robert.sternberg@yale.edu Phone: 203-432.

Sternberg, R. (1997). *Successful Intelligence*. New York: Plume.

Sternberg, R. (1999). *Handbook of Creativity*. Cambridge: Cambridge University Press.

Sternberg, R. (2000a). Intelligence and wisdom. In R. Sternberg (ed.), *Handbook of Intelligence* (pp. 631–50). Cambridge: Cambridge University Press.

Sternberg, R. (2000b). *Handbook of Intelligence*. Cambridge: Cambridge University Press.

Sternberg, R. and Davidson, J. (1986). *Conceptions of Giftedness*. New York: Cambridge University Press.

Sternberg, R. and Grigorenko, E. (2000). Practical intelligence and its development. In R. Bar-On and J. Parker (eds), *The Handbook of Emotional Intelligence* (pp. 215–43). San Francisco, CA: Jossey-Bass.

Sternberg, R. and Lubart, T. (1999). The concept of creativity: prospects and paradigms. In R. Sternberg (ed.), *Handbook of Creativity* (pp. 3–15). Cambridge: Cambridge University Press.

Stone, A., Neale, J., Cox, D., Napoli, A., *et al.* (1994). Daily events are associated with secretory immune responses to an oral antegen in men. *Health Psychology* 13: 440–6.

Stone, A., Schiffman, S. and DeVries, M. (1999). Re-thinking self-report methodologies. An argument for collecting ecologically valid, momentary measurements and selected results of EMA studies. In D. Kahneman, E. Diener and N. Schwartz (eds), *Well-being: The Foundations of Hedonic Psychology* (pp. 26–39). New York: Russell Sage Foundation.

Strathman, A., Gleicher, F., Boninger, D. and Edwards, C. (1994). The consideration of future consequences: weighing immediate and distant outcomes of behavior. *Journal of Personality and Social Psychology* 66: 742–52.

Stratton, P., Heard, D., Hanks, H., Munton, A., Brewin, C. and Davidson, C. (1986). Coding causal beliefs in natural discourse. *British Journal of Social Psychology* 25: 299–311.

Stroebe, M. (1993). Coping with bereavement: a review of the grief work hypothesis. *Omega Journal of Death and Dying* 26: 19–42.

Stroebe, M., Stroebe, W. and Hansson, R. (1993). *Handbook of Bereavement: Theory, Research, and Intervention*. New York: Cambridge University Press.

Subcoviak, M., Enright, R., Wu, C., Gassin, E., Freedman, S., Olson, L. and Sarinopoulos, I. (1995). Measuring interpersonal forgiveness in late adolescence and middle childhood. *Journal of Adolescence* 18: 641–55.

Subotnik, R. and Arnold, A. (1994). *Beyond Terman: Contemporary Longitudinal Studies of Giftedness and Talent*. Norwood, NJ: Ablex.

Suh, E., Diener, E., Oishi, S. and Tiandis, H. (1997). The shifting basis of life satisfaction judgements across cultures: emotions versus norms. *Journal of Personality and Social Psychology* 74: 482–93.

Swann, W. (1983). Self-verification: bringing social reality into harmony with the self. In J. Suls and A. Greenwald (eds), *Social Psychology Perspectives* (vol. 2, pp. 33–66). Hillsdale, NJ: Lawrence Erlbaum.

Swann, W. (1997). The trouble with change: self-verification and allegiance to the self. *Psychological Science* 8: 177–80.

Sylva, K. (1994). School influences on children's development. *Journal of Child Psychology and Psychiatry* 35: 135–70.

Szasz, T. (1961). *The Myth of Mental Illness*. New York: Dell.

Szasz, T. (1963). *Law Liberty and Psychiatry*. New York: Macmillan.

Tannen, D. (1990). *You Just Don't Understand: Women and Men in Conversation.* New York: Ballentine.

Tavris, C. (1989). *Anger: The Misunderstood Emotion* (revised and updated). New York: Touchstone.

Taylor, G. and Bagby, M. (2000). An overview of the alexithymia construct. In R. Bar-On and J. Parker (eds), *The Handbook of Emotional Intelligence* (pp. 40–67). San Francisco, CA: Jossey-Bass.

Taylor, G., Bagby, M. and Luninet, O. (2000). Assessment of alexithymia: self-report and observer-rated measures. In R. Bar-On and J. Parker (eds), *The Handbook of Emotional Intelligence* (pp. 301–19). San Francisco, CA: Jossey-Bass.

Taylor, S. (1989). *Positive Illusions: Creative Self-Deception and the Healthy Mind.* New York: Basic Books.

Taylor, S. and Brown, J. (1988). Illusion and well-being: a social-psychological perspective on mental health. *Psychological Bulletin* 103: 193–210.

Taylor, S. and Brown, J. (1994). Positive illusions and well-being revisited: separating fact from fiction. *Psychological Bulletin* 116: 21–7.

Taylor, S., Dickerson, S. and Cousino Klein, L. (2002). Toward a biology of social support. In C.R. Snyder and S. Lopez (eds), *Handbook of Positive Psychology* (pp. 556–72). New York: Oxford University Press.

Taylor, S., Kemeny, M., Reed, G., Bower, J. and Gruenewald, T. (2000). Psychological resources, positive illusions and health. *American Psychologist* 55: 99–109.

Tellegen, A. and Waller, N. (In press). Exploring personality through test construction: development of the Multidimensional Personality Questionnaire. In S. Briggs, J. Cheek and E. Donahue (eds), *Handbook of Adult Personality Inventories.* New York: Plenum.

Tennen, H. and Affleck, G. (2002). Benefit-finding and benefit-reminding. In C.R. Snyder and S. Lopez (eds), *Handbook of Positive Psychology* (pp. 584–97). New York: Oxford University Press.

Terman, L. and Ogden, M. (1959). *Genetic Studies of Genius. Volume V. The Gifted Group at Mid-Life: Thirty-five Years follow-up of a Superior Group.* Stanford, CA: Stanford University Press.

Tesser, A. and Phalus, D. (1983). The definition of self: private and public self evaluation management strategies. *Journal of Personality and Social Psychology* 44: 672–82.

Thomas, A. and Chess, S. (1977). *Temperament and Development.* New York: Brunner/ Mazel.

Thompson, R. (1999). Early attachment and later development. In J. Cassidy and P. Shaver (eds), *Handbook of Attachment* (pp. 265–86). New York: Guilford.

Thompson, S. (2002). The role of personal control in adaptive functioning. In C.R. Snyder and S. Lopez (eds), *Handbook of Positive Psychology* (pp. 202–13). New York: Oxford University Press.

Thurstone, L. (1938). *Primary Mental Abilities.* Chicago: University of Chicago Press.

Tiger, L. (1979). *Optimism: The Biology of Hope.* New York: Simon and Schuster.

Topping, K., Holmes, E. and Bremner, W. (2000). The effectiveness of school based programmes for the promotion of social competence. In R. Bar-On and J. Parker (eds), *The Handbook of Emotional Intelligence* (pp. 411–32). San Francisco, CA: Jossey-Bass.

Winter, D. (1991). Measuring personality at a distance: development and validation of an integrated system for scoring motives in running test. In A. Stewart, J. Healty, Jr and D. Ozer (eds), *Perspectives in Personality: Approaches to Understanding Lives* (vol. 3, pp. 58–89). London: Jessica Kingsley.

Winter, D. (1996). *Personality: Analysis and Interpretation of Lives*. New York: McGraw-Hill.

Witvliet, C., Ludwig, T. and Vander Laan, K. (2001). Granting forgiveness or harbouring grudges: implications for emotion, physiology, and health. *Psychological Science* 121: 117–23.

Wolitzky, D. and Eagle, M. (1997). Psychoanalytic theories of psychotherapy. In P. Watchel and S. Messer (eds), *Theories of Psychotherapy: Origins and Evolution* (pp. 39–96). Washington, DC: APA.

Wood, J. (1996). What is social comparison and how should we study it? *Personality and Social Psychology Bulletin* 22: 520–37.

World Health Organization (1992). *The ICD-10 Classification of Mental and Behavioural Disorders*. Geneva: WHO.

World Health Organization (1996). *Multi-axial Classification of Child and Adolescent Psychiatric Disorders: ICD 10 Classification of Mental and Behavioural Disorders in Children and Adolescents*. Cambridge: Cambridge University Press.

Worthington, E. (2001). *Five Steps to Forgiveness*. New York: Crown.

Wortman, C. and Silver, R. (1989). The myths of coping with loss. *Journal of Consulting and Clinical Psychology* 57: 349–57.

Wright, R. (2000). *Nonzero: The Logic of Human Destiny*. New York: Pantheon.

Yalom, I. (1981). *Existential Psychotherapy*. New York: Basic Books.

Young, J. (1998). 'Professional Tennis Players in Flow. Flow Theory and Reversal Theory Perspectives'. Unpublished Doctoral Dissertation, Faculty of Science, Monash University, Melbourne, Australia.

Zahavi, A. and Zahavi, A. (1997). *The Handicap Principle*. New York: Oxford University Press.

Zeidner, M. and Endler, N. (1996). *Handbook of Coping: Theory, Research, Applications*. New York: Wiley.

Zubin, J. and Spring, B. (1977). Vulnerability: a new view of schizophrenia. *Journal of Abnormal Psychology* 86: 103–26.

Zukerman, M. (1985). *Manual for the MAACL-R. The Multiple Affect Adjective Checklist – Revised*. San Diego, CA: Educational and Industrial Testing Service.

Index

abstinence violation effect 346
abuse 245
achievement motive 192, 200
acquaintances 24
action 307, 316–17, 346
adaptation 32–3, 45
Adolescent Coping Orientation for
    Problem Experiences A-COPE 230
adolescence 269–72
affectivity, positive and negative 2–6, 45
affiliation motive 192, 200
agreeableness 200
alexithymia 132–3, 143
altruism 193, 200
analytic intelligence 167, 179
anger, grief 276; self-help 43
anxiety, defence mechanism 236; grief
    227; self-help 43
Apter motivational style profile 58
Apter's reversal theory see reversal
    theory
Argyle, M. 7–11
arousing emotions 312–13
assertiveness 245
assessing coping 228
assessment see measurement
attachment theory 287–8; measurement
    298
attachment, emotional competence
    124–6; styles 126, 143
attributional retraining 86–8, 106
autistic spectrum disorder traits 131–2,
    143
autotelic activities 74

Balte's predictors of wisdom-related
    performance in adults 166

Bar-On, Reuven, model of emotional
    intelligence 112, 114; personality
    model of social and emotional
    intelligence 112–14
Beavers Family Systems model 299
brain processes see neurobiology
brainstorming, self-help 178
broaden and build theory 13–15, 45

catharsis 219–20; measurement 247
causes of happiness 16–19
change 301–47; abstinence violation
    effect 346; action 307, 316–17, 346;
    arousing emotions 312–13; children
    333–7; communication 320–1;
    consciousness raising 311–12,
    347; contemplation 306, 311–14,
    347; countering 319–21, 347;
    environmental re-evaluation 313, 347;
    goal-setting and monitoring 314–15;
    maintenance 310, 317–22, 347;
    negative beliefs 319–20; planning
    307, 314–16, 347; precontemplation
    306, 311–14, 347; problem-solving
    321; relapse prevention 322–3; reward
    321; self-help 345; self-liberation
    316–17, 347; self-re-evaluation 315;
    social liberation 313–14, 347;
    stimulus control 318–19, 347;
    strategies 324–5; strengths 302–4;
    termination 310, 322–3, 347
change, self-help 345
character strengths 51–3, 70, 74
children 260–9
circumplex model, emotions 4; family
    functioning 299; interpersonal
    behaviour 288–9, 299

Client Satisfaction Questionnaire 343
cognitive development, wisdom 162–5
communication 320–1; self-help 295
conscientiousness 200
consciousness raising 311–12, 347
contemplation 306, 311–14, 347
Cooper's EQ-map 116–17
COPE 230
Coping Inventory for Stressful
   Situations 228
Coping Responses Inventory 230
coping strategies 213–30, 249;
   Adolescent Coping Orientation for
   Problem Experiences A-COPE 230;
   catharsis 219–20, 247; COPE 230;
   Coping Inventory for Stressful
   Situations 228; Coping Responses
   Inventory 230; crying 221, 248;
   distraction 227; reframing 226–7;
   exercise 223; faith 221–2, 247;
   Functional Dimension of Coping
   scale 228; humour 227–8;
   measurement 228–9, 247; meditation
   222; problem-solving 217–18, 244,
   247; relaxation 223–4; social support
   218–19, 247; Ways of Coping
   Questionnaire 228
countering 319–21, 347
couples 257–8, 262
creative intelligence 168, 179
creative problem solving, self-help 178
creativity 150–7, 173–4; brain processes
   157; childhood giftedness 150;
   Csikszentmihalyi's systems model of
   creativity 151–2, 179; culture 152;
   family life 153; individual differences
   155–6; intelligence 156; measures
   179; motivation 157; personality 156;
   society 153; stages 155; Sternberg
   and Lubart's investment theory 154,
   179; teaching 178
crying 221; measurement 248
Csikszentmihalyi 46; flow 58–74;
   systems model of creativity 151–2
culture, creativity 152; flow 61–2;
   happiness 19

day-care 266
death 275–81
Decisional Balance Questionnaire 309
Defence Mechanism Rating Scales
   239

defence mechanisms 230–49; adaptive
   235; correlates 237; Defence
   Mechanism Rating Scales 239;
   Defence Mechanisms Profile 240;
   Defence Style Questionnaire 239;
   development 238; maturity 232;
   measurement 238, 248
Defence Mechanisms Profile 240
Defence Style Questionnaire 239
denial and repression 78–9, 106
depression, self-help 42
desirability of control 212–13;
   measurement 245
development, emotional intelligence
   120–6; mature defences 238;
   optimism 84–6; positive illusions
   79–82; self-esteem 205; traits 185–8;
   wisdom 162–5
dialectical operations 179
dispositional optimism 82–3
distraction 227
divorce 281–7; self-help 296–7
drinking, self-help 346
drug-abuse, self-help 346

eating disorders, self-help 345
education 30; preschool 266–7; school
   267
effectiveness of psychological therapies
   327, 344–5; adolescents 333–7; adults
   328–33; children 333–7
effects of happiness 9–16
emotional awareness 133–4
emotional behaviour, a framework for
   analysis of 135
emotional competence 120–6
Emotional Competence Inventory 115
emotional creativity 43, 143
emotional intelligence 107–43;
   attachment 124–6; Bar-On's
   personality model of social and
   emotional intelligence 112–14;
   Cooper's EQ-map 116–17;
   development 120–6; Emotional
   Competence Inventory 115;
   enhancement 117–20, 139; EQ-Map
   116; Goleman's model of emotional
   Intelligence 115–16; Mayer Salovey
   and Caruso Emotional Intelligence
   Test 109, 111; Mayer, Salovey
   Caruso's ability model of emotional
   intelligence 108–12; measures 143;

Multifactor Emotional IQ Test 111;
Multifactor Emotional IQ Test
111; neurolobiology 127–30;
resilience 126; Reuven Bar-On's
model of emotional intelligence 112,
114; self-help 143
emotional intelligence tests 143;
Cooper's EQ-map 116–17;
Emotional Competence Inventory
115; Mayer Salovey and Caruso
Emotional Intelligence Test 111;
Multifactor Emotional IQ Test 111
emotions, adaptive but distressing
35–6; emotion focused coping
strategies 216; emotional competence
121; emotional creativity 143;
measurement of emotions 44–5;
positive emotions 2
enabling themes 53, 74
environmental re-evaluation 313, 347
Erikson's psychosocial stage model 159
eudaimonic 45
evaluation *see* measurement
evolution 31–6
exercise 29, 223
expectationism 93–7, 106
expert knowledge, wisdom 165–7
extraversion 200
extrinsic motivation 70, 74

faith 24, 221–2; measurement 247
family 250–300; creativity 153;
giftedness 148
family lifecycle 250–300; couple
formation 257–8; divorce 281–7,
296–7; extra stages entailed by
separation or divorce and remarriage
282; families with adolescents
269–72; families with children 260–9;
later life 275–81, 297; launching 272;
leaving home 251; marriage 258–60,
295; midlife re-evaluation 272–5; new
relationships 286; separation 281–7;
stages 252
Family Process Model 300
Family systems models 289–91;
measurement 298
flow 46, 58–74; concentration and lack
of self-awareness 60–1; conditions
61–3; Csikszentmihalyi 46, 58–74;
culture 61–2; Experience Sampling
Sheet for assessing flow 67; Flow

Experience Questionnaire 64; goals
and immediate feedback 60; intimate
relationships 63; measures 63–9;
physical activities 63; relationships
with our children 62–3; skilful
challenging activities 59–60;
strategies for enhancing well-being
using flow 70; transformation of time
61
forgiveness and atonement 254–7;
measurement 299; self-help 295
friendship 23–4, 251–2; forgiveness and
atonement 254–7, 299, 295; gratitude
257, 299; trust and betrayal 253–4,
299
Functional Dimension of Coping Scale
228

genetics, giftedness 148; happiness set
point 18–19; personality traits 17–18,
184–5
giftedness 144–50, 172, 176–80;
adult creativity 150; brain processes
149; definitions 145; early
gifted performance 148; family
backgrounds 148; genetic and
environmental factors 148; gifted
children 147; multiple intelligence
146–7; psychological adjustment
148–9; Renzulli three ring model of
giftedness 146; self-help 178
goals 31, 60
goal-setting and monitoring 314–15
Goleman's model of emotional
Intelligence 115–16
government policies 348–9
grandparents 264–6, 271–2
gratitude 257; measurement 299
grief *see* loss

habituation 32–3, 45
happiness 1–45; acquaintances 24;
Argyle 7–11; causes 16–19; culture
19; education 30; effects 9–13;
enhancement 36–7; environment
25–31; exercise 29; friendship
23–4; geographical location 28;
goal attainment 31; health 29;
kinship 22–3; longevity 15–16;
marital status 21; marriage 20–2;
measures 6–11, 43–4; personality
traits 16–17; physical state 28–9;

productivity 29–31; recreation 31; relationships 20–5; religion 24; religious service attendance 25; set point 18–19, 45; spirituality 24; strategies 37; wealth 26–8; work 30
hardiness 212–13, 249
health 29, 97–8
hedonic treadmill 45
helping relationships 323–6
heritability *see* genetics
hope 88–98, 98–100, 105
humour 227; measurement, 248

illness 275–81
improvement in psychotherapy 326
intelligence, analytic 167, 179; creative 168, 179; creativity 156; multiple 146–7, 179; practical 168, 179; triacrchic theory 167–8, 180
intrinsic motivation 47–50, 70, 74

Kansas Marital Satisfaction Scale 261
Kansas Parental Satisfaction Scale 265
kinship 22–3

later life 275–81; self-help 297
lateral thinking, self-help 178
leaving home 251
Life Orientation Test-Revised 83
locus of control 212–13, 249; measurement 245
longevity 15–16
loss 275–81; acceptance 277; anger 276; anxiety 277; bargaining 277; guilt 277; sadness 276; self-help 297; shock and denial 275–6; yearning and searching 276

maintenance 310, 317–22, 347
marital satisfaction 258–60; measurement 261
marital systems models 291; measurement 299
marriage 20–2, 258–60; divorce 281–7; forming a couple 257–8; happiness 20–2; Kansas Marital Satisfaction Scale 261; marital satisfaction 258–60; marital systems models 291; self-help 295–7; separation 281–7; types of couples 262
Mayer Salovey and Caruso Emotional Intelligence Test 111

Mayer, Salovey Caruso's ability model of emotional intelligence 108–12
McMaster Model of Family Functioning 300
measurement, Adolescent Coping Orientation for Problem Experiences A-COPE 230; Apter Motivational Style Profile 58; attachments 298; catharsis 248; control-related constructs 245; COPE 23; coping 228, 247; Coping Inventory for Stressful Situations 228; Coping Responses Inventory 230; creativity measures 179; crying 248; Defence Mechanism Rating Scales 239; Defence Mechanisms Profile 240; Defence Style Questionnaire 239; defences 238; defence mechanisms 248; Emotional Competence Inventory 115; emotional intelligence 143; emotions 44–5; EQ-Map 116; Experience Sampling Sheet for assessing flow 67; family functioning 298; flow 63–9; Flow Experience Questionnaire 64; forgiveness 299; Functional Dimension of Coping scale 228; gratitude 299; happiness, 6–9, 43–4; hope 105; humour 248; interpersonal behaviour 298; Kansas Marital Satisfaction Scale 261; Kansas Parental Satisfaction Scale 265; Life Orientation Test-Revised 8; marital functioning, 299; Mayer Salovey and Caruso Emotional Intelligence Test 111; metamotivational constructs 57–8, 73; Metamotivational State Interview and coding schedule 57–8; Multifactor Emotional IQ Test 111; narcissism 299; optimism 105; Positive Affectivity and Negative Affectivity Scale (PANAS) 5; problem-solving 247; religious coping 247; Revised Oxford Happiness Scale 10; Satisfaction with Life Scale 8; self-concept 245; self-deception 104; self-efficacy 211; self-esteem 204, 245; social support, 247; strengths 43; Telic-Paratelic State measure 57; Time Horizon Questionnaire 95; traits 184; trust 299; Values in Action Inventory of Strengths 53,

73–5; Ways of Coping Questionnaire 228
meditation 222
Metamotivational State Interview 57–8
metamotivational states 55–8, 73
midlife re-evaluation 272–5
modifying positive illusions 82
motivation 47–50; creativity 157; extrinsic 70, 74; intrinsic 47–50, 70, 74; metamotivational construct measures 57–8, 73; metamotivational states 55–8; telic and paratelic metamotivational states in reversal theory 56
motivation, creativity 157
Motives 182, 192–200; achievement 192, 200; affiliation 192, 200; altruism 193, 200; assessment 195–6; implicit and explicit 196; power 192–3, 200; state-like motives 194–5
Multifactor Emotional IQ Test 111; multiple intelligence 146–7, 179; giftedness 146–7

narcissism 299
negative affectivity 2–6, 44–5
negative beliefs 319–20
negative self-schema 79, 106
neurobiology, creativity 157; emotional intelligence 127–30; optimism and hope 98–100; trait-related strengths 190–1
neurophysiology see neurobiology
neuroticism 200

openness to experience 132, 200
optimism 82–8, 97–106; attributional retraining 86–8; development of optimism 84–6; dispositional optimism 82–3; 106 health 97–8; measurement 105; neurobiology 98–100; optimistic explanatory style 83–4; 106; self-help 104
optimistic explanatory style 83–4

parenting 263–4
peer group 268–9
personal action constructs 200
personality, creativity 153–6; genetic and environmental determinants 17–18; happiness 16–17; traits 181–91, 197–200; wisdom 158–62, 159

planning 307, 314–16, 347
pockets of incompetence 79, 106
positive affectivity 2–6, 44–5
Positive Affectivity and Negative Affectivity Scale (PANAS) 5
positive emotions 2–6, 44–5
positive illusions 77–82, 106; denial and repression 78–9, 106; modifying positive illusions 82; negative self-schema 79; pockets of incompetence 79, 106; positive illusions, development 82–79; selective attention and benign forgetting 79, 106; self-deception 78–82
power motive 192–3, 200
practical intelligence 130–1, 143, 168, 179
precontemplation 306, 311–14, 347
pregnancy, self-help 296
preschool 266–7
prevention of psychological problems 337–41
problem-solving 217–18, 321; measurement 247; self-help 244
psychological mindedness 133, 143
psychological well-being 36, 44, 45
psychotherapeutic relationships 326–7

quality of life 38, 44, 45

recreation 31
reframing 226–7
relapse prevention 322–3
relationships 250–300; assessing relationships 287–91; attachment theory 287–8; divorce 281–7; family systems models 289–91; forgiveness and atonement 254–7; forming a couple 257–8; friendship 23–4; grand parenting 264–6; gratitude 257; happiness 20–5; helping 323–6; Kansas Marital Satisfaction Scale 261; Kansas Parental Satisfaction Scale 265; kinship 22–3; marital Satisfaction 258–60; marital systems models 291; marriage 20–2, 258–60; measurement 298–9; new relationships 286; parenting 263–4; psychotherapeutic 326–7; self-help 295–7; separation 281–7; trust and betrayal 253–4; types of couples 262
relaxation 223–4

religion 24–5, 221–2
Renzulli three ring model of giftedness 146
resilience 126, 188–9, 270–1, 300
Reversal Theory 55–9, 73–4;
    Apter Motivational Style Profile 58; autotelic activities 74; Metamotivational State Interview 57–8; metamotivational states 55–8, 73; telic and paratelic states 74; Telic State Measure 57; Telic-Paratelic State Instrument 57
Revised Oxford Happiness Scale 10
reward 321
risk homeostasis theory 93–7, 106
Ryan and Deci's self-determination continuum 48–9

Satisfaction with Life Scale 8
school 267
selective attention and benign forgetting 79, 106
self 201–49; object and agent 203–4; self-efficacy 210–13, 249; self-esteem 204–9, 249, 245
self-deception 78–82, 104
self-determination continuum 48–9
self-efficacy 210–13, 249; general self-efficacy 212–13; measurement 211; outcomes 212; sources 211–12
self-esteem 204–9, 249; correlates 207; defensive self-esteem enhancement 207–9; development 205; improvement 209; measurement 204, 245
self-help, aging 297; anger management 43; anxiety 43; assertiveness 245; brainstorming 178; change 345; communication 29; coping with abuse 245; coping with living single 295; creative problem solving 178; depression 42; divorce 296–7; drinking 346; drug-abuse 346; eating disorders 345; emotional intelligence 143; forgiveness 295; gifted children 178; lateral thinking 178; loss 297; marriage 295; optimism 104; pregnancy 296; problem-solving 244; self-esteem 245; sexual problems 296; stepfamilies 297; stress management 244; studying 179; trauma 245; weight control 345–6

self-liberation 316–17, 347
self-re-evaluation 315
Seligman, optimism 83–4; positive psychology 1–2; signature strengths 54
sense of coherence 212–13, 249
separation 281–7; self-help 296–7
set-point for happiness 45
sexual problems, self-help 296
signature strengths 50–1, 54, 70, 73–5
single lifestyle 295
Snyder's Hope Theory 89
social comparisons 33–4, 45
social liberation 313–14, 347
social support 218–19; measurement, 247
social well-being 38, 44, 45
society, creativity 153
spirituality 24, 221–2
stages of change, action 307, 316–17, 346; contemplation 306, 311–14, 347; maintenance 310, 317–22, 347; planning 307, 314–16, 347; precontemplation 306, 311–14, 347; termination 310, 322–3, 347
Sternberg and Lubart's investment theory 154, 179
Sternberg's balance theory of wisdom 168–70, 179
stimulus control 318–19, 347
strategies for change 324–5
strategies for enhancing happiness 37; based on research on giftedness, creativity and wisdom 171; based on research on self-esteem, self-efficacy, positive coping strategies and adaptive defences 241; based on the family lifecycle 292; based on traits and motives 197; by building emotional intelligence 139; by promoting positive change 301–47; by promoting positive illusions, hope, optimism and positive expectations 101; using strengths, intrinsic motivation and flow 70
strengths, assessment of trait-related strengths 184; change 302–4; character strengths 51–3, 74; five factor model of personality 182–4; measurement 43; signature strengths 54, 74; strategies for promoting strengths 70, 197, 241, 292; Values in

Action Inventory of Strengths 53, 73–4
stress management 244
studying, self-help 179
subjective well-being 12
surveys of happiness 7

tacit knowledge 170
techniques for change, arousing emotions 312–13; communication 320–1; consciousness raising 311–12, 347; countering 319–21, 347; environmental re-evaluation 313, 347; goal-setting and monitoring 314–15; negative beliefs 319–20; problem-solving 321; relapse prevention 322–3; reward 321; self-liberation 316–17, 347; self-re-evaluation 315; social liberation 313–14, 347; stimulus control 318–19, 347
telic and paratelic states 74
Telic State Measure 57
Telic-Paratelic State Instrument 57
temperament 184–8, 200
termination 310, 322–3, 347
Time Horizon Questionnaire 95
traits 181–91, 197–200; development 185–8; genetic and environmental factors 184–5; measurement 184;

neurobiology 190–1; resilience 188–9; theories 182–4; well-being 189–90
trauma 245
triacrchic theory of intelligence 167–8, 180
trust and betrayal 253–4; measurement 299
twin study 18

Values in Action Inventory of Strengths (VIA-IS) 53, 73–4, 75
virtues 51, 75

Ways of Coping Questionnaire 228
wealth 26–8
weight control, self-help 345–6
well-being, optimising 19–20; personality traits 189–90; psychological 36, 44, 45; social 38, 44, 45; subjective 12
Wilde's risk homeostasis theory 93–7, 106
wisdom 157–80, 179; expert knowledge 165–7; final stage of cognitive development 162–5; final stage of personality development 158–62, 159; Sternberg's balance theory 168–70, 179; tacit knowledge 170
work 30